IN THE EYES OF THE ANCESTORS

IN THE EYES OF THE ANCESTORS

Belief and Behavior in a Maya Community

by June Nash

New Haven and London, Yale University Press, 1970

Published with assistance from the foundation
established in memory of Amasa Stone Mather of the
Class of 1907, Yale College.
Copyright © 1970 by Yale University.
Library of Congress catalog card number: 70-81425
Standard book number: 300-01135-0
Designed by Marvin Howard Simmons,
set in Granjon type,
and printed in the United States of America by
Vail-Ballou Press, Inc., Binghamton, N.Y.
Distributed in Great Britain, Europe, Asia, and
Africa by Yale University Press Ltd., London; in
Canada by McGill-Queen's University Press, Montreal; and
in Mexico by Centro Interamericano de Libros
Académicos, Mexico City.

To my parents

Contents

Contents

Appendixes

Plates

following page 198

Tables

Figures

Acknowledgments

My study of the people of Tzo'ontahal was made in four field sessions, the first in 1957 with return trips in 1958, 1964, and 1965, for a total of eighteen months. Brief visits were made in 1966 and 1967. With each returning visit it was possible to penetrate more deeply into the lives and experiences of the villagers, most of whom were highly resistant to an outsider on the first contact. I began writing the book in 1966, and some of the predictions I made came true before I finished it in 1968. These included the demise of the ceremonial leadership of the *alfereces*—the officials in charge of religious celebrations—the waning of the community status of curers, and the killing of one of my principal informants who had taken a leadership role before acquiring the traditional validation of age and experience in office. The transformations over the period of my study in this community created difficulties in recording and organizing my material. I owe whatever clarification has emerged to the efforts of Jane Olson and Gale Griffin of Yale University Press.

I am indebted to the National Institutes of Mental Health, which made possible the research for this study. I owe an intellectual debt to Sol Tax, who introduced me to the problems and potentialities of the area as a locus for field study, to Norman McQuown, who gave me the first instruction in Tzeltal and provided a grammar which facilitated learning the language, and to Manning Nash, who provided some of the earlier formulations of the culture from which I have borrowed. I am grateful to Duane Metzger and Gerald Williams, who generously provided equipment and facilities for work with informants in San Cristóbal Las Casas in the summer of 1964. Alfonso Villa Rojas, who was director of the Instituto Nacional Indígenista, was of great assistance in the first summer's field trip, introducing me to leaders within the town and in the Instituto's headquarters in Las Casas. His encouragement and support of investigations by foreign students set an example in international cooperation. I am personally indebted to Mary Marshall for the companionship and assistance she offered during our summer of residence in the public bathhouse of the town; she is responsible for the observations in Appendix 3A and 3B. Terrence Kaufman checked the Tzeltal words appearing in the glossary. I am grateful for the hospitality and friendship of the family of the schoolmaster, Louis Tavernier. Without the patience, the insight, and the friendship of Juliana Lopez Shunton, Mariano Lopez Lin, Simón Perez Kantirón, and their families, the book would never have been written. Vera Deutsch provided encouragement and assistance in the final typing of the manuscript. My children, Eric and Laura, shared the hardships of fieldwork and of producing the book.

Preface

And so we shall be able to do what our mothers
did and what our fathers did here where our
Holy Father sees **us** and our Holy Mother sees us.

> *From the prayer said at the
> time of taking offices in
> the civil hierarchy*

In all societies, some of the ideology and behavior of the past persists after their relevance to current problems has ended. How much this continuity eases the absorption of change by providing meaning and motivation and how much it hinders the ability to deal with current issues and to plan for the future is a long-standing social problem. It is of special relevance to developing nations undergoing changes that transform all social institutions. Developing nations have focused their planning on economic change in the hope that other institutions will respond automatically. This hope has not been justified.

Mexico has shown a growing awareness of the strength to be drawn from its rich cultural heritage in the five decades of development since the revolution. The changes that were transforming the cities a generation ago are now drawing enclaves of Indian populations into the mainstream of national development. In the 1930s government policy was directed toward transforming Indians into modern nationals. Since the 1950s there has been an increasing effort to incorporate Indians without suppressing their distinctive customs and languages. The old melting pot policy has given way to a new policy of selective adaptation.

For the Indians, adhering to the ways of the ancestors is the means of surviving as a people. Their sense of cultural survival is threatened by the very adjustments and adaptations that make economic survival possible. Cut off from other Indian communities around them since the Conquest, when their ceremonial centers were destroyed and the political hierarchy which drew them into a single polity was replaced, the Indians were able to retain a sense of cultural independence within the corporate communities (Wolf 1957b). Each community developed a distinctive style of life in which the old pre-Conquest beliefs and customs were reworked with the colonial Spanish introductions. Validation of their behavior lay in the belief that they were doing as the ancestors did, and that they were living "in the eyes of our ancestors."

This social fiction is now threatened by a growing disbelief in the presence of these supernatural figures. The crisis caused by the disjunction between belief and behavior is forcing the Indians to reassess their present condition. Awareness of the contradictions between what they do and what they think they ought to do is forced upon them by events over which they have no control.

This study of a Maya Indian community in the state of Chiapas, Mexico, deals with the problem of the relation between belief and behavior in a changing world. It is a problem that we have failed to solve in our own society, if the labels of our time—The Age of Anxiety, The Society of Alienation—have meaning. I have studied this small Indian society not in search of a solution but as a way of phrasing the problem in the widest possible context.

I selected Tzoʔontahal because the people seemed to have retained a traditional Indian culture even though the community is on the Pan-American Highway linking them with the departmental and national capitals. The question of what changes had affected their lives and how they had responded to them was relevant to my interest in the effects of national changes on local groups. In the last year of my study my interest broadened from an enquiry into responses to external changes to a study of the meanings assigned to both internal and external changes.

Like many other predominantly Mayan communities of the Chiapas highlands, the community is the context of all meaningful social relations. Endogamy and a belief that the people who live in the center and the nearby barrios are descended from the same ancestors give a sense of eth-

nic unity extending back to the beginning of time. The people set boundaries by such external symbols as a locally specified costume for men and
women, a distinctive dialect of Tzeltal, and specialization in the production of pottery. Implicit boundaries are established by socialization processes that inhibit response to the outside world and that define a code of
behavior understandable only in its own context. The completely socialized member of the community is not expected to seek recognition, nor
could he find prestige, outside these boundaries. The community com-
prises the moral universe: cooperation and reciprocity are limited to members of the community, as are most cases of homicide and theft. Lacking
concrete evidence, people assume misdeeds to have been committed by
someone from the community.

The boundaries that separate these Indians from other Indian communities as well as from non-Indian, or *Ladino*,[1] communities are social artifacts that give a sense of security to members of the in-group. They call
themselves "the true men" (*b'atz'il winik*), and their world is defined in
"the true word" (*b'atz'il k'op*). The latter is their term for the Tzeltal dialect of Maya which is the language of the house and of the street, the
courthouse, and the church in the absence of the Spanish-speaking priest.
Tzeltal names differ from Spanish names for most of the surrounding
towns, the earth, the heavens, and the cosmological bodies. Catholic saints
are incorporated under a Tzeltal name or a Tzeltal version of their Spanish name. All of the members of the community have a Tzeltal patronym
in addition to the Spanish surname with which they are baptized. The
given name is that of a Spanish saint but is shortened and pronounced
with Tzeltal phonemes, and female names have the feminine prefix *š*.
Their world is labeled in their own language.

The people assume that their expectations will be met and their projec-

1. The term Ladino has a range of usage throughout Middle America. In Mexico City,
people define Ladino as any person who abuses his superior skills to take advantage of
others. In Oaxaca, a Zapotec Indian defined Ladino as "an Indian who knows Spanish, has
adopted western-style clothing, and takes advantage of other Indians because of his knowledge of the language and ways of life of the non-Indian society. He is like a fox." In
Chiapas, the term is applied to any non-Indian without derogatory connotation, and the
same is true in Guatemala. In the metalanguage of anthropological monographs, it is
used in this latter sense.

tions of self will find a responsive audience only within these linguistic and physical boundaries. The sense of insulation is a denial of regional and national political institutions in which they interact with the other Indians and Ladinos who are part of their present world and share their history. The town itself is a product of the Spanish colonial *congregación,* which drew together diverse Indian populations that had been scattered in small settlements. The outlying barrios are occupied by Indians who have moved out from the center, as well as foreign Indians who had worked in the *fincas,* or large plantations, within the township. These latter people are referred to by a derisive term, *Kurik,* meaning roughly "country hick." Beyond these, and still within the municipal limits, there are a series of *colonias,* settlements populated by Indians who have moved here from other towns and by *mestizos,* or acculturated Indians. These settlers acquired land in the time of Juarez or later in the Cardenas period. Ladino men are called *Kašlan* and women *Šinlan;* foreigners who do not appear to be of the country are called *Alemán,* the Spanish term for German.

The focus of this book is on the lives and thoughts of people living within the center. The people of Tzo'ontahal live in a square world, surrounded by a round universe. From the square hole, cut in the earth at the center post of their square house to receive the sacrifice of a live chicken when the house is built, stretches a square village (it appears as a rectangle on the map, but they draw it as a square).[2] The fields are measured in squares of twenty-five arms' breadths, with five handspans measuring the square between each plant. Within this square world, they have elaborated techniques for dealing with spiritual and human co-residents in curing rituals, offerings for crops, burial practices, and baptism rites. Their present cultural stock reveals a selective absorption of Spanish colonial features along with twentieth-century innovations. They have techniques for planting and harvesting milpa, marketing the pottery manufactured in all the households, curing an eclipse of the moon, divining causes of illness and curing the maladjusted social relations which cause it, manufacturing and

2. This view of the world as square is shared by Tzeltal and Tzotzil neighbors in Larraínzar (Holland 1963:69), San Pedro Chenalhó (Guiteras Holmes 1961:254), and Pinola (Hermitte 1964). The four-direction concept of the village and world noted by Landa (Tozzer 1941:135) suggests a square-space concept.

marketing contraband liquor, minimizing discord and settling disputes locally, and preserving continuity in a town administration marked by the annual rotation of officials.

These are the techniques acquired for dealing with the world in which they were born. For the world into which they are being propelled, they are combining new skills with old, creating a semblance of continuity but with a recombination of elements. Fitting this square community into the round post-Columbian world is a task consciously undertaken by the Mexican government. Within the town, strategies are being developed to meet the new demands made on the community as economic and political horizons widen.

The problem focus on the relation between belief and behavior in a changing social environment can be restated by asking how behavior is conditioned by custom and how it responds to cues from the environment. The first class of responses is adjustive, fitting the behavior of the individual to a given environment, and the second is adaptive, changing the external environment (Kluckhohn 1962:46). I shall use the distinction Mowrer and Kluckhohn (1944:258) have made between adaptation, "which develops and changes inherited ways of behaving," and adjustment, "which develops and changes habits," with the former referring to socially acquired responses and the latter to individual responses. A moving equilibrium is found when changes in adjustive and adaptive responses fit a persisting framework of understandings and explanations. Both adjustive and adaptive responses follow rules. These rules enable social groups to generate consistent, understandable, and appropriate behavior in response to a variety of settings. The "rules of the game" set the parameters for adjustive behavior; the "rules of strategy" generate behavior adaptive to change. The rules of the game are validated by the belief system of the society; the rules of strategy can be justified on the same premises, but if they are so fundamental as to challenge existing values, they require a new ideology.

The model of change which takes into account the techniques of adaptation and adjustment occurring within small-scale societies is that of moving equilibrium. Wallace (1962:142) has stated the dimensions of this model:

> A culture, under certain conditions, during a period of time can be said to be an open system in a state of stable but moving equilibrium: that is to say, it maintains a boundary, accepts inputs and produces outputs at approximately equal rates, and changes continuously but gradually in internal structure.

The concept of equilibrium is one way to talk about the constraints which make behavior congruent with beliefs. Given a constantly changing ecological setting due to an expanding population and a changing man-land ratio, the stability of the system depends on the adequacy of existing institutions to handle conflict and of shared understandings to explain events. Movement stems from the tension between individual and social goals and the adaptations to bring them into closer harmony. The basic condition for the kind of change characteristic of a moving equilibrium is that conflict is contained within the community.

I have organized the data to clarify features maintaining equilibrium and to show the direction in which the society is moving. First I describe formal, prescribed behavior for each institutional complex and relate it to the beliefs that underlie it. Following each of these chapters I analyze strategies formulated in response to changes coming from within or outside the community. The formal behavior providing a framework for continuity is related to place spirits in Chapter 1, to economic activities in Chapter 2, to customs and rituals in the family and neighborhood in Chapters 4 and 5, to civil and religious government in Chapters 7 and 8. Changing strategies are related to economic activities in Chapter 3, to social relations as revealed in curing practices in Chapter 6, and to political relations in Chapter 9.

Implicit in the organization is an ordering of institutions from most static to most dynamic. In the economy, agricultural technology has been stabilized at the colonial level of adaptation at which the wooden plow, hoe, and machete were added to, but did not displace, the digging stick, while in pottery manufacture, both techniques and products have remained unchanged. The organization of work groups remains limited to the household except for the introduction of cooperatives in recent years. In domestic institutions there has been an adaptation to living in a compact settlement with the emphasis on the bilateral kinship group. The authority of the elders in settling conflicts in the family and the community is weakened, although the hierarchy remains intact. In religious institutions, the personnel has remained the same, but the authority of the religious officials has weakened and the belief in the deities and ancestral figures has been undermined.

Political leadership is the most dynamic area of change. The power of the *principales* had already been taken over by young civil officials when I first went to the town in 1957. The curers, who retained the power derived from belief in their control over the supernatural, were the core of resistance to change in the decade that I knew the community. But this control was being challenged by civil officials and factional leaders, who were aware of its repressive effect. The dynamic aspect of the political sector is linked to the fact that the new leaders saw the necessity of seizing power from those who were privileged in the traditional society. They were reworking the social structure to pave the way for the acceptance of development opportunities being offered by the national government.

In Chapters 10, 11, and 12 I have summarized the structuring of behavior in roles, place, and time and described how these patterns have been affected by change. The following questions are raised in the summary chapters:

1. The role system: How are people recruited into roles? How are roles coordinated? How are performances evaluated? The matrix of roles provides the patterned expectations of what others will do in a given situation. Some of the decisions made in assigning people to roles allow little room for choice. In other cases, new functions, such as those imposed upon governing officials, have replaced traditional bases for making decisions and in turn upset the balance of power between elders, curers, and leaders in civil office. (Continuity and change in the role structure are analyzed in Chapter 10.)

2. The setting: How is appropriate behavior defined for each institutional setting? What kinds of behavior are replicated in each setting? How are changes in role relations reflected in positions assumed in each setting? Observations of behavior in the church and the

school included in Appendix 3 provide the data for an inductive analysis of conventions established by place. (These are compared and
analyzed in Chapter 11.)

   3. Timing of behavior: How does time enter into the consciousness
of people's planning of activities? Time is a resource the use of which
indicates the values assigned to activities and the relative power of
people in bargaining positions. As such, it is a sensitive index to changes
in strategies for allocating effort. (The sense of time is examined in
reference to the scheduling of performances and interpreting the behavior of others in Chapter 12.)

The summary chapters provide the basis for testing the following hypotheses in the final chapter:

   1. The stability of the society varies directly with:
      a. the degree of control over time and place
      b. the efficiency of its procedures for adjusting conflict
      c. the ability to validate behavioral innovations in terms of exist-
         ing values
      d. the effectiveness of the techniques for transforming old power
         positions whose functions contradict changed social conditions
         into ceremonial posts
   2. The lability of the society varies directly with:
      a. the gap between expectations and experience
      b. the degree of dissonance between traditional explanations and
         current interpretations of events

During the period I worked in Tzoʔontahal, the fundamental propositions on which behavior was predicated were being challenged. When old
beliefs are waning, the question is whether the techniques developed to
maintain the old conditions for equilibrium will persist in the future.

   Fortes (1959:25) has pointed out that the "serious defect . . . of general-
ized enthnographic descriptions" is that they do not show "how ritual or
belief is actually used by men and women to regulate their lives." My purpose is to indicate not only how belief and ritual serve the ends of regula-
tion but also how beliefs are transformed in the process of performing ri-

tuals and everyday tasks. The dialectic of change lies in the interpretations people make of new experience.

My method of study in the field was that of participant-observation combined with extensive eliciting. The assumption implicit in participant-observation that "seeing is believing" denies not only the symbolic significance of the acts one sees, but the relevant social features which are part of their definition of the situation. Rather than impose my own perceptions on the simplest field description, I relied on informants' statements about where, when, what, to whom, and how things were happening. In the case of formally programmed events, I elicited in advance in Tzeltal from two or more informants the sequence of activities as they expected them to transpire. I asked informants to segment the experience they were recounting in as minimal units as they had the descriptive vocabulary to do. This was done for instrumental activities—agriculture and pottery production —as well as ceremonial events in the life cycle and in religious and economic institutions. Implicit in the informants' segmentation of experience is the concept of "molar acts"—purposive and cognitive behavior.[3] The informant says for example that he "eats," not that he raises food to his mouth and chews it. The importance of eliciting descriptions in the performers' own language is indicated in the different way in which experience is lumped or split in Tzeltal. For example, when a curer takes a pulse he both "feels" and "hears" ($\check{s}\mathit{?awai}$) the messages communicated by the blood. On the other hand, the verb "to eat" has several terms depending on what is being eaten (Berlin 1967). Their translations into Spanish do not make the same distinctions.

Observation of events in process provided not only a check for validity and completeness of the informants' accounts, but also a means of analyzing the process of change. The attempt to analyze divergence in actual behavior from normative statements in terms of Murdock's ideal-real dichotomy or Kroeber's value-culture and reality-culture is based on an assumption that there is a single perception of the way things ought to be done in

3. Psychologists such as Lewin (1951:72) and Tolman (1961:89) who have studied animal behavior have emphasized that the minimal unit of significant behavior is both purposive and cognitive. Most of my descriptions of behavior are limited to molar behavior, and the analysis of gesture systems is confined to those which have symbolic significance in a ceremonial context.

a given culture, and that real behavior is a not always successful attempt to approximate those ideals. This formulation has proved inadequate because the actors have a number of ideas as to what appropriate behavior is, and the permissible range of behavior varies in each setting. In questioning informants about the divergences between the account I elicited prior to an event and the acts I observed, I was able to sort out these kinds of variation from those which indicate adaptation or social change.

Past events in the history of the community, selected, described, and interpreted by the participants in those events, provide a framework for analyzing structural and social change. Deviation from the norms is not in itself an index to social change, as Faron (1964:202ff.) and others have pointed out. The impetus to social change depends upon awareness of dissonance between the way things are done and social goals. Past events are assigned significance according to this awareness of changing social conditions. Lies about the past and guesses about the future are as important sources of data as history. When people lie about what they do or have done or will do, they lie in terms of the norms, and when they guess, they guess in terms of patterned expectations. These data are of significance in exploring the patterns underlying both formal and dynamic behavior.

Communities such as Tzoʔontahal represent a paradox in Latin America since the Indians pretend to be the same when they are changing, while non-Indians exaggerate the changes which have occurred. In Indian communities, the old cultural forms persist even while the community responds to the changing cues in the environment. The Indians are aware that the corporate community is an important resource base in easing their transition into regional and national networks, not on the bottom rung of the Ladino social ladder as when individuals leave the community, but in a competitively favorable position. Their insistence that they are following the customs of the ancestors is a means of keeping their boundaries intact and protecting themselves against external encroachment.

Chapter 1

Spirits and Places

Social space is the cognitive pattern of relationships imposed upon any terrain. In Amatenango del Valle [1] there are two superimposed patterns. One is defined by the nation for the purposes of political administration. This follows the pattern of colonial administration of *municípios,* or townships, with a *cabecera,* or administrative center, containing the church, town hall, and school house, and serving a number of colonias and *rancherias,* local hamlets or nuclei of populations. The other pattern is defined by the inhabitants using Tzeltal terminology or a Tzeltal rendition of a Spanish name. In this pattern, domains of good and bad spirits are defined, and behavior appropriate to each place is specified in myths and rituals. Persistence of this pattern has had profound implications for continuity of pre-Conquest culture. It provides a ground plan for the system of social control and security exercised by the old gods and their human intermediaries.

In the following section, I will discuss first territorial divisions defined by national law and modified by indigenous categories, and then the interaction between the spirits of persons and places.

THE TERRITORIAL DIVISIONS

The township of Amatenango del Valle is located at 92°30′ longitude and 16°30′ latitude in the highland zone of the state of Chiapas. The town center is located no more than fifty yards from the Pan-American Highway twenty-five miles southeast of the departmental capital of San Cris-

---

1. I use the national designation derived from Nahuatl, Amatenango del Valle, to refer to the township, and the Tzeltal term Tzoʔontahal to refer to the center.

tóbal. The altitude above sea level varies from 2,000 meters in the hilly periphery to 1,720 meters in the valley where the town center is located. Ejido lands acquired in the 1930s have extended the boundaries of the township to lower lands at 1,500 meters altitude.

Pre-Conquest settlement patterns in the Chiapas highlands were characterized by independent communities occupying the headlands around flat-bottomed valleys (R. M. Adams 1961:341). The choice of sites seems to have been based on defense against invading Toltec or other conquest groups (Calnek 1962:25). The sites investigated by Adams and Culbert (R. M. Adams 1961:347) in Amatenango belong to the late-Classic and early post-Classic period. They were marginal to the centers of Maya civilization in the Yucatán peninsula and Guatemala. Test excavations in the modern town indicate that it was occupied only after colonial times.

The town of Amatenango del Valle is first mentioned in the year 1528 when it was included in tribute lists with both the Nahuatl name, Amatenango, and the Tzeltal name, Tzobontaghal (Calnek n.d.). The tribute lists of 1761 include 33 families in the *parcialidad,* or Spanish political unit based on an indigenous settlement, of Zacatepec in Amatenango and 75 families in the parcialidad of Amatenango (Trens 1957 I:217). The first census done in 1778 shows a total population of 576, with 374 men and 202 women. The racial breakdown is listed as 8 white, 2 negro and mestizo, and 560 Indians (Trens 1957:221). By 1824, the population had increased to 1,620. The present population of 3,179 represents natural growth as well as inclusion of additional outlying settlements added in the latter part of the nineteenth century and during the 1930s with the enactment of the land reform act. The population changes indicate steady but not great increases. The capacity of the town to incorporate additional population has probably passed its peak. The present trend is for out-migration to newly opened ejido lands.

The subdivisions of the town, which provide the framework for administration by the national government, are included in Table 1.

The center. The center of Tzoʔontahal is called the "center [or navel] of the world." The residents of the center, with the exception of the schoolteacher's family, are all Indian. Although the town center forms

TABLE I. Population of Political Subdivisions of the Township
of Amatenango del Valle

Name of subdivision	Men	Women	Total
Center			
Tzo?ontahal	938	894	1,832
Colonias			
Bočibal	109	113	222
Te?tikil	81	91	172
Pathuitz	36	30	66
San Caralampio	50	46	96
San Vicente	46	48	94
Ranchos and rancherias			
Buena Vista	1	5	6
Candelaria	5	3	8
Carmen	8	9	17
Carmen las Delicias	6	7	13
Cruz Quemada	5	10	15
El Porvenir	12	13	25
El Rabinal	11	9	20
El Rosario	12	17	29
La Esperanza	3	6	9
La Libertad	3	4	7
La Merced Buena Vista	4	5	9
Llano Grande	11	16	27
Porvenir	2	6	8
Rosario Tulanca	3	2	5
San Agustín	11	9	20
San Antonio Buena Vista (a)	63	76	139
San Antonio Buena Vista (b)	12	7	19
San Caralampio	8	9	17
San José Cruz Quemada	14	14	28
San José La Reforma	10	10	20
San José Yujulum	10	8	18
San Pedro Soledad	12	10	22
San Ramon Buena Vista	4	5	9
San Salvador	12	11	23
San Sebastian	1	1	2
Santa Anita	6	3	9
Santiago Buena Vista	11	10	21
Tulanca	5	6	11
Fincas			
San Nicolás	26	28	54
Tejonera	8	5	13
Total	1,559	1,546	3,105

SOURCE: 1960 census.

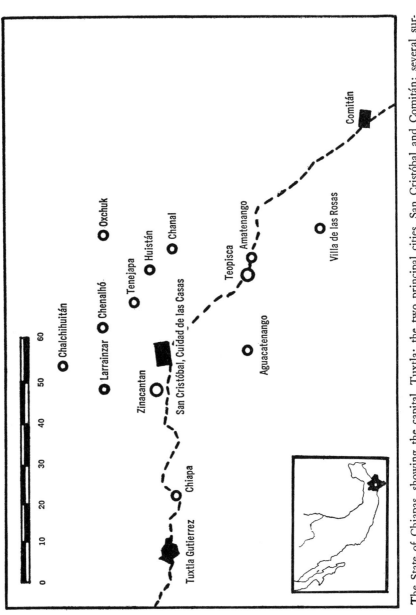

The State of Chiapas, showing the capital, Tuxtla; the two principal cities, San Cristóbal and Comitán; several surrounding Indian towns; and the Pan-American Highway (dashed line).

a rough rectangle on Map 1, the people think of it as being a square.[2] This conforms to the cultural ideal of a square applied in house, milpa, village, and probably world, although when anyone is asked about the last, he cautiously answers, "I have heard that it is round." The center is the unit that the people think of when they say *hteklum,* my land or my village. House lots are not sold to outsiders, particularly Ladinos, but the prohibition applies as well to other Indians living within the limits of the township.

The residents of the center identify themselves with the former residents of the two pre-Conquest sites occupying the hill of Amawitz[3] northwest of the center, and the hill of San Nicolás (called Lelem in Tzeltal) to the southeast. The following account is given of the founding of the present town in the valley:

Our ancestors lived in Amawitz. There wasn't enough water there, but there was a great deal that passed here in the valley. The ancestors came out of their cave to look at where the people should move. They told the people where they should go. The people "thought in common." They cut the trees here; then, when it was dry, they burned it with fire as they do for milpa. When it was cleared, they began to build their houses. Others saw this and came to build their houses. When they finished building their houses, everyone began to think of building a church. The first church was built in Alannantik [the low side] for San Pedro the Martyr. This was torn down because the witches used to come to get the permission of San Pedro to do witchcraft. When the new church was built, there was a division of the town into the upper and lower sections.

It is significant that the people attribute the initiative in the resettlement to the mythical ancestors, although archaeological evidence indicates that the present center was settled after the Conquest. The Conquest is not a part of their mythico-historic past. The ancestors are given credit for establishing everything.

2. The pre-Conquest term for local center was Tzamgholal (Calnek 1962:25), signifying "square head." "Head" town was possibly a ceremonial center.

3. Hermitte (1964:48) notes that in Pinola the "police" of the spiritual government are sent to outposts in Amawitz and Me?wakaš in Amatenango. This suggests that it may be considered the ancestral home of other Indians of the area.

A territorial distinction not recognized by the federal government is the division of the town center into two sections, or sides, by the street running in front of the church. The two sides of the division are called Ahk'olnantik, upper side, and Alannantik, lower side. The upper side is in the direction of higher lands in the southwest called Ahk'olk'inal, and the lower side is in the direction of lower lands to the northeast, called Alank'inal. The emphasis on relative altitude implicit in place nomenclature is a central fact in the Indians' ecological adjustment. Marriage is endogamous within each division by explicit rule, and in fact 87 percent of all marriages conform to the rule, according to a census I took in 1958. A man who marries a girl on the opposite side is forced to make a payment of eighteen liters of liquor to the bachelors of the opposite division. In addition to regulating competition for marriage partners, the dual division is the basis for allocating civil and religious offices.

Whether the dual division was an indigenous trait or not is a moot point. The pattern for dual organizations existed in both Spanish and indigenous societies (Foster 1951:5). There is some speculation that the dual divisions are a product of the Spanish colonial policy of the congregación, when populations of different origins were drawn together. However, local historical accounts indicate that several ethnic groups were introduced at various periods. After the initial congregación, foreign Indians were incorporated in the sixteenth century, in the latter part of the nineteenth century (Secretaría de Gobierno Constitucional, October 26, 1893), and as late as the 1930s in response to the land reform program. As each ethnic group entered the region, it was either incorporated into one of the existing divisions or was isolated. The persistence of polarization must be explained on other grounds. The widespread distribution in the Chiapas highlands of dual divisions defined by territory and descent in communities of both dispersed and nucleated settlement patterns suggests the indigenous origins of the division. A dual division of upper and lower sections based on endogamy and equal representation is found in San Pedro Chenalhó (Guiteras Holmes 1961:64), Chanal (Eva Hunt, NSF II report), Oxchuk (Villa Rojas 1946:424), and Cancuk (Siverts 1964). The Nahuatl term *calpul* is applied in some cases to these divisions. The towns where calpulles are found are *paraje,* or vacant center, types (Tax 1937) which

were not affected by the congregación. The fact that there is no mention
in the post-Conquest documents of the introduction of dual divisions suggests that the model was indigenous to the area.

The Indians of Tzoʔontahal state that the dividing line of the division
was established in its present position when a new church, replacing the
first one which was burned, was built on the present site. Judging from a
date carved in a beam of the church, this must have been about the year
1746. The endogamous restriction on marriage has not led to a sense of racial distinction between the two populations. Both groups feel that they
are descendants of the same ancestor figures and under their guardianship.
The same Tzeltal patronyms are distributed on both sides of the division,
although there is a clustering of some of them on one or another side.
Table 2 shows the distribution of patronyms of 714 male and female
adults; 88 percent of the patronyms are found in both divisions.[4]

The functions of the division in organizing social groupings have been
eroded, but some survive. Equal representation by civil officials from the
upper and lower sections, when there are two or more posts at the same
rank, is still in effect. The principle of alternation of the single posts of
president and *síndico,* his administrative assistant, so that one term the
incumbent is chosen from Ahk'olnantik and the following term from
Alannantik has not been a decisive factor since the 1930s, when Indian
communities were being drawn into more active participation in national
programs of change (Chapter 9).

Residential expansion within the center has been almost entirely in
Ahk'olnantik because of the addition of ejido lands formerly belonging to
the finca of San Nicolás on this side of town. This one-sided increase in
population finally resulted, in 1965, in a breakdown of the principle of
equal representation in the ceremonial posts involving high expenses,
those of the four *alfereces.* Although attempts were made to find candidates in Alannantik, there were no men with sufficient funds who had not

4. Carrasco (n.d.:5) quotes a document in the *Archivo General de Indias de Sevilla,
Guatemala* 16 indicating that Spanish patronyms were given to the heads of calpules and
that these were to be extended to all members of the calpul. The present distribution
of name groups in the dual divisions cannot support this, nor can it refute the possibility
that Spanish patronyms were related to some larger kin or territorial grouping more than
three hundred years ago.

held that post formerly, and all four alfereces were for the first time taken from one side.

TABLE 2. Patronyms in the Dual Division

Patronym	Alannantik only	Ahk'olnantik only	Alannantik and Ahk'olnantik
Alvarez			37
Arguella Jimenez	1		
Bautista		1	
Bautista Čail			52
Bautista Čo		5	
Bautista Koʔton			14
Bautista Saʔben			20
Cepeda			1
Cepeda Čilol			29
Cruz Mendez	1		
Diaz			6
Diaz Čamo			5
Diaz Ton			8
Diaz Uz			42
Gomez		2	
Gomez Bot			39
Gomez Kompaš			73
Gomez Kut			49
Gomez Waris	1		
Gonzalez	1		
Gonzalez Ikob		3	
Guitierrez	1		
Hernandez	1		
Hernandez Čela	1		
Hernandez Tenan	4	1	
Jimenez		2	
Leon		2	
Leon Či			21
Leon Čulik			14
Leon Malatz	2		
Lopez			1
Lopez Lab'	1		
Lopez Lin			31
Lopez Mai	11		
Lopez Pokoš		13	
Lopez Tapiya		5	
Lopez Šunton		18	

Patronym	Alannantk only	Ahk'olnantik only	Alannantik and Ahk'olnantik
Lopez Tz'uʔu			12
Lopez Wolto			50
Lopez Yutz			16
Perez			9
Perez Huhan			4
Perez Kam			11
Perez Kantiron			23
Perez Os			17
Perez Otol			16
Perez Tut			18
Perez Ventura			11
Sanchez		3	
Santis Peč	1		
Vasquez		3	
Total	26	58	629

The curing hierarchy was organized on the basis of the dual division until the 1940s. There were two leader curers, one on each side, who were in charge of guarding their own side against intrusion of evil spirits. During the 1940s a breakdown in the hierarchial principle led to some lessening of the power of the group and a collapse of the leadership. People now patronize curers from either section, but there is some feeling that it is safer for the curers if they cure only on their own side.

The dual division persists as a basis of economic organization only in the case of the cattle owner's associations. Pasturage on communal lands is allocated according to residence in the upper or lower division. Since cattle raising for beef has increased the size of herds the cattle owners on each side have formed an association to clear the waterholes and celebrate fiestas at the major waterhole on the Day of the Cross. None of the other new enterprises in town organize on the basis of the territorial division.

In the etiquette of social interaction, the dual division is still taken into account. When a resident of one side walks in the streets of the other side, he is not expected to greet passersby or people in their houses with the usual *b'onme wiš* or *b'onme tat* (I go, elder sister or father, or whatever the appropriate extension of kin terms may be). Such street greetings are mandatory on one's own side of the town. It is considered much safer to drink in a bar on one's own side, but those men who pride themselves on being widely respected brag that they can drink on either side without becoming involved in a fight. When people must pass to the other side of town, they prefer walking on the Pan-American Highway, a socially neutral network, to passing through the streets of the opposite division, where their presence arouses curiosity and comments, such as "He must be looking for a lover!"

The colonias. The six colonias (Table 1) are populations of Indians who have moved from the center to take advantage of the lands granted under the ejido program of 1937 and "foreign Indians" who were formerly workers on the expropriated plantations. The Indians distinguish the close-lying settlements, or *barrios,* of Yetawitz, Pathuitz, B'očib'al, and Teʔtikil from the remaining colonias listed in the census (Table 1). The populations of the barrios are more closely identified with the center since they are closer to it and there is a higher proportion of migrants from the parent group. They are linked to the side of the dual division to which they are most closely situated. Marriages can be contracted between members of the two settlements, and house lots can be acquired by residents of the town in the barrio with which they are associated. An exception was made to the association on the basis of proximity in the case of Teʔtikil, which lies nearer to Alannantik but was linked with Ahk'olnantik in order to balance the population ratios at the time of its settlement. Police are appointed from these colonias and serve in the local *cabildo,* or town hall, along with other police from the center. The colonias of San Vicente and San Caralampio are farther away, and the rural judge and police appointed to these populations appear only once a week and during ceremonies in the local cabildo. The foreign Indians of San Vicente, who migrated from Chanal, and of Yetawitz, who came from Huistán to work in the finca of San Nicolás before acquiring ejido lands, are discriminated against in the local political organization. Their representatives never reach the high positions of president and first or second judge.

Ranchos and rancherías. The populations of these small settlements have only the most formal kind of social, economic, and political ties to the center. They register births and deaths in the township center, but they do not have any representation in the cabildo. The populations have no identification with Indian subgroups, speak Spanish, and are oriented to the regional rather than the local economic center. The plantations remaining in the area, classified as *ranchos* in the national census, employ Indians from the center. Their only relationship to the central authority is to get help in recruiting additional laborers. Recruitment of labor is no longer coercive as it was prior to the 1930s when the low wage rate could not attract the help needed. Announcements of the need for workers are made by the president on the loudspeaker system of the town, and men voluntarily go to the plantations.

Spirit Domains

The link between people and place is through the media of the spirits (*č'uleletik*) of persons and of locale. The relationship is maintained through a set of rules governing the behavior among spirits of people and of places. These rules derive from myths and stories of encounters which define the character of the spirits in each of the domains. Danger is localized in a series of caves which are avoided. Benevolent, or guardian, spirits inhabit a different set of sites, where ceremonies are conducted that maintain the well-being of the individual and of the community. By locating and circumscribing places of danger and guardianship, the members of the community can supplicate helpful spirits and avoid evil; they are delivered from fear of the unknown and provided with a rationale for dealing with fear of the known.

The places where spirits meet are outlined in Table 3. The first group includes spirits which are supplicated, the second, dangerous spirits which are avoided or approached only by powerful persons.

The house spirits. The spirits of inhabitants and of the house meet at the center post at the rear wall of the house. The spirit of the house lives in this post. Those who claim to have seen the house spirit say he is a small Ladino child. He is capricious, and if he is not happy, he may admit the evil spirits who will eat the souls of the inmates. His appetite must be satisfied when the house is first occupied and when the children of the house fall ill from a sickness diagnosed by a curer as a result of their souls being eaten. The souls of the inmates of the house hover near the center post when they are not in the body. The soul calling ceremony is held near this center post. If someone is cured in a house not his own, he must not sit near this post because his soul will be confused with those of the inmates of the house. The curing arch is erected directly before the center post, over the square hole in which the ceremonial offering of a sheep's head is buried when the house is built. A live chicken is buried in this spot if the illness is severe.

TABLE 3. Spirits and Places

Place	Place spirit	Person spirit
Loci of spirits to be supplicated		
House	Spirit of the house (*sč'ulel na*)	Spirits of children (*sč'uleletik yuntikil*)
Spring of San Nicolás	Little Ladino (*č'in kašlan*)	Spirits of male patients (*sč'uleletik yu?un keremetik*)
Spring of Pahaltón	Little Ladina (*č'in šinlan*)	Spirits of female patients (*sč'uleletik yu?un ?ač'išetik*)
Cave of Ancestors	Lopez brothers (*Šuntonetik*)	Spirits of towns-people (*sč'uleletik spisil teklum*)
Loci of spirits to be avoided		
Cave of Don David	Ladino moneylender (*Klabil*)	Petitioners for wealth
Cave of the Black Man	Devil, or black man (*?ihk'al winik*)	Witches
Cave of Juan Santos	Deceased recipient of wealth from Cave Hwan Santil	Petitioners for wealth
Stone Cave	Owner of cave (*Yahwal sč'en*)	Petitioners for wealth
Cave of Elotes	Owner of cave (*Yahwal sč'en*)	Petitioners for wealth
Cave of the Star	Owner of star (*Yahwal ?ek'*)	Curers and witches

The four sides of the square house are protected by palm crosses which were nailed to each of the four corner posts during the ceremony of the initiation of the house. These crosses prevent the entry of evil. A fifth cross on the door post, replaced each year on the Day of the Cross, ensures the guardianship of San Pedro the Martyr, the Lord of Lightning.[5]

The idea of the similarity in substance between a house and its inmates originates in the notions about soil (*lum*) and mud (*ʔač'al*). An origin myth concerning the creation of man indicates that God created man out of soil and this mythical identification is reiterated in prayers when the fleshy part of the body is referred to as *hlumeletik,* our soil, and *kač'aletik,* our mud. Whatever soil man comes into contact with—in his house, in the backyard, or in his travels, may contain some of his soul. This belief is demonstrated in the following practices: When a person's soul is lost because of a fright, such as falling or "seeing a spirit," the soil where the incident occurred is scraped into a shirt or skirt belonging to him and deposited in the soil below the head of his bed. Some older informants say that the soil from beneath the bed is scraped up and deposited in the coffin of a deceased inmate of the house, but I have never seen this done. This intimate relation between soul and soil was best illustrated to us when our landlord refused to let us put a cement floor in the interior of his house since it would interfere with the practices described above and other customs in the house ceremonies mentioned below.

The house is constructed in two stages. The completion of each stage requires a ceremony linking the spirits of the inmates to that of the dwelling. The first stage is the erection of the house posts and the wooden frame. When the roof is covered with wood shingles, thatch, or tile, the family may set up temporary walls of boards. They wait until the rainy season to complete the second stage of building up the walls with mud. The first ceremony, called "fiesta for the house," is for "the spirit which resides in the posts," and the second, called "meal for the house," is to feed "the spirit of the house earth." People believe that the mud walls, like their fleshy counterpart, the human body, require nourishment.

5. San Pedro Martyr is referred to by the Indians as *Tatik Martil* and is identified with the pre-Conquest deity Lord of Lightning, or *Tatik Čaʔuk.*

First house fiesta. In preparation for the fiesta to inaugurate
the wooden frame of the house, the older men of the household and the
curers make palm crosses called *Tatik Martil,* another reference to San
Pedro Martyr. Older men are chosen to do this task because their procrea-
tive powers will not be endangered by handling this powerful symbol.
Branches of the bushes growing near the springwater of San Nicolás are
cut by the younger men of the household to be arranged in an arch, while
the women make incense burners and clay candle holders. The protective
symbols used in the fiesta—the arch of branches and flowers, the candles,
liquor, handrolled cigarettes, palm crosses, and springwater in a gourd—
are arranged before the center post of the back wall of the house.

Fig. 1. Relatives Present at House Fiesta

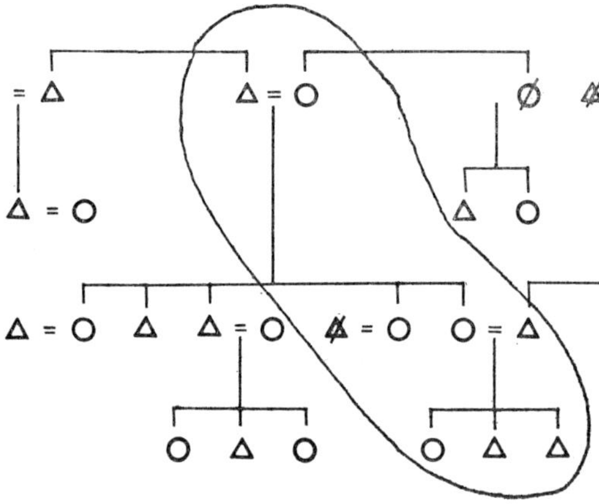

Encircled group will live in house.

The activities of a house fiesta observed in 1966 are described below.

*The future occupants of the house sat in a row facing the curing arch.
Two curers officiated, the elder a resident of the side of the dual division
in which the houseowner lives and the second from the barrio in which
his son-in-law, Santiago, was born. The elder curer lit the candles at the
center post of the back wall, while the younger curer lit those at the center
post in the middle wall. The mother of Santiago lit the incense and placed*

it before he arch. The younger curer then took a bunch of the branches of spring bushes and brushed each person over the head, shoulders, back, arms, and legs. Liquor was passed around to the visitors and participants. The elder curer took the bunch of branches, prayed, and brushed the future occupants. The younger curer followed him with another brushing.

The elder curer put some powder in the springwater. He then took a rattle, stuck it it in a bunch of the leaves from the spring, gave it a couple of shakes as though testing it, and handed it to one of the b'alnial (young male assistants). He then stood before the candles at the back center post, bowed to it, turned, and bowed to the opposite center post. He poured the springwater in a gourd and gave it to Juliana, the houseowner's daughter, who passed it to each member of the household. The curer then took out four cigarettes and put them on either side of the candles. He greeted everyone present and delivered the following prayer:

> *May no witchcraft enter.*
> *May all the children be cared for.*
> *I can see and hear who enters.*
> *Of one heart are the women, of one heart are the men.*

Santiago began to play the guitar as his wife, Alberta, brought in the coffee and rolls. She handed the first cup to the elder curer. This was followed with a serving of rice and tomatoes. Before he began to eat, the curer said, "good afternoon" to all present.

After the meal, the elder curer led the household members outside. He held one of the palm crosses at the corner post of the house and prayed; then Santiago pounded in a nail to hold it. Each member of the household, including the small children of Alberta, went up and kissed the cross in turn. They went on to the other main posts of the exterior of the house where they did the same thing. They entered the house and continued drinking the rest of the afternoon. Cigarettes were passed around, and the men began to joke. Drinking is compulsory: everyone who attends must drink equal amounts of the liquor served.

Each of the ritual items is introduced because it contains a powerful soul. The branches and the springwater contain souls associated with the spring. The gourd is used as a container for the springwater because, like all growing plants and unlike metal or glass containers, it has a soul. The soul of the tobacco plant is considered particularly strong. The smoke of the candles and incense are the media through which prayers to the spirit of the house are transmitted.

The house fiesta serves three functions: (1) introducing the spirit of the house inmates to the house spirit, (2) creating a harmonious setting for spiritual interaction of the members of the household and the house spirit, (3) protecting the house against the intrusion of evil. The introduction is achieved by brushing the household members with the branches from the spring, and the harmony is brought about by drinking liquor, playing the guitar, and dancing. The music of the seed gourd, the guitar, and sometimes a radio or phonograph makes the residents, their guests, and the house spirit happy, or "of one heart." Protection is insured by nailing the palm crosses representing the Lord of the Lightning to the house posts.

Second house fiesta ("meal for the house"). When a meal is given to the spirit of the house earth, the house is arranged as for the house fiesta with curing arches set in front of the center posts at the back and middle walls. The same guests are invited as for the first fiesta. The family buys a sheep and slaughters it in the morning by stringing it up to the center post by it paws and slashing its jugular vein. When the blood has drained into the square hole opened at the base of the center post, the curer removes the head and buries it in the hole. Some curers bury the four paws as well, while others prefer to add an offering of five pieces of bread in a new pottery jar, twenty measures of chocolate, thirteen cigarettes, and a bottle of liquor covered with a new cloth. The head of the sheep is placed so that the eyes look up to watch over the inhabitants. Some refer to it as the *me?iltatil,* identifying it with the curers (who are called me?iltatil in the context of guardianship) and thus with the ancestor guardians.

During the house fiesta I observed in July 1967, an old curer who had officiated at the first ceremony served again. A neighbor, who was not related to the houseowners but who was skilled in butchering, slaughtered the animal. *The curer received from him the severed head and paws which he placed in a large gourd. Then the curer served a potion of herbs in springwater to all of the members of the household. The final ritual act was for the curer to smoke an article of clothing belonging to each member of the household over the incense burning in front of the center arch at the back wall. Liquor was served continaully throughout the ceremony, the first drink always being given to the curer followed by one to the elder houseowner. The first drink was served immediately after the cutting of the jugular vein of the sheep. Flowing blood, water, and liquor are spirit media symbolically linked in ritual behavior. Between each of the major ritual acts—the slaughtering of the sheep, the burial of the head, the serving of the springwater and herbs, and the smoking of the clothing with incense—the curer prayed, but his prayers were so mumbled that I could not hear or record them. Informants said that it was a variation of the prayer given at the first house fiesta. After the rituals, a stew made with the sheep meat was served with tortillas to all the visitors. The music of guitar and gourd rattle, played during the ritual by young male relatives continued after the meal, and the guests remained in the house drinking and dancing for the rest of the afternoon.*

Elements of these house fiestas are repeated when any of the children of the household is ill. A severe illness, diagnosed as being caused by the devil eating the soul of the patient, requires offering a meal to the house spirit. The square hole is reopened, and a live black chicken, male if the patient is a boy and female if it is a girl, is placed inside. A food offering of one-fourth liter of liquor, one peso's worth of bread, and 50 cents' worth of chocolate is placed inside with the chicken, and a square board is fitted on top of the hole "to keep the chicken alive for eight days so that the house spirit will hear his cries." When the curing arch is removed, the hole is filled in with dirt over the chicken, now dead, which provides a meal for the spirit house earth.

When the houseowner is sick, an appeal for health is made to the spirit in the house post. The members of the household kiss the post, a splinter is removed and burned in an incense burner with *pom,* the resin of pine. This odor is pleasing to the house spirit.

When a serious illness caused by witchcraft has been cured, the patient must be protected against reentry of the evil by a gift of medicine to the house. Palm crosses are made for the corner posts and the entry, and a medicine consisting of a mixture of garlic and creosote, the seeds of mustard, and *poščan,* a "hot" herb, is mixed. As the crosses are nailed on the posts, the curer marks a cross with the medicine over the palm cross. This "covers the eyes of the evil spirit" so that it will not enter the house.

The relationship between house spirit and the spirits of the residents is an uneasy one. Fear is associated with this capricious spirit, who might make an alliance with evil spirits, and whose power is evident only in sickness and in death, never in good deeds. A sense of alienation is conveyed in the fact that the house spirit and the spirits of the spring are conceived of as Ladinos. Spirits of the house and of the landscape are exacting landlords from whom the tenants expect nothing in return for their offerings but freedom from harm. Acceptance of the offerings seals a contract between spiritual occupants that must continually be renewed in order to maintain the balance of security expressed in the phrase "to be of one heart." The payment of a "tribute" in the form of food, liquor, and entertainment is part of a larger strategy by which these Indians ensure their survival by appeasement of overlords, demanding government officials, and the very rats which live in their houses and feed on the corn they store in the eaves.

The springs. Other meeting grounds for the spirits of people and places are the springs. The major spring, San Nicolás, is located on the southwestern periphery of the town. It provides drinking water and water for irrigating the cultivated lands. A second spring, called Pahaltón, lies closer to the village and provides a smaller stream of water directed into the canals irrigating the fields of the center. Some say the spirit of San Nicolás is a small Ladino boy; others say he is a man. The spirit of Pahaltón is a female non-Indian, or *Ladina.* The spirits of these waters are able to effect miraculous cures for patients who have lost their souls or those who are of two hearts because of upset social relations in the home. Male patients are brought to San Nicolás and female patients are brought to Pahaltón to seek a miracle. In the curing ceremony an arch of flowers entwined in pine boughs is constructed as closely as possible to the spring waters. The curer brushes the patients with branches of the cooling bushes and herbs growing near the spring, the same ones used in the fiesta of inauguration and the curing ceremonies conducted in the house. The strategy of making the house spirit happy by providing music, dancing, and drinking is repeated at the spring to make the water spirit happy. Some of the family of the patient must remain in the house as "waiters" (*maliwanehetik*) to receive the spirit if it should arrive before its owner. The maliwanehetik must drink as much liquor as the participants at the spring.

The Cave of the Ancestors. The ancestors, the *me?tiktatik,* were believed to have lived in a cave in the hills lying on the peripheries of the township. In the myth that follows, they are given a historical identity as two brothers, the Shuntonetik. Shunton is one of the Tzeltal patronyms of families still living in the town, and in fact the narrator of this version of the myth is Mariano Shunton, whom people consider a descendant of the ancestors.[6]

Formerly a priest asked for a document to be delivered to Antigua in Guatemala. Two messengers were sent with it, but they did not return. Another messenger went and did not return. Four or five more messengers were sent out and did not come back. Finally they sent a man from the cabildo with his younger brother. They left early in the morning, and the elder brother said as he left the other town officials, "If I succeed, I want a fiesta. Look for my sign of four arches [rainbow]."

The two brothers first went to a hill. There they called upon their swayohelik *[animal spirits]. First the animal spirit of the elder brother spoke. He said, "I am a stone." Then the animal spirit of the younger brother said, "I am a stick. Moreover, I am a snake and a maguey plant." The elder brother said, "Then we are well off. Let us go."*

6. The same identification of a lineage patronym with the most important sacred hill is found in other Tzeltal- and Tzotzil-speaking communities (Holland 1963, Hermitte 1964). The pattern may have originated in a period of pre-Conquest expansion when the dominant lineage was assiged a custodial leadership over the new settlement, with their spirits remaining as guardians of the community. Members of the contemporary communities who bear the same patronym do not have any privileged position. These associations of past and contemporary belief are, as Vogt (1964:216) cautions, still hypothetical.

As the two brothers were walking, the elder brother said, "Do you see what that man is doing?" He was referring to a black man lying near the road. "He is sleeping," said the younger. The elder said, "Let us go on."

They approached closer to the sleeping man. The elder brother said, "Let us pass." Just as they were passing, the black man said, "Where are you going? Come back! Come, enter here."

They entered a cave. The black man said, "Here you are going to die." "So be it," said the elder.

"Put your head here," said the black man. He went to get his machete, but instead of hitting the head with it, he drove it into the great stone which was the elder brother's swayohel. "Ah, the devil, who are you?" he asked. Turning to the younger brother, he said, "Now it is your turn!"

The younger brother came, and the black man struck him with his machete. The machete broke.

"Now it is your turn, black man!" said the younger brother. The devil began to cry, "Go along, I will not trouble you." "Yes, you will always trouble us," said the elder brother. "I shall give you money," said the black man. "No, I have money," said the elder brother. "Then I shall carry you," said the black man. "I do not want that. You must die!" said the elder brother. "Come, boy [to his younger brother], cut a stick and make two points on each side. Stick it there and a wind will carry him aloft.".

Then a snake came and settled right there where the stick was planted. The black man fell, and the stick entered his anus. It came out of his mouth and he died. The brothers cut off his head and brought it to Guatemala. They delivered the paper to the priest, who was very frightened.

"Which way have you come?" asked the priest. "We came along the road," answered the brothers.

"But didn't you see anyone?" asked the priest. "No one," answered the brothers. "But where did you really go?" asked the priest.

"Since you force us to answer, we did meet someone," answered the brothers, "covering the road where we passed midway. We brought him here."

"I want to see him," said the priest. The elder brother said, "Look, I brought him in this box. I cut off his head."

The priest looked, and when he saw the head, he cried. He ordered the soldiers to come and throw the Shunton brothers in jail. He ordered a meal brought to prison with a servant.

"I do not want it," said the elder brother and returned it with the servant. "Tell him [the priest] that I do not want it but thank him."

The servant told the priest that the brothers did not want the good meal.

"Good," said the priest. "If they don't eat in a little while they will be dead. Go leave them liquor so that they will not feel how they die."

"Good," said the servant. She went to the jail and said, "My master wants to know if you want to drink."

"I don't want any. I have some too. I brought a liter of trago." There they were drinking inside the prison.

At ten in the morning, they came to tie a blindfold on the brothers. They shot at them, but the bullet did not hit. They shot again, but it did not hit. "Who are these people?" asked the priest. "Send out another soldier!" The other began to fire, but the bullets did not hit the brothers. Many soldiers came out and fired, but the bullets did not hit them.

"Then," said the soldier, "you know what we shall do? We shall burn them in this hide."

"Good, go look for the hide. When the hide comes we will prepare it," said the priest.

They began to sew the hide. When they finished sewing, they began to throw wood and lit a fire. They waited until the fire started. They came to see the brothers. They were very drunk.

"Bring them here." said the priest. "Not yet. They are still drinking." But the priest answered, "They have drunk enough. Go bring them and we shall burn them."

On their second return, the fire began to burn the pueblo. The people began to cry. Half the pueblo was burned when the Lord of Lightning and Rain came. A shower hit the fire.

"Good," said the elder brother. "We have won. Now the fire is out and we shall go. Let us see if they are waiting for us in our town. If not, I know where we can find some pretty women in Chiapa."

"Good. Let us rest a little," said the younger brother.

"Good, I am thirsty. Let us go where there is water," said the elder.

"Good."

They waited a while and the water came. "Are you going to drink?"

They drank, and then they made the sign of the rainbow. The president sent his sindico to meet them. The sindico got drunk on the way. He sat down halfway in the road. The brothers met him there. They were angry that a fiesta was not prepared for them. And for this they left town, and went to live in Chiapas.

This tale is known to everyone in town, and there is no doubt as to its authenticity expressed by those who have given versions of it. When I took some of the Indians on a trip to Guatemala, they pointed out the rocks where the brothers encountered the devil. When they arrived in Guatemala and saw a bus marked Antigua they expressed amazement that the town was still in existence.

Some people claim to have seen the ancestors, whom they describe as wearing the old style costume—a long shirt with the hat now worn by the alfereces. The ancestors are believed to have watched over the village from a mound rising abruptly before the mouth of the cave, called Hol Shan, or Head of Palm, because of the trees growing on it (Plate 1). From this eminence they could watch the streets of the village and see whether anyone was trying to bring in evil (Plate 2). They were able to discern the power of evil in the souls of the newborn and could snatch the soul before its possessor grew up to cause evil. Their human agents in guarding the town against evil were the curers (*ʔuʔuletik*), who in the context of guardianship were called *meʔiltatil*.[7]

Each year on the Day of the Cross, May 3d in the Catholic calendar,[8] a fiesta is held in honor of the ancestors. It refers back to the fiesta which ought to have been held for the returning Shuntonetik, and is performed in the interest of the whole community as a means of ensuring good relations with the ancestors.

Formerly the curers were responsible for conducting this fiesta. An informant recalled the ritual:

7. The guardianship role of the curers is related to the functions of pre-Conquest officials, called *ghcanalum*, "caretakers of the soil" (Calnek 1962:25).

8. The date of the Day of the Cross was changed by the Vatican in 1964. When the local priest tried to reschedule the fiesta in the community, he encountered strong opposition. The Indians continue to celebrate the Day of the Cross on May 3d.

The curers used to go up to the cave with the alfereces, the mayordomos *[religious officials], the prayer reciters, and the people of the village. When they arrived there, the mayordomos played the guitar and gourd rattle. They lit candles and incense, and the leading curers would go inside the cave. All the people contributed money for the liquor and candles which was collected by the officials. They said that they spoke to the ancestors inside, where there was a lake and a beautiful field. They asked for rain and good crops. They would come out and tell the people waiting outside what the ancestors had said.*

Then one year [in 1957] during the fiesta of the cave, the curers went into the cave. The people said to the curers, "We want to see the owners." The curers said they would come out, but they didn't. The people waited and waited. A boy went inside with the curers. They tried to prevent him, saying, "Won't you be afraid?" He said, "No, let's go in." They entered twenty feet inside the door. The curers said, "Let us stay here." The boy asked them where was the river, the lake, and the milpa that were supposed to be inside. The curer replied, "It is all a lie. Now you know; don't tell the people." But when he came out, the boy told the people it was all a deception.

Since the late 1950s the ritual has changed. The curers no longer officiate, nor do they enter the cave and speak to the ancestors as they did formerly. The *fiscal,* or assistant to the priest, leads the mayordomos, alfereces, and prayer-reciters to the cave on the Day of the Cross and simply replace the palm cross at the entrance to the cave just as they do with the palm crosses fixed to the wooden crosses marking the roads leading into the town. The curers have attempted to revive the belief in the presence of the ancestors by saying that their nephew is in residence now, but no one I ever spoke to believes this. Most people agree that the ancestors live permanently in Chiapa de Corso.[9]

The hill and cave owners. While people try to maintain a good relationship with the spirits of the house, of the springs, and of the Cave of the Ancestors, they avoid the dangerous spirits of the hills and caves

9. A similar myth concerning the departure of the ancestors to go live in Chiapa de Corzo exists in Pinola (Hermitte 1964).

which have the power to mislead, give illness, or capture people to work for them. Only the most powerful curers and witches, and the very greedy approach these spirits for they are reputed to be very "live" and maliciously clever. Snakes are the offspring of the hill and do the bidding of the hill owners.

Wealth in the form of livestock, corn, or gold can be gained from some of the cave owners upon request, but there is danger in receiving these gifts since they must be reciprocated. Among the cave owners who give gifts is Don Klabil, a deceased moneylender of the neighboring town. After his death in the 1940s, his spirit went to live in the hill bordering the two towns. People say that when he was alive he used to get money from the true owner of the cave. Those who have been inside the cave say it is filled with animals—cattle, horses, rabbits—which drink at a large interior lake. The appropriate approach for requesting wealth is to go on Thursday, "when the earth is open," and burn candles and incense. When the request is granted, the recipient must light candles at the cave every Thursday, and after his death he must work forever for the cave owner. It is said that at his death his wealth dies with him—usually all has been spent, and in fact children are left poor. Some say the spirit of the firstborn child of the recipient must be given to the owner to work for him. For this reason, there is no envy felt by neighbors when they see the increasing wealth of a man who has visited the caves and received such gains and he is doubly protected because no one can hurt an "enchanted man" (one who has entered the cave) with witchcraft.

Ladinos' belief in the cave owners gives support to the Indians' credence in their power. Ladinos inquire of Indians where they can find treasures. Once the request to the hill owners is made, it is essential to follow through correctly. Everyone in town knows the story of Martin Bautista, a curer who went to speak to the true owner of the hill in which Don Klabil lives.

He knew how to talk to the owner. The owner told him that at midnight on the following day, he would give him what he wanted. At midnight Maria, his wife, was alone in the house. She heard a noise and the sound of "Andale, burro!" Then there was a knock at the door. When the woman opened the door, she said, "Ay, Dios!" The owner of the cave did not like this, and at that moment, he disappeared. Her husband returned the next morning. He beat her when he heard of the arrival of the hill owner and his disappearance when she invoked the name of the Lord. From that day on, he lost his luck and remained a poor man.

The personalities of the cave owners are more fully defined than those of the spirits which reside in the forests. These tree spirits are able to talk to people, or they may sing, "as a mother sings to her child." They sometimes play tricks, misdirecting those who are lost in the woods. A man who intends to kill his enemy may go to talk to the tree spirits to gain their advice. Some plant spirits, such as tobacco, are stronger than others. Indians sometimes address the tobacco plant as "our grandfather" when they approach it, asking leave to pass. Some say that if you chew the tobacco plant you will have strength to overcome evil spirits when you walk in the woods.

An especially fearful group of spirits called *bohwaletik* roam the wooded hills in the late afternoons. These spirits, who look like Ladinos, are feared because they cut off people's heads to feed to the church bell in a neighboring town or to give to the spirits of major construction projects, such as dams. Suspicions are immediately aroused when a solitary Ladino is seen on the outskirts of the town near evening, and if several Indians sight him, they may even kill him.

Persistence of belief and rituals related to the old gods and demons that were part of the Maya pantheon is directly related to the fact that the Indians continue to live in the same place surrounded by the hills and caves that were the habitations of both good and bad spirits. The landscape serves as a mnemonic device, keeping alive the myths of the past. Everyone accepts the knowledge that the spirits once lived here; the only doubt is whether they continue to inhabit their appropriate places, particularly in the case of the ancestors who were responsible for crops and security. This is not a crisis of loss in belief, but a phasing into history of the mythological past. Since there is no longer acceptance of the curers' claim to communication with the spirits, the Indians believe they may have gone elsewhere. It is characteristic of these Indians that they do not reject their past as they appraise their present conditions, but rather fit it into a historic continuum. It is the core of their self-awareness that makes possible the kind of change which I have characterized as a moving equilibrium.

Chapter 2

Traditional Economic Activities

The traditional occupation of every adult man is working in the milpa and of every adult woman, making pottery. The fiction is maintained that they do this work, even if they are actually engaged fulltime in some other activity. In response to the census question, "What is the work of the man or woman?" men answered universally that they were agriculturalists and women that they were potters. Men who work outside the community, in the fincas or in the sawmills, consider this a temporary means of gaining cash income and do not define themselves as sawyers or laborers for others. They work outside the community only when they do not have sufficient land to provide themselves with corn to eat and a surplus to sell, or when they must pay debts incurred by bethrothal or assumption of religious posts. Many women who do not make pottery for extended periods of time, or make it only for a special fiesta, still consider themselves pottery producers.

Persistence of the same occupations and the daily effort to make a living strengthen the link between generations and to tradition. The primary emphasis in child training is teaching both boys and girls to work efficiently and industriously in these traditional occupations. The techniques for codifying and perpetuating a given way of doing things, particularly evident in pottery production, provide clues to the way in which other kinds of behavior are schematized.

AGRICULTURAL PRODUCTION

Agricultural production involves two areas of decision making: what to grow and when to schedule each activity related to production. Decisions in both these areas are based upon custom and time-proved results. I shall indicate these bases and assess the efficiency of the agriculturalists in allocating resources of labor, land, and seeds.

Land use. The historical factor of the greatest significance in establishing the present economic position of the town was the act of possession of ejido lands in 1937. The first grant included 4,873.53 *hectares* [1] of land of the following categories:

irrigated flat land	139.77
non-irrigated plots	1,018.37
pasture	1,659.65
hill land	2,055.74

The high hill land with its cover of pine and scrub oak was set aside for use of all members of the community for hunting and gathering firewood. The pasture lands are similarly controlled by the civil authority for common use. The cultivable lands passed into the hands of 385 ejidatarios, each of whom received one-half hectare. A further grant in 1954 provided an increase of 2,578 hectares, including:

low mountain land	2,277.60
pasture land	300.40

The possession of land by individual small-plot cultivators reversed the trend toward large-scale commercial agriculture begun in the last quarter of the nineteenth century. The land of the Indians that had been expropriated in the latter part of the nineteenth century by forced sales was to be held in the possession of the townspeople, "benefiting all with its products and uses" (Act of possession, 1937, Town Archives).

With the increase in ejido lands acquired in 1954, the share of each ejidatario has been increased to one hectare. This is usually split between low land in San Caralampio and high land in San Isidro and Tulancá, giving two growing seasons. The advantages of different growing seasons are that there is a more balanced work schedule and that there are two harvests, one in November and one in July. The ejido land grant has stabilized subsistence crop cultivation in the economy of the town and in-

1. A hectare is equal to 2.46 acres.

creased the economic independence of the Indians. The present total of 613 ejidatarios in 1965 has increased 59 percent since the original grant. The dependence of the town's economy on the ejido land can be assessed in the fact that 63 percent of the pasture land is held in ejido grants. The use of land resources in the township is summarized in Table 4.

TABLE 4. Agricultural Productivity by Size of Landholding

Size of landholding (hectares)	Weight of produce (kilograms)	Value of produce (pesos)	Land used (percentage)
Less than 5 hectares			
Corn	200,000	120,000	83.
Wheat	29,000	27,550	16.8
Fruit	3,000	9,000	.2
1 hectare of ejido land			
Corn	319,688	223,781	49.
Corn (with beans)	30,320	21,224	6.
Beans (with corn)	14,000	17,360	
Wheat	185,580	181,580	28.
Beans	84,322	104,322	17.
More than 5 hectares			
Corn	67,388	45,117	34.
Corn (with beans)	96,550	68,108	51.
Beans (with corn)	42,985	56,740	
Alfalfa	350,000	42,000	4.6
Fruit	14,508	9,720	4.4
Other			6.

SOURCE: 1960 census, Mexico.

According to the 1960 census figures on productivity per hectare, privately owned plots under five hectares yield the highest return in corn (1,097 kgs. per hectare), privately owned plots over five hectares the next highest return (925 kgs. per hectare), and ejido plots of one hectare the least (810 kgs. per hectare). In the census evaluation of wheat and corn production on privately owned plots of less than five hectares, wheat apparently yields a higher return (807 pesos per hectare of wheat compared with 658 pesos per hectare of corn). This relative return is nearly the same for the corn produced on ejido lands (820 pesos per hectare return on wheat compared with 603 pesos for corn). However, this is figured at the maximum market price for wheat of 124 pesos per 100 kgs. The Indians usually sell their wheat at 90 pesos per 100 kgs. to Teopisca truckers, or at best gain 110 pesos per 100 kgs. by bringing it to the mills themselves. From their perspective corn is the more valuable crop, not only from the point of view of subsistence, but also for sale since if they hold it in storage they can sell it at double the price at which the values are calculated in the census (.60 peso per kg.). They do not have facilities to store wheat in order to take maximum advantage of price changes.

The census I made in 1964 of land ownership and use by the 304 families living in the center of the township (Table 5) shows that 47 percent of the households have no land other than the ejido grant of one hectare. Because of the growing population, the land per household has decreased. A comparison with the 1958 census of land ownership of 280 households in the center indicates that 89 families now have less land than they had at that date, 72 have the same amount, and 44 have more land; 99 unknown cases include new families which have been created since the earlier date, families which were no longer in existence in 1964, and households in which there is a lack of data on the question of landholding.

The strong sentiment against the sale of one's own land, well documented in the monographic literature,[2] is expressed here:

> If a man sells his land without sickness, people say he is lazy. The best thing to buy if you have money is land. Unlike cattle, it does not die, it does not get lost, and it does not need watching. It is not the same with a horse. When you buy one, you have to watch it and care for it and when it dies, all is over. You lose all your money. But with land, in two years you have the land paid for and it remains as a gift. It gives us what we eat.

Land is rarely sold to outsiders. If a man needs money and has a buyer from out of town, the civil authorities raise the money and buy the plot, selling it in pieces as they find buyers. Only one small plot of land has been sold to an outsider in my knowledge of the community. This plot

2. See Tax (1957), Wagley (1941). Oscar Lewis (1963:125 indicates that in Tepotzlan the breakdown of the resistance to selling land was associated with a growing awareness of profits to be made in the regional and national economy.

TABLE 5. Land Ownership and Crops Grown by Households, 1964

Crops	Owners of ejido land (2 tablones*)	Owners of ejido and inherited land No. of tablones					Owners of ejido and bought land No. of tablones					Owners of ejido, bought, and inherited land No. of tablones					Total
		1	2	3	4	5	1	2	3	4	5 and over	1	2	3	4	5	
Corn	45	6	2				1			1							55
Corn and wheat	92	25	13	1		2	2	3	2	2	2	1	6	5	2	3	161
Corn and beans	3	23	16	4		2	8	11	1	2			3		3	2	78
Unknown	2							2						1			5
Total	142	54	31	5		4	11	16	3	5	2	1	9	6	5	5	299

* A tablón is equal to 25 square meters roughly figured; there are 4 tablones in one hectare.

was in a low gully where crops would not grow, and no one within the community would buy it.

Land is frequently pawned by farmers as security on a loan. The title to the land is left with the lender, who can foreclose on the debt if the interest payments of five percent per month are not paid. Often the land pawned may be worth far more than the loan. Loans in town are rarely backed with security, and if something is pawned, it is usually clothing or household items.

With the growing significance of ejido lands and land sale, inheritance of land is of less importance in the economic expectations of each successive generation. The rules controlling inheritance are theoretically simple: equal inheritance for all children regardless of sex. The parents usually give some land when the child establishes a separate household; the remainder is then given at the death of the parent or when old age makes it impossible for the parent to work any more. The youngest child remaining at home works his father's land, or if he is living with his wife's family, his father-in-law's land, until the latter's death. His family inherits the house site as well as an equal share of the privately held lands. Complications arise because of modifications of the basic rule of equal inheritance by provisions for care and maintenance of the aged parents. Frequent disputes over inheritance are settled in local courts or passed on to the Department of Indian Affairs in San Cristóbal.

The selection of which crop to grow is related to the kind and amount of land a farmer owns. The most important crops are corn, beans, and wheat. Some squash and sugarcane are grown in the lower ejido lands of San Caralampio. Cabbage is grown by one Indian who possesses fertile irrigated lands in the center. Most Indians, however, are unwilling to undertake the risk of raising a cash crop since there is greater chance of the crop being stolen and they cannot afford a bad market price when they harvest.

Relating the size of holding to the crop grown, according to figures in the Mexican census of 1960[3] (Table 4) one can see that in privately

---

3. The census figures are based on estimates received from town officials, who submit them monthly to the census bureau. The officials of the town question the household heads as they see them in the streets or in their houses about how much seed they planted. They then estimate what the yield per almud for good and bad land is, from their own crops.

owned plots of less than five hectares, corn is clearly the major crop, with 83 percent of the land devoted to its production. In the ejido lands, it is cultivated on less than 50 percent of the land, with wheat and beans sharing the remaining lands. Included in the category of ownership of five hectares or more are three large fincas where cattle fodder is grown. These fincas employ eighty-three laborers, some of whom live in the town center.

Since the Mexican census figures do not take into account the total land holdings of the household, I shall refer to the data on land use from my own census in 1964 (Table 5). Beans are grown (except in three cases) only if the household has more than the one hectare of ejido land grant. Corn and beans are grown together only on irrigated lands, both in high lands and in low country. Most farmers with ejido land grow wheat in addition to corn only when the land is in continual production, since it is believed that wheat gives "heat" to the land and improves the soil. This belief is supported by the real value of crop rotation.

Decisions concerning what crops to plant where are based on two sets of criteria: topology and soil characteristics. These criteria, furthermore, are the basis for determining what kinds of seed should be planted and what techniques of cultivation should be utilized.

Topological criteria. Because of the relative wealth of land resources, the steep hills are left uncultivated. All of the steep hills are communally owned, and the second growth of pine and scrub oak provides firewood. Tall pine growing in the higher lands of the colonia of San Vicente is sold by the community to private lumber companies.

The "belly of the land," the mound-like hillocks at the bottom of the hills, are sometimes cultivated or used for pasturage. On hilly lands farmers put rocks in the banks or curve the rows of corn to avoid erosion. The very low lands of the valley floor must be drained by digging ditches.

The flat irrigated lands of the valley floor are the most desirable lands for cultivation. The Indians are reluctant to sell these lands, and hold on to them until they are forced to sell.

When the officials reach concensus on what the mean yield (or *medio calculo* as they call it) is, they multiply this by the known amount of seed planted. Every six years a house-to-house census of what was planted is made.

Soil characteristics. The potential productivity of flat irrigated lands is evaluated on the basis of two criteria: color of the soil and consistency of the soil. The preferred land for cultivation is the black loam mixed with some sand, (*ʔihk'al hiʔiletik lum*). The better, quicker growing corn seed is planted here. These very productive soils are called "hot" lands (*k'išin lum*). (Heat is associated with fertility in both lands and people: a pregnant woman and her husband are considered to be in a state of heat, and the contrast state of being cold is attributed to someone who is sterile.) The red (*tzab'alum*) yellow (*k'analum*), and white soils (*sak lum*) are poorer soils and the slower seed is planted here. These soils are considered "cold" (*sik*) and are thought to be "tired."

The loss of soil productivity is attributed either to the loss of the soul of the crop or to the fact that the soil gets "tired." Farmers have noticed that in the first five years of planting in Tulanca, the ejido land grant, the soil was "hot" and gave good crops. When this productivity was lost, people said the soul of the crop left. It is considered dangerous to start crops in the lower lands of hot country because when the location of crops is changed, the soul leaves its original residence. The notion of crop soul loss does not conflict with the awareness of natural causes of soil productivity. Fields are left fallow for four or five years when productivity diminishes and the soil is "tired." The irrigated lands are in continuous use because there is some replenishment of fertility with the overflow of the ditch waters. Cattle fertilizers are used sporadically. Those who have many head of cattle construct corrals into which they herd the cattle each night. The location of the corral is changed yearly. Corn and beans are then planted in the old corral with superior results. The dozen or so corrals in the town are owned and worked cooperatively by extended families and are referred to by the Indian patronyms—for example, *skoral Linetik* (corral of the Lins) or *skoral Čailetik* (corral of the Čailes). The one attempt to use commercial fertilizers provided by the Ejido Bank proved a technical success but an administrative failure (chapter 3). Indians noted the increased yields, but none have attempted to purchase fertilizers.

Soil consistency is evaluated on the basis of how easy it is to work. Wet, sticky, or clayey soil (*šučilium*) and stony soil (*kešilum*) are least desirable. Sandy soil is easier to work, but soil productivity depends on a loam base, so the farmers prefer to plant the better, quicker-growing corn seed in a mixed sand and loam soil.

The final evaluation of land is based on results at harvest. The range of variation is large: from 48 liters of yield per liter of seed to 80 litters of yield per liter of seed. Township officials say that the average harvest is five *fanegas* (1 fanega equals 12 liters) or 60 liters per liter of seed. Market prices are of less importance in deciding what crops will be planted than are considerations of what the soil "wants" and what labor is involved. Corn is grown on all kinds of land, whereas beans and special crops such as cabbages can be grown only on the more fertile soil. Wheat can be grown only where there is irrigation. One farmer raised cabbage in cooperation with a Ladino and earned 1,000 pesos, four times the amount he earned with his wheat crop the previous year. Despite the greater return for cabbage, the farmer did not plant it the next year when the Ladino, who had supported the first venture, withdrew his support. The reason he gave for this was the fact that there was more work involved and he could not accomplish it alone: first the crop had to be planted, then transplanted, then irrigated every three days in the early growing period, and cultivated two or three times; every eight days he had to get rid of worms. He estimated that growing cabbage involved well over four times the amount of work necessary for growing corn.

Labor. Most agricultural work is performed by members of households with exchange or hired labor. There is no specialization of labor when the work force includes two or more men since the men cooperate in doing each task. Communal labor is restricted to the maintenance of the main irrigation ditches. Each year the ditches are dug out where the sides have eroded and cleaned of brush and leaves. The president and judges unite to decide on a time for this work and announce it on a loudspeaker of one of the cantinas. This usually occurs around the twenty-fifth of December. Formerly, all the men of the community helped in this work whether or not they owned irrigated fields. In 1958 those who did not own such land "got smart" and refused to work.

In 1962 the civil officials decided that a cement canal should be installed near the source of the spring. They tried to finance it with contributions from all men of the township, but again they were refused by the farmers who did not own irrigated land. The officials then sold trees in the communally owned lands to support the project, which cost 2,000 pesos. The farmers without irrigated lands still bore the cost although indirectly since community resources were expended in subsidizing the work.

The scheduling of agricultural activities follows an annual cycle for the three major crops, corn, wheat, and beans.

Corn. In corn production, the greatest discrimination comes in the selection of seed.[4] Seed is chosen from cobs which have the most grain. The farmer must look carefully to see that none of it is rotten, since if one grain is bad, the entire five grains put into each hillock will rot. There are two major kinds of corn: a quick-growing variety and a slow-growing variety. The first is preferred, but not all soils "want" it. The bitter soil "wants" the slow corn which must be planted about the first of February. A new corn seed introduced by some developmental engineers in 1957 yielded more grain, but it was not as flinty as the old variety and rotted quickly.

The soil is prepared by cross-plowing the land three times in one direction and two times in the other. Those who do not own their own oxen team do it just once because of the additional expense. In planting, the farmer is careful to measure rows evenly, five handspans between rows, and five handspans between each hillock, forming a square which permits the maximum growth of each plant. Five seeds are placed in each hillock. In hot country, the land has not been worked over as well, and as a result it cannot be measured as accurately because of rocks and trees. This upsets the agriculturalist's sense of symmetry and beauty.

Once the corn has been planted, the scheduling of activities is based on the maturation of the plant rather than on a calendrical sequence. The scheduling of activities in corn production is shown in Table 6. The starges of growth in the corn plant and the activities related to them are listed in Table 7.

Cultivation is performed twice, to kill the weeds and to pile up earth at

4. The botanist Anderson (quoted in Lévi-Strauss 1966:73) points out that the careful separation of seed planted in each plot distinguished Indian from non-Indian agriculturalists in other Middle American communities.

the roots of each plant so that it will be protected. One farmer commented on this process: "The face of the earth remains loose. Thus the corn remains of one heart. Nothing dies because the soil is moved, and the tender shoots begin to grow. When the second hoeing is finished, God looks at it to see that the corn matures." In the second hoeing, any corn which has grown between hillocks is pulled out so it will not deprive the main stalks of strength.

When the corn has matured, the stalks are doubled over to hasten the drying process. The mature cobs are left on the doubled-over stalks for about two weeks to ensure the maximum drying of the kernels before har-

TABLE 6. Schedule of Activities in Corn Production

Activity	Month	No. of days necessary for task	Helpers	Tools
Clear irrigation ditches	Oct.	6		Machete, forked stick
Fence fields	Nov.	4		Machete, ax
Cut stalks of last year's crop; burn leaves and weeds	Dec.	4		Machete, forked stick
Plow land 3 times	Jan.	3	Oxen	Plow
Clear irrigation ditches	Feb.	2		Machete, forked stick
Irrigate land and leave 6 days	Feb.	2		
Select seed and put in water, leaving overnight	Mar.	1	Wife	
Measure rows and distance between hills so there will be 5 handspans between each hillock; plant corn	Mar.	1		Digging stick, string, net bag
Irrigate planted corn	Mar.	1		
First hoeing	Apr.	4	2 or 3 men	Hoe
Second hoeing	May	3	2 or 3 men	Hoe
Fix irrigated ditches	June	1		Machete
Outside employment	July–Aug.			
Double over corn and leave 15 days	Sept.	4		
Pick corn; put in net bag and degrain cobs with few kernels; carry home harvest.	Oct.	5	Wife, horse	Net bags, sticks,

SOURCE: Information from a farmer possessing ½ hectare of irrigated land in center. He has no sons and one married daughter, whose husband works in sawmill.

vest. Harvesting is done by all the members of the household, sometimes with the assistance of exchange or hired labor. Women help by going to the fields and degraining the cobs with few kernels of corn so that there will not be an unnecessary burden to carry to the houses.

A small fiesta for the corn is made following the harvest. The purpose of the fiesta is to reciprocate the spiritual owner of the corn by giving him a "gift." Two candles are lit and set on top of the piles of corncobs. Two other candles are placed near the heaps of corn grains gathered by the

TABLE 7. Stages of Corn Growth and Agricultural Activities

Stages of growth	Activity	Time (after planting)
Šlihk sčital (begins to grow)	First hoeing	8 days
Čištal lik ʔišim (well-grown; about 4 feet)	Second hoeing	1 month
Čištal stekan sniʔ (begins to form husk)		2 months
B'al tzuto (begins to bud)		
Lok'iš tzutohal (flower comes out)		3 months
Yihiš sk'ab'enal (begins to mature)		4 months
Lok'iš yihkatz (cobs fill out)		
Sčam hol (its head dies)	Pick cobs to eat fresh	5 months
Yihištal sk'anubiš (now more yellow)	Double over stalks	6 months
Yihubiš (more yellow)		
Tahkiniš (dry)		
Sk'ahik lok'el (harvest time)	Pick dried corn	7 months

women. The candles cause the spirit of the corn to rise and give its "gift to the world" in the following harvest. Failure to make a fiesta would mean an end to all corn harvests.

Corn is brought to the house and stored in the rafters, since there are no corn cribs or separate storage facilities of any kind in the village. Most of the houses are infested with rats as a consequence. When the harvest is brought in, there is an attempt to rid the rafters of these "thieves." The men and boys armed with slingshots stand posted in the yard as the children rustle around in the rafters chasing the rats out. Although they are remarkably good shots since they use this tool from early childhood, the houses are never completely free of rats, and the inhabitants learn to put up with them.

Wheat. In selecting the seed, the farmers choose those heads with the most kernels—there may be from thirty to eighty on each head. The same kind of seed must be used in planting each plot of land or the soil "does not give well." A new wheat seed was introduced by an American agronomist in the 1950s. The following reaction by an informant reveals why most of the farmers decided not to use it:

There is a quick-growing wheat, called foreign wheat because a foreigner brought it and planted it in the soil. Those who wanted to try it were given some. It was difficult to harvest because it was very dry and broke easily. Most of the grain was left behind on the ground. When it got to the threshing floor, most of it was broken. Therefore the town did not want it. So we continue planting the common wheat and it doesn't break.

The inefficient harvesting techniques force the people to consider loss of grains in deciding what wheat they will seed. However, a few of the farmers continue to grow the new wheat.

The scheduling of wheat production is shown in Table 8. The *arada* plow, introduced by the Spaniards (Foster 1951) and made locally by farmers for their own use, is commonly used to prepare the land. A few farmers borrow the plow of a relative, or sometimes a metal plowshare is bought in the departmental capital.

The harvest is the most arduous work in wheat production, but because it is done with the assistance of four or five helpers, usually brothers or compadres, it is a gay occasion. There are about a dozen threshing shelters which are individually owned and rented for 5 pesos a day. At the height of the harvesting season, the farmers have to wait for their turn to use the shelter. After the threshing, a fiesta is held in the house of the owner of the wheat at which liquor and a meal of beef stew is served. Since the labor involved is based on exchange rather than payment, the owner will take part in the harvest and celebration of those whom he has helped.

Beans. The choice of locale and the time of planting vary more radically for beans than for other crops because of the greater differences in type of seed. The two major types of beans are (1) ground beans, of which there is a black variety and a colored variety, and (2) climbing beans, of which there are four subclasses: "painted," white, yellow, and black. Beans must be grown only in irrigated lands of highest productiv-

TABLE 8. Schedule of Activities in Wheat Production

Activity	Winter wheat	Summer wheat	No. of days necessary for task		Helpers	Tools
			Winter wheat	Summer wheat		
Clear land	Dec. 7	May 12	5	2	2 paid workers	Machete, forked stick
Irrigate land; leave soaking	Dec. 7	May 15	1	1		
Plow	Dec. 15	May 23	1	2	Oxen team	Plow
Sow seed broadcast; cover, crossing over twice	Dec. 16	May 24	1	1	Oxen team	Plow
Cut wheat	May 1	Oct. 5	2	2	2 or 3 un-paid work-ers	Scythe
Thresh						
Carry wheat to shelter	May 3	Oct. 7				Net bags
Horses trample wheat	May 4	Oct. 8				
Shake stalks						Forked stick
Scoop grains into wooden box and sift to get rid of chaff			3	3	4 or 5 unpaid workers, 5 horses	Box with wire mesh
Put grain in burlap bags; carry to houses on horse-back	May 5	Oct. 9				Burlap bags

SOURCE: Information from two informants, one who grows winter wheat and the other who grows summer wheat, both cultivating ½ hectare of irrigated land.

ity. The land in the center, except for the fertilized corral areas, has lately yielded a very poor harvest. People say that the soul of the bean departed when they introduced the crop to their ejido plots in hot country. The scheduling of bean production is shown in Table 9.

Guarding the crops. The crops must be guarded against intruders. The farmers sometimes sleep in the fields when they expect animals to steal the ripening corn. They observe the habits of these intruders and develop belief systems which help them organize opposition:

The raccoon steals maize seeds. He pushes down cornstalks when they are in elote and steals the cob. He is very smart. He can tell whether the owner is sleeping or not by putting his hand on his own anus. If his anus is cold, the owner is awake; if it is hot the owner is asleep and he enters.

Some men who live below in Alannantik have good dogs. They planted their milpa, and the next night wanted to hunt. "You stay with one dog,"

TABLE 9. Schedule of Activities in Bean Production

Activity	Date	No. of days necessary for task	Helpers	Tools
Cleaning and preparation of soil is same as for corn (Table 6)				
Ground beans				
Plant between rows of corn	Mar. 1	2	3 exchange workers	Digging stick
Cultivate	Apr. 19	3	2 exchange workers	Hoe
Harvest, pulling up entire plants and putting them in burlap bags	July 10	2		
Store in eaves of house				Burlap bags
When pods are very dry, beat bag with stick to depod beans	Sept. 1	2	women of household	Stick
Pole beans				
Plant, following the second hoeing of corn, setting seeds near each hillock of corn	May 2	1		Digging stick
Wind the vines up on corn stalk; tie	June	1		
Cut pods and store in burlap bags in eaves of house	Nov.	1		Burlap bags
Shell beans as they are used				

SOURCE: Same as for Table 6.

they said to me, "while we go over with the other two." I fell asleep. Then the raccoon entered. And so I believe the raccoon is very bright.

Also there is the wild pig, who is less bright than the raccoon.

Another "thief" of the milpa is a small black insect which eats beans. These are eliminated in the following way:

When we plant beans, the women go with us wearing a new skirt and a new shawl. They walk near the plants, waving the shawl. The animals die. It has to be a new skirt. My mother proved it. She went with an old skirt, and she saw that they did not die. They just fled to the mountain out of shame. It is the smell of the old skirt that scared them away.

If many animals are eating the crops, Indians buy three twenty-cent candles. They take them to the fields and light them, praying in Tzeltal: "God, holy world, please look at me and speak to the little animals. God, holy rock, holy forest, please look at me, hear me, speak to the animals."

The candles are media through which communication is made with the gods as well as gifts which seal the contract with the gods ensuring their protection and guardianship over the crops.

Guarding the crops also involves avoidance of certain kinds of behavior by the farmer and his wife. Farmers must always avoid irritating the spirits of the heaven who control the elements which make the growth of the crop possible. One informant explained:

One should not have sexual relations with anyone in the milpa because the Father Sun [Tatik K'ak'al] gets angry or "ends his heart." He will not give crops. He gets very hot. One time, many women in town were looking for lovers. They would have sexual relations with boys in the daytime. The Father Sun got angry and caused the crops to burn. There was very little corn. The price went up to twenty cents a liter. People bought bread and mixed it with the nixtamal.

It is different if a man is married to a woman in the church. The Tatik K'ak'al does not get angry. The Tatik K'ak'al does not have a woman of his own, and so he gets jealous if he sees people having sexual relations in the milpa in the daytime.

But if you have relations at night with a man in the milpa, Our grand-

mother the Moon gets angry. This might cause an eclipse of the moon, and the crops will suffer because there will be no sun.

There is no prohibition, however, against having sexual relations prior to planting or at other crucial stages, as there are for other Maya Indians (Wagley 1941:34).

During the growing season, candles are lit in the milpa as protection against wind as well as robbers, who "lose their luck" when this is done.

The spirits' care of the crops. The crops have souls, given by the spirits, which will be lost if they are not cared for. The spirits "watch over the crops as parents watch over their children." The term for seed (*yal*) is a metaphorical extension of the term for "child of a woman."

The following myths give different, occasionally contradictory versions of the origin of crops. This central truth emerges in all of them: The spirits have given us our crops and will continue to do so as long as we offer thanks in the form of ceremonies and gifts to them.

Santo Tomás [the patron saint of Oxchuk] had intercourse with Santa Lucía. She wanted [asked for] the soul of corn, and he gave her the seed of corn. Then there came forth beans, corn, and wheat. But then all the saints of San Bartolo and San Miguel [neighboring towns] asked for the soul of corn. Then the soul of beans left us and went to hot country. Now it does not grow well in the pueblo. Also, the avocado has gone to Comitán. The matasano and ground beans went to Oxchuk when Santa Lucía fought with Santo Tomás.

The myth of the origin of crops overlays an older myth which has parallels in other groups of Maya-speaking Indians (Castro 1965, Wagley 1941:20).

Formerly, during a famine, there was hunger. The tzisim, *an insect of Ariola, came to take the corn from underground. Thus the ancestors got their first seed. For this reason, people say that corn was born underground, brought up by the tzisim. But I believe God sent us corn.*

Another version has synthesized the role of the saints and that of the animal agent.

The ant [alielo] brings corn out of the house. They say that a saint passed on horseback. The ant came to the saint, bringing a grain of corn. He stood before the saint, and the saint said, "Where are you going with the corn?" The ant replied, "To the storeroom." The saint inquired, "Which one?" The ant went to show the saint a stone as large as a church into which he entered to take out corn. There was white, yellow, and red corn.

The saint returned to heaven and spoke to San Bartolo. San Bartolo asked, "Where is it?" The saint replied, "I will show you."

San Bartolo went with Santo Tomás to see the stone. Santo Tomás said, "Good, let us figure out how to destroy this stone." San Bartolo said, "Let us go talk to a carpenter." At this moment, a carpenter came. They asked him to cut the stone. "Good," said the carpenter, "I will do it."

But the carpenter could not open the stone. They went to another carpenter—there were three in this mountain. The first couldn't, nor could the second. The third carpenter said, "Let us talk to the tunselek *[woodpecker]. He is a good carpenter."*

The first two birds had broken their beaks, and the saints warned the woodpecker that he should be careful or he would fail with the stone. The woodpecker broke open the stone, and all the corn seed—yellow, red, and white—fell out. People should not kill these birds because they broke open the rock where the seeds were kept.

The necessity for showing respect to crops because of their relationship to the saints is expressed in the following account:

Corn must be treated with respect, since it is the body of the Virgin. You cannot step on anything which is for eating—beans, corn, or wheat —or the Virgin will become angry. Particular care has to be taken at the harvest to avoid offending the saints.

Some of the saints serve man by helping to spread the cultivation of crops, as in the case of San Isidro, the patron saint of milpas.

The Padre told us that San Isidro helps the farmers. Formerly there was only milpa here where there is irrigated land. San Isidro went up to the hilltop with a digging stick. He knelt and prayed, asking for rain. At that very moment, the rain came. He put the seeds in the holes he made, and from then on people have been planting in the hills.

Other saints are charged with providing rainfall. The saint of greatest importance in this respect is Santo Tomás, the patron saint of Oxchuk. Some Indians have gone to the church there to light a candle and ask for rain, and on their return the rains came. During an extended drought in August 1967, over one hundred people walked to Oxchuk to pray for rain. The people of Tzo?ontahal are somewhat bitter about the Oxchuqueños' neglect of Santo Tomás since over half of the town has converted to Protestantism. Whenever there is a drought, they blame it on the failure of the people of Oxchuk to take care of Santo Tomás.

In addition to the Catholic saints, the ancestor spirits help man to watch over the land. They are responsible for giving the rains in the planting period and early growing season. The fiesta on the Day of the Cross (Chapter 1) is primarily a plea for rain. Until the 1950s, the curers would hold a celebration at the Cave of the Ancestors to ask for rain during a drought. The waning belief in the presence of the ancestor spirits in the town has meant that there is less attention given to such fiestas. Some go to seek the ancestors in Chiapa de Corzo in the cave in which they are supposed to reside, as the following story illustrates:

One time my three brothers-in-law went to Chiapas to ask the ancestors for better crops. When they arrived there, nobody knew where the cave was. They said only a certain mayordomo there could find it.

Another time, two of the prayer-reciters went to the cave. They talked to the guard of the cave, saying, "May we speak to our ancestors?" The guard said, "Are you prepared? Did you bring two liters of trago? The ancestors like to drink."

The prayer-reciters went to get two liters of trago and all three drank it. While they were drinking, they saw a cow and chickens appear. The guardian said that if they came back in May with "food" for the ancestors —candles, incense, and firecrackers—they would get rich crops. I think the prayer-reciters succeeded because now they have a cow and chickens and a horse. They are afraid of the envy of their neighbors.

People with lands in hot country recount that during droughts the Indians from the neighboring town of Chamula have held rainmaking fiestas for which they solicit contributions from other Indians.

The Chamulteco came to us and said, "Let all of us who have milpas contribute five pesos for a fiesta." He brought the candles. In the little hill there the people brought drums and flute. We ate chickens and drank liquor. For eleven hours he prayed, and in the afternoon it rained.

The *kuriketik,* rural inhabitants of the colonia of San Vicente who migrated to Amatenango from Chanal, have no irrigated lands and depend directly on rainfall throughout the growing season. Indians of the center know of their practice of sticking their digging sticks into the ground with the points toward the sky "to puncture the clouds" when they have planted their milpa, but they do not imitate this practice. Control over the supply of water in the irrigated lands has apparently led to the neglect of supernatural appeals even where the canals do not supply water. Under pressure of extended drought, they will resort to spiritual intercession through Chamula or Oxchuk practitioners in whom they have some faith.

Acquiring the protection of the gods does not obviate the practical activities necessary in the cultivation of crops. Fiestas for the saints are a repayment for services rendered in watching over the milpa. The sponsorship of fiestas for the saints by the community ensures the protection for all of the crops, and general crop failure due to drought or high winds is explained as a result of mismanagement of these community-wide fiestas. The offering of candles to the spiritual owner of one's own milpa is a kind of individual insurance policy for future crops as well as a repayment for the gift of the corn harvest. The peasant notion of surplus value is implicit in this reciprocal relation: the payment, or gift, of two candles to the milpa spirit is far less than the value of the harvest. But the account is balanced by the expenditure of this surplus in communal fiestas.

POTTERY PRODUCTION

Making pottery has been a speciality of the town since pre-Conquest days. The old site of the town contains sherds of pottery which is remarka-

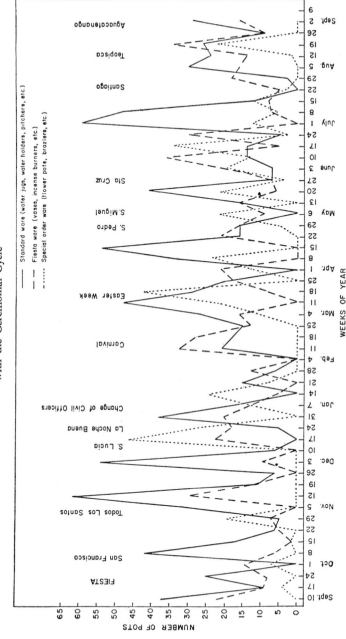

Fig. 2. Pottery Production in the Household and Its Correlation
with the Ceremonial Cycle

SOURCE: The above was printed in *Man* (219:186-91) in an article by Manning
Nash entitled "The Social Context of Economic Choice in a Small Society."

bly similar in texture, design, and form to the pottery made now. Just as a
man defines himself as an agriculturalist, a woman defines herself as a potter. Men complain if their wives do not produce pottery, and I know of
two cases of separation on the grounds that the woman was not fulfilling
one of her functions as housewife by helping the family budget with pottery production. Most women like to make pottery: it helps them to pass
the day, and they say they would be bored without it. Some of the women
who have gone with their husbands for extended stays in hot country have
tried to make pottery out of clays available there, but because of its inferior quality, they have not had much success. Unlike women of neighboring towns, the women of Tzoʔontahal usually do not accompany their
husbands to the fincas "because they have their work at home."

Making pottery. The women make a wide variety of household
and ceremonial objects, but the item which has the widest market distribution is the water storage jar (See Plate 7). They introduce new items in response to local needs, such as the funnel used in channeling liquor into
large containers from the retort of the still. One vessel which is disappear-
ing from production is the large ceremonial cooking pot. The only woman
who knew how to do this (or who admitted to knowing, since it is unpaid
work) died in the 60s, and no one has replaced her. One woman who had
a reputation for eccentricity, introduced several elaborate vases and ash-
trays. Her creative imagination was best exemplified in a combined ashtray and vase which featured four frogs poised on the lip of the tray, presumably drinking from a fountain. Reina (1962–1963) has pointed out
that women of the Guatemalan community of Chinautla who wish to be
accepted in the community must limit themselves to conventional forms,
and the same restriction seems to apply in Tzoʔontahal.

The women of a household work as a group in collecting clay and in
firing pottery. Clay is free since it is found in the communally owned hills
on the perimeter of the town. It is collected preferably during the rainy
season when it is easier to gather from the open gorges in which it is
found, but if the supply runs out, other trips are made. All of the women
of the household go, sometimes with neighbors or relatives in groups of
five or six. They collect large clay balls weighing from forty to fifty

pounds which they carry in a net bag on their backs with a tumpline. The sand which is mixed with the clay is found nearby. In preparing it for use, the clay has to be chopped with a hatchet and soaked. A temper for cooking pots is made of ground sandstone, called *baš*. This is found near the border of the neighboring town of Aguacatenango, and sometimes Indians of that town bring pieces which they exchange for a soup bowl or other small pottery item.

Variation in the color of the clay—it may be white, white mixed with yellow, true yellow, black, or blue-green—provides the basis for discerning its quality. The white clay is thought to be best since it doesn't break as much in firing. The preferred clay is very soft, and the women test deposits by feeling them with their hands.

The rhythm of work is regular. Children under three years of age climb on their mother's back or lap or sometimes stand by her side nursing. The women do not interrupt their work when this happens, although they may shift their body to accommodate the child. In the organization of work, there is no discussion of what is to be done or who will do it. Orders are given only to the young children. When the women are working, all motions which would require a break in activity are assigned to children who bring unfinished pots to be worked on and shoo away chickens or dogs. The standardization of production rhythm is evidenced in the uniformity in time required for each operation. Timing one potter's production of 10 *apastes* (soup bowls) on two different days, I found that she spent one hour and 10 minutes for each set, an average of 11 minutes per pot. Another woman made a *comal* (platter) in 26 minutes and a second one in 28 minutes. A pair of larger bowls produced by another woman took 15 minutes each.

The continuity in tradition of pottery production stems from a tightly organized behavioral schema with defined units of motion and stages of production. I follow Piaget in his definition of behavioral schema which Flavell (1963:54) has summarized as follows:

> Thus, an action sequence, if it is to constitute a schema, must have a certain cohesiveness and must maintain its identity as a quasi-stable, repeatable unit. It must possess component actions which are tightly

interconnected and governed by a core meaning. However elementary the schema, it is a schema, precisely by virtue of the fact that the behavior components which it sets into motion form a strong whole, a recurrent and identifiable figure against a background of less tightly organized behavior.

Piaget (1952:244) has stated:

It is due to the fact that schemata present this kind of structure that mental assimilation is possible and any object whatever can be incorporated or serve as aliment to a given schema.

This has significant implications for the continuity of tradition. The persistence of behavior depends on control in the organization of the work and in the training of new producers. As yet we do not have a means to measure the degree of organization or transfer of cognitive maps so that we can make comparisons across behavioral domains. The best source of data lies in the language which provides the cognitive mapping of the behavior. Table 10 provides a preliminary breakdown of the major stages and the distinct but similar action sequences which they include. Individual motions are replicated, in combination with other elements in the action sequence, to make up the component actions of different stages of production. The classification of actions implied in the Tzeltal verbs is shown in Table 11.

TABLE 10. Schedule of Activities in Pottery Production

Time	Step	Activity
1st day	1.	Yah tzes yaʔbi yaʔlel (Moisten; give water to clay and leave one day)
2d day	2.	Ya swotz lum sok hiʔ (Mix clay with sand)
	2.1	Yah sčičin hiʔ (Sift sand)
	2.2	Yah lihk swotz (Begin to mix)
	2.3	Sah sk'ap sok hiʔ yuʔun ben pikiš (Add sand until grainy)
	2.4	Yakto parte ma to yaiyehuk hiʔ (Put aside some that doesn't have enough sand)
	2.5	Yaʔbe ča? mel sk'ut * sok hiʔ (Give 2 passes, kneading with sand)
	2.6	Ya tzob ya swol (Collect it and make a ball)
	2.7	Ya sba snaʔan ta suhk sč'ute (Go set it on a board)

Time	Step	Activity
3d day	3.	Ya slihkesbe hiťʼ (Begin to make the base)
	3.1	Ya swol (Make a ball)
	3.2	Ya sčob (Work into it)
	3.3	Ya snakan te čuhte (Set it on a board)
	3.4	Ya skubeyit (Poke it)
	3.5	Ya slihk sbis moʔel (Begin to press it to rise)
	3.6	Ya snit mo'el (Pull it up [a process of pressing clay from inside pot against palm of hand and forcing clay upward])
	3.7	Ya stuisbe stiʔil (Level; cut off edge)
	3.8	Ya sčʼewanbael (Lay it out)
	3.9	Ya skʼehilel swai (Keep it while one sleeps)
4th day	4.	Yaʔbe stalbilum (Stick on clay on the base)
	4.1	Ya sbʔal te lum yuʔun ya tzak (Make a tube to stick on)
	4.2	Ya smakbe ʔa (Cover over where it is stuck on)
	4.3	Ya šlič mo''el (Let it up)
	4.4	Ya sčʼulmoel (Make it rise by rubbing against hand on outside)
	4.5	Ya stuisbe stiʔil (Cut off edge [evens it])
	4.6	Ya stalhilel hil swai (Let it stick overnight [some leave it for only 2 hours])
5th day	5.	Ya šyubmoʔel (Raise the sides)
	5.1	Ya yaʔbe bʔal lum (Give it a tube of clay)
	5.2	Ya tzak šyubmoʔel (Stick it on sides making it rise)
	5.3	Ya yaʔbe sčuht (Make the belly [round out side walls])
	5.4	Sbʼisbetal yutil (Smooth inside)
	5.5	Ma snuksba ya yaʔbe šan čʼinuk (If it doesn't meet, make another piece)
	5.6	Tzak šan yuʔun sčube stiʔil (Stick on more to make it close at the mouth)
	5.7	Ya yaʔi baʔa te haʔ yei ya yaʔbe slumil yuʔun pahal sila spimile (Feel where it is thin and give it more clay so it is same remains double)
	5.8	Lah šyubmoʔel skʼahilel šwai (After raising side leave overnight)
6th day	6.	Ya yaʔbe snukʼ (Make the neck)
	6.1	Ya yaʔbe yaʔlel stiʔil yuʔun skunubai tenaš ʔa ta yaʔbe slam yit (Scrape pot with knife; put water on mouth to make it soft and more clay at edge)
	6.2	Yah sbʼalbe slumil snukʼ (Form roll of clay for neck)
	6.3	Yah tzʼakbe stiʔil (Stick it on the mouth)
	6.4	Yah šlihk sbʼisbe te yutil (Begin to smooth it inside)
	6.5	Yah šlihk stuisbe stiʔil (Even the edge)

(cont.)

Time	Step	Activity
	6.6	Yah lihk sb'is ta snukul (Smooth the edge)
	6.7	Yah lihk spusko?el sok nukul (Double over the edge with leather piece)
	6.8	Ya sb?albeko?el (Roll down lip of jug)
	6.9	Ya sibetal yutil (Spread it out inside)
	6.10	Ya ya?be sbelbel lumil (Put little pieces on edge where the neck is stuck on)
7th day	7.	Yah ya?be sčikin (Make the handles [ears])
	7.1	Ya sb'albe slumil (Roll the clay)
	7.2	Ya sp'is ?ošeb (Measure out three pieces)
	7.3	Ya tzakbe sčikin (Stick on ears)
	7.4	Ya sku?be sčikin (Press on ears)
	7.5	Ya spusbe (Double over)
	7.6	Ya sb'isb'e sčikin sok yal sk'ab (Smooth with little finger [child of the hand])
	7.7	Ya sb'isbe sčikin sok sme?sk'ab (Smooth with thumb [mother of hand])
	7.8	Ya sčulbe lek sok sme? sk'ab (Spread it out with thumb [mother of hand])
8th day	8.	Yah smes ta k'ib' sok ?ul (Wash the pot with corn grind)
9th day	9.	Yah tz'ibawe kib' (Design pots)
10th day	10.	Čik'omahel (Fire pottery)
	10.1	Ya ya?be sčute?al ?a k'ib'e yu?un mak swok'a (Put down boards and accompany pottery in order that it does not break)
	10.2	Stos' si?wok (Chop wood)
	10.3	Ya šlihk sk'ak'al (Light fire)
	10.4	Ya holtik si? (Take off wood)
	10.5	Yah ta sik'ub ya him lok'el (Cool and take off wood)

* Same term used for grinding corn; motion similar.

The segmentation of activities shows that in a major schema such as pottery-making, similar motions are found at different levels, modified by direction in which motion occurs (up or down) or by the part of the pot being worked on. The classification of such motions simplifies teaching. Some of the motions included in Table 11 are classified with behavior in other contexts. For example. kneading the sand and clay (2.5 sk'u) is expressed by the same verb used for grinding corn, and a very similar motion is involved. Tz'ib'ayel, or painting the designs, also refers to writing.

The word for the act by which a tube of clay is formed, *ya sb'al*, has the connotation of creativity. In the *pat?o?tan*, a prayer form with many variations which introduces ceremonials, informants explain the terms *sb'al lum* and *sb'al ?ač'al* as a reference to the creation of man's body formed out of soil and mud by the ancestors. Sometimes the verb *sb'al* is used instead of the usual word for planted, *tz'un*, to refer to the seeding of crops.

The parts of pottery are metaphorically equated to those of the body; the belly of the pot and the neck, ears, and mouth all have parallels in English metaphors. But among the Indians, pottery also has a soul. Metal or enamel containers do not have souls as do gourds and handmade pottery.

TABLE 11. Classification of Motions in Pottery Production

Motion *	Step †	Context
Sb'is + (smooth +)		
-mo?el (raise)	3.5	Pressing walls of base with curved index finger inside pot against flattened fingers outside, working clay upward
te yutil (inside)	6.4	Smoothing interior of vessel
ta snukel (its neck)	6.6	Smoothing neck with piece of leather
-b'e sčikin sok yal sk'ab (its ears with "child finger")	7.6	Smoothing handles on inside with little finger
-b'e sčikin sok sme? (its ears with "mother finger")	7.7	Smoothing handles on outside with thumb
Šyub' + (shape +)		
-mo?el (raise)	5, 5.2, 5.8	Shape and raise pot upward
Tzak + (stick +)		
yah tzak (stick on)	4.1	Stick on tube of clay to hardened base
-šyubmo?el (shape and raise)	5.2	Stick on another tube of clay to side, shape it upward
šan (another)	5.6	Add another tube of clay to side
-b'e sti?il (mouth)	6.3	Add roll of clay to hardened mouth
-b'e sčikin (ears)	7.3	Add measured, flattened tube of clay to walls of pot for handles
Swol + (make a ball +)		

(*cont.*)

Motion *	Step †	Context
yah swol (make a ball)	2.6, 3.1	In mixing sand with clay, finish by making oval ball; also preliminary to making base, form ball
Spus + (roll +)		
yah lihk spusko?el (begins to roll down)	6.7	Turn down lip of neck
yah spusb'e sčikin (doubles over ears)	7.5	Curve tube of clay over to form handle
Stuis + (cut +)		
-b'e sti?il (edge)	3.7	Push clay with thumb; even edge by removing higher levels of clay at upper edge of base
" " "	4.5	Same, but edge is top of half-formed pot
" " "	6.5	Same, but edge is top of opening of jug
B'al + (make a tube +)		
ya sb'al te (make a tube of clay)	4.1	Build up sides with coils of clay
ya ya?b'e b'al lum (give a roll of clay)	5.1	Continue building up sides with coils of clay
yah sb'alb'eko?el (roll down)	6.8	Roll the tube of clay fitting on neck of pot to form a lip.

* Additives preceded by a hyphen form a single word with the verb stem; others are separate words in a phrase with the verb.
† Numbers refer to step numbers in Table 10.

The nine stages of production provide a basis for the organization of the work in five-day intervals. The usual output is in lots of one dozen water jugs or ten bowls. This staging of production indicates an incipient rationalization of production that maximizes efficiency for the individual producer: a woman repeats the same limited sequence of motions for the lot. Leaving the item overnight permits drying and hardening so that in building up the pot there is greater stability. The staging of production also provides a basis for the division of labor in households with more than one producer. Certain stages require greater skill and/or discrimination: mixing the clay with sand requires the greatest discrimination to achieve the consistency which allows both maximum manipulability and strength and durability; building up and shaping the walls of the pot requires the maximum skill and dexterity. These tasks are performed by the more experienced potter in the household, sometimes with the help of a trainee. Older women prefer doing the lighter tasks, such as putting on the handles and mouth or applying the slip of watered clay, to raising the sides which requires greater force and exertion of the back muscles. A second basis for the division of labor is the kind of item produced: older women for example, make bowls in preference to large water jugs and containers.

Learning to make pottery. A girl begins to make pottery about the age of eleven. First she makes small replicas of the articles her mother produces. Then, under her mother's direction, she learns to prepare the clay. The mother feels the clay with her fingers, telling her daughter to add more sand if this is lacking. She is taught to knead the clay three times. In making the pot, the most difficult phases are mixing the clay, forming the base, and rounding out the walls of the vessel as it is raised. The child is expected to learn slowly and is encouraged gently to improve each step. While the child works on her first pot, the mother makes a similar one; three or four times they exchange vessels, and the mother shapes her daughter's pot into a better form.

About two generations ago, marriages at the age of eleven or twelve were the rule. Since most of the intensive learning of pottery techniques begins at that age, pottery was taught to the bride by her mother-in-law if she resided in her husband's house (Blom and La Farge 1927). Most marriages now are contracted for girls from fourteen to seventeen years of age. By this time they are already proficient potters and accustomed to working with their mothers. Therefore there is greater stress on their remaining in or near the parental home after marriage.

The pottery is fired in the streets of the town outside the house, usually after the women have made four or five dozen items. The pots are set on planks forming a rough square around the fire in the center. Charcoal is added to the fire as the brush or corn husks set between the pots begin to burn. The women tend the pots, turning them every five minutes until the surface is well dried and hardened. Wood is added to the fire, and then the jugs are stacked in a pyramid, each one protected from the one it touches with a broken piece of pottery. The stacking is crucial to permit even firing and must be done carefully so that none are broken. Once the pyramid is complete, wood is laid against the pots in a tepee formation. When the sawmill in the vicinity was in operation, flat boards—scraps of cut lengths—were used, but now only logs are available. Corn husks or dry straw are stuffed between the planks or logs. When a large number of pots are being fired, the men usually help at the final stages to remove the charred planks with poles. If men are not available, the women of the household often call upon their neighbors for help. In this operation, the women wear sandals and hats for protection from the heat. When the pots are cooled, the women, sometimes with the help of the men, stack them in net bags, six to a net with straw protecting the pots.

About fifteen year ago, a kiln was introduced by the government in the interest of conserving wood. Those who tried it claim that the pottery did not fire well and that many of the pots were broken. I.N.I. (the Instituto Nacional Indigenista) planned to introduce an improved kiln, and while most of the people we questioned expressed a willingness to try it, the proposal was never put into action.

The men do most of the marketing of pottery. Loads of one or two dozen may be taken by bus or truck to San Cristóbal or to Comitán. When there is large-scale production throughout the community, as occurs just before major fiestas, truckers come from the neighboring town of Teopisca to contract for delivery.

The amount of pottery produced in households varies with the following factors:

1. Household composition: (a) Number of women in the family. If there is only one woman, very little or no pottery is produced because of the demands of domestic duties. Households with two or more women are able to sustain the ideal output of at least a dozen water jugs a week (I use "ideal" here to suggest their notion of what they produce when asked to guess. As Fig. 2 indicates, this varies considerably during the year.) (b) Age of women and ages of children. Older women over sixty do not independently undertake pottery production. They may assist in washing pots with corn gruel or making the neck, mouth, and handles, but they are unable to endure the harder task of collecting clay. A woman with infants under two years of age makes little pottery if

there is no other woman in the house. (c) Number of men in the family. If there are productively employed men, women of the household tend to make less pottery, since they are busy cooking and washing and have their basic subsistence needs supplied. Pottery is then produced to supply cash for fiestas only. Widows make a great deal of pottery since they must either hire men to work in the milpa or buy corn.

2. Wealth of the family: Relatively wealthy families make almost no pottery. In other cases, the scheduling of production is related to consumption needs. Figure 2 charts the pottery production by type of item produced for a family which included two unmarried women, their mother, father, and grandmother. The peaks in production occur just before the major fiestas when the family wants additional money to buy meat, fruits, and clothing. Although this family produced more pottery than the majority of households because of the presence of four women, its production typifies the high periods of activity relating to the fiestas. Production is also related to the seasonal changes: during the rainy season (from June to October) many households curtail production, except to earn money for the fiesta of Santiago (July 25), because of the difficulty of firing without closed kilns.

Variation in production means that an overall estimate of income from pottery cannot be made. It ranges from none to nearly 90 percent of family income in the case of widows without land or male helpers. I would guess that an average family might earn 200 pesos a year, about 10 to 15 percent of the money value of crops. One family of two widows and five children who work constantly throughout the year averages an income of about 600 pesos, or about one-half what an agriculturist can make on one-half hectare of land.

The Motivation to Produce

The motivation to work is tied directly to consumption needs of the household. Failure to meet expenditures with income from agriculture and pottery is met by men hiring out as agricultural workers or as laborers in the sawmill. This alternative is chosen over that of increasing the size of the farm by renting additional land, as European peasants typically did,[5] since there is very little land available for rent and the returns are not immediate. Farmers will try to avoid this by acquiring land grants to increase subsistence agriculture.

Expenditures and earnings were studied in six families over varying periods of time from ten days to one year. The data are summarized below.

Family No. 1, consisting of a husband, his wife, and their married daughter separated from her husband and child, is able to meet all of their need for corn and brown sugar and most of their need for beans by the crops they raise on one-half hectare of ejido land in hot country, one-half hectare of ejido land in the township, and three-quarters hectare of privately owned, irrigated land in the township. On their irrigated land, they grow one-half hectare of wheat and one-quarter hectare of corn. In hot country they grow corn, beans, and sugar cane on the margins of the field. The cane is ground in a cooperatively owned mill, and their crop in 1965 produced 144 *tapas,* or measures of one kilogram worth 5 pesos. In addition to 200 pesos earned for the wheat crop, 100 pesos for the bean crop, 298 pesos for corn, this farmer earned 808 pesos for outside work. His high wage income is due to his working for an American at twice the usual daily pay. The farmer buys coffee by the twenty-five-pound bag costing 62 pesos in hot country, a saving of about one-half the retail price of coffee in the town, where it is sold at 5 or 7 pesos at pound. In twelve months of recorded expenditures, the family spent 609.50 pesos or 83 percent of their budget on food, 40 pesos or 5 percent of their budget on clothing and 82 pesos or 11 percent of their budget on medicine.

The high expenditures in the case of family No. 2, consisting of a man, his wife, and two mature sons, was due to the fact that one of the boys was carrying on a betrothal suit. The bride-price had been fixed at 500 pesos, toward which the family was contributing whatever excess of income over expenditures it had. The son who was seeking a wife worked fifty-six days in the sawmill at a wage of 15 pesos per day during the six-month period recorded, earning 255 pesos. In addition, he and his brother earned 169

5. Chayanov (1966:7) demonstrated that Russian peasant families expanded the size of their farms when the subjective needs of the family increased, not as a response to market prices for crops or rents.

pesos for agricultural work for other families in the village. The expenditures of this family on meat, brown sugar, and liquor were required for the house celebrations carried out almost every Sunday. Like family No. 1 they spent 83 percent of their budget on food, a total of 714.80 pesos, and a larger percentage on clothing, 138 pesos. They sold their surplus corn for 292 pesos and their beans for 247 pesos. These crops were produced on one hectare of privately owned, irrigated land, one hectare of privately owned, non-irrigated land and one hectare of ejido land.

Family No. 3 consists of a widow and her widowed daughter-in-law who had five children. The oldest son, aged sixteen, worked their one-half hectare of ejido land and one-half hectare of irrigated land with some hired help during harvest. During the three weeks recorded, there were no returns from their crops, which include wheat and corn, and the family relied entirely on returns from pottery. This household produces more pottery than any of the others recorded, earning 61 pesos in the three weeks, because there are no adult male producers. They spent 63 percent of their budget on food, a total of 42 pesos, and 34 percent or 23 pesos on clothing.

Family No. 4 consists of a married couple with three children seven years of age and under. The husband works occasionally in the sawmill, but since he drinks a great deal, he does not contribute much of his 70-peso weekly wage to the family. He grows wheat on one-half hectare of irrigated land and corn on one-half hectare of ejido land. In the ten days recorded, no money was gained on harvest, but the woman earned 19 pesos from pottery. The family spent 77 percent, or 17.20 pesos of their budget on food and another 22 percent, or 5 pesos such as soap, kerosene, etc.

Family No. 5 consists of a married couple, their married son and daughter-in-law, and three grandchildren. They own one and one-half hectare of irrigated land, on which they grow wheat and corn, and one-half hectare of ejido land. The husband and his son supplement their earning from farming by distilling liquor, earning 108 pesos in the ten days recorded. In addition, the women of the household earned 54 pesos from pottery they made. They spent 143 pesos, or 97 percent of their budget on food and 3 pesos, or 2 percent of their budget, on clothing.

Family No. 6 consists of a young couple with two children. The husband owns one-half hectare of irrigated land, and one-half hectare of non-

irrigated land in addition to their one-half hectare of ejido land. He sup-
plements his income with work in the sawmill for some periods of the
year, at a wage of 90 pesos a week, making a total of 165 pesos in the ten
days recorded. The family spent 81 percent or 36 pesos of the budget on
food, 13 percent or 6 pesos on clothing 2.3 percent or 1 peso on household
supplies, and 3 percent or 1.20 pesos on medicines.

These family budgets show that most of the corn and beans can be supplied by subsistence agriculture. Garden crops of chile, chayote (a green
vegetable which produces a fruit and an edible root), and fruit trees, including lime and anone, are raised in the house yard. Tomatoes, fruit, and
cabbages are bought in neighboring market towns.

In comparison with household consumption expenditures in the United
States and other foreign countries, these budgets show a much higher proportion of cash income spent on food. The percentages of food expenditures range from 63.2 to 97.0 in the families studied, whereas in the United
States the average percentage is only 26.3, in Argentina 59.2, and in Zam-
bia 66.5 (Conference Board Economic Almanac 1967). This reflects the
fact that the people of Tzo?ontahal have no expenses for house rental, that
wood for fuel and light is available in communally owned forests, and
that most of the household utensils such as jars, jugs, and bowls, are
locally produced. However, failure to report items must also be noted—no
one reported purchasing matches although everyone uses them, and only
half of the families reported use of soap, although this is universally purchased.

A gross estimate of the land necessary to fulfill consumption needs of
corn for a family of two adults and four children would be approximately
one and a half to two hectares. The yearly average consumption of corn
for such a family is about 2,000 kilograms. One hectare produces from 1,-
200 to 2,000 kilograms in addition to 80 kilograms of beans. Of the 299
families whose land ownership is given in Table 5, 142 have only one hectare of ejido land and 85 more have only one-half additional hectare of privately owned land. This means that 227 households, or 61 percent do not
have enough land to meet their subsistence needs. 160 household heads

have recently sought additional lands in the ejido of Brindis to meet these minimal requirements. This preference for expanding subsistence agriculture to hiring out as laborers is the best index to the persistence of traditional economic pursuits.

Farmers who do not have a cash crop in wheat may be forced to sell corn even when there is no surplus. Because they usually need the cash as soon as they harvest their crop, they must sell when the prices are low. Thus their consumption needs exacerbate the disadvantage they face in the market.

Clothing, whether traditional or modern in style, requires cash outlays. Women have kept the traditional costume while men are modifying their clothing. Even when they go to hot country, older women wear the heavy cotton skirt bound with a thick sash and topped by an embroidered blouse; some younger women have adopted the long cotton dirndl skirt and peasant blouse. A white cotton shawl is added for ceremonial events or for warmth in the evening. All of their clothing is either bought or made of materials woven on looms in Comitán or San Bartolomé. The navy blue skirt, which they say is black, and the red and yellow sash are sold for 40 to 50 pesos by Ladina vendors who come to town. The blouse is made from two meters of heavy white cotton sold in the local stores or in Teopisca and San Cristóbal. Most prefer the more expensive cotton woven on bed looms in San Bartolomé, but it is not always available. They embroider the wide bands of yellow and red around the neckline with embroidery floss sold in the local store. The fringed shawl from Comitán is also sold locally, but is often purchased during the annual fiestas in the town. These items are replaced every two or three years, depending on the wealth of the family. The newer clothing is worn on ceremonial occasions, and the older clothing is worn every day. Women wear sandals and hats for protection only when they are firing pottery. For jewelry they wear bead necklaces, sometimes with crosses attached. Their hair is braided with ribbons for fiestas, or simply left hanging when they work.

Men buy a woolen jacket called *kotonču,* which is brought illegally from the Department of Huehuetenango, Guatemala, where it is made, and sold in Comitán. It is the same as the costume worn by the Indians of that area. A similar garment is made in Comitán but is considered inferior to the contraband product. Shirts and wrapped trousers made of coarse cotton are stitched and sold in Teopisca. The trousers are bound with a red woven sash. These items make up the modified costume worn by most of the boys and men. Men over sixty wear a long, coarsely woven shirt with a slashed neck made in San Bartolomé. This is caught at the waist with a woven band and worn over short trousers. In the evening or during ceremonies the kotonču is always worn. The older men wear high-backed sandals attached to rubber-tire soles with thongs, while younger men wear the *huarache* of crossed leather bands secured to a rubber-tire sole found in many parts of Mexico. Increasingly men are taking on the western clothing worn by Ladinos—the belted cotton trousers, shirt, and underclothing sold in the local store and in the neighboring towns. In 1957, only a half-dozen men, all of them former students in the boarding school established in Cárdenas' term of office, wore this dress, but today over twenty middle-aged men and dozens of youths in their teens wear it. Those who wear modern clothing have substituted a zippered "air-force" jacket for the kotonču. All men wear factory-made straw hats, under which, on ceremonial occasions, they wear a red bandanna bound over the forehead and tied at the nape of the neck. A high-crowned palm hat with black designs, ordered by the alfereces when they enter office, used to be woven by a few specialists; now only one man can make them.

The changing styles in men's clothing reflect three stages of acculturation. The older style worn by elders is said to be the costume worn by the ancestors who live in the cave. Since all of the items are and have for some time been purchased from outside the town, the changing pattern of consumption—the change from modified peasant to ladino-style clothing—has not affected local production.

Girl's wear a machine-embroidered peasant blouse and a mid-calf gathered skirt made of cotton or rayon and purchased in the neighboring towns. They change to the woman's costume when they reach their teens. Boys wear the same clothing as their fathers, except for the old costume. Table 12 shows the cost for these items.

Houses are built of materials locally produced or gathered from communal resources, but new construction materials, such as tiles, require cash outlay. The average house area is thirty-six square meters divided into two main rooms. Building is usually done in February or March. After the

TABLE 12. Clothing Expenditure and Origin

	Price (pesos)	Place of origin
Men's clothing		
Kotončи from Guatemala	60	Huehuetenango
Kotončи from Mexico	40	Comitán
Shirt worn by elders	60	San Bartolomé
Underpants	15	San Bartolomé
High-backed sandals	25	San Cristóbal
Wrapped pants	25	Teopisca
Tailored shirt	30	Teopisca
Factory-made shirt	7	San Cristóbal and Comitán
Straw hats	10	Teopisca and San Cristóbal
Factory-made pants	15	Teopisca and San Cristóbal
Belt	5	Teopisca, San Cristóbal, and Comitán
Sash	7	Comitán
Huaraches	20	San Cristóbal
Women's clothing		
Wrapped skirt	40–60	Comitán
Huipile, factory-made cloth	50	San Cristóbal
Huipile, hand-loomed cloth	60	San Bartolomé
Reboza	12–16	Comitán
Apron	5	San Cristóbal
Children's clothing		
Girl's skirt	7	Teopisca
Girl's blouse	5	Teopisca
Boy's shirt	3.5	Teopisca
Boy's hat	3–4	Teopisca, San Cristóbal
Boy's pants	5	Teopisca

materials have been collected, the construction of the house frame takes about eight days' work with the cooperation of five or six men. Filling in the walls with mud takes another three days. Table 13 gives the cost of materials and transportation for one house built during my stay.

The biggest change in housing has been in the roofs. The old type of construction used thatch or palm leaves carried from hot country. These cost only the price of renting a horse, if it was necessary, for transportation. Roofs made of these materials have to be replaced every seven or eight years. Each rethatching requires three days' work with four or five helpers, and the houseowner must provide a meal for them and their families. He spends about 25 pesos for meat and uses two or three liters of corn; the total cost is about 75 pesos. Another kind of roof is made of wooden shingles bought in the neighboring town. These are fixed to the housetops with wooden pegs, and the total cost is about 200 pesos. This lasts ten or twelve years with replacement of individual shingles. Tile roofs have the highest initial cost, 800 pesos, but the lowest maintenance in labor.

TABLE 13. Construction Costs for House, 1965

	Cost (pesos)
Supplies	
Roof tiles (1,000)	800
Posts and poles	*
Planks	40
Door	100
Window frame	30
Services	
Transportation of tiles	30
Transportation of posts and poles	206
Carpenter	50
Food for helpers	75
TOTAL	1,331

* Obtained free from communal woods.

House walls are preferably made of mud mixed with lime poured into an interlacing of cane poles set between the house posts and tied with a handmade fiber rope. Another temporary type of construction, which does not offer as good insulation, is made of board planks. Sweatbaths are made by digging out a floor about 2.5 meters square, raising stones in an oval shape over this, and plastering them with mud. The I.N.I. tried to introduce latrines, but no more than a half dozen of the cement toilet seats they gave away as demonstrators were put into use. Latrines are considered to be dirty since the pigs and dogs cannot scavenge the feces. Mothers train their children to have bowel movements in the evening when darkness offers them privacy in the houseyard.

Changes in house types in the seven-year period from my first census in 1958 to the second in 1964 are tabulated in Table 14. There has been a general improvement in the standards: tile roofs have increased from 1 to 20.1 percent. The increase has been at the expense of both wood shingle (declined 8.3 percent) and of thatch and palm leaf (declined 9.8 percent).

TABLE 14. Types of House Construction

	1958 *		1964 †	
	Number of houses	Percent of all houses	Number of houses	Percent of all houses
Roofs				
Tile	1	1	58	20
Shingle	27	23	41	14
Thatch or palm	87	76	190	66
Walls				
Board plank	17	15	66	23
Wattle and daub	98	85	223	77
Sweatbath				
Have	60	52	120	42
Have not	54	47	169	58
Unknown	1	1		

* Based on sample of 115 houses.
† Based on total survey of houses in center with 22 unspecified.

The numbers of houses with wood plank walls has increased from 14.8 percent to 22.8 percent. This is a temporary arrangement, and the planks are usually replaced with wattle and daub, so the increase may simply reflect new construction. The percentage of houses having sweatbaths has declined from 52.1 to 41.5. No new sweatbaths have been made for the last ten years or so, and many of those recorded are not in use.

The changes in housing type reflect the greater prosperity of the town as well as the increasing receptivity to outside influence. The increase in tile roofs means a greater dependency on external markets. Ten years before the final census, a man who put on a tile roof feared the consequences of witchcraft. Today probably 95 percent of the new roofs are made of tile. Often the old roofs cannot be replaced with tile because the rafters were not built to support them. One result of the change has been the dependence on a carpenter to construct the gables, since they have to be lined up more accurately than they do with thatch or palm roofs.

House lots in the town center are preferred to those on the margins. As residents of house sites on the ejido lands at the margins of the town acquire wealth, one of the first things they try to do is acquire a house closer to the plaza. These lots are smaller, averaging about 500 square meters, while those farther out average 900 square meters. In a sample measurement of 100 house lots, the size ranged from 180 to 1,440 square meters, and the average size was 77 square meters. Considering the advantages of a large lot in growing chile fruits and corn, the preference for smaller central lots reveals the strong prestige factor influencing choice.

House furnishings include both purchased and homemade items. Sleeping accommodations consist of wooden bedboards, either nailed on a frame or simply laid on blocks and covered with a straw mat. Woolen blankets from Comitán are sold locally at a price of 24 pesos or for 20 pesos in San Cristóbal and 18 pesos in Comitán. Most households own two or three wooden benches which line the walls of the porch and are made locally. Small chairs are purchased from Chamula carpenters at a cost of 2 to 4 pesos, as well as a small table costing about 4. A higher table is provided for the saints' pictures and candle holders, incense burner, and flower vases or tin cans. Hooks are fashioned from the crotch of trees and suspended on the house posts. Wooden boxes are bought from Ladino carpenters in San Cristóbal at a cost of 10 to 20 pesos depending on size and workmanship and are used to store clothing. In addition to the homemade water holders, water carriers, comales, strainers, and bowls, handmade glazed ware from San Cristóbal, factory-made porcelain dishes, metal cooking pots, knives, and spoons are purchased. Gourds provide serving ware for ceremonial occasions. Stone grinding platforms and rollers are purchased in San Cristóbal for about 10 pesos. Two new items have become increasingly popular in the past five years: a metal grinding machine for corn, hand operated and costing from 40 to 60 pesos depending on the size and quality, and a hinged press for tortillas, costing 15 pesos if made of metal and 10 pesos if made of wood. These are lined with waxed paper which the local storekeeper cuts from cracker-box wrappers and sells for 5 cents each.

Electricity, first used in the cooperative store and later in the liquor shops, is now being installed in houses. 83 families had electricity installed in their homes by 1967. Street lights have been in operation since 1966, although the first attempt to install them was blocked by residents on the streets to be lighted who did not want to pay the tax of 1 peso per month per household to meet the cost to the community of 75 pesos a month. Most people have a flashlight, and lighting in the house is provided by pitch pine or by small kerosene lamps. Candles are used only in ceremonies.

The inventory of items sold in the cooperative store in town includes the most frequently purchased items of consumption. Hardward includes buckets, hoes, kerosene lamps, batteries, Gillette blades, shotgun bullets, canned goods such as sardines, chiles, and powdered milk. Packaged foods include rice, sugar, salt, oatmeal, cornstarch, flour, coffee, biscuits, cookies, gum, and candy. Beer is sold along with soft drinks and cigarettes. Household supplies include candles, soap, D.D.T. powder, thread, matches, and kerosene. Medicines dispensed most frequently include sulphur pills, aralin, Desenfriol, Alka-Seltzer, and Sonrisal. Yard goods for shawls, children's wraps, and men's clothing are sold along with manufactured shirts, blouses for girls, and rubber capes. Eggs as well as money are taken in payment and then sold. Except for one can of Chocomilk, which sat on the shelves for a year, all of the items are in constant demand, and provide an index to the level of living and dependency on external markets.

The preferences in changing consumption are limited by communal standards of what is appropriate. I once asked a man who was acquiring more than the usual income by brokerage activities what he would buy with more money. He replied, "I would get more land and cattle." I interrupted to ask what he would do to improve his standard of living. "I wouldn't get better clothing—what would I need that for? I would get a house built with good materials like this [the government-built clinic] with a cement floor. But I couldn't get it now because of envy. When my children grow up, they [the neighbors] will see them working and maybe

I can get one then. Last year I bought a transistor radio for nine hundred and ninety pesos. My wife said she would leave me if I got it because all the children would get sick. But I got it anyway and no one was sick. I am stronger than my enemies."

Innovation on the consumption level is adding a stimulus to innovation in economic activities. The successful innovator must invent a rationale for his improved standards of living and then prove that he can survive the possible evil consequences of envy. The process of adoption is one of a shift in the incidence of choices made in the direction of improving levels of living. The new is often incorporated with the old rather than replacing it. For example, after the rough preparation has been done with the mill, grinding stones are used for the final grinding of corn to get the dough into the preferred consistency for making tortillas. Tin plates are used along with crockery and gourds. Some items are linked in change: for example, tailored pants are worn only with buttoned shirts and belts and with zippered jackets. The old forms are continued in a ceremonial context: kotončʉ is preferred when a man undertakes an official role, and gourds are preferred to any other container for ceremonial foods. The technology of production lags behind the changes in consumption that have increased the need for greater income—agricultural tools have not been modified since the colonial period when the wooden plow, metal hoe, machete, and plow used with draft animals were added. Changes in consumption needs rather than in productive technology are expanding the economic horizons of the Indians.

CHOICES AND STRATEGIES IN AGRICULTURAL PRODUCTION

In agricultural and pottery production, decision-making concerning the use of land and labor resources is controlled not only by a traditional technology but more importantly by a given state of cognitive orientations that determines, in Goodenough's words (1966:54), "what states of affairs they have learned to discern, what they believe to be the relations between them, and what they understand to be the processes by which one state can be transformed into another." Agriculturalists have a fine perception of what seeds grow best in which soils. Good, fast-growing seed is not sowed indiscriminately but is limited to use on more fertile irrigated lands. The size of a family's holdings is the primary factor in deciding what proportion of the three major crops—corn, beans, and wheat—they will grow. Where they grow each of these crops depends upon the quality of the soil categorized by topological criteria, consistency, color, and proved fertility. Decline in productivity is attributed to wearing out of soil fertility because of overuse as well as to loss of the soul of crops. The first explanation leads to adaptive behavior, in which the land is "rested" or turned over to cattle grazing, and to crop rotation, alternating wheat and corn crops. The second explanation leads to adjustive behavior in which the agriculturalist takes care of ceremonial obligations to the saints and to the "owner of the milpa."

The scheduling of activities is determined by the knowledge of time required for maturing of the crop and by expectations concerning seasonal fluctuations as they affect rainfall. Although the farmers have some control over water supply through irrigation, dependence on rainfall for the non-irrigated fields means that sporadic appeals to the ancestors or saints are made to ensure rain in the growing period. These rituals are not as integrated in the agricultural production cycle as they are in the neighboring towns of Chamula and Oxchuk or in the colonia of San Vicente where irrigation facilities are lacking.

Traditional techniques of pottery production are maintained by a tightly organized schema of procedures which allows for little variation in technique or form. Learning of productive techniques is facilitated by a fine segmentation of tasks. Knowledge of local clays and tempering has been stabilized for at least five hundred years of occupation in this area. Women's work is entirely lacking in rituals to ensure the success of their efforts.

These given sets of cognitive orientations in economic activities do not exclude the possibility of considering new ways or means of doing things. Agriculturalists have tried the new seed introduced by agronomists, but have found them wanting in their resistance to mold, in the case of corn, and in their portability, in the case of wheat. Fertilizers have been tried, but the credit costs proved too high for the agriculturalists to continue. Women were willing to try a kiln in place of open firing, but either the model introduced was faulty or they were not taught to use it properly. Notions about the supernatural relation between souls of crops, man, and the saints do not interfere with experimentation or adaptation at the instrumental level. Obligations with respect to them are carried on as a supplement to other practical measures.

The organization of men's work in agriculture contrasts with that of women's work in pottery. Men's work, when performed cooperatively by two or more of an extended household or exchange labor team, is mechanically organized, in Durkheim's terminology. Each of the men does the same task, working closely in the rows of the milpa. Women's work groups are organically organized since segmentation of the pottery production in the stages described above makes possible specialization within a domestic production group including two or more women. Preferences and special abilities can be taken into account. The potters with more experience do the jobs which require more judgement and skill, such as mixing the clay or making the bases, and then the work is passed on to less proficient workers. Or an older woman can leave the more strenuous tasks, such as mixing clay or building up the sides of the larger pots, to younger women and perform the lighter tasks, such as putting on the neck and handles.

These differences in the organization of male and female work tasks suggest the need for a reformulation of the classification of whole societies as organically or mechanically integrated. In assessing the potential for change, internal variations in the organization of production might provide the clues for implementing development programs.

The division of labor according to sex is nearly absolute: women do not learn to work in the milpa nor do men learn to make pottery or perform household tasks. However, women will gather firewood, and men will transport clay (although they do not collect the clay deposits in balls) and help in firing pottery. Women can live without men in the household economy of the town, but men cannot live without women. This is because male labor is a market commodity while female labor in household activities is not. A widow can hire a man to work her fields, but a man cannot hire a cook. If he is widowed, he must remarry, move into his mother's house, find a wife for a grown son, or find an unattached female relative to live with him.

Traditional agricultural and pottery production contained within household units has limited specialization and the formation of classes. Whatever exceeded consumption needs was absorbed in a ceremonial fund that served to maintain existing standards. The aim of production was to maintain a given level of "poverty and suffering" as they said in prayers of thanksgiving. These old standards are no longer adequate. Family budgets reflect a range of alternatives requiring an increasing amount of cash expenditure on goods made outside of the community. Because of land limitations, these new preferences are met by wage labor rather than increases in the size of the farm. The new enterprises discussed in the following chapter provide the income streams which are disrupting the present distribution of wealth and the social system based on it.

Chapter 3

New Economic Activities

The role of the Indian in the regional and national economy is being shaped more and more by supralocal institutions in public and private enterprises. The Indians of Tzoʔontahal have mobilized their own resources to incorporate these opportunities. In this they reveal a selective perception of the economic and social advantages of innovation and a tendency to translate form and function into a local idiom. The success of planning at national or regional levels depends upon incorporation of projects at local levels, while the survival of the local group depends upon acceptance of the new opportunities to absorb rising populations.

The major institutional settings in which innovation is occurring are (1) the ejido program, (2) employment in agricultural and nonagricultural enterprises outside of the community, and (3) economic enterprises originating within the community. My discussion of the economic potential of the local community to adapt to change will be organized in terms of these settings.

The Economic Potential of the Ejido

Mexico's ejido program, as one of the oldest and most extensive attempts at land reform in the hemisphere, provides a basis for assessing the economic potential of such programs. Here I shall consider only the effects of ejido administration in the community and what this case illustrates of the potential for development in the future.

Manuel Giraul (quoted in de la Peña 1951:327) summarizes the negative effects of the ejido program:

> In Mexico, the ejido system constitutes an institutionalized block to the reform of the social and economic structure; it corresponds to a

72

highly stratified primitive society, which remains static: it lacks the flexibility and mobility that exists in modern societies.

The history of the ejido program in Tzoʔontahal in the first few years after it was organized in 1937 seemed to confirm this conclusion. Its immediate effect was to block the flow of labor and goods in the regional and national markets. The ejidatarios were no longer forced to sell their labor at the prevailing rate of 25 cents a day, a wage which was not enough to supply the needs of even one man much less those of a household. Children and women formerly had to work with their husbands in the coffee fincas in order to meet their most immediate consumption needs. The independence that the ejido tract gave meant that men could withhold their own labor and that of the subordinate members of the family from such exploitation. The second harvests coming from the ejido plots in low country freed the Indians from having to buy corn in July, August, and September at the inflated market prices which took advantage of the scarcity of this basic necessity.

The political effect of the ejido in the early days was to fortify the corporate community against the shocks of the outside world. The first lands acquired were primarily allotments of corporate lands alienated by the laws of 1856 and 1876. Populations remained in situ, whether they were foreign Indians working on the expropriated estates, or residential communities created in the sixteenth century as crown towns.

The township of Amatenango acquired its first ejido land grant in 1937. One of the early promoters of the ejido, a *revestido* Indian (one who has adopted western clothing) from Huistán who had been a laborer on one of the fincas within the township limits, threatened to become a rural *cacique,* or local boss, comparable to those who emerged from the agrarian revolt in the central plateau (Friedrich 1962). This leader was elected president, but during his term of office he was expelled because of his attempt to secure house plots in the center for himself and other Huistecan Indians residing in the barrio of Yetawitz (Chapter 9).

The stabilizing effects of the ejido in its earlier phase have been upset in recent years. As the population of the center expanded, new families migrated to the nearby barrios contiguous to the town center. These new settlements were assigned to one of the two sections of the division in the center with an attempt being made to maintain a demographic balance. Incorporation of the new settlements was more effective in the case of the barrios than in the case of the colonias, which were farther away from the town center and included Indians of diverse communities. The process of breaking away from the old community is illustrated by the 1961 move for independence made by the original settlers of the colonia of Caralampio. The following account was given by a man who was then secretary of the ejido:

The first settlers of San Caralampio, José, Pablo, Luciano, and Santos were self-appointed principales, *or head men, of the colony. Santos and Luciano were from the town center, and José and Pablo had worked on the ranch when it was privately owned. The colony was well populated and the people lived well—there were no fights nor any problems. In 1956 the four principales decided that they should separate from the center. They told the people that if each person would contribute twenty-five pesos, they would raise the issue of the division in the* Departamento Agraria Mixta. *José invited Mateo, a man who knew how to read and write, to help them.*

"Let's divide from the town so that we alone will run the colony," he told them.

The principales took the money contributed and went to Tuxtla. There, in the Liga de Communidad Agraria *they asked for the separation, and were referred to the* Departamento Agraria Mixta. *When they arrived there with their request, the commissioner said that he would have to communicate with the chief in Mexico.*

After this, Pablo came one day to the center. He spoke to the ejido commission: "Look here, José, Luciano and Mateo went to Tuxtla."

"What for?" asked the ejido president.

"They asked for a division from the town."

"Que pendejo!" said the president. "What happened?"

"What do you think?" asked Pablo.

"We are against it. If it was a new center, we would support you. But

we are against division," said the president. *"How much did you have to contribute?"* he asked Pablo.

"Twenty-five pesos. They told us if we do not give money, we will be thrown out of the colonia."

We advised him that it would be better not to continue giving money to the principales. "You can't make this division," we told him.

One Sunday all the pueblo united in a mass meeting. Everyone was present. People asked about the affair of San Caralampio, and the Ejido Commission explained to them what had happened. The people said, "Let's get rid of them [the four principales of San Caralampio]."

When the three principales returned to San Caralampio from Tuxtla they asked each household head to contribute fifty pesos in order to send them to Mexico to talk personally with the Chief of the Ejido Division. Pablo came the next day to talk to the president in the center and advised them that the principales had gone out. There was another meeting. The president's decision was to get a contribution of one peso from each person in the center so that they would have six hundred pesos to prevent the division. They feared that if this occurred the people of the center couldn't work down there.

When the leaders of the central Ejido Commission had received the money, they went to the departmental capital to explain to the chief of the ejido zone what had happened. They said that the leaders of the colonia had gone to Mexico.

"Let's to go work!" said the chief. *"Did you bring the money?"*

"Yes, we have six hundred pesos."

"Go to the bank and change it into one-hundred-peso bills," said the chief. *"Let us send two hundred pesos to the chief of the division in Mexico so that he will prevent the division."*

We sent the money airmail. Before the principales of San Caralampio had arrived, we had their way blocked. Our money went to work for us. In five days, the chief in Las Casas said the money had been well received, and the leaders of San Caralampio had not been received.

A week later, Pablo came to see how the affair had proceeded. We asked Pablo if he had contributed money. He said no. We told him,

"*Don't give any more money. The Ejido Commission won't let the division happen since we are the same pueblo.*"

The four principales returned from Mexico. They said that they had a paper and that an engineer would come. They asked for another contribution of 25 pesos. They said that those who wouldn't pay would be thrown out. Pablo came and told us. We told him not to be afraid. The principales now knew that Pablo was with us. He had two brothers, Pancho and Ignacio, whom he advised not to go along with the principales since he knew that they would not win the case. When the principales returned to ask for more money for their trips to Tuxtla, both brothers refused.

Since these three brothers did not cooperate, the principales got angry and decided to kill Pablo. One day, when Pablo was on his way to Teopisca, he was shot in the back. He continued riding 76 meters. The horse returned to his house. His wife ran to tell his two brothers that the horse had come home without a rider. The brothers ran out and found Pablo dead. The civil authorities of the town went. A few days passed. The brothers never asked for justice. But since they knew who did it, one of them took Pablo's 16-centimeter rifle. Pablo's wife had been thinking of selling it to pay for the expenses of the funeral. Pancho [Pablo's brother] said, "No wait. I will buy it as soon as I have money."

He borrowed it for several years. One Sunday there was an order for all of the people of San Caralampio to go to the pueblo. They got up early and wakened all the others with a horn. Pancho got up with his rifle. He went to Juan's house and shot him. Luciano had Pancho jailed in the department capitol. He declared his crime, and said that he had killed Juan because the latter had shot his brother. He made a good statement. For this reason, he got out very cheaply—1500 pesos—which he paid with his crop of beans and corn. He was in prison in San Caralampio three months. Now he lives in Teopisca. His sons go to work there, but he doesn't. One day, Pancho was shot in the back—I don't know how many centimeters the bullet penetrated, but he did not die. The brothers of Juan and José have all left the colonia.

José was the one who caused all of the trouble. His wife was the younger sister of Pablo and she left him. Now José is going around begging for food to eat.

The action of the Ejido Commission of the town reveals the knowledge of how to manipulate political and economic power. By sending the 200-peso bribe, they were able to block the independence movement before the leadership had arrived. The extreme tactics used by the independence leaders in killing their opponents approximates the kind of political homicide characteristic of the central plateau (Friedrich 1962). The Indians of the center have been able to maintain their ejido grants intact. However, the political discrimination against residents of both colonias and barrios—no resident of either (except for the Huistecan mentioned above) has been elected president, and they never serve in any post higher than that of assistant judge—will undoubtedly lead to further unrest as the populations expand.

Bureaucratic inefficiency and corruption minimize the potential effectiveness of the ejido organization at local, state, and national levels. Projects undertaken by the national government lose their effectiveness when they are promoted by fraudulent claims, taking advantage of the presumed illiteracy and ignorance of the peasantry. The following case illustrates both the tactics of the ejido agents and the countertactics of the local Indians, resulting in a stalemate in the development projects planned and projected at the national level.

In August, two years ago, the Ejido Bank agents came to town with an offer to lend money on crops. We didn't want to borrow it, but Francisco, carbrón! [then president of the town], said we should do it. "Good," we said. We accepted their terms. They said, "We will give fertilizer. It won't cost you a cent. We have tried it. It will give a good crop. We will give you money every six months, and you will pay the interest of nine percent. We will pay for all the costs. It won't cost you anything for the fertilizer."

In six months, when the bank agents came to get the interest, they charged us six hundred pesos for the fertilizer. We did not want to receive the second load of fertilizer. We presented our case to the Jefe and told him, "Why did you say it would not cost anything?" He replied, "No, muchacho [boy], I told you [using the familiar form te dije] that the fertilizer is going to cost."

We used seven bags of fertilizer on each hectare for which they charged us 65 pesos per bag. It was the first time we had used it and we had very good crops. We got together and decided not to pay for the fertilizer. We called the bank agents and requested that we be relieved of the charge because the crops had failed. We showed him a milpa which is a low plot that is too wet for a good crop. We just throw the seed there, but don't work on it because it isn't worth the trouble.

We went to a lawyer in Tuxtla. He told us the bank would have to pay for the fertilizer since they had promised it. The lawyer is the helper of the campesinos [*poor farmers*].

Several points of significance can be noted in this case: (1) the Indians are reluctant to take credit risks because of unfortunate experiences in the past; (2) they react to deception with their own deceptions, showing the engineer the land which had not only not been fertilized but had never been weeded or cared for; and (3) they seek professional legal aid in dealing with government agents in order to equalize the contest in which they feel disadvantaged. These first two behavioral syndromes are culturally conditioned responses; the third represents an innovation. By seeking professional aid for which they pay a fee, the Indians are breaking the monopoly of power held by the caciques to whom they were formerly bound in a network of personal obligations incurred in such transactions.

Recent colonization of national lands since the 1950s has introduced a new kind of ejido settlement. Since most of the lands contiguous to settled towns were absorbed in the early days of the ejido grant, movement has been into lands outside the domain of established centers. This spontaneous colonization of unexploited land has followed the penetration of new highways in Quintana Roo, Campeche, Chiapas, Tabasco, and Vera Cruz (de la Peña 1951:348). In defense of their rights to the new lands, the colonists, often of diverse origins, develop a political consciousness. Mestizos and Indians of different towns work together in securing official ejido status for their lands. Acculturation to the national language and ways of life is much greater in these mixed centers than in the settled populations that were part of the original ejido tracts. Consciousness of their rights under national law and independence from traditional loyalties means that these new settlements may be the basis for welding Indians into the national economy and polity at a more rapid pace than has ever occurred in the past. Typical of this new movement is the recently established ejido of Brindis, formed by a core of landless Indians from the town working with acculturated Indians from Teopisca. Whether the political unity which has developed in the course of establishing their claim to the land will continue to provide a base for community development will depend on the encouragement and support by national institutions.

Within Indian communities of highland Chiapas, the ejido program has weakened age-authority principles in the family and in the civil hierarchy (Day n.d., Edel n.d.). Sons are no longer primarily dependent on their fathers for acquiring economic independence. Ejido Commission leaders have broken the monopoly of power by a gerontocracy of principales. Outside of the community, however, the political and economic potential of the ejido has not yet been fully realized. As the new ejidos such as Brindis develop, they may break the old community boundaries that contained and limited the power of the ejidatarios. With rising literacy, many Indians now read the *Codigo Agraria* sold in neighboring markets, and they are increasingly conscious of their rights. If unity across township boundaries could be achieved, the new ejidos might become an effective political force in regional and national spheres.

WAGE LABOR AND OCCUPATIONAL SPECIALTIES

The agriculturalists of the community do work as both exchange and paid laborers in the following forms: reciprocal exchange, part time labor and part-time independent agricultural work, and forestry.[1] Wage work is considered only a supplement to independent self-employment for all but twenty agricultural employees who work full-time on a finca within the township.

Payments for agricultural labor within the community are lower than the prevailing rate outside of the town and are higher in the fincas of hot country than in the highlands. When men work on the fincas of landowners in the neighboring township, they prefer payment by the task (*tarea*) rather than by the day, since they can usually complete two tareas by

1. See Richard N. Adams (1964:48) for a discussion of the forms of rural labor.

working long hours. Thus they receive 12 pesos for about one and a half times as many hours as is worked locally for the prevailing wage of 6 pesos (ten hours in comparison with the usual day's work of six to seven hours in the town). For this reason they maximize the effort expended in getting to fields outside of their own township. The lower payment in town entails an obligation on the owner's part to reciprocate the labor, but the payment relieves him of an immediate demand on his time. Exchange labor without payment requires reciprocity within the same activity schedule: thus if a man assists someone else during harvesting, he expects that person to assist him during the same harvest period. If, however, he will be unable to reciprocate immediately, the payment of 6 pesos terminates an immediate obligation, but he will be expected to respond when he can if other requests should be made by this same farmer. Exchange labor without payment is contracted between relatives, compadres, and neighbors, using the network of established social ties to reinforce the obligation to reciprocate.

Agricultural work in the fincas in hot country is undertaken only when there is extreme need for supplementary income, or when a man is escaping the threat of being killed as a witch. In the 1920s, when the Indians had limited land resources and prevailing wages were low, some were forced to go to the fincas of the Argentino and Aregovia near Tapachula. Despite the economic necessity for their undertaking this work, the social pressure was so strong against it that they would leave early in the morning to avoid being jeered as they passed in the street. The women rarely accompanied them because they could produce pottery at home and supplement earnings. The prevailing rate now is 15 to 18 pesos per tarea, a half-day's work, but Indians work in the finca only when urgently pressed.

Nonagricultural labor in the sawmills is a source of employment for twenty-two Indians of the town. Lumber companies operating in the forested areas of Montebello Lake have employed Indians of the town for the past year. The wage offered, from 15 to 18 pesos a day, exceeds the 12-peso wage paid to agricultural laborers in the immediate area, but corresponds to that paid in hot country. The men must live at the sawmill, and supplies of tortillas made by their families are brought in on Wednesdays

by the company truck to replenish supplies they bring with them. Most of
the workers are young men in their twenties and thirties. They return Saturday evening in a truck supplied by the company and go back to work
on Monday morning. Weekly wage payments have upset the usual controls over budget management. Money earned from crops is handled by
women. The sawmill workers have resisted passing over their paychecks
to their wives or mothers, and several court cases have been precipitated as
a result (Appendix 2b).

All of the work in which men are engaged outside of the community is
voluntarily undertaken for cash compensation. Formerly, forced labor of
two kinds was frequently demanded of the Indians: communal labor in
the neighboring ladino town when Tzoʔontahal was an *agente municipal*
of that town, and work in neighboring fincas for wages of 50 cents a day.
Forced communal work came to an end when the town became an independent municipio in 1931, and the labor roundups at substandard wages
were ended when Indians became conscious of their rights guaranteed in
the *Ley Federal del Trabajo* in the late 30s. Copies of the *Colección Juri-
dica Ley Federal del Trabajo* are sold in the departmental marketplace
along with the *Codigo Agraria*. Awareness of their rights as workers is
concomitant with increasing entry into wage labor employment outside of
the local community. As yet, Indians do not have any organized labor interest groups to champion their rights. The Commissioner of Indian affairs in the departmental capital is an intermediary in individual cases that
arise. But wage levels and conditions of work are set in a free market in
which the Indian's only control is to refuse to work.

The few special occupations in the town, such as butchering, caponizing, weaving bags, carpentry, and midwifery, have never developed into
full-time professions.[2] The failure of the development of specialization is
related to the tradition of ritual offerings of gifts of liquor and consumables and to the lack of a marketplace in the town.

Most of the livestock raised in the town is sold to butchers of the neighboring town because of lack of storage or of market facilities for the meat.
Pigs and bulls are slaughtered in town only on the occasion of a celebra-

2. Curing is treated in a separate chapter since it is an exceptional case of specialization
related to social control.

tion or when the animal is sick. For ceremonial occasions, the assistant of one of the mayordomos is expected to kill the bull which will provide the meat for a common meal. On other occasions, someone who is known to have a hand which gives flavor to the meat is asked to do it. The owner of the animal gives the butcher a half-liter of liquor.

Caponizing is a skill learned by some men with a few head of cattle by watching someone who knows how to perform the operation. If a man's wife is pregnant, he cannot perform the operation himself or even approach the bull, since his glance is very hot and will cause the bull to die. The procedure for making the request and for performing the operation is described below:

The owner goes to speak to one who knows how to caponize. When he arrives at the house of the caponizer, he says, "Are you in, Mam Gomez?" "I am," he replies if he is in. "Come in and sit down," he says.

"Pardon me, I have come to speak to you. Please, for the sake of the Virgin and for the sake of God, will you do nothing more than take out the little scrotum of my bull tomorrow?"

"Yes," replies the caponizer. "Do not worry, I shall take it out tomorrow."

"Good," replies the owner. "I shall wait for you in the house."

The next morning, the caponizer comes. The owner gives him some coffee to drink with a little bread. After they drink, they go to the hills to find the bull. They bring him to a wooded place and tie him by his hind legs to a branch of a tree. They then cast the body on the ground and tie the forelegs to the hind legs with a leather strap. They tie a string around the scrotum and sever the testes. After this, they drink a little. The owner's family joins them. The men blow up the scrotum to make a ball and the children play with it. They cut up the testes and broil them in a pan on the fire. After this is cooked, they pass it out to all of the people present with a tortilla and salt. Two liters of liquor are served. After the common meal, everyone goes to the house of the owner, and there they have a meal of chicken soup with two more liters of liquor. Those who do not drink liquor are served soda.

Very early the next day, the owner goes to see if his bull has died. If he dies, the owner announces on the loudspeaker of the local bars that he will sell meat at 5 pesos a portion. He preserves the hide to make saddle packs and tumplines. But the loss is great because he will not be able to buy a new bull with what he earns. If the bull lives, he will be better in three weeks and can carry loads. It is a very dangerous operation since the scrotum of a bull is very large. It is easier with a horse.

Surrounding the event with a ceremonial complex minimizes the development of commercialized relations between the caponizer and the owner. Most men who acquire several head of cattle or horses eventually learn to do the task themselves.

Handicrafts performed by men include rope-making from the tails of horses or from plant fibers, and weaving net bags. Most of the men who are assigned to the civil hierarchy spend their spare time in the cabildo making these items.

Carpentry is a skill now being practiced by two Indians of the town who "just learned by watching." They are called upon to help people in constructing the house frame, for which they receive 50 pesos in wages. A Ladino living on the margin of the town is a full-time specialist with his own shop. In addition to supervising house construction, he makes furniture and caskets to order.

New Economic Enterprises

In the operation of the new enterprises, which include cattle raising, cooperative ownership of a store, bars, and trucks, and liquor distilling, several patterns of organization have emerged. Some of these are based on preexisting social groupings, while others represent innovations. The social resources of management, credit operations, and the development of new skills within these local enterprises are of significance in preparing Indians for new occupations in the wider society.

Cattle raising. The most traditional organization is found in the case of cattle raising. Cattle have been in the town at least as far back as the 1915 revolutionary period when informants indicate that most of the cattle was seized by bandits or soldiers. It is "new" only in the size of the holdings, which have expanded from ownership of one or two head per household, primarily useful as draft animals, to a herd as large as two hundred head belonging to the wealthiest man in town. Cattle rearing is now a capital investment for resale as well as for draft animals in plow agriculture.

The increasing herds have stimulated competition for community resources. The control of communal grazing and waterhole rights is exercised through the traditional dual division of the town, with rights to pasture allocated on the basis of residence in the upper or lower barrio of the center. An association of cattle owners has developed in each of the sections, and the leaders of each association call together all members to clean the water holes and repair the troughs. A recent project of the cattle association of the upper section has been the erection of a large cross at the water hole. The water had dried up the year before, and the installation of the cross was an attempt to ensure a continuous supply of water in the future. The priest blessed the cross in the dedication, and the fiscal and prayer-reciters adorn it each year on May 3, the Day of the Cross in the old Catholic calendar, along with other crosses of the village.

Cattle grazing is the source of much of the conflict in the town. The cattle roam freely in the woods and communal pasture lands, and many are lost or stolen. The cattle association has not fenced in the pasture in order to control it. Their tactics have been punitive; they have raised funds from among members to hire men to kill suspected cattle thieves. In the last twenty years, six men have been killed as cattle thieves, and at least three of those were known to be killed by men hired by the association, which then paid the court fines to set the killers free. The leader of one of the cattle associations was killed after an incident in which he fined a man who had failed to assist in cleaning the water holes. The fine of 2 pesos per head of cattle represented a large fee for the man, who had sixty head. He refused to pay more than half, since he said he had not been notified. When his daughter later died of illness, he blamed her death on witchcraft exercised by the cattle association leader, and later killed him.

Cattle are only minimally exploited as a resource. The cattle are not butchered locally since there is not a large enough market, but are sold to

Ladino butchers in the neighboring town. The cows are not milked either for local consumption or sale. Fertilizers are for the most part wasted since the cattle roam freely in the communal pasture lands except in the case of a few corrals owned by families. Hides are cured rather crudely and are used for saddle packs or protective aprons by the men, but none are sold.

The cooperatives. The notion of a cooperative to mobilize capital had been introduced by the I.N.I. in 1957 with the inauguration of a store owned by over one hundred members of the community. In the first years of its existence, the cooperative had some difficulties, primarily in convincing the Indians that when the returns on shares were lower in any year from prior levels, it did not indicate that the agents were stealing the money.

The cooperative store was bought by the Indians of the town from the I.N.I. in 1964 after the members had some trouble receiving returns on their shares. There are now one hundred and twenty-two members. The profits of 1965 were reinvested in the purchase of the corn-grinding mill. Current profits at the store are lent at 5 percent per month interest. The store grosses 80 to 100 pesos in sales daily, and the mill grossess 100 pesos. The wages paid to the storekeeper are 300 pesos and to the miller 250 per month.

Now that the cooperative is independent of the government, one of the stated policies is not to sell a single share to a Ladino or member of another community. "We do not want to give gifts to the Ladinos," the secretary of the cooperative told me. He added, "There was a Ladino in Teopisca who wanted to join with 5,000 pesos, but we wouldn't let him in. If you let them in, they would come to dominate the pueblo." The cooperative store does not share profits with the consumers but gives dividends. The 11,380-peso assets in the year 1965 were reinvested in stock and in the purchase of corn at harvest which was then sold at one and a half or two times the sale price.

The Indians developed their first independent cooperative in the ownership of a *marimba,* a musical instrument like a xylophone, operated by eight men of the community. This enterprise failed because the players never developed sufficient skill to be commissioned to play outside of town. However, other cooperatives have been successfully organized to finance small-scale oeprations. Five record players with loudspeakers have been installed in the houses of members who sell liquor. Once the initial investment is made, the operating costs are low: 27 pesos for electricity, 25 pesos for a liquor license, 30 pesos for *hacienda* or state tax, and 10 pesos for the township tax. Liquor bought at 60 pesos for an 18-liter jug is resold at 72 pesos. The total monthly cost of 92 pesos yields a net profit of about 300 pesos. The cost of the installation, 5,000 pesos, was low enough for some of the richer members of the community to finance individually, but as one of the operators told me, it was too risky—that is, too profitable. The envy the neighbors would feel on seeing the profits made would never result in witchcraft against all of the members, whereas an individual owner could expect that he himself or a member of his household would become ill or die as the victim of witchcraft. These early entrepreneurs recognize the value of the cooperative in overcoming the force of envy which has effectively inhibited acquisition or display in these corporate Indian communities. Instead of socializing losses, one of its functions in modern capital organizations, the cooperative in Tzo ?ontahal serves to socialize gains.

The most enterprising action of the new cooperatives has been the purchase of a truck, initiated by the entrepreneur, Santos. The purchase of the truck was inspired by the example of the Ladino secretary, who with his wife and son had a monopoly on the transportation of pottery, people, and wheat out of the village. Furthermore, in the neighboring town of Zinacantan the Indians were successfully operating two trucks. Santos went with his brother to the director of the I.N.I. in Las Casas to ask for a co-signer on the installment purchase of a Chevrolet truck, since without a Ladino sponsor Indians could not get credit with the company. According to one informant, I.N.I. officials advised them that they would not be able to profit from this venture and that they should buy a tractor with their money. The brothers persisted and went to the Dodge company in the state capital. The company agreed to sell to the Indians without Ladino co-signers on the basis of a down payment of 10,000 pesos. The initial payment was raised with thirty Indians putting up the money. Some gave no more than 150 pesos, but as the instigators of the purchase remarked, "The more members we have, the more power it gives us."

The truck is the focus of the desire for self-improvement, for fighting the Ladino monopoly of the road, for the antagonisms and factional strife and conflict within the community. When they bought the truck, the Indians hired a Ladino in the neighboring town as chauffeur. One of the conditions of his employment was that he would teach his Indian assistant to drive. The Ladino tried to avoid doing this since he knew it would be the end of his job. But the Indian assistant learned by observation and is now operating the truck with an Indian assistant.

Accounts of the cost and profit of the truck operation indicated a running loss. A new tarpaulin cost 1,200 pesos; there were repairs and bribes to the highway patrol. But the truck was kept in operation because the major shareholders were impressed with the power it gave them. "They [their enemies, the members of the other co-operative owned by the Ladino along with twenty members of the community] are afraid of us because of the truck," one said, and added that it was better than having a *swayohel,* the animal spirit that gives power to the curers. At the time of my last visit in 1967 the truck was making a profit. The owners were thinking of selling it and replacing it with a five-ton model.

Structural realignment has been most marked in the organization of the truck-owning cooperatives. Membership cuts across the dual division for both of the truck-owning cooperatives. The cooperative is the most important factor in local political elections (Chapter 9). The truck has become both the symbol of power and the basis for the contest for power between the factions within the community.

Contraband liquor. The number of distillers has grown in the last ten years from five to forty. The distillation process was learned by Indians from Ladinos in neighboring towns fifteen years ago. There has been no local innovation in the basic process, but a new item, used in distillation, has been introduced into pottery production, a funnel decorated in the traditional manner of the water jars and other vessels. The capital investment in the equipment for operating the still is put up by individuals or partnerships of relatives. The still is rented to people who have charge of the celebration for a saint's day, or who are involved in courtship.

Private enterprise is the favored form of organization of the distillers because of the limited capital involved and the fear of discovery with the expansion of the enterprise. A loose syndicate of distillers provides an insurance protection by raising fines for members who are apprehended by federal agents. Security measures are taken to avoid discovery, and the presence of a federal agent is announced in Tzeltal on the loudspeaker system of one of the bars. One federal agent is on the payroll of the four operating bar owners, who give him 5 pesos a week to avoid legal action on the sale of contraband liquor. Individual distillers pay the tariff of 10 pesos or two liters of liquor a year to the civil officials and to the ejido commission, a tariff justified by the fact that they use wood from communally owned land to cook the sugar. The syndicate is a community-wide organization, mobilized in emergencies only.

The New Social Resources

In the course of operating the new enterprises, knowledge of and experience with supralocal institutions and agents are developing social resources in (1) entrepreneurship, (2) management of capital and credit, (3) knowledge of markets, and (4) dealing with government agencies. In entering into these new economic activities, the Indians have not lost a sense of belonging to the local community. Self-identification as poor, indigenous farmers is both a screen of protection and a means of ensuring continuity with local control systems.

Entrepreneurship. Local entrepreneurs explain their motivation in a rhetoric which emphasizes their interest in community welfare. This validates entering into nontraditional activities, but retaining their position in local society inhibits the expansions of their activities. The case of Santos, the promoter of the trucking cooperative is instructive. Santos had picked up some accounting techniques while he served in the army in Michoacán. He returned to the village because his father walked from Chiapas to Michoacán to tell him he should come back and get married. When he returned, he kept careful account of his costs and returns from the milpa. He realized soon that it wasn't "worth his work" (the Indian has not as yet learned the idiom or the value system which goes into the phrase "worth my time"). He therefore persuaded a Ladino of Teopisca to lend him 5,000 pesos. He went down to hot country and bought corn when it was scarce in the village, brought it up the hill, sold a little to pay for his needs, but held the rest until the price went up in the next three months. In a two year period of buying and selling with his 5,000 peso investment, he grossed 400,000 pesos. Afterwards he began to hire men to work in his milpa. At a meeting of the cooperative association in 1966, Santos defended his investments of the association's funds by showing his carefully kept accounts. He held up his pencil saying proudly, "This is my machete! This is my hoe!" The phrasing is an imitation of Ladino rhetoric of the provinces.

Santos served as treasurer of the ejido commission and of the town. In 1965 he was made a *nič'nal martoma,* or junior religious official in charge of caring for the saints. His appointment was an attempt made by the former president, a member of the Ladino-owned trucking concern, to cut down Santo's operations in passenger traffic on Sunday by keeping him occupied in religious activities. While in office, Santos began an enquiry into the use of the funds collected in donations to the saints. The priest had gained control over these funds, and had not subjected the collection to the public review and accounting procedures by which funds had been handled by the civil administration. Santos demanded an explanation by the priest, who refused to make a statement. The issue was raised in a general assembly of the men of the community which occurs sporadically on Sundays. Meanwhile Santos was taking advantage of the money associated with each of the major saints. In the cargo system for the care of saints, a fund of money is passed over in the installation ceremony from the outgoing mayordomos to the incoming mayordomo. This fund has always been passed over to the incoming officials with an increment of about 10 pesos. Santos requested the use of these funds to "make them grow," and he thus gained uncontested access to low interest funds which he used in his brokerage activities. In addition to the interest, he gave a gift of clothing to the saint to maintain good credit relations.

Santos' administration of funds in his public capacity as town treasurer, storekeeper, and treasurer of both the ejido commission and the truck cooperative won him a reputation of honesty and reliability. His knowledge not only of how to manage money, but also of how to *manejarlo,* or drive it, and to "make it grow" indicated an insight into capital operations which made him a leader in local enterprises. In his post as shopkeeper, he invested the store's capital in corn bought at harvest.

Santos' career as an entrepreneur was ended when a bullet was fired into his back in 1966. He had relaxed his observation of the rules which permit survival for those who challenge traditional ways: no drinking, no trips to the mountain alone, and no boasting of gains. As yet, he has had no parallel in the community, but the truck drivers are becoming aware of the possibilites for profit in trade and commercial deals.

Capital and credit. The Indians' knowledge of capital and credit operations has been acquired in the role of debtor, not creditor. In the legends concerning money the creditor is an outsider, a *pukuh* or devil, usually a Ladino. I had accepted a story about a Don Klabil, owner of a mountain in the town adjacent to the neighboring Ladino town Teopisca, as being of ancient origin. It fit with the many stories collected in Mesoamerica of owners of the hills who give out money on request to those who come knocking at the entrances to their caves. After their death, the recipients spend their spirit life in the mountain, working off the debt. Don Klabil was said to be responsible for the wealth of one of the outstandingly wealthy men in town who had gone to his hill and asked for cattle and money. Once while riding in a bus from Tzoʔontahal to Las Casas, I was engaged in conversation with a woman of Teopisca, who was dressed in widow's weeds. I commented on the story of Don Klabil as we passed the hill, and she said, "Oh, yes. That was Don David, my husband. He used to lend money to the Indians." When he died, the Indians say he went to live in the cave from which he got money when he was alive.

The Indians feel at a disadvantage to Ladinos when they enter into capital and credit operations. They tell a story of how, many years ago, when all the Indians of Tzoʔontahal were rich, the mayordomos got drunk on *Paswamal,* the day of gathering flowers and greens to decorate the church. When the true day of the fiesta came, they looked about them and realized that the church was undecorated, so they strewed green peso notes on the floor of the church. The Ladinos from Teopisca came for the fiesta as usual, and seeing the pesos, picked them up. The "spirit of the money" left the village forever. The story reveals not only the sense of deprivation Indians feel in losing wealth to Ladinos (historically land the Indians had lost through fraud or legal trickery during the Porfirio Diaz period), but also their realization of their own responsibility for letting their assets slip out of their control.

Payment of interest on money borrowed is justified in the calculations of the Indians for loans made within as well as outside of the community. Interest, called *shol tak'in,* or "head" of money, makes it possible for the borrower to work, and thus to earn, so the "owner" has the right to charge for the use. The rate on loans made within the pueblo has risen from 2 or 3 pesos a month for 100 pesos to 5 pesos, thus equalizing the rate with that charged in the neighboring Ladino town. The same rate is applied between relatives as nonkin. The advantage of intracommunity borrowing is that the lender does not demand an immediate return, or as high security. Ladinos of the neighboring town tend to demand items of greater value than the debt held as security—one Ladino held title to land worth 1,000 pesos for a 50-peso debt, and threatened to foreclose. Within the pueblo, security of about the same value as the loan is asked except in the case of neighbors and relatives who can be reminded every day of the debt. And they are.

Markets. In marketing, the Indians of Tzoʔontahal have neither extended nor gained control over the selling and buying operations that have been pursued since before the opening of the Pan-American Highway in 1955. The pottery which is produced locally was formerly carried on horseback to the smaller towns within a radius of fifty miles. The pottery was marketed directly by the men of the household which produced it, with no specialization in trading by commercial travelers, as had happened in the Zapotec and other areas of Mexico. Since the penetration of the Pan-American Highway, the men take the pottery produced in their households by bus or on the trucks to either San Cristóbal or Comitán. This tends to polarize trading operations and dry up the traffic into small towns not connected by the highway. As a result, the wholesale trade in San Cristóbal and Comitán has increased in the past decade, with dealers coming from the smaller towns to buy. The Indians still bring pottery to sell retail in towns that they visit during a fiesta. One of these is the barrio of Lok'ibal in the município of Villa Carranza, where people go on the third Friday of Lent to get holy water from the spring.

The Indians have not taken advantage of the truck to buy pottery wholesale and market it directly in the smaller towns, selling from the truck in the plaza as some of the wholesale fruit truckers do. Another operation which they have failed to profit from is buying the wheat harvest and selling to government warehouses, as some of the Ladino truckers do.

Lack of capital is the major reason for failure to exploit these opportunities. In marketing the contraband liquor, which is the most flourishing of the new enterprises, the Indians have not yet entered into the external markets except in the case of one young unmarried mother. Wholesale purchases are made by Ladinos, primarily women, from other towns who resell the liquor in Comitán and on the coast. There is however, a well-developed home market since all contracts are sealed with the offering of liquor, the "gift of the gods," all court fines are paid in liquor, and the main gift in betrothal is liquor. The cantinas with phonograph players opened by the cooperatives operate very successfully on Saturday night and during fiestas. The internal market for liquor is controlled by a syndicate of the forty-two independent liquor distillers. The price is set at 4 pesos per liter for all buyers, with the buyer providing the bottle.

Agricultural production is not geared to a market, and Indians do not take advantage of fluctuations in price. Wheat yields a lower return per unit of land than corn, but it is grown for two reasons: the Indians believe that crop rotation of corn and wheat prevents depletion of the soil, and wheat requires less work since no cultivation is needed. Wheat is a cash crop and none of it is milled or consumed directly in town. Poor families sell their wheat "standing" to Teopisca truckers. The price given the grower is usually about 90 pesos per hundred kilograms, and it is resold at 110 or 120 pesos in Tuxtla or to the government storehouses. Wheat is sometimes brought directly to San Cristóbal millers who give 120 per hundred kilograms. Corn is primarily a subsistence crop when grown in the center. Corn grown in hot country ejido land is now sold in Teopisca and San Cristóbal. The local truck cooperative has a special permit which gives members entry to the ejido colony, an area where traffic was formerly ex-cluded because of the monopoly by the large trucking companies. Both the fruit and root of chayote are sold in August by some families who have a supply over consumption needs. It is brought along with pottery to the market of San Cristóbal where it is sold to *regatones,* retail sellers who have stalls.

Decisions as to what crops to plant are not responsive to market fluctua-tion. With the major emphasis on subsistence crops, the farmers have little margin of land on which to experiment with profitable but risky ventures. They have little knowledge or experience. There are no full-time special-ists in market operations, although the truck drivers may gradually as-sume a greater role in this respect.

Very few Indians of the region, and none of those in Tzoʔontahal sell corn to the National Warehouses (Almacenes Nacionales de Deposito), al-though the warehouses offer prices higher than the going market price for corn. (940 pesos per ton in comparison to 500 to 600 pesos at harvest or 800 pesos offered a few months later by wholesalers who come to town). The reason for their failure to take advantage of the higher market price is that they do not have sufficiently large crops to pay the transportation costs of 28.75 pesos or the "tip" to ensure that their crops will not be declared sub-standard because of impurities, rotten kernels, insects, or excessive water content. In addition to that, they must spend time at the warehouses and in traveling. The alternative to the sale of crops to national warehouses is sale to wholesalers.

Dealing with external agencies. Entering into competitive areas where they were formerly excluded, the Indians are encountering opposi-tion from competitors and are the prey of departmental and state govern-ment agents. The reduplication of bureaucracies at the state and depart-mental level means that they will be subject to the double "bite" or *mor-dida* if they pursue their enterprises. Operating on minimal capital, they are not able to fulfill all the requirements, or buy all the necessary permits and licenses. Because of monopolization of certain traffic by the larger syn-dicates of truck owners, they proceed without permits and are often caught.

The strategies the cooperative members have developed in their frequent tangles with state police illustrate the combination of custom and innovation. When caught red-handed, they may respond by playing the stereotype Indian role. "We don't know anything. We are just poor Indians. How do you expect us to do what the law says?" This is hard for the Ladino authorities to resist, since it feeds their own sense of superiority. But it does not always work, and so the Indians have devised secondary resources. They put the departmental police at each terminal of their usual route between Las Casas and Comitán on a regular monthly mordida payroll of 50 pesos each. When trying to extend their operations, they hire a lawyer. A recent coup has been the acquisition of a permit to truck corn from Villa las Rosas and other ejido settlements that have been recently colonized. The appeal was made on the basis that they are a nonprofit cooperative of ejidatarios. With the permit, they now undercut the price of their own competitors in the town as well as of the large companies. Lawyers are beginning to advertise themselves in newspapers as "Friends of the Indians" and are in some cases specializing in this new patronage, which they receive from other communities as well as Tzoʔontahal. The professional relationship bypasses personal ties which formerly limited the development of Indian leadership.

The self-development occurring in Tzoʔontahal may appear paradoxical if we do not understand the internal dynamics by which change is contained within an existing equilibrium. The cooperative association has been adopted as a technique for socializing the risk of making a profit. The truck, although currently used in an uneconomic operation, is a symbol of power in the struggle for a position in the regional markets and in the intracommunity factional strifes. The usual patron-client system is being reversed as the Indian puts the Ladino on his payroll to secure evasion from the law. In the changes which are occuring, the defensive structure of the corporate community is a means by which the Indians are entering into national life not on the lowest rung of the social ladder, but on terms they are setting for themselves. In the new enterprises, the Indians combine old ploys with new strategies. Confronted with legal threats from the outside world, they play the colonial game of defensive ignorance.

When this fails, they turn to the professional help of lawyers rather than to the old caciques with whom they had formerly maintained patron-client relations. The traditional structural alignment of upper and lower barrios is retained as the basis for organizing the growing cattle herds, but the cooperative provides flexibility and power for developing new enterprises.

The minimal changes in the material environment and the technology of the peasantry are countered by the development of social resources which should facilitate Indian integration in the wider society. In operating the new enterprises independently of Ladino control, they are developing entrepreneurial skills and an awareness of the relationship between capital and profit. The restriction of their operations to nonproductive use of capital for profit, such as buying crops at harvest and reselling as the price rises, reveals the limited dynamics of intracommunal development. The town will look to the regional and national networks for fundamental changes in its economy.

The fear of exciting envy acts as a brake on productive activity and the enjoyment of improved consumption resulting from wealth. Santos' death is a symbolic warning to others who would follow in his footsteps. An earlier case occurred when the ejido land grants were made in the 30s:

The brothers Čaʔiletik became "very rich" as a result of careful operation of their ejido and privately owned land. They owned ten pair of oxen and about fifty horses. When they brought in their crops on horseback, it looked like a line of ants. They built a good house in Alkob', and a good threshing shelter. The people of the town began to talk about getting them off the land. The ejido commissioner took their land away and turned it over to others in the town. Until this day, the brothers Čaʔiletik are without land. Now they do no more than work like other men. They live poorly. All their cattle and horses are sold.

The organization of the cooperatives is one means of diverting envy directed against individuals and permitting some increase in productive efforts, but the society still lacks the means of validating higher consumption standards. The richest man in town eats better than his neighbors, but his style of living is indistinguishable from theirs. The only difference is the larger number of dogs he keeps to guard his wealth stored in the form of surplus crops in the eaves of his house.

The kind of economic change occurring in Tzo ʔontahal fits the model of a moving equilibrium. Tightly controlled behavioral schema preserve the traditional productive activities in pottery and agriculture. They provide the framework into which the new enterprises are fit. Increasing dependence of cosumption choices on external markets is slowly transforming the content but not the pattern of community life. This kind of change is limited to societies that form a distinct corporate group. In an open society where many alternatives are available, the painful process of accommodation of the new to a customary pattern would probably not be undertaken given the tendency for social change to follow the course of least resistence. The absorption of economic innovation in Tzo ʔontahal illustrates the ability of closed corporate communities to participate in commercial undertakings and reformulate them to fit their own pattern.

Chapter 4

Family Authority
and Community Control

All residents of the center consider themselves to be "true men" descended from the ancestors who lived in the cave. In Murdock's terminology (1965:63), the Indian community constitutes a *deme,* or local group of genealogically related residents who cannot trace the exact kinship tie. This sense of kinship sustains a model of paternal authority for assigning positions of power and prestige in the wider community. The key to persistence of the Indians as a culturally distinct population lies in these age-ordered hierarchies sanctioned by the ancestors and the elders who act as their intermediaries. The reward for remaining within the social control system is security and the right to their guardianship; the sanction against violating the norms is exile or exposure to the evil spirits they hold at bay.

The bilateral extension of age-relative collateral terms to all members of the same side of the dual division is a successful adaptation of the kinship model to the government of a compact nucleated community. The system of terminology is similar to that of the neighboring nucleated settlement of Aguacatenango which shares many of the same features of behavior (Hunt n.d., Metzger in Romney 1967:231). These systems are closer to those of the Coatlan Mixe (Merrifield and Hoogshagen 1961) and the Chinantec of Palantla (Merrifield 1959) than they are to the nearby Tzeltal-speaking communities of Cancuc (Guiteras Holmes 1947) and Oxchuk (Villa Rojas 1947). In the case of the Mixe and Chinantec, the strong emphasis on relative age is correlated with age-graded positions in the political-religious hierarchy (Merrifield 1959, Merrifield and Hoogshagen 1961:225).[1] The lineage-clan pattern found in the vacant center, or *paraje,*

1. In the Coatlán, Oaxaca case of Mixe Indians cited by Merrifield and Hoogshagen (1961) they state that the classificatory terms utilizing the criteria of age relative to ego

type of communitives such as Oxchuk and Cancuc depends on communal land holding and contiguity in residence of the agnatic kin. The corporate identity of these groups is breaking down with the fragmentation of land holdings and movement of men from the paraje of their fathers (Guiteras Holmes 1947, Villa Rojas 1946).

Symmetrical bilateral extension of kinship terms can be seen in Figure 3. Relative age modifies generation in terms for collaterals. In ego's generation, older brother and sister are distinguished from younger siblings. In parents' generation, siblings of father younger than father are referred to and called elder brother or sister, and those older than father are called father or mother. In grandparent's generation, siblings older than grandparent are called grandfather or grandmother, and those younger than grandparent are called father and mother. If the grandparent should die, leaving only a younger sibling, the term grandparent is used referentially and vocatively. There is no sex distinction made between siblings or collaterals younger than ego in the referential terminology. Referential terminology for lineals younger than ego does not make sex distinctions, but the distinction may be made with one's own children by using the possessive form of the vocative term, such as "my little man" (*htatil*) or "my little woman" (*kantzil*). Women refer to their children with the term *ʔalal*. The stem *ʔal* signifies the verb to give birth. Men refer to their children as *niěʼan*. The collective term for children of both parents combines the two terms in a possessive form, *kalniěʼan,* our children.

The bilateral system of Amatenango is not in conformity with the Spanish model. Along with similar systems mentioned for Aguacatenango, Coatlan, and Palantla, it differs from the Spanish model in that collaterals in ascending generations are classified with lineal relatives, and age relative to ego modifies generational separation. These systems appear to be an

---

obscures that of generation. Just as in Tzoʔontahal, all members of the community address others they meet on the street with the term indicating age relationship to ego, and grandfather and grandmother terms are reserved for the very old. The authors conclude that this terminological behavior reflects the rigid age-grading found in social groups throughout the community. I would venture a generalization that requires further research to the effect that age-grading provides a pattern for appropriate behavior among members of endogamous, closely settled communities whereby conflict is reduced by channeling competition for prestigeful positions.

adaptation to conditions imposed by nucleated compact settlement which may have been prehispanic.

Terminology for affinals differs according to the sex of speaker and the age and generation of referent. Men refer to brother's wife, wife's brother's

Fig. 3. Kinship Terms for Consanguineal Relatives

Generation	Collateral Male	Lineal Male	Female	Collateral Female
Older than grandparent	Mam	Mam	Meʔčič	Meʔčič
Younger than grandparent	Tat			Meʔ
+2				
Older than parent	Tat	Tat	Meʔ	Meʔ
Younger than parent	Bankil (Šiʔlel)			Wiš
+1				
Older than ego	Bankil (Šiʔlel)			Wiš
		EGO		
Younger than ego	Kihtz'in			Kihtz'in
−1				
	Kihtz'in	Ničʼan (Alal)		Kihtz'in
−2				
	Kihtz'in	Mam ničʼan		Kihtz'in

Terms in parentheses are female spoken terms.

wife, and wife's sister with the term *mu?*. This same term is used by women to refer to sister's husband, and to husband's brother. Men refer to sister's husband, wife's brother and wife's parents' brothers as *b'al,* while women refer to brother's wife and husband's sister as *ha?wan.* The rule is that siblings-in-law of opposite sex of speaker are classified as mu? and siblings-in-law of same sex as speaker are differentiated by sex of speaker so that men classify them as b'al and women classify them as ha?wan. Parents-in-law are referred to as *tat ni?al* and *me? ni?al* and called father and mother. Wives of sons and brothers' sons are referred to as *kalib'* by men.

Fig. 4. Kinship Terms for Affinal Relatives

Collateral		Lineal		Collateral
	Nial <u>Tat</u>	Nial Me?	
+1				
Bal	(Hmamlal) Kinam		Mu?
−1			
	Kihtz'in		

Underlined term is vocative.

Affinal terminology is not applied to spouses of parents' siblings; the terms for father and mother or elder sister and elder brother, depending on their age relative to ego, are extended to them (Fig. 4).

The term for assistant in a ceremony, *b'alni?al,* using the combined terms for ego's generation and parental generation in-laws, may indicate that this group formerly served in household ceremonies. They are still called upon for assistance, but nonrelated neighbors and compadres or godchildren may also assist and the same term is applied to all.

Significant reference groups are designated by the Spanish derived terms *yermanotak, kumparetak,* and *bersinatak.* The yermanotak is comprised of siblings, their spouses, and siblings of parents; the term is derived from the Spanish *hermanos;* kumparetak, meaning the ritual co-parents, is a term derived from compadres; and bersinatak, meaning the neighbors, is derived from *vecinos*. When informants are asked to summarize who participates in rituals, these three groups are always mentioned. They are not exclusive groupings; neighbors or siblings may be chosen as compadres, in which case the reference and vocative terms for compadres are preferred to any previous terminology. Activation of any of these ties depends on choice and convenience. Proximity of residence is of greater importance in day-to-day exchanges of assistance or visiting than closeness of genealogical tie. Interaction rates have been quantified in an earlier study of the community (J. Nash 1960; 1964).

Another way of referring to the yermanotak is with the plural form of the Indian patronym. Members of the Shunton family would, for example, be called the Shuntonetik. Several Indian surnames are linked to a Spanish patronym. For example, the Shunton, along with Lin, Mai, and Wolto? are linked to the name Lopez. In other Tzeltal and Tzotzil-speaking communities, these Indian surname groups have a greater cohesiveness, and in the recent past held corporate lands which they worked in common, as in Larraínzar (Holland 1963), Oxchuk (Villa Rojas 1947, Siverts 1960) and San Pedro Chenalhó (Guiteras Holmes 1961). In these towns, the Spanish patronym designated a clan marked by exogamy and responsibility of the elders for maintaining social control. In Tzo?ontahal, the tie of descent has given way to an emphasis on collateral links. Exogamy of the Indian name group is the only surviving function of the lineage, and when this has been violated, there are only minor repercussions.

While the Spanish-derived collective terms are restricted to domestic groupings, the Tzeltal collective term for elders, me?iltatil, refers to the three central groups responsible for social control in the community. Derived from the terms for mother, *me?*, and father, *tat*, it is metaphorically extended to include the sponsors in household ceremonies, the curers acting as guardians of their side of the dual division, and the civil officials. Each of the groups is vested with a different level of authority in the community. This is summarized briefly below.

1. Household sponsors: The Spanish institution of ritual godparenthood has been fused with the indigenous system of sponsorship by me?iltatil. When a child is baptized, his god-parents are included as

members of the meʔiltatil along with relatives and sometimes neighbors. They are his sponsors at subsequent life crises—rituals of betrothal, marriage, and death. All of these people become co-parents to each other and to the child's parents. This relationship lasts throughout his and their lifetime. If the marriage bond is threatened, the meʔiltatil gather to hear the complaints and try to resolve the problems. When a person dies, his meʔiltatil go to his wake to watch over his spirit. He in turn is expected to help in the household of his meʔiltatil when they have a ceremony by bringing wood or serving food and drink to guests.

2. Civil officials: The civil officials as a group may also be called the meʔiltatil; the term has special reference to the judges who represent the ancestors in their judgment of wrongdoers. In their passage through office from lower to higher positions, they are ranked in age-graded sets of junior officials (policemen), senior officials (regidores), and elder officials (judges), with the highest respect in ceremonial occasions accorded to the principales, two men, one from each side of the dual division, selected from those who have served in all offices. Drinking order, marching order, and seating order reflect the age-ordered rank in all ceremonial occasions.

The link between the meʔiltatil of the household and the meʔiltatil of the civil authority is provided by a group of officials called the *nakawanehetik*. These men are chosen from among bilaterally related relatives, ritual co-parents, and neighbors who have served in office in the church or the town hall and know the prayers. They direct ceremonies in the house at times of baptism, betrothal, death, and when the household head enters a community office. They are the ones who know how the ancestors did things and "watch and see" that all is done in accord with custom. They instruct the new official in the prayers he must memorize. Their wives direct the preparation of food by the younger women, and one of them may serve as chief woman speaker greeting guests.

3. Curers: Curers are similarly ranked according to age and years in practice. The elder curer on each side of the dual division is charged with guarding his side against the intrusion of evil spirits in the form of his own animal spirit. It is in this function of guardianship that the curers are referred to as meʔiltatil.

The meʔiltatil is the core institution preserving cultural continuity in the community. The exercise of authority and social control depended on a system of checks and balances in which the ancestors watched over the community, the judges watched over the curers to see that they did not abuse their power, and the curers watched over their side of the dual division to see that no witches or evil spirits caused harm. The validation of power is based on the kinship model of age-authority. The recruitment and functions of each of the three manifestations of this ancestral authority will be discussed in the following chapters on life crisis rituals, curing, and civil government.

The Household and Family

The household unit is a crystallization at a given point in time of consanguineously and affinally related people within a wider kinship matrix. It is the most important structural unit providing for economic cooperation, socialization of the young, and care and sustenance of the aged. It provides the setting and the personnel for the transmission of traditional prayers and ritual procedures of the civil and religious hierarchy. The composition of the unit is constantly changing due to internal changes in the life cycles of its members as well as changes in the wider kinship matrix. The decisions made in response to these changes reveal both traditionally established adjustments to life crises and adaptations to social changes originating outside the family. The kinds of choices made in residence after marriage as well as in inheritance and succession to leadership in the household do not always conform to the cultural formulae for handling them. The exigencies of space, time, economic, and social considerations may outweigh the ideological considerations of what ought to be done.

The formula for the developmental cycle of the household is the following: when a man marries, he lives with his bride's family for one year, working in her father's fields. He then returns to his father's household to live and work with him until his father is too old to manage the work in the field. The father then gives equal shares of his land and animals to each of his children, both male and female. The youngest child, or the last one to get married, remains in the parental house, taking care of the aged parents. This role is institutionalized and the youngest child is referred to as *k'oš*, the last one.

The choice of residence after marriage is influenced by the following factors:

1. The couple live with whatever family has less pressure from immature siblings remaining in the household. If there is no other child in one family, there is a strong likelihood that the new family will remain in that household.

2. If there is any wealth difference, the couple tends to live with the richer family. "Wealthy" families prefer to have their children live near them and will make an effort to build a house within their compound or nearby.

TABLE 15. Trends in Household Composition, 1958–1964

Family type	Alannantik No. of families	Alannantik Percent of total families	Ahk'olnantik No. of families	Ahk'olnantik Percent of total families	Total No. of families	Total Percent of total families
Remained the same						
Nuclear	49	76	38	57	87	67
Virilocal	7	11	11	16	18	14
Uxorilocal	4	6	7	11	11	9
Joint sib	1	2	1	2	2	1
Grandparent- grandchild	1	2	2	3	3	2
Incomplete	2	3	7	11	9	7
Total	64	100	66	100	130	100
Percent of all families		44		34		39
New families created						
Nuclear	16	89	48	88	64	88
Uxorilocal	1	5.5	1	2	2	3
Incomplete	1	5.5	6	10	7	9
Total	18	100	55	100	73	100
Percent of all families		12		28		21
Families which changed *	64	44	74	38	138	40
Total number of families	146	100	195	100	341	100

* Direction of change indicated in Table 16.

Changes in the household composition in the period from 1958 to 1964 between the two censuses I made in the field indicate some of the trends toward nuclear family units or bilaterally-rather than predominantly patrilineally-extended units (Tables 15 and 16). Comparisons are made between the same household in each period. Comparison of family forms in the six-year period indicates a high rate of change, with 39 percent remaining the same and 40 percent changing. The remaining 21 percent are the newly created families. The direction of change favors nuclear families (40 cases or 29 percent of changes) and virilocal forms (27 cases or 20 percent of changes). Nuclear families were the most stable, with 62 remaining the same and 62 changing to another form. This contrasts with uxorilocal households which are the least stable, with 11 cases remaining the same and 23 changing, and virilocal households which follow a similar pattern with 14 cases remaining the same and 25 changing. Nuclear families account for 88 percent of the new families created by marriage in the period studied. The trend is toward a greater proportion of nuclear families, as measured by the various indices.

TABLE 16. Direction of Change in Household Composition, 1958–1964

Family type	Alannantik No. of families	Alannantik Percent of total families	Ahk'olnantik No. of families	Ahk'olnantik Percent of total families	Total No. of families	Total Percent of total families
Change to nuclear from						
Virilocal	14	22	4	5	18	13
Uxorilocal	5	8	9	12	14	10
Joint sib			1	1	1	1
Grandparent-						
Grandchild			1	1	1	1
Incomplete	1	2	3	4	4	3
Unknown			2	3	2	1
Total	20	32	20	26	40	29
Change to virilocal from						
Nuclear	8	12	10	14	18	13
Uxorilocal	2	3	1	1	3	2
Joint sib			1	1	1	1
Incomplete	1	2	4	5	5	4
Total	11	17	16	21	27	20

(cont.)

Family type	Alannantik		Ahk'olnantik		Total	
	No. of families	Percent of total families	No. of families	Percent of total families	No. of families	Percent of total families
Change to uxorilocal from						
Nuclear	4	6	4	5	8	6
Virilocal	1	2	1	1.5	2	1
Joint sib			1	1.5	1	.7
Grandparent-grandchild			1	1.5	1	.7
Incomplete			1	1.5	1	.7
Unknown			1	1.5	1	.7
Total	5	8	9	12.5	14	10
Change to joint sib from						
Nuclear	1	2			1	.7
Virilocal			1	1.5	1	.7
Uxorilocal			1	1.5	1	.7
Total	1	2	2	3	3	2
Change to grandparent-grandchild from						
Nuclear			1	1.5	1	.7
Total			1	1.5	1	1
Change to incomplete from						
Nuclear	8	12	4	5	12	9
Virilocal	1	2	1	1.5	2	1.4
Uxorilocal	2	3	1	1.5	3	2
Joint sib	1	2			1	1
Unknown			2	3	2	1.4
Total	12	19	8	11	20	15
Change to disintegrated from						
Nuclear	11	17	10	14	21	15
Virilocal	2	3			2	1.4
Uxorilocal			2	3	2	1.4
Grandparent-grandchild			2	3	2	1.4
Incomplete	1	2	4	5	5	4
Total	14	22	18	25	32	23
Change to avunculocal from						
Nuclear	1	2			1	1
Total	64	100	74	100	138	100

TABLE 17. Choice Made in Response to Changes in Constitution of Family

Individuals with change in status	Lives with parents	Lives with children in same house	Lives with in-laws	Lives with married child	Lives alone	Children of first marriage live with him/her	Children live with his/her parents	Moved to barrio	Moved to another town	Total
Woman separated	6						1			7
Man separated	2									2
Widowed woman	1	14	3	2	1			4	1	26
Widowed man		3	1	1						5
Man remarried	1					1		1	1	4
Woman remarried	1	1				4	1		2	9
Total	11	18	4	3	1	5	2	5	4	53

The household into which an individual is born remains a resource base throughout his life. In nine cases noted in Table 17 in which separations occurred, the spouse returned to his or her natal home. In most cases involving the death of a spouse, the widow or widower stays in the household established during the marriage. If the children are too young to be economically useful, the surviving parent may return to the parental household with his or her children, or they may move in with married siblings. If the family was living with the parents of one of the spouses, the surviving members usually remain there even if the elder couple are not the parents of the widow or widower. A young widow living alone is the prey of drunken men during fiestas and requires a protector.

The stability of marriage can be seen in the statistics on changes in conjugal status in the period from the first census in 1958 to the second census in 1964 (Table 18). Of 264 marriages formed at the time of the first census, only 15, or 5 percent, were voluntarily dissolved; 16 percent were broken by the death of one or both spouses, and another 1 percent by the death of both partners. 10 widowers and 4 widows remarried, an index both to the greater availability of women for remarriage as well as to the necessity for a man to have a woman in the house.

TABLE 18. Changes in Conjugal Status, 1958–1964

Conjugal status	Alannantik	Ahk'olnantik	Total
Same	92	89	181
Separated	3	11	14
First marriage	28	65	93
Widowed	13	26	39
Two wives		1	1
Remarried			
Widower	6	4	10
Widow	2	2	4
Both died	3	1	4
Returned to wife	3	1	4
Unknown	3	21	24
Total	153	221	374

BEHAVIOR DEFINED IN THE FAMILY

Socialization in the family provides the individual with the idiom for behaving in the wider community. The basic principles ordering behavior are respect and obedience toward those who are older, and care for those who are younger. Obedience, expressed by the verb *č'un* which means both to believe (or to be gullible) and to obey, is instilled by cultivating a sense of fear and shame. Fear is communicated by the parent to the child by invoking evil spirits and by the threat or use of punishment, especially whipping with a leather strap. Shame is aroused by ridicule, jeering, and chastising. A good child is a quiet child; questioning is discouraged either by refusing to answer the child or by telling him to keep quiet. The negative aspect of good behavior is stressed. Significantly, the phrase "Behave yourself!" is translated into Spanish as "Don't do anything!" Good behavior is not rewarded either by praise or by gifts. The only public demonstration of affection toward children I have seen is by grandparents toward grandchildren: an elder might give his sweet roll at a ceremony to his grandchild and even fondle him. Parents show affection to youngsters under three years of age, although the last child may be coddled somewhat longer. Mothers and young children show intimacy and affection in delousing each other or combing each others' hair. Kissing is not a sign of intimacy but of formal respect in ceremonies.

Beliefs concerning conception show awareness of both the male and the female contribution to the fetus. The man's sperm (*snal*) enters the womb, *yo?tan,* (also the word for heart) and mixes with the woman's flow, to bring about conception. The blood of a child is believed to come from its mother and the skin, bones, and brains from the father. During pregnancy, the father must have intercourse with his wife because his sperm nourishes the fetus. This continues right up to the birth of the child. Men too are believed to have wombs, and some men have trouble with "dropped wombs" caused by lifting heavy burdens.

The only people in attendance at the birth of a child are the women of the immediate household, the mother of the woman giving birth if she is not a part of the houshold, and the midwife. Children are kept out of the house, and the men usually leave the scene. Women are ashamed of their husbands seeing the afterbirth because they joke about it with other men. (I do not know what the joking is about—possibly it is related to the frequency of sexual intercourse during pregnancy, since the placenta is believed to be increased by male sperm.)

There is no ceremony attending childbirth. Although some women are assisted by one female relative, most call in a midwife, who is referred to as "grandmother of the child" and who comes when the birth pangs begin. There is only one recognized midwife in Tzoʔontahal; she is the sister of one of the practicing curers and a niece of one of the former leading curers of Alannantik. She has patients on both sides of the dual division. On rare occasions, caused by witchcraft the Indians believe, a woman fails to give birth after two or three days of labor, and then a curer is called in.

The child is delivered with the mother kneeling on the floor. The midwife cuts the umbilical cord with a knife, and the child's navel is tied with a cord. The child is wrapped in cloths which have been smoked over incense, and then a woman's sash is wrapped around him from shoulders to feet, firmly binding the arms and legs so that they cannot move. It is felt that if this is not done, the child will snatch at everything and eventually become a thief. The body remains bound in this way for fifteen days. The umbilical cord and placenta are buried in the houseyard. Some say that a boy's umbilical cord may be tied in a tree "so that when the child grows, he can climb trees and cut fruit." The mother is given a drink of coffee, and the midwife binds her stomach with a band. Three days later the woman enters the sweatbath to cleanse herself. The midwife goes in with her and rubs her with branches of orange leaves and massages her stomach. If the child is born away from his own house, he is brought to it with great care so that his soul will not be dislodged from his body. The midwife makes a pad with branches of bushes growing near the springs, and the father sprays the child's body with springwater from his mouth.

In the first "twenty days or one month" of life, the child's contacts with the world are limited to the immediate family in order to guard against soul-loss and illness from "hot" glances of outsiders. When anyone not of the household approaches the house in which there is a newborn child, he must announce his arrival at the gate so that the mother can cover the child from view. In this period, the mother sleeps with the child apart from her husband.

Infants remain swaddled in wrapped skirt pieces—the woman's sash is not used after the first fifteen days—throughout the first year of life. Their arms are bound to their sides by kerchiefs crossed over the chest and drawn around the back with the ends tucked in; this makes it easier to carry the child on the back, wrapped in a large carrying cloth. Mothers sometimes lay sleeping infants on their bed when they are working in the house, but much of the time they carry them on their backs.

The child is given corn gruel to supplement nursing during his third or fourth month. Weaning may be consciously done after the child reaches the age of one and a half or two years. If the child persists in trying to nurse, the mother may put chile sauce or draw a face on her breasts to discourage him.

Much of the care of children from two to four years of age is done by elder siblings. Both girls and boys of from seven to ten years of age carry younger siblings in a carrying cloth on their backs, even when playing very active games. They pacify the child by holding a flower or twig for him to chew or grasp, and they usually share with him any cookies or scraps of food they are given.

School is commonly considered the most joyful time of a person's life. There the children, especially boys, make friendships which last throughout life. School recess is a time for unrestrained running, shouting, and laughter such as I have rarely seen in the houseyards when children play together.

In teaching their children how to work, parents are expected to inculcate not only competence but also a sense of the value of work, for industry is one of the most esteemed traits in both boys and girls. Small girls do errands for their mothers from the age of about four years. When a woman is occupied with pottery, she rarely disturbs herself to get needed items, but calls upon her children to fetch a pot which is out of reach or to bring water for the painting. She gives these orders in a quiet undertone, and I have never seen any need to prompt or cajole the child into fulfilling the errand. By the age of ten or eleven, girls begin to make small pots like the larger ones their mothers make, but their products are usually not commercially saleable until they reach the age of marriage. Their responsibility in preadolescence is to bring water from the faucets installed in every other block of the town, and to degrain corn, tend the fire as the *nixtamal,* or corn dough mixed with lime, cooks, and help their mother grind it. The careful assessment of the child's capacity to perform tasks is exemplified by the gradations of water-carrying jars given to each child: the older the child, the larger the jar, with minute variations in scale. The close, usually wordless cooperation between women in a household comes from years of working together and knowing their part in cooperative tasks.

Boys accompany their fathers to the fields after they reach the age of six and when they are not attending school. They do not participate in the work of the milpa until they are eight or older, but they pick up twigs for the fire or gather the wild berries or plants which supplement the diet of the family. They usually carry slingshots with which they kill field rats and birds, which they bring home to cook and eat. Teaching a boy the tasks involved in agriculture is consciously undertaken by older brothers or the father when the child reaches the age of twelve or thirteen. The following reminiscence of this training is given by a man who had been brought up by his widowed mother and brother.

I went to the field with my brother who is eighteen years older than I, when I was thirteen years old. My brother brought me to clean the milpa, saying, "Let us go and you will learn how to work. See what I do and you do the same. You will learn what I do and you can do the same."

One day I finished six rows. My brother said when he saw my work, "Good, just give a little more soil at the foot of the corn because the little corn must have a little soil. Now you do it well." "Yes," I said. He saw it was good, and he told me, "You have learned your work. You are going to forget it when you enter school. When you come out of school, go do two or three rows of work. When you hear the bell strike, go back to school."

He told my mother that I had learned to work, and she said, "Good you know how to cultivate." I learned to do my work better by going along with my elder brother in his work so that I would not forget.

The relationship of respect and obedience between parents and children is expected to last throughout life. When a boy reaches the age of eighteen, his parents are expected to provide him with a wife. Wealthier families tend to fulfill this obligation at an earlier age than do poorer families, in which the boy may have to work in the fincas or in the sawmills to acquire the money for his own marriage.

Instruction in sexual behavior and reproduction is not characterized by continuity, as is instruction about work tasks. Children are given no information about sex prior to marriage, and girls remain entirely innocent. They may be pregnant several months before they are aware of what is happening. The complete sexual segregation in work tasks and play during adolescence makes the relationship between sexes strained.

Even after marriage, the parents are concerned with maintaining their child's marital situation, or, if they judge their child's spouse to be incorrigible, to help him get rid of his partner. In the case of women, in particular, parents continue to provide a refuge in case a daughter's husband should die, be sent to prison, or prove incompatible. Parents usually accompany their children if they are called into court, and failure to attend is tantamount to admitting the guilt of the child.

In successful marriages, the parents-in-law are equivalent to parents and are called "mother" and "father." The parents of both spouses attend the life crisis ceremonies of their children and grandchildren. Grandparents provide support and care for grandchildren if their parents should die or remarry.

When parents reach the age of about sixty-five, they are no longer expected to work actively. A man will then distribute all of his land and animals among his children. He will expect to be taken care of by all of his children, but special responsibility falls on the youngest who will inherit the house. Sometimes aged parents move from one of their children's houses to another, spending a few months or years with each. Children are expected to pay for any curing ceremonies necessary in their parents' old age and to provide a good funeral appropriate to their wealth. Failure to do this incurs loss of respect with the neighbors and collateral relatives of the deceased. If the parents die after they have distributed their possessions, the crisis following the death is minimal. At the funeral, mature children of a deceased parent exhibit to the community their filial respect.

Kinship is one of several bases for recruiting reciprocal or cooperative labor. Table 19 compares kinship with nonkinship-defined work groups in terms of the kinds of exchanges, the type of work done, the time span permitted for reciprocity, and the sanctions against failure to reciprocate.

TABLE 19. Labor Exchanges of Kinship- and Nonkinship-Defined Groups

Conditions	Within household	Beyond household, within community	
		With kin (ritual, compadre, affinal and consanguineal)	With nonkin
Interchange	"Cooperation"—reciprocity based on implicit understandings	Reciprocity—explicit, defined by traditional expectations	Reciprocity—explicit, often defined by contract as well as tradition
Sanctions	Authority of elder member, male in men's work group, female in women's work group	Authority of elders of bilaterally-extended kin group; Recourse to cabildo if no strong elder	Informal—fear of gossip of neighbors; formal—reliance on local judges and president or recourse to district courts
Time Span	Extended, indefinite	Extended, usually some defined limit on repeated tasks (harvest); no limit for non-repeated tasks (house-building)	Immediate return expected, or explicitly stated time allowance
Kind of Task	Pottery-making, milpa agriculture, care of cattle, preparation of food	Ploughing, cultivating, harvesting, firing pottery, housebuilding	Same.

Fathers and sons, or sons-in-laws may work together on family-owned property. Because all men can acquire ejido land after marriage, and since 47 percent of the households claim to have only this land, the cooperative tie between fathers and sons is not based on inheritance. If they work well together, they may continue to cooperate after the son has become independent. Father and sons, brothers and brothers-in-law are expected to cooperate with each other in building a house, rethatching a roof, and threshing wheat. In the case of house-building or maintenance, they must pay for a substitute if they are unable to fulfill the obligation.

Compadres, or ritual kin, are the next most important pool from which to draw assistance. The same restrictions on exchanges between actual kin apply to those between ritual kin. The one task which is confined to brothers and not extended to compadres is that of house-building.

Relationships between members of the household are defined by daily work tasks, commensality, sharing a living space, and participation in the same ceremonial events. The same rules which govern behavior in the family are extended to the wider community. The extension of the terms elder brother and elder sister, father and mother, and younger sibling to all of the people in one's own side of the dual division implies a pattern of behavior similar to that of the family. The fundamental equation in social relations is age-respect-deference-prestige.

The bilaterally extended kinship group provides the pattern structuring relations throughout the community. It is a framework allowing wide choice in selecting individuals with whom ceremonial and work relations are contracted. Relative age has superseded generation and descent as the principle governing relationships of authority and respect from the nuclear family to the hierarchy or community officials. These patterns will be traced in other institutions in following chapters.

Chapter 5

Rituals of Life Crisis

The ceremonial occasions marking baptism, betrothal, and death define the network of bilateral relatives, neighbors, and compadres who will guide and help a person throughout his life. These people make up the group called meʔiltatil. The constitute a corporate group, but one which is tied to a single transaction. The sense of corporate identity is strengthened by the same group being called upon to act in subsequent household celebrations. But for each set of meʔiltatil there is almost always a different membership since the participants are selected for a particular event. The behavior during these ceremonials is marked by formality and replication of a limited number of ceremonial acts. Through this replication, the rituals dramatize continuity with the past and foster a sense of changelessness. The symbolic act establishing the bond is the embrace, called *smeʔispetb'ak*. Within the ritual setting, the child learns whom he can turn to for help and what he is expected to do in his home and community.

Baptism

After a month of seclusion when the child is hidden from public view, the soul is expected to have found its place in the child's body. A ceremony called *ḳiʔn haʔ* (water ceremony) then takes place with the mother and grandmother in attendance. The three enter the sweatbath, and the mother and child are bathed in hot water and then cold.

If the child cries frequently, it is suspected that his soul is still not firmly lodged and has been wandering in the streets where it encounters animal spirits that frighten him. This requires a soul-calling ceremony performed in the house in which he lives. The midwife, the only person present besides the mother, performs the ritual. She puts cold water in the child's mouth and then goes to the door, saying, "Enter if you arrive, little boy [or little girl]." Then she brushes the child with pine branches dipped in springwater, and smokes with incense of pitch pine the clothing which is then put on the child. The incense "makes a path for the soul to find the body of the child." As she does this, she says, "May your heart be one now that you are in the house." This ceremony is always performed when the child is born outside his parents' residence is order to guide his soul to its proper locale. Three days later, a ceremony called *sti? mut* (eat the chicken) takes place. Only women attend this meal. In one case I observed, the child's mother, her three sisters, mother, and husband's cousin attended. Each woman brings a peso's worth of bread, some chocolate, and ten tortillas. Two hens are cooked in boiling water, and the food is eaten by the women.

Baptism, called "throw the water" (*?ič ha?*) occurs as soon as possible after the new-born child's twentieth day of life. If the parents of the child live with either the mother's or the father's family, the grandparents will choose the godparent, or *padrino*. The actual decisions recorded for four families in Table 20 can be compared with statements of preference as to who should be godparents. People say they prefer nonrelatives ("We are not deceived by them"), people of the same section of the dual division ("We like to greet them in the street") and finally people of good reputation. The individual or couple chosen as godparent becomes *compadre* or co-parent to the parents of the child.

People seem to be successful in realizing the preferences they state. 81 percent of compadres are chosen from their own side of the dual division, and only 4 percent are chosen from out of town. 71 percent of compadres are chosen from among nonrelatives. A significant factor in the choice of compadres is maintaining good neighbor relations. Most families surround themselves with a ring of compadres which neutralizes both the fear of being the object of witchcraft and of being accused of witchcraft. Factors of wealth, prestige, and status positions—particularly that of fiscal—are also taken into consideration in choosing a compadre. Most of the padrinos of baptism are chosen from among older members of the community, but on other occasions they are as likely to be chosen from among peers of the parents.

The occasions on which the first informant in Table 20 acquired compadres are spelled out in the following diagrams to show the growth of the network of compadrazgo relations in the course of a lifetime.

Compadres of C. K., sixty-five-year-old man. C. K. chose as compadres on the occasion of the baptism of his first child an older man who lived in the same section of town. The diagram shows the composition of the baptismal party. The darkened symbol in this and the following diagrams represents the child baptized.

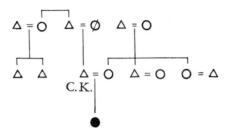

C. K. addresses all of the guests by the term "compadre" and refers to the group as "kumparetak." The second child has the same padrino, and the same group of relatives attended the ceremony. For the third child, C. K. chose a Ladino shopkeeper from the neighboring town. He chose him because, "I sold wheat to him, and I saw he was honorable." C. K. had a house fiesta to which the shopkeeper came with his wife. This is somewhat unusual and occurred because the compadre was from another town. C. K. chose as the padrino of his fourth child another Ladino he knew in the same town, but the padrino did not attend the house fiesta to which only his sister, her husband, and her husband's brother came. A woman prayer-reciter of the same section was chosen as *madrina* of his fifth and sixth child when C. K. was fiscal. A younger man of the same section was chosen as the padrino of the seventh child. C. K. helped his son select the padrino of a grandson born in his house, a man from the same

TABLE 20. Relationship of Individual to Compadres

Informant's family status	Occasion	Residence of compadre					Relationship		
		Same section	Opposite section	Other barrio	Neighboring town	Total	Relative	Non-relative	Total
65-year-old man, wife, 5 grown children	Baptism of godchild	13	5			18		18	18
	Wedding	31				31	12	19	31
	Baptism of own child	3			2	5		5	5
	Total	47	5		2	54	12	42	54
42-year-old man, wife, adopted daughter	Baptism of godchild	12	1			13	2	11	13
	Wedding	13	3	5		21	6	15	21
	Confirmation		2			2		2	2
	Blessing of loudspeaker	2			2	4		2	2
	Total	27	6	5	2	40	8	30	38
35-year-old man, wife, 5 children	Baptism of godchild	7				7	4	3	7
	Baptism of own child	4			1	5		5	5
	Wedding	4				4		4	4
	House saint	2				2	1	1	2
	Total	17			1	18	5	13	18
34-year-old widow	Baptism of godchild	17	1	1		19	15	4	19
	Wedding	7	3			10	2	8	10
	House saint	2	1		1	4	1	3	4
	Confirmation	1				1	1		1
	Total	27	5	1	1	34	19	15	34
	TOTAL	118	16	6	6	146	44	100	144

section. Attending this house fiesta was the group of relatives represented in the diagram.

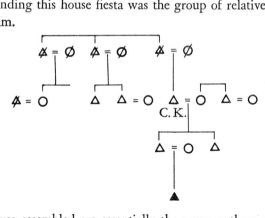

The relatives assembled are essentially the same as those who attended the birth of C. K.'s first child. They are the core of the meʔiltatil for his family, a core which expands to include additional compadres and neighbors for special house rituals. The second and third grandchildren had as padrino a man from the opposite section.

In summary, C. K. has chosen four Indian compadres and two Ladino compadres for the baptisms of his own children. Other members of the meʔiltatil who became compadres on these occasions include five men and three women who are bilateral and affinal relatives.

C. K. has been asked to be padrino of baptism by four persons:

1. A neighbor asked him to be padrino of his child. At a small fiesta, he became compadre of the father and godfather of the child.

2. A man from the opposite section asked him to be padrino of his son's child, and he acquired the group of compadres shown in the diagram.

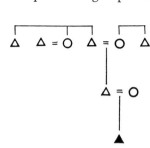

3. A man of the same section asked him to be padrino, and he acquired 6 compadres and 7 comadres.

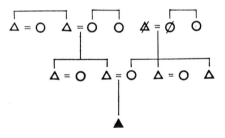

4. A man of same section asked him to be padrino, and he acquired 5 compadres and 5 comadres.

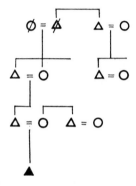

He has been asked to be padrino of marriage ceremonies, also by four parties. The darkneed symbols represent the individuals married.

1. A man of the same section.

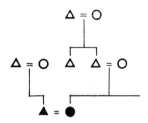

2. The sons of his brother's son.

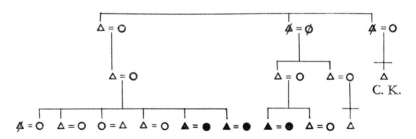

3. A neighbor's son.

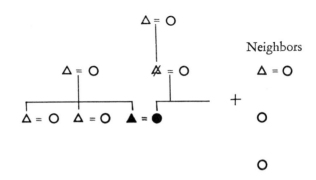

4. A man of the same section.

In becoming a padrino of baptism and marriage, C. K. has acquired 33 compadres, 31 comadres, 4 godchildren of baptism, and 7 godchildren of marriage, 4 of which are his nephews. Adding to the 6 compadres of baptism for his own children, he has 39 compadres and 37 comadres, a total of 76. Most people by the time they have reached 60 have acquired well over 50 compadres.

The relationship between compadres is one of respect, and the referential and vocative terms, *kumpare* and *kumare,* or compadre and comrade in Spanish, take precedence over any other relationship term. The godchild is expected to bring a load of wood to his padrino's house when the latter has a household ceremonial, and when the godchild is old enough, he will serve as b'alnial, or assistant. All the people who attend the household ceremony following the church baptism become compadres and constitute the kumparetak. Compadres attend each other's household ceremonials, acting as nakawanehetik (attendants who are present at all household ceremonials) or b'alnialetik. Compadrazgo is patterned on a pre-Conquest institution establishing ties between attendants in household rituals called maliwanehetik.

The relationship of protection and guidance that is to characterize the tie between co-parents, godchildren and their godparents for the rest of their lives is symbolized in the behavior formally prescribed in the baptism ceremony. On the day of baptism, the child is dressed in clothing given by his godparents. The parents and grandparents of the child go together with the godparent to the church. While the child is being baptized by the priest, he is held by his godfather if he is a boy, or by her godmother if a girl. The priest throws water and salt on the child and prays over him, baptizing him in the name of the Father, the Son, and the Holy Ghost. After the ceremony the participants embrace the child and each other in front of the church, symbolizing the status they now occupy in respect to the child, his grandparents, and parents. Without this performance, the ritual terms of comadre, compadre, or padrino cannot be used.[1]

---

1. This behavioral definition of the ritual kinship tie in the sme?ispetb'ak is illustrated in the following incident: The wife of a man who had been asked to be a child's godparent was absent when the priest arrived for the ceremony. Her husband went to the church with the parents and grandparents of the child and embraced them at the church steps. Although

The church ceremony is followed by another ceremony in the house of the child's parents. As the group returning from the church enters the house, they are greeted with the patˀoˀtan by the maliwanehetik who are waiting for them in the house. As they enter, each of the returning party says, "You go forward, kumpare." They embrace all of the waiting party, an act which establishes their relationship as compadres with the entire company. When the padrinos leave, the grandparents and parents of the child go to a spot before the eaves outside the house; there the father of the child serves liquor to the padrinos and the grandparents of the child. The drink is called "the finale as the compadres leave." The group must finish the entire liter "since it is a gift," and if there are only one or two grandparents, they may get fairly drunk. As the compadres leave, the grandpaernts say, "Over the soil, over the mud where you take your holy godchild, your holy flower, your holy candle." The child, referred to metaphorically as holy flower, holy candle, is identified with the most sacred symbols of the culture.[2]

The emphasis on the group relationship in Tzoˀontahal contrasts with the form of compadrazgo found in the central plateau of Mexico where the dyadic tie between two compadres provides flexibility in achieving instrumental ends in political or economic life.[3] Some of the new leaders in economic enterprises are beginning to emphasize the dyadic contract in their compadrazgo relationships to achieve political support, but its greatest importance is still based on creating or reinforcing group solidarity.

BETROTHAL AND MARRIAGE

The Indians of Tzoˀonthal are initiated into the community of the living and depart from it with ceremonies deriving from the Spanish colonial culture. The courtship and marriage ceremonies continue indigenous re-

---

she later attended the household ceremony, she was never called kumare because of the omission of this act.

2. See Laughlin (1962) on the symbolism of the candle and flower in Zinacantan.

3. In regard to the occasions and the kind of respect relation established, compadrazgo in Tzoˀontahal is similar to the institution in other parts of Mexico (Foster 1963, Nader 1964, Wolf and Mintz 1950). The difference lies in the elaboration of the number of ties acquired through compadrazgo at each event.

tual practices and are carried on in the home. Sometimes a church and/or civil marriage is held in addition, but the union is not consummated until the traditional home marriage has taken place.

The betrothal, or *č'om,* is an extended series of negotiations in which the boy's representatives plead with the girl's family to accept the suit. Anytime in a boy's late teens or early twenties, he may initiate the suit by speaking to his father, or the father may undertake to find a wife for his son. The parents of the boy then request an older woman who has some skill in speaking the formal speeches to serve as the me? *Č'om,* mother of the betrothal, and an older man to serve as the *statal č'om,* or leader of the betrothal (sometimes he is called mam č'om or grandfather of the betrothal). These intermediaries may or may not be related to the family initiating the request. Nonkin are usually chosen from among compadres or a neighborhood group. When the father requests that they act as intermediaries, he brings a gift of liquor, chocolate, and bread.

Before any negotiations are begun with the girl's family, the boy's family calls together the representatives. These include his grandparents, uncles, and aunts, his padrino of baptism and confirmation, and possibly neighbors or nearby compadres of his parents. The gathering then questions the boy to learn whether his interest in the girl is sincere and exclusive of any other infatuation. In this session, called the *?ič' yo?tan* or "taking of the heart," the boy goes to each of his representatives and kneels before them as they question him, asking him if he wants that girl and only that girl. He is told that marriage is an important relationship, not to be treated "as a toy"; the boy should be interested in only this girl, and if he should cause them to have to go to the cabildo "the day after tomorrow," it would cause embarrassment to the entire company.

At the final gathering, called the *?ič' rason* or "taking of the understanding," the assembled me?iltatil of both the boy and the girl give the couple further advice. The boy is told what is expected of him in the marriage. It is a minimal statement: he should not leave her tomorrow, he should not beat her, he should bring home corn and beans, and all will be well. The girl is told that she should prepare her husband's meals and be waiting for him in the house when he comes home from work. Respect, called "hearing" and "feeling" (both combined in the verb *š?awayi*), is stressed for both. The boy is again warned not to bring the meʔiltatil embarrassment by causing them to go to the cabildo.

During the six months to a year between the first and the last gatherings, the boy's representatives make up to a dozen visits to the girl's house. The patterning of behavior during these visits reveals cyclical and progressive tendencies of which the participants are consciously aware. These progressions involve time, the number of people involved, and the size of the gift.

Time progression affects two aspects of the courtship: the hour of the visit of the boy's mam čʼom and meʔ čʼom, which becomes later, and the length of the visit—it is longer each time. The first visit is a tactical maneuver involving the early-bird ploy. The meʔ čʼom, having stayed awake after the all-night ceremony of the "taking of the heart," arrives at the girl's house at the "dawning dusk of the world." She stays only long enough to leave the gift and announce her intention of continuing the suit indefinitely. The timing of the last visit when the "taking of the understanding" occurs contrasts with this in that the members of the boy's wedding party arrive late in the evening and do not leave until four or five in the morning. The time of arrival and departure is plotted for each visit in Figure 5. The progressively later arrival time indicates increasing security on the part of the members of the betrothal party that the girl's family will be there to receive them, while the extended staying time indicates growing confidence and the breaking down of the barriers of reserve. Even up to the last visit, however, the members of the betrothal party take two quick parting shots of liquor as they leave the boy's house to "rid themselves of their embarrassment."

The increase in the number of members of the betrothal party who go to the girl's house is tied to the increase in the amount of the gift. The role terms of the members of the betrothal party indicate their association to the gift, as shown on Table 21.

Finally, the progression in the value of the gift is the cultural item most commented upon by the people, both within the village and in comparing customs with other Indian towns. This permissible variation indicates the relative wealth of the boy's family and the relative resistence of the girl's family. While the quantities vary from one čʼom to another, in all cases

Fig. 5. Timing of Arrival and Departure in Čʼom Visits

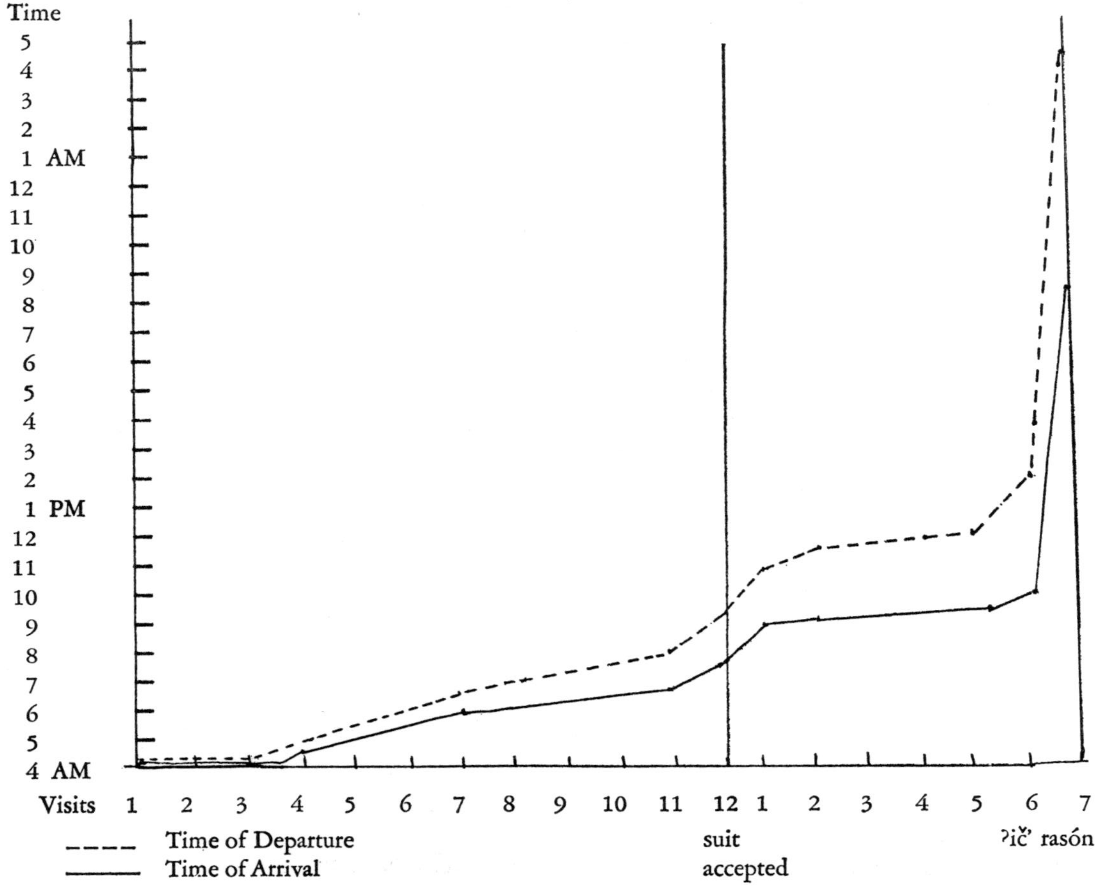

there is an increase with each trip. Except for the transfer of money in the last trip, the gift is completely in consumables—chickens, bread, liquor, chocolate, and sugar. With many of the older men becoming teetotalers, soda has become an established part of the gift exchange as well. Two elements of the gift exchange are stable in all marriages—the four chickens each cooked and wrapped in fifteen tortillas with a chile placed inside, and the chocolate. In a traditional exchange system, the quantities of some items of exchange are fixed while those of other items fluctuate; gifts of bread, liquor, and money, for example, are of varying quantity in Tzoʔontahal. The fixed quantities of chicken, chocolate, and tortillas establish conformity to community standards while the fluctuating ones indicate the relative prestige of the family.

TABLE 21. Relation of Members of Betrothal Party to Gifts

Member of the betrothal party	Time of participation	Function
Mother of the betrothal (Meʔ čʼom)	Initiates action	At first, carries the gift of bread, chocolate, and brown sugar. Burden lightens as others take over these gifts, so that at end she carries only corn gruel and one large piece of bread
Elder of the betrothal (Mam čʼom)	On fourth visit, accompanies mother of the betrothal	Carries liquor until Measurer of liquor takes over, then carries only sweetened liquor served to women
Measurer of liquor (Pʼ is haʔ)	About seventh visit, accompanies mother and elder of the betrothal when suit is accepted	Carries white liquor served to men and that given as gift
Basket carrier (La smoč, usually wife of Pʼis haʔ)	Accompanies mother and elder of the betrothal and Measurer of liquor when suit is accepted	Carries bread throughout final visits before "taking of the understanding"
Carrier of brown sugar (Čʼup ʔaskah)	On last visit before "taking of the understanding," accompanies mother, elder, measurer, and basket carrier	Carries sweet liquor and soda for last visit and for "taking of the understanding"

The links between members of the meʔiltatil of a couple united in marriage are reinforced if another marriage occurs between the two households. While this does not provide a basis for prescribed or preferred mating, those who have such exchanges say they prefer it because the negotiations in the čʼom proceed more amicably, especially in the earlier stage.

Solidarity of the group is reinforced when the meʔiltatil are called upon to help settle conflicts that arise in the marriage. The household review of marital conflict requires a formal gathering of all the members of the betrothal party who represented both the husband and the wife. Parents of the couple state the evidence and recite the events which led up to the conflict. The husband or wife may interject, speaking in their own defense. The elders suggest how the person judged guilty (usually the man) ought to behave and what his reponsibilities are. A transcription of one such case is included in Appendix 1A. This concerns a couple who had separated two years after the marriage. The following statement of the padrino of the wedding ceremony, speaking in lieu of the leader of the čʼom who could not be present, shows the techniques they use to adjust relations:

Now he [the husband] wants to change for the better. You [speaking to the husband] ought not to drink. It is better to eat meat and vegetables and find corn and beans for your wife and child. Now we have arranged it, and you can take your wife and child to your house.

A successful outcome depends on all people in the dispute accepting the judgment of the elders. If this cannot be achieved, the abused partner seeks redress in the courts. Women are most frequently the plaintiffs. The plaintiff is supported by her parents who appear with her in court and help argue her case. The defendant may appear with his parents, if they support him, but very often they feel shame and do not.

In court cases, two judges hear the evidence and they, along with the president and other civil officials deliver the verdict. The quality of interpersonal relations does not differ much from that which one finds in the household review, as can be seen in comparing the court review included in Appendix 1B with the household review. In the former case, the woman's wrath had been aroused by her husband occasionally returning to his first wife, and by his failure to give her money for expenses. Since he

worked in the sawmill, he was not as willing to hand over his wages to
his wife as is the farmer, who according to established custom gives the
proceeds from the sale of his crop to his wife. The judges advise the man
to stay sober, adding, "If you want a woman, you ought to support her.
You shouldn't fight." They entreat the wife to return to her husband's
house "and make a fire there." They refuse to release the marriage license,
and the woman's father reluctantly agrees. He has the last word, warning
the husband: "The day after tomorrow, don't come back here with a couple more children and say, 'I don't want you; go back to your mother's
house.' You are lucky to have a wife. If you don't have a wife, you go get
drunk every day. But with a wife, life is good. She will give you coffee
and corn to eat. Don't go on fighting whether drunk or sober. Both my
compadres [referring to the judges] have advised you."

The curing ceremony as a means of adjusting interpersonal conflict is
discussed at greater length in the following chapter. Padrinos of baptism,
compadres, and other members of the patient's meʔiltatil attend, both to
see that the curer is performing his duties properly and to lend spiritual
support. Like the household and court review of conflict, it permits the
open airing of grievances and relies on the authority of elders. Drinking
liquor is a means of restoring good feelings, either as a follow-up to the review of court cases or as a continuous measure of goodwill in curing.

The responsibility of the meʔiltatil for repairing personal relationships
in the family underwrites the importance of this institution in the community. In these institutionalized means of settling conflict the society recog-
nizes the inevitability of friction in intimate relations and draws upon the
resources of personnel and techniques developed in the life crisis rituals.

The meʔiltatil are the guardians of individuals. The security that they
provide depends upon the individual conforming to the group norms.
They are a personal reference group maintaining customary ways of behaving. I shall show in the following chapters how they are linked as the
inner core to a system of guardianship provided by curers within each side
of the dual division and by civil authorities at the community-wide level.
These are the agents who, by providing models of how the progenitors
behaved and by channeling responses to social change, maintain the sense
of equilibrium and the illusion of changelessness. The sense of continuity

with the past is preserved in the ceremonials in which these officials act, but nonceremonial activities no longer reinforce the values symbolized in ritual.

DEATH AND BURIAL

When a person dies, his soul is believed to go out from his tongue. The family is responsible for finding a resting place which will be satisfactory to the soul. If the dead person has died of a "good" (not caused by witch-craft) illness, the soul lingers for eight days and then goes to heaven. If the dead person has been killed, his soul stays in the village for "a month or twenty days." The reason given for this is that "the gods did not choose the hour of death, and the soul doesn't know where to go." During this waiting period the dead person "finishes his heart," or ends his emotional ties with friends and relatives.

Following the death, a sister of the parents of a child or some other adult woman washes the body and puts a wrap over it. The body is always laid out with the feet toward the door; the eyes are shut, and the jaw is wrapped with a kerchief to hold the mouth closed. Two candles are placed at the head and two at the feet. Flowers and a bowl to collect offerings of 2 pesos from each visitor are placed at the head of the body. The contribution given at the burial assures the giver of a hearing with Christ:

Everyone gives a contribution of 50 cents or a peso. Each one considers how much he can give and gives it. God listens to and speaks to those who give gifts. Those who give a candle or a little contribution of corn or flowers give an account of the dead man's life. If he had no crime on his conscience or only one crime, whoever killed him by violence or by witchcraft bears the guilt. Christ listens to the account of those who have given good contributions. Thus the help is given so that Christ will see that he did a favor to one who is poor and who has nothing to bury himself, not corn, or money, or anything to sell, not land, or cattle, or wheat. Therefore everyone who is a relative or a compadre or a neighbor brings one-fourth [bottle of liquor], a half measure of brown sugar, fifteen or twenty corn-cobs and one or two candles. And all men who arrive at the grave and give five or ten pesos are helped by God. Those who give nothing end at their burial with nothing.

If the death occurs in the night, the body will be buried on the following day. During the wake, called "watching over the dead," relatives of the father, mother, and spouse of the deceased, as well as compadres and neighbors, watch over the body so that the devil cannot enter and steal the soul. If the dead person's padrino is alive, he serves as first *nakawane* and greets the guests. Liquor is served constantly. The women serve coffee and tamales or tortillas to the visitors at midnight.

At midnight the woman who is closest of kin cries for the dead. This is a stylized crying in which the mourner speaks of how the dead man passed his life. If she is his widow, she weeps for the misery she will face. Mourning for herself, she repeats:

How can I eat now with my children?
You will not see how I shall live.
You are of one heart in the ground.
But you do not see how I shall eat with the children.

If the death has been a violent one, the widow may express her sentiments about the blamelessness of her husband, or she may suggest that accusations that he was a witch are true by saying she knew nothing of what he did at night. In any case, people listen carefully to what she sings because it may give some basis for speculating whether there will be an attempt to avenge his death.

On the day of the burial, the coffin is lined with a new straw mat, and all the dead man's used clothing except for his kotončʉ is placed inside. A gourd drinking cup with *posol,* a spiced corn gruel, is placed near the dead man's mouth along with a tortilla. A metal cup cannot be used to hold water in the coffin because it does not have a soul as does the gourd vessel, which comes from a living plant. If the deceased is a man or boy, his hat is placed next to his head and his sandals are set beside his feet. A cross made of palm is put in the coffin to ward off the devil. If the deceased is a child, his head is adorned with a wreath of paper flowers set on a kerchief which is bound around his head.

The funeral procession leaves for the cemetery about three in the afternoon. Attending the body are the padrinos, **parents**, aunts, and uncles. If
the deceased is a child under two years of age, he is carried by his madrina. One of the former fiscales or someone who knows how to pray goes
along. Smaller siblings or children of the dead are left at home with the
maliwanehetik, who in this case are chosen from among the more distant
relatives, compadres, and neighbors not attending the funeral. As they
walk, the women cry and the "owner of the dead," the woman closest of
kin, wails constantly in the stylized mourning cry. She stops wailing only
when the company stops to pray at the cross at the exit of the town and
just before entering the graveyard. At each resting point, the fiscal, who
holds a rosary, reads the prayer book, while a neighbor or compadre uses a
geranium to sprinkle holy water on the spot. An older male relative holds
a palm cross.

When the party arrives at the opened grave, the godmother sits down
near the coffin to make the final arrangements. The grave has been opened
prior to the arrival of the party, but sometimes the men widen the hole. If
they come across a bone, the fiscal shakes holy water over it with the geranium. When a nursing child is buried, the mother leans over the coffin
and puts her breast in the child's mouth just before he is lowered into the
grave. This is done so that the child's spirit will not think any longer of
returning. The godparent or some other attendant dips the geranium in
water and shakes it over the body. Handfuls of dirt are then thrown into
the coffin. It is at this point that the assembled group, including the men,
breaks into loud wails. The wails of the funeral party, though they do not
lack feeling, are most important as a controlled communication, uttered
when it is appropriate and by particular persons who are expected to cry
before a select audience.

As the neighbors who have come to help the bereaved relatives shovel
dirt on the grave, the padrino of the deceased approaches the fiscal and recites the pat?o?tan of blessing for the gift of liquor. The liquor is measured in a shot glass and passed around to the company. The women leave
soon, and the men remain drinking. At this point a kind of trial is held to
see who is responsible for the death. Since almost all sickness is believed to
be caused by witchcraft, it is important to decide who the guilty person

might be. The father or closest male kin of the dead person is careful to recount all the consultations he has had with curers, both to absolve himself of the guilt of neglect or unconscious witchcraft and to search for the true culprit.

A proper burial with holy water, flowers, grave offerings, and prayers assures the survivors that the soul of the deceased will rest and his bones will lie in peace. Lacking any of these features, the dead will disturb the living, as is recounted below:

During the revolution, many were buried without a funeral or without blessed water. On Thursday, the bones burn and cry. You can still see a blue flame rising above the old graveyard on Thursday. You can find money that the ancestors left there, but you have to go at night to dig it up.

An important safeguard to ensure that the soul will lie in peace is burial among people with whom the deceased lived. When a married adult dies, he is buried with his dead spouse. If he had two dead spouses, he is buried with the first spouse on the right hand and the second on the left. A child is buried with the grandparents of the household in which he lived—that is, if he lived with his mother's parents he is buried with them, and if with the father's parents, then with them. When people know that they are going to die, they express their preference as to where they wish to be buried. Usually they will elect to be buried between their dead parents, but if they were unhappy with their parents, they might choose a padrino or uncle. If dissatisfied in its resting place, a soul, even when properly buried, cannot find peace and wanders back to the house. Fearing this, relatives try to comply with the wishes of the dead.

My grandfather used to say that he wanted to be buried between his mother and father. But when he was about to die, he said, "I don't want to be buried there because my father beat me. He will continue beating my soul. I want to go on the side [of the cemetery]. Please don't bury me near my parents." My father said, "All right, we will put you on the side."

The funeral must meet the expectations of the community as well as those of the deceased and his relatives. The mature children of a man who dies are expected to give a funeral appropriate to his station in life and his wealth, as is expressed in the following account:

When my father got sick, he told his wife not to put him in a black box. He had heard a story that when the dead man is in a black box, his spirit cannot see. He wanted to be in a white box. He told this to his brother. But his brother wanted to get a black box. He bought one black box for three hundred pesos when my father died, because it is the custom of the pueblo to bury adults in a black box. The people would talk if we did not buy a good box because they knew he had animals. We spent six hundred pesos for the funeral. We presented the body in church for a mass. We had a singing mass for thirty pesos, and the box cost three hundred pesos. We had a common meal of beef in the house, and we spent two hundred and sixteen pesos for three garrafones of liquor. Each of his sons contributed sixty pesos for that. If we hadn't given him a good funeral, people would have said, "His children are very lax not to buy a good box to bury their father."

The padre says that all bodies should be presented in the church. He says if you don't have money, you don't have to pay for the mass. But we are ashamed if we don't pay because he does work for us. He charged only twenty-five pesos because he said my father worked hard for the town. We took a collection from all the people who were there, and it amounted to one hundred and thirty pesos. We paid the padre for the mass and gave a contribution. All the people in whose houses he had passed when he was alive came to see him. They said, "Ah, his children gave a very nice box for their father."

If all of the family is poor, no one talks if the funeral is not a good one. But if there is anything that can be sold, it will have to be to make a good funeral. When my father died, he had eighteen horses. We had to sell one, and each of the children gave one hundred pesos.

Some say the souls play the harp and drink liquor when they arrive in heaven. On All Soul's Day they visit the village where they had lived and where they are known. For each member of the household who had died, a specific portion of food is laid out. Special likes are catered to: a bottle of liquor will be set on the table for a deceased father, soda pop for children who have died, or candy and gum. Luxury foods, particularly fruits, meat, and sausage are prepared. Only those dead relatives who were known to the present residents of the house are honored. The celebration of All Souls' Day is not a celebration for the ancestors as a general group.

In addition to the feast given in the house, food and drink are carried up to the graves of the relatives. The cemetery duplicates the residential pattern. When people have relatives buried on the side opposite to where they live, because of a marriage violating the rule of endogamy within sections, they "have shame" to go light a candle at the graves, and they return hastily to the relatives on their own side. The women cry for the recently dead in the stylized wail for the dead. While souls are honored relatives on this one day, if they appear at any other time there is great fear of them.

Chapter 6

Curing and the Curers

Sickness is a sign of upset relations between the spirits or people and those of relatives, neighbors, or places. In the curing ritual, the curers not only treat the disease, but also try to bring about spiritual readjustment by dramatizing the ill effects of animosity. Because they claim to be able to counteract witchcraft, the curers exercise a great deal of power. This power is limited by institutional requirements controlling entry into the profession and exercise of their skill and knowledge. The breakdown in the authority of elder curers during my study of the community, and their attempts to reinstate themselves, made explicit some of the structural principles of the institution.

THE CURING HIERARCHY

Recruitment into the hierarchy. Until the 1950s, each side of the dual division had an age-ranked order of curers and recognized the leadership of a single elder, called *statal ?u?ul.* The older, more experienced curers, called the *b'ankilal,* or elder brothers, had authority over the novice curers, called the *?ihtz'inal,* or younger brothers. With the breakdown of the hierarchy during my stay, this distinction was becoming less clear. In 1964 there were seven curers in Alannantik and six in Ahk'olnantik; on a return visit I made in 1967, their numbers had been reduced by homicide and exile to five in Alannantik and five in Ahk'olnantik.

Entry into the profession occurs during an epidemic when the civil authority calls upon the curers to gather in the town hall to determine who is bringing the "heat" that causes death from disease. The curers decide whether there are any promising young men who have the third soul, swayohel, which gives them the ability to cure. If a young man is deemed

137

suitable, the president and judges give permission to the curers to allow him to enter the profession at this time. The novice provides three liters of liquor which are drunk "in common" by the curers and the civil officials.

There is some evidence that, formerly, novice curers were asked to yield the soul of one of their children:

My dead husband was given permission by Julian Gomex, the leader of the curers of Ahk'olnantik, to enter the curing profession. When my husband told me he wanted to cure, he said that Julian had asked him for a child "for the ancestors to eat." My husband was going to give a child of his brother since we didn't have any, but I said it would be a pity. Then he said he would give trago. This he did. I forget how many liters.

When the contagion came, the curers went to take out the heat. A policeman called my dead husband, and he went. The policeman said the leading curer had called him. The judges told him, "It is better for you to enter in common with the other curers."

He began to cure. The curers then asked what offering we were going to give.

"We have no children," said my husband. "We will give you liquor. I cannot give my brother's child or my sister's children."

He must have brought them about ten or twelve liters of trago and two packs of cigarettes.

The third soul, swayohel, may be acquired, or one may be born with it. Those who acquire the third soul by capture of the soul of a dead person within twenty days after the death are considered to be potentially dangerous. They are more likely to use the soul for evil than those who have acquired it from the ancestors at birth. Swayoheles can be acquired from a saint named ʔAhau in the neighboring town of Oxchuk.[1] The following account illustrates how one asks this saint for a swayohel:

If you go to the saint with a black face named ʔAhau with two candles of twenty cents you can ask for a swayohel. You say, "I want one č'ulel that is very strong. I have an enemy. I need one." You sleep there, and wake

1. Lombardo Otero (1944:73) says that in Oxchuk, Mukulajau, or Chulajau, is identified with Trinidad, and is associated with the pigeon, which is the animal spirit of powerful curers.

up with a swayohel. One man near San Vicente said his friend went there to ask for one. Next day, the enemy died. One man who went there said when he woke up he was sure he had gained a swayohel. He had dreamed of two animals. "Are they my swayoheles?" he asked. They were jaguars.

When he got to his house, the same two animals came. They thought about how to get his enemies. But when the jaguars had killed his enemies, they were not content. Then they went on to kill many people. Finally the man was shot. The spirits of all those who die as a result of a swayohel received from ?Ahau go to him after their death.

Curers are classified as potentially good or dangerous on the basis of what kind of swayohel they have. Good curers have swayoheles of animals which eat leaves or grass—horses, sheep, bulls, or other herbivorous animals. Potentially dangerous curers have the souls of carnivorous animals —vultures, dogs, cats, mountain lions, coyote, and others. They may not use these swayoheles for evil, but possession of such a soul is a basis for suspicion. Usually the curers keep secret the nature of their swayohel, but sometimes when they are drunk they brag about its power. Good swayoheles fly or walk straight down the main roads of the town, while evil swayoheles lurk at the outskirts of the settled area.

Only one woman has a swayohel and practices curing. She is reputed to have acquired her swayohel in the following manner:

There was a woman named Andrea Ča?il and another named Fernanda Ča?il. They were not sisters, but they were of the Ča?iletik. Fernanda died. She was a true elder woman, a very strong woman. She lived in Madronal and Andrea lived in the center.

One day Andrea said, "Let us go collect wood," to two girls.

"Let's go," said the girls. "Where shall we get the wood?"

"Let's go in the woods behind Madronal," replied Andrea. "Let's go."

The women arrived in the mountain to cut wood. When they had the wood, Andrea said she saw a mulberry bush. "Let us eat some berries," she said.

Andrea went to the mulberry bush. She saw a white ball of Čišol under the bush. "What kind of an animal is that?" she asked.

The girls looked at it and said, "We don't know."

Andrea told them to go and eat the mulberries and she would see what kind of an animal it was. The animal said, "Come here." But when they got there, there was no animal.

In two or four days, people asked them, "What kind of an animal did you see?"

"It was a dog that we saw. Not a real dog, but the soul of the dead Fernanda. Andrea caught it," the girls said.

"Did you truly see where it was?" the people asked.

"I caught it," said Andrea.

"Why did you catch it," the girls asked.

"I caught it because it is a pity it died. Since there is no one to take it, I grabbed it because it made me sad that she [Fernanda] died."

Now Andrea is a me? u?ul [woman curer]. She fights sickness because she has this extra soul.

Ordinarily, soul-catching is dangerous since it is sezure of power which has not been granted at birth by the me?iltatil. Andrea, however, has never been accused of doing harm, and people emphasize that she did it out of sympathy for her dead kinswoman.

There is some sentiment that curers should not enter too young into the curing profession. If they do, they should be extremely deferential to the elder curers, and not claim greater powers. The informant quoted above concerning the initiation of her husband into the curing profession maintains that the older curers did not support her husband when he was accused as a witch because of jealousy of his youth.

My husband was very young when he entered curing. He had gone to cure in the house of a man living near Domingo [his enemy]. Domingo saw him come out drunk. He had a companion, Lorenzo. About eight people gathered. They put a nail in his jaws. He lived three nights. He told me who did it. I went to the cabildo with my father. They got many witnesses to deny they had been near. It was during the fiesta of Carnival.

My father and I spoke with the authorities in Las Casas. But nothing was done. I did not know how to speak well in Spanish; I went and spoke to Domingo. He told me, "It was your husband's own fault."

"What crime did he have?" I asked.

"He looked for trouble!" Domingo replied.
I said, "You killed my husband!"
He said, "It was not I! It was not I!"
It doesn't serve to enter curing early. People will kill you right away.
Another young man wanted to enter. The curers did not permit him since
they said he was a witch. People heard he was a witch, and they killed
him. He was the same age as my husband [about twenty-seven].

The curers who have survived to an old age were introduced into the profession by an elder relative. They choose their clients carefully, refusing to cure a man who is on the point of death, and remaining within their own section of the dual division. These rules of survival are ignored by some of the younger men who wish to impress their elders with their powers.

The changing image of the curers. The curers of today are unfavorably compared with those of the past who used their power for good. The prototype of the old curer was the fearful Tatik Čaʔuk, Lord of the Lightning, possibly a local manifestation of the Maya god Chac.[2] The dialectic of power is exemplified in his control over beneficial and destructive forces. His beneficence is demonstrated in his ability to bring rain to crops, while his vengeance is revealed in lightning bolts which can kill people and destroy houses. Anyone who is struck by lightning is believed to have had some sin for which the Tatik Čaʔuk has punished him. His destructive force is equated with a rifle—called "the elder brother of the Lord of Lightning"—and with the "heat" which brings death in illnesses. His habitation is believed to be the Cave of the Star where the heat which causes epidemics is found.

The curers were intermediaries for the Tatik Čaʔuk in their control over both destructive and beneficial forces. Formerly, the swayohel of the curers patrolled the streets of the town to prevent the entry of evildoers bringing heat. It is in this role that they are referred to as me'iltatil. If an epidemic occurred, the two leading curers from each side of the town con-

2. In other Tzeltal- and Tzotzil-speaking communities, the god Čaʔuk is named as the chief figure from pre-Conquest theology (Hermitte 1964, Holland 1963:93).

sulted with each other to determine who was bringing in the heat. They privately disposed of the evil by causing the evildoer to die of an illness. At the time of my stay, suspicion of the curers meant that a public hearing was held in the town hall to determine who the guilty person was; usually one of the curers themselves was suspected (Chapter 9).

The curers formerly demonstrated their beneficial power by bringing rain during a fiesta held in the cave of the ancestors. This is described by an informant:

When the pueblo lacked rain in the growing season of corn in May and June, the leading curers went with the other curers, the fiscal, the alfereces, the mayordomos, and the women prayer-reciters to the cave. All the women carried candles of a peso or fifty-cent size and incense burners. They drank a great deal of liquor at the mouth of the cave and then entered to dance. The mayordomos played the guitar, the drum, and flute as the women danced and the curers prayed to the meʔtiktatik. There used to be a spring in this cave, people say, and the ancestors granted water from it when they were given a fiesta.

The last fiesta for rain occurred about 1950. The whole town contributed two pesos for the liquor and candles. The leading curer then was Juliano, a man recognized for his powers in curing and in bringing rain. He told the people that he spoke to the meʔtiktatik who, he said, were dressed in the old style [a shirt worn over short cotton pants still used by older men of the town, and the handwoven hat worn by alfereces today]. The curers told the people that it would rain, and the afternoon of the fiesta, it came down hard.

There is no longer faith that the ancestors live in the cave, nor that the present curers could speak to them if they did.

The growing discontent with the curers, the suspicion that they are responsible for much of the witchcraft, is reflected in the account of an older informant.

The curer O. K. told me that the curers ate the spirits of sick people who were going to die. The sick people would come to ask the curers for medicine. But why should they ask for medicine if the curers were going to eat their souls as he told me? I asked him, "How do you eat their souls?" He said that the five or six curers would make a common meal. They looked for a frying pan, and when it was well cooked, they would call all the curers and say, "Come, let us eat in common." When people came to ask for medicine, they would say, "Please, give us medicine." The curers would give the medicine, but the sick ones did not get well. The curers were only deceiving them. How could they get well if they wanted to eat their souls? They only wasted their money.

It is this that O. K. said to me. He told me himself that he had eaten the souls. Then I felt that he was bad because of what he himself had told me. To this day, I believe that he himself did the evil to his patients.

The personality of the curer. In view of the hazards of entering the curing profession and the low material rewards, the question of what motivates a curer to practice is of some interest. The older curers claim that God spoke to them in a dream and made known His desire that they cure. They conceive of it as a responsibility to the people, and maintain that their power comes from God. This contradicts parallel statements made by the same curers that their power comes from their swayohel. The younger curers say that the curers of their side selected them because they saw that they had a swayohel.

Direct questioning yields only limited understanding of what motivates these extraordinary people. The behavior of some of the curers reveals facets of the role which could not be elicited from them in questioning. Curers are able to defy tenets of the moral code of the community which stress softness and slowness, a moderation which is fundamentally based on fear of the world of spirits and of men. When drunk, the curers brag about their strength and fearlessness. They try to avoid the usual negative sanctions to such behavior by asserting the strength of their swayoheles and their imperviousness to harm.

My elder brother Albino was drinking with the dead Nicolás, leader of the curers of Alannantik. When both were half drunk, my elder brother asked Niholás what swayohel he had.

*"You won't be afraid if I show it?" Nicolás asked. He then flipped his
kotončk four times and a black bull appeared. It disappeared, and they
drank some more. Nicolás made the bull appear again.*

*Nicolás was ejido commissioner when I was president. We began to
talk one day in the cabildo. "Who is the strongest of all the curers?" we
asked. One said that now it was the elder brother Nicolás.*

*Čiko turned to Nico and said, "Tell us who is the strongest of all who
know curing." Nico replied, "Ah, you want to hear. There is no one who
is strong as the dead Mamal Komesil [elder Gomez] and I." Čiko said,
"Mam D. is good."*

*"Less so," said Nico. "One time we tested it. I took out a sheep and a
black dog. He [D.] took out a goat and a pig, and we ordered the animals
to run. And I saw that the swayohel of D. could not run. Mine ran well,
and his couldn't arrive before mine. It was then that I saw he was not as
strong."*

Formerly, when bullfights were held in the town as a feature of the
fiesta of Santiago, curers took the great risk of riding the backs of the
bulls to demonstrate their bravery. The fight became a symbolic defiance
of culturally instilled fears. The fights are organized in this fashion:
one man mounts the bull which has no saddle, bridle, or grip of any
kind. His feet are tied under the belly of the bull, which increases the haz-
ard if he is thrown since he can easily be dragged under the hooves of the
bull. A man stands with a cape before the bull, trying to unseat his opponent. The curer Minko regularly entered the fights as a rider. He drank
copiously before mounting the bull. He himself would try to goad the bull
into jumping by leaning backward and biting its tail or kicking its sides.
People rated even more highly than Minko's performance that of another
curer, Bon, who, they said, never even shook when he climbed onto the
bull as did Minko. They realized that Minko needed the liquor to face the
threat of being crushed by the hooves of the bull, but that Bon was beyond fear. In these displays of fearlessness, some of the curers enjoy a
sense of power and freedom from the inhibitions conditioning the behavior of ordinary men.

Competition and the assertion of power among the younger curers is symptomatic of the present breakdown in the hierarchical controls which formerly maintained the authority of elder curers. Informants say that in the old days there was no such competition, and the leadership of the elder curers was unchallenged.

Another clue to the personality of the curer can be seen in the statement of a young curer, who expressed in a kind of stream-of-consciousness style the fears and worries that plague him. After responding to the questioning about what he did when he cured, he proceeded to talk of his own concerns as he cured patients:

And when I arrive at Pahaltón [curing spring], I set aside my hat and blanket so that they do not get burned. If a dog should come and chew my sandals or if I should leave them outside the house where I am curing and a house rat chews them, then it will cost me thirty pesos to buy a new pair. When I come out late at night, a cat spirit sometimes appears on the road, and I throw a stone at it so it will not carry off my spirit; or a dog comes and I must beat him with my hand because I have no machete with me, or I must throw a broken bottle at the devil. When I get home, I take off my jacket and hat and go to sleep. My woman must tie up the sandals with a string on the rafters so that the rat will not eat them. Then it is the woman's fault if the devil dog gets them.

Late at night the spirits of the curers come to play and go at cock's crow. And at two o'clock the spirit of a sheep comes out with the devil, and these spirits do not go to sleep in their house until dawn. And if they [the curers' spirits] arrive in bed drunk and take off their huaraches and bother their wife she will put them in prison and then they have to pay a fine of two liters of the "gift" [liquor] and one handful of cigarettes. If their woman leaves the curers and they come out of prison, then if they do the same thing again, they send then to Santo Domingo. In prison they make net bags and if they have a wife, she goes and gives them tortillas and coffee. If their wife or father and mother help and give money, then they can pay for a lawyer and get out. Or if they have a daughter, then they receive the gift of a suitor and eat the bread.[3] Later there will come the chicken and sweet liquor and trago, and then she will marry. Later

3. "Eating the bread" signifies that the betrothal negotiations are accepted.

they will go to the church wedding. The parents of the couple embrace
the godparents. They go dance in the house.

The paranoic fantasies of this young curer, a man in his early thirties,
characterize the world of fears, both real and demonic, which the curers
sometimes manipulate and by which they are sometimes victimized. The
young curers in their thirties and forties tend to have more domestic disputes than most men in town. Emilio, a man in his forties who has been
trying to assert his stature as leading curer of Alannantik since his prede-
cessor was killed for witchcraft, was deserted by his wife. She fled to a
neighbor's house. In a drunken rage, he tried to burn it to the ground.
When his attempt failed, he threatened to bring "heat" from the Cave of
the Star to cause an epidemic after which, he said, he would "eat the souls
of the children by the dozen." In the line of duty, curers are often required to get drunk, and drunkenness loosens the cautions which control
behavior. Gloating in the power of their swayoheles, there seems to be no
limit to the threats or acts they commit. While drinking has probably always been part of curing ceremonies, the behavior noted in the cases described seems to be a response to the growing insecurity on the part of the
curers about their status.

The curer reveals in his speech and acts the motivation of power. In
Tzo?ontahal, power means freedom from one's own fears as well as from
the human and supernatural sanctions imposed on those who ignore the
norms governing behavior. The proof of his power lies in the ability to in-
spire fear in others. For this reason, the curer brags of the evil deeds he
has committed or is capable of doing, even though this may bring about
his own destruction.

CURING BEHAVIOR

In their role as "doctors" for the individual patient, curers are referred
to as *?u?ul* and are addressed with the honorific title *tatín*. Despite the declining belief in their guardianship function, there has been a retention of
belief in their power to overcome witchcraft. Only the curer, because he
possesses a swayohel, can deal with illness caused by witchcraft. Even if

the curer is a potentially dangerous witch, he can be persuaded to fight the evil power of another. One of the most dangerous and powerful witches, until he was killed five years ago, was a man who boasted as he was curing a patient, "The evil [pukuh] in me will win over that of the witch!"

Curing behavior is classified in Tzeltal according to five major schema: (1) pulsing (*pikel č'ič*), (2) drawing out the evil (*slok'es ʔak'čamel*), (3) calling the soul (*tamohel*), (4) medicating the illness (*poštawane camel*, and (5) medicating the house (*poštawane na*). Each behavioral schema represents the highest level of a behavioral taxonomy which includes discrete actions described below.

Pulsing. The course of the cure for all illnesses is set in motion by the diagnosis through pulsing Throughout the cure, pulsing is performed to gauge the effectiveness of each step. The curer is chosen on the basis of his ability to pulse; when anyone is asked why a curer was chosen, the consistent answer is, "He knows how to pulse." The significance of the curer's ability to pulse is related to the fact that the first level of contrast establishing a taxonomy of diseases is that between "evil" and "good" determined by pulsing. The essence of the pulsing is a diagnosis of the patient's social relationships. It is a kind of exploratory "sociopsy" comparable to the stage of biopsy in modern medicine, resting on a notion that the witch "leaves his signature in the blood." and the curer "hears/feels" it. He does this by placing his thumb over the pulse at the wrist, inner elbow, and sometimes the inner knee joint and temples. The logic is that the blood passes from the heart and "talks" at the pulse points, revealing the condition and needs of the heart. The blood of the curer enters into communication with that of the patient when he holds his own thumb pulse against the patient's pulse. He does not look for the physiological symptoms on which modern medicine bases diagnosis, but for what the blood tells about the patient's relations with people in his social environment and for what the heart needs. Disease symptomology, such as fever and locus of pain, provides the basis for assigning medicines at a later stage in the cure.

Some curers use thirteen candles set before the curing arch to corroborate diagnoses made in the pulsing: if, for example, the candles bend inward, the illness is interpreted as a result of trouble within the family. But the use of candles is often interpreted as showing the curer's lack of ability to pulse properly.

Taking out the evil. The evil is drawn out by bleeding or by sucking. Bleeding is diagnostic, curative, and preventative in function. Confirmation of the preliminary diagnosis made in pulsing comes in the bleeding: "clinical" examination by pulsing is reviewed by the "laboratory" findings of the blood analysis. Bleeding is used in cases of surface pains to draw out the evil which is causing the pain. The patient enters the sweatbath so that the heat will stimulate the flow of blood and lessen the pain. The curer makes scratches with broken glass near the source of the pain. Cupping, called *la ventosa,* is done by placing hot water, a piece of pitch pine, and thirteen handmade cigarettes in the gourd. These are very "hot" items, not in the sense of caloric content but of soul power. When these hot items have heated the gourd, they are thrown out and liquor is poured in and burned. When all the liquor is burned, the gourd is slapped onto the cut, so that it "grabs" the flesh, and the blood flows into the vacuum. The diagnosis comes in burning the blood. The curer takes the gourd into the yard so that the odors containing the evil will not linger in the house when the blood is burned. He is accompanied by the guests while the patient remains in the house with an attendant. He gives an account of what the witch has put in the blood. Some of the items I have seen discovered were a wood splinter, explained as evidence of the envy the witch felt because the patient's husband was making a fence; lard, evidence that the witch coveted a pig of the patient; grain of corn or bean, evidence that the witch envied them their harvest. These items are probably inserted by the curer in some slight of hand trick.

The curer prevents the recurrence of the disease by sealing the cuts with garlic and liquor, elements which the devil does not like. The power of the curer is exhibited when he draws out the evil. At this moment he is confronting the enemy directly, fighting the animal spirit of whoever is causing the witchcraft.

The items found in the blood are always attributed to the envy of the witch who is causing the illness. Envy can be countered by the curing rituals. The resources expended in the process of curing counterbalance the patient's greater wealth which provoked the envy initially. The witch starts the sickness by going to one of the caves in the hills where he burns a candle, drinks a liter of liquor, and prays that the object of his envy fall ill. The essential element in the fight against the witch is the act of drinking by all those present at the curing. In consuming their own liquor, often paid for by the sale of cattle or crops, they mitigate the envy of the witch. If the witch persists, he must continue to spend money on the liquor necessary to initiate the witchcraft after each ceremonial cure. Part of the tactic of a rapid series of cures is to demonstrate willingness to use all of the family's resources if necessary to counteract the rituals of the witch. The statement that they drink "in order to finish with the money" takes on significance in this strategy of limiting envy by expending resources.

Medicating the illness. The cure of the disease comes in the bathing or heating of the patient and the application or ingestion of medicines, usually a combination of patent medicines purchased in the nearby Ladino town. The specific cures called for depend on the secondary classification of the disease: if it is a "cold disease," hot medicines are applied; if it is a "hot disease," cold medicines are used.

Two kinds of bathing are performed, one a kind of steam bath, called "rise over the fire," for cold illnesses, and another a cold bath for hot illnesses. Chills and fever require both treatments. In the first case, a large charcoal fire is made inside the main room of the patient's house. When the fire is strong, two thick green logs are placed on it to create smoke. The patient mounts on a stool over the fire, and a straw mat is held over him to capture the steam. When he is sweating a great deal, the curer gives him a drink of cold medicines.

The cold bath is given with thirteen branches from bushes which grown near the spring.[4] Patent medicines dissolved in Spring water include syrup of *isidro,* cloves, vapor rub, epsom salts, aspirin, and other cold herbs or juices such as lemon, grapefruit, *cintula,* and *tok'o.* If the trouble is chills and fever, hot herbs such as *inajo, lumahiya,* and apple may be added to restore the body's hot-cold balance. A bad curer may reverse the medicines,

4. These include plants called *tihiliha?, yokmut, tzitzil hič, čelwamal* and *yetalbulha?.*

giving hot medicines for hot diseases. If this is discovered, he will be subject to accusations of witchcraft. The relatives of the patient are present as witnesses "to see what medicines are given."

In the case of infections, the curer cauterizes the wound, a process called "take out the odor." First he smells the wound, checking on the severity of the infection. He mixes chile and hot charcoal and puts them on the wound to "cause the evil to rise to the surface." He then sucks on the wound, and spits out a "worm" which indicates the kind of evil caused by witchcraft. He covers the wound with mentholated cream and binds it. The patient is kept covered.

Calling the soul. The major effort in soul-calling (tamohel) is concentrated on preparing the patient and the house for the return of his soul. This is done for illnesses caused by fear and resulting in soul-loss. Here a knowledge of the setting is crucial to understand each act. An arch of pine boughs is set at the center post because it is here that the souls of the inmates of the house cluster (over the square hole at the foot of the post where the sheep's head is buried during the inauguration of the house). Thirteen candles, including a large, 50-cent one in the center and twelve 20-cent ones, are set before the arch. If the patient is being cured in the house of the curer, which happens when he goes to another town for a cure, the arch is put near the door in order that his soul not mingle with the souls of the curer's household. The patient is laid out on a mat in front of the curing arch, or if he is a small child, he is held in the arms of his mother. The curing is scheduled so that the arrival of the soul occurs when it will not be seen by people passing in the street. This would cause it embarrassment, and it would not enter the house. The patient continues to sleep under the arch each night until it is removed nine days later. As he sleeps, his soul enters in a dream and is reunited with the body. A guitar and seed rattle are played continuously during the ceremony to make the spirits of guests, patient, and house "of one heart." Many rounds of liquor are served in order to "finish with our money" and thus reduce the envy of the one who caused the witchcraft.

The soul-calling is combined with a cold bath to cure the illness. The patient is disrobed, and the curer brushes him with branches of plants from the spring and a live black chicken which draws the heat from the patient, taking it into its own body. The branches are dipped in a mixture of raw cocoa, pieces of melon mixed in water, and other "cold" items. A new set of clothing, smoked over an incense burner in which pitch pine is burned, is put on the patient. A common meal of chicken or beef stew is served with tortillas to all the guests.

In the case of more persistent illnesses, the bathing may take place at the springs. Male patient go to the large spring of San Nicolás and female patients to Pahaltón. A curing arch is erected near the spring. The curer calls upon the spirit of the spring to perform a miracle. Some members of the family stay behind at the house so that if the spirit of the patient should return before he does, it will be welcomed. The people waiting in the house, called maliwanehetik, must drink as much liquor as do those at the spring.

Sometimes the soul of a child is called at the place where fear caused it to be lost. The cure is started at the house, and then part of the group goes to the place which the curer has designated as the location of the fright. Soil is gathered in a kerchief or item of the patient's clothing and is placed at the head of his bed. As the group returns to the house, one of the child's relatives plays the guitar at the gate, and the curer sweeps a path for the soul with branches he has taken from the spring. Inside the house, the soul is again called while the curer brushes the child with spring branches. The mother embraces the child as incense is smoked over him and all his clothing. The child is then pulsed to determine whether the soul has returned.

Medicating the house. The strategy of medicating the house is tied to an understanding of the interaction of the spirit of the house and those of the inmates. When the evil sent out by the witch enters the house, it first asks permission of the house posts to enter the soil of the house. The house is adorned with pine branches and flowers to make the house-soul happy. Old men make palm crosses for the center post and corner posts of the yard. One large 50-cent candle is lit at the center post with small 20-cent candles on each side. When these candles are lighted they "blind the eye of evil spirits who can see only in the dark." A black chicken is buried alive in the square hole where the offering of the sheep has been made at the time of the house inauguration. Food for the chicken—bread, chocolate, tortilla, and liquor—is put in the hole so it will stay alive for eight days.

The logic of the meal is that the house needs nourishment and for this reason has been fighting with the inmates and causing their illness. After the guests have been fed, the curer marks a cross with a mixture of garlic, creosote, seeds of mustard, and a "hot" herb called poščan, on the center post inside the house and on the corner posts. Like the candles, the cross serves to "blind the eye" of the evil spirits so that they will not reenter the house and talk the spirit of the house into causing harm.

This ceremony replicates that of the house meal at the time of the inauguration (Chapter 1). The music of the guitar and gourd rattle is intended to make both the soul of the house and the souls of the inmates content. Why the curing of the house is always done on Thursday, when "the holy earth is open," is not fully understood by the curers I have questioned; they say, "We have forgotten how to talk to the earth." Chamula curers are reputed to be able to talk to the earth, and consultations may be sought with them if the illness continues.

Prayer. The curers talk with the soul of the thirteen ancestors of the world,[5] to the "spirits of the heaven and of the church," and to saints of neighboring towns, asking for a good cure. The following prayer is one given by the oldest and most honored of the curers:

Sacred earth, sacred world
Thirteen holy world, holy flowers
In the center of another holy world

Look mother, its clay
I am a child, its clay.
Holy heaven, Jesus Christ
Holy herbs give the spirit

5. The number 13 has significance in the Maya cosmology in the 13 levels of heaven (Thompson 1964:125). The 13 candles set before the curing arch symbolize the 13 holy worlds. The meal for the house spirit includes 13 cigarettes.

The companions of the patient
  are gathered here with his father
In the center of this other holy
  earth
Holy earth, take out the fever.

The curer then calls upon each of the saints of the surrounding towns, asking for help in bringing about a miracle. First he calls upon the major saints of the pueblo (Santa Lucía, San Francisco, Santiago, San Pedro the Martyr, and the Virgen de Rosario), then those of Teopisca (San Augustín and the Virgen de Mercedes), of San Cristóbal (San Cristóbal and Justo Juez), of Villa Carranza (Señor del Pozo and San Bartolo), of Socoltenango (the Virgen de Candelaria), of Villa las Rosas (San Miguel and San José), of Comitán (Santo Domingo, San Caralampio, and the Virgen de Santa Teresa), and finally Señor Esquipulas of Tulanca. Thus he defines the meaningful spiritual universe of the village, building a kind of hegemony of defense and protection.

At any point throughout the cure the patient may consult the doctor sent by the I.N.I., the priest, or the schoolteacher, all of whom compete with each other in gaining clients by dispensing medicines. This does not undermine the role of the curer since curing the disease is considered a separate issue from stopping the witchcraft which is causing it. The disease may be cured, but the persistence of the witchcraft will eventually cause death through spiritual malaise unless treated by the curer.

All the people of the village know the common herbs and the sicknesses for which they should be used. The basis for the curer's power thus is not specialized knowledge of medicines, but the strength of his swayohel in fighting that of the enemy, and his esoteric knowledge of pulsing.

Formerly curers received minimal pay for practicing. The family of the patient offered about 20 pesos or worked in the fields of the curer. Curers refused larger payments because they said their skill came from God, and it would be a sin to accept money for it. This practice is continued today by one old curer for patients within the community. However, he receives from 100 to 200 pesos from out-of-town patients. A Ladina from the neigh-

TABLE 22. Types of Diseases, Medication, and Curing Agents

Category of disease	Etiology	Cure	Medication	Curing
Bad illnesses				
Hot illnesses	Witchcraft	"Taking out the evil"	Cold medicines and bathing with cold herbs	Curer doctor, and/or druggist
madness	Caused from start by witchcraft	tamohel (soul calling)		
headache, dysentery diarrhea, yellow fever	May start as "good disease," and become entry for witchcraft			
Cold illnesses				
swelling	Caused from start by witchcraft	tamohel		
diarrhea, white rheumatism	May begin as "good disease" and become entry for witchcraft	tamohel and bleeding		
Hot and cold illnesses				
chills and fever	May start as "good disease" and become entry for witchcraft	tamohel	Alternating hot and cold liquids	
Good illnesses				
Hot illnesses				
toothache			Apply cold leaves, remove tooth	I.N.I. nurse

Illness	Belief / cause	Treatment	Patent medicines	Curer
"embarrassment"	Any embarrassing incident will later result in swelling of limbs or surface cuts	bathing in springwater		
Cold illnesses				
broken bones		pull, tie with splint		Bone-setter
"two hearts"	Spiritual depression and malaise resulting in illness	tamohel		Curer
"soul fear"	Fearful incident, fall, may result in fear of soul or loss of soul	tamohel		Curer
Illnesses of God				
Hot illnesses				
contagious diseases: measles, whooping cough, influenza	Given by God	Formerly required tamohel. Now only a few call in curer	Patent medicines: aspirin penicillin	I.N.I. doctor, and curer
epidemic illnesses	Given by God, but when many begin to die, suspect witchcraft	Gathering of curers to "take out evil"	Patent medicines: aspirin penicillin	Curer

boring community who is reputed to practice both witchcraft and curing receives fees of 200 to 300 pesos regularly. She has been accused of killing more than one patient in giving injections.

Since most diseases are not static conditions, a master classification must take into account physiological process. The only absolutely evil diseases are those which are found to be incurable. When diseases which start out as apparently "good," or not caused by evil intent, fail to respond to patent medicines, the patient or his family begin to suspect witchcraft. They then turn to the curer who will diagnose this. Category 1 of Table 22 includes those diseases which, depending on duration and intensity, indicate the presence of evil.

In the case of the illnesses of God, Category 3 of Table 22, an additional complication enters. As in the case of Category 1 diseases, they may begin as "good" diseases, but the introduction of evil by a witch means that the illness can cause death to many people. This category includes the contagious diseases, the most common ones being measles, whooping cough, and heat, which may refer to typhoid, grippe, or to an increase in the virulence of other contagious diseases.

The designation "sickness of God" is one inspired by the priest. He has been active in trying to discourage witch-killing and has insisted that the contagious diseases are sent by God. The villagers have accepted this as far as the origin of the disease is concerned, but as the deaths mount, people begin to suspect witchcraft.

Sudden attacks causing almost immediate death are classified as judgments of the ancestors rather than as illness. These include "seizure, because the very cold leg and arm of the ancestors touch the body [of the victim]" and "ancestors grab the soul." Asphyxiation and heart attack may be some of the modern classifications for such diseases. If a child should die suddenly, the logic applied in Tzo?ontahal is that the *me?iltatil kananatay lum,* the mother-father ancestors who care for earth, see a potential danger in the soul of the child and seize it so that he will not develop into a witch. These are the only deaths I know of which are not attributed to witchcraft.

THE LOGIC OF CURING

Diagnosis of illness in Tzoʔontahal is a kind of checklisting against a native taxonomic hierarchy of disease (Frake 1963). The curer is concerned primarily with establishing whether the illness is evil or good, secondarily whether cold or hot, and his prestige depends upon his ability to classify the disease at these highest levels of contrast.

In questioning the meaning of each act, I encountered no hesitation in giving answers, as I have in investigating other performances. Each act is understood in terms of the part its plays in the diagnosis and curing of the patient, and is in turn tied into a cognitive reference scheme which takes into account the patient's relations with kin and neighbors, environmental conditions, and the state of the patient's constitution. The notion of process underlying the classification of diseases explains some apparent contradictions in behavior. Good illness may so weaken the patient that he is vulnerable to the invasion of evil, and the tactic must shift to counter witchcraft. The alternation of chills and fever means that cold medicines must be administered followed by hot. The curer maintains communication with the blood in frequent pulsing to check whether he has overcome the evil and to ascertain what the blood wants.

The logical premises underlying diagnosis can be summarized as follows: Social relationships are primary causes of illness, while the conditions of the environment, such as cold wind or rain in which the patient gets drenched, provide conditions favorable to the entry of the disease. The effect of the evil projected depends upon the condition of the patient. Thus a mature adult may have the internal resistance to reject disease, while children, the aged, or women after childbirth are more vulnerable. Accidental wounds may render the victim more vulnerable to witchcraft as well as to "sickness of God." The malefactor achieves his goal if any member of the household or even a chicken or cow of the person against whom he has a grudge falls ill.

The emphasis on the origin of illness means that the study of symptoms is of little significance. People involved in some conflict may define themselves as patients or be defined as such by their intimate social group even without having any apparent physical illness. Sometimes a colicky baby may become the focus of a curing ceremony designed to "cure" the conflict between husband and wife. In one case, the parents of a healthy young wife separated from her husband staged a curing ceremony to dramatize her marital plight to the in-laws.

The breakdown of the curing hierarchy and the recruitment procedures which were maintained by the elder leaders (see Chapter 10) has led to a reevaluation of the role of the curers in the community. They have lost their position as meʔiltatil representing the ancestors who guard over the community. Curers are increasingly being accused of sorcery, and over ten of them have been killed in the past decade as witches (Nash, J. 1967). Paradoxically, it is the belief in their evil power which leads to their persisting role in the society. Clients feel that the more evil the curer is, the more able he is to combat evil. In a community dominated by belief in witchcraft, they are both feared and valued for their ability to control it. From a position as arbiters of morality, they have become the chief targets as deviants from the moral code. Despite the loss of confidence in curers as guardians, they are still called upon to fight the evil of witchcraft, and nearly every day a ritual is performed. The regimen of the curing ritual has not been upset by the undermining of the curers' position. Tied to a diagnostic system emphasizing the state of the patient's social relations, the same procedures are carried out even when modern medicines are used.

In curing practices, the Indian sees himself as the key figure in the drama of his own self-victimization. His illnesses come from within his own world, usually from within his family or close neighborhood. They are a mark of guilt for having excited the envy or hatred of associates. While the Indian is often portrayed in the role of passive victim to outside domination, in his own self-projection he sees himself dominated by powers within the community. Greater participation and equality in the wider society may in the future release him from these fear-provoking figures in his own environment.

Chapter 7

The Formal Organization
of Local Government

The formal organization of civil and religious offices in Tzoʔontahal is based on the pattern of a locally independent, democratically elected officialdom introduced by the Spaniards. Variations in the pattern from that of other towns of the highlands have resulted from differences of interpretation of the functions, the range of power, and the course of succession of offices. This flexibility has preserved structural continuity as organizational adjustments are made. The Indians have transformed an alien governing mechanism into one that meets their changing needs and contributes to their independence in the modern world.

The independence of the local township has a base in the pre-Conquest social organization of Chiapas. Robert Adams (1961:347) has noted the absence of architectural or other features indicative of functional specialization that would arise in a politically integrated region. At the time of the Conquest, Chiapas was divided into warring principalities, revealing the extreme political fragmentation of the area (Calnek 1962:8). Each town was divided from the neighboring town by *mojones,* hilled-up boundaries (ibid:36). A minimum of political unity was achieved by holding certain towns subject to the dominance of others (ibid:27); local autonomy persisted, however, in the administration of landholding as a community enterprise.

During the colonial period the Spanish Crown established the independence of towns directly under their control and provided them with a civil-religious hierarchy which has persisted as the form of government to the present (Carrasco 1961: Wolf 1957b).

Comparative studies of the civil-religious hierarchy indicate the range of variation on the Spanish colonial model (Camara 1952; Cancian 1963, 1965; Carrasco 1961; Siverts 1964; Tax 1964). In the many community studies of the highland Maya, we have reports of the roles and functions of the hierarchy as they are played out in a specific context (Adams 1957; Bunzel 1952; Guiteras Holmes 1961; La Farge 1947; La Farge and Byers 1931; MacArthur 1961; M. Nash 1955; Siverts 1960, 1964; Valladares 1957;

Fig. 6. Civil and Religious Officials *

Officials in the town hall	Officials in the church
President	Fiscal
Secretary	Women Prayer-reciters
Síndico	

Principales (Krinsipaletik)
Second Principal
First Principal

Judges (Alkaletik)	Cofrades (Kobrarietik)
First Judge, Alannantik	Cofrade of Sacramento
Second Judge, Ahk'olnantik	Cofrade of Santa Lucía
Assistant Judge, La Grandeza	Cofrade of San Pedro the Martyr
Assistant Judge, Madronal	Cofrade of San Francisco
Regidores (Rehiroletik)	Mayordomos (Martomaetik)
First Regidor	Mayordomo of Christ of Ascension
Second Regidor	Mayordomo of San Antonio
Third Regidor	Mayordomo of Virgin Rosario
Fourth Regidor	Mayordomo of San José
Policemen (Mayoletik)	Mayordomo of Santiago
2 First Police	Alfereces † (Alperesetik)
2 Second Police	First Past Alférez
2 Third Police	Remains Past Alférez
2 Fourth Police	Second Past Alférez
2 Last Police	New Alférez
	Assistants to cofrades (alib'aletik)
	Assistant to Sacramento
	Assistant to Virgin Santa Lucía
	Assistants to elders for lesser saints
	(Nič'aniletik)

* Boxed-in terms refer to age-graded hierarchies. Other posts are outside of this "ladder" as explained in text.
† Alfereces may be chosen after taking higher posts in the religious hierarchy, but cannot become first or second regidor before serving in this post.

Vogt 1965; Wagley 1949; Wisdom 1940; Zabala 1961). Comparison of the structure and functioning of the hierarchy reveals differing applications of the same principles of allocating roles (age, sex, territorial identification, and previous service) and differing assignments of the same tasks (administrative, judgment, and maintenance).

In this chapter, I shall analyze the civil-religious hierarchy in Tzoʔontahal as a formally prescribed system of roles and behavior. The data on which the analysis is based are: (1) the system of roles and the principles of allocation, (2) careers in office of household heads, (3) instrumental behavior prescribed for officials, and (4) ritual behavior. The following chapter will be concerned with the exercise of power within the limits set by the formal organization of offices.

THE MATRIX OF ROLES

Civil officials. Civil offices in Tzoʔontahal are a segmented, ranked set of posts, each of which has an internally age-graded ranking. Outside of these segments are two leadership positions, those of president and his assistant, *síndico,* which are not controlled by the same criteria of entry—service in lower posts of the civil and religious hierarchies and age. Multiple posts at the same level have equal representation of officials from the upper and lower divisions of the center, Ahk'olnantik and Alannantik, and single posts are held alternately by residents of each side. Theoretically, the post of president should alternate as well, but in fact the scarcity of qualified candidates limits consideration of this condition. Since 1948, of the twelve presidents, only four were from Ahk'olnantik.

The four ranked segments (Fig. 6) from higher to lower are *krinsipaletik,* or principales, *alkaletik,* or judges, *rehiroletik,* or regidores, and *mayoletik,* or policemen. The relative rank of the post is expressed in terms of its power, and the relative rank of the post-holder in terms of age (the term used to describe an older office holder, *mas mamališ,* has the extended meaning of greater power[1]). Age-ranking of officials complements

---

1. Siverts (1965) points out that in Cancuk the term *mamal,* or elder, was applied to a young man who held a post of high authority because of his skills in literacy and language. By terminological reference, he was graduated into the senior age group.

the household principles of authority in which seniority gives one the right to command. This principle is violated in the case of an older man who has served as regidor and sometimes even judge and returns to the lawer post of ceremonial leader of the policemen. Some of the officials say that this is an "ugly" custom because it means that the hierarchy "is not a straight road." Due to obstacles in the individual's career in the hierarchy, within any segment there may be older men in the lower posts than in the higher. However, except for the barrio judges, posts within each segment are occupied by men of roughly the same decade in age (Table 23).

A complement of age-grading in the designation of officials is the principle of residence. In the upper two ranks of judges, one is chosen from the upper division, Ahk'olnantik, and one from the lower division, Alannantik. The remaining two judges are chosen from the outlying barrios of Madronal and Bočib'al. Judges representing the colonias of San Vicente, San Caralampio, and Cruz Quemada do not regularly attend the town

TABLE 23. Rank and Age of Civil Officials

Post	Division	Age
Judges (Alkaletik)		
First Judge	Alannantik	75
Second Judge	Ahk'olnantik	52
Barrio Judge	Madronal	42
Barrio Judge	Bočibal	50
Regidores (Rehiroletik)		
First Regidor	Ahk'olnantik	43
Second Regidor	Alannantik	44
Third Regidor	Alannantik	43
Fourth Regidor	Ahk'olnantik	48
Police (Mayoletik)		
First Police	Ahk'olnantik	27
First Police	Alannantik	28
Second Police	Ahk'olnantik	25
Second Police	Alannantik	30
Third Police	Ahk'olnantik	32
Third Police	Alannantik	30
Fourth Police	Madronal	25
Fourth Police	Bočibal	35
Martomorey	Ahk'olnantik	48
Martomorey	Alannantik	48

hall, but always appear at major ceremonies and at the inauguration of the
new officials. Residents of the barrios and colonias can never rise to any
position above that of assistant judge, but once they have served in this
post they may become principales in their own localities. One week the
first regidor from Ahk'olnantik serves with the third regidor from Alannantik, and the next week the second regidor from Ahk'olnantik serves
with the fourth regidor from Alannantik. The ten police are ranked in
five levels with representatives from each side at every level in the series
except for the fourth level, which is occupied by police from the barrios.

These civil officials, called as a group the *hu?eletik,* those who are "able"
(in control), constitute the traditional ladder of the hierarchy. To reach a
high post, an official must first pass through each of the lower positions in
the hierarchy. Outside of this ranked hierarchy, the posts of president and
síndico are occupied by young men who are able to read, write, and speak
fluently in Spanish. Literacy was, until the present generation, limited to a
few men in their thirties. With increasing literacy, the competition for
these posts is growing.[2] Men who have such skills are called upon as signers of official documents and are called *firmanetik.*

Also existing outside of the traditional hierarchy is the post of secretary
which had, until 1965, been occupied by a Ladino. This was the only post
which was paid; it also provided opportunity for earning extra income by
preparing "acts," or official documents, and fines from court cases. The
present incumbent is an Indian of Alannantik.

Because Tzo?ontahal's hierarchy is still a linked series of civil and religious posts, the structure of the civil hierarchy cannot be considered independently from that of the religious hierarchy. The major segments of the
religious hierarchy are the *martomaetik,* mayordomos or caretakers, and
alperesetik, alfereces or captains of the fiestas. The internal ranking of the
sixteen mayordomos depends on the number of religious posts the incumbent has filled and on the rank order of the saints he serves.

The alfereces, or captains of the fiestas, provide a ceremonial link be-

2. Julio de la Fuente (1964:30) has summarized the effect of literacy in breaking the
homogeneity of the community since the literate Indians have received greater privileges and
release from communal work. When the entire community is educated, the monopoly of
literacy is broken.

tween civil and religious authorities. They are in charge of the fiestas for the saints whom they represent: San Francisco, San Pedro the Martyr, Santa Lucía, and Sacramento. The internal ranking of this set of officials is based on time of entry. This varies in the annual cycle since the new alférez enters just before the fiesta for which he will be responsible. He will be expected to give deference to the three who have preceded him during the year. The terms applied to this fluctuating ranking system in order of highest to lowest are *hilon ta pasaro* (remains as past), *pasaro* (past official), *sčebal ʔač' ʔalperes* (second new alférez), and *ʔač' ʔalperes* (new alférez).

Outside of the traditional religious hierarchy are roles performed by functionaries on the basis of specific skills. These include the fiscal, assistant to the priest, and the *meʔeletik,* women who serve as prayer-reciters. The fiscal takes orders from the priest when the latter is in town, and in the absence of the priest he directs the activities of the mayordomos within the church. He is chosen on the basis of his knowledge of Spanish and willingness to perform the priests' bidding. He remains in office as long as he wishes, or until he is forcibly retired by the priest or by the mayordomos. When retired, he has an ex officio role saying prayers at funerals, and is often called upon for house ceremonies and as godfather in baptisms. The retired fiscales attend mass more often than the rest of the townspeople and sit in the front near the altar. The prayer-reciters are usually widowed or single women of the town whom the lay sisters have organized as support in responding to the catechism.

The officials who have served in five posts in the civil hierarchy and six posts in the religious hierarchy become *pasaroetik,* the Tzeltal rendering of *pasados* or former officials. Any one of these men may be eligible to serve as one of two principales, one chosen from Alannantik and one from Ahk'olnantik. They remain in office until they are too old to serve or until death. Each of the outlying barrios has two principales chosen from among men who have served in office.

Entry Into and Exit from Office

The constitution assures local autonomy in the election of civil officials. The officials of Tzoʔontahal, including the two principales, president, síndico, four regidores, ten policemen, four judges, and the "signers" meet in the town hall on the twentieth of November. Except for the post of president, which is now a contested position, each incumbent names his own successor. The president opens the meeting with an address to the principales, saying, "Now, *Mamal* Principales, whom will we name to leave in power in the town hall to pass the year?" The principales reply with the question to each officer: "Whom have you thought of naming?"

Each officer gives a name, which is written down by the secretary. When the officials have heard who will be the new officials, the first judge speaks with the principales and the "signers" using the formal speech of the patʔoʔtan to ask permission to serve the "gift" of trago. Eight days later an assembly of all the male household heads takes place. The president announces the names of the nominated officials in Tzeltal and the secretary announces them in Spanish. The president asks for a show of hands of all those who support the nominations. If the man who is named does not want to take the office, he may request withdrawal of his name. The president accepts refusal by all nominees for civil posts if there is adequate excuse.

The great majority of men begin their careers between the ages of twenty-two and thirty. Only seventeen men, or 5 percent of the 311 household heads censused (Table 24), had reached the age of thirty without serving in any office. Among men fifty and over, only two men had not filled any religious post (Table 25), and all had served in some civil post.

There are two major channels of mobility in the civil hierarchy. The more common course is for a young married man to enter as a policeman, either at the third or fourth level. Next, he will again be named as policeman, or possibly third or fourth regidor, if he is a poor man and has little hope of rising to the higher posts. If the man or his father is well off, he will be asked to serve as alférez. The appointment may be made with or without prior service in the civil or religious hierarchy, and the main prerequisite is having sufficient money to pay for the expenses. Once he fills this post, he will be eligible for first or second regidor since he will have learned the major speeches required in ritual gatherings. Formerly he took on at this point the post of assistant judge. These positions are now assigned to incumbents from the outlying barrios, and the number of posts a man in the center must fill in order to become a pasado has been reduced

TABLE 24. Civil and Religious Careers of Household Heads

(Civil)

Age of house-hold head	No office	Police (1 term)	Police (2 terms)	Síndico	Síndico, police	Police, regidor	Police, regidor, judge	Police, regidor, judge (2 terms)	Police, síndico, president	Síndico, president	President	Un-known
19	2											
20	20	3										
21	6											
22	11	1										
23	1	2										
24	7											
25	19	2										
26	6	1										
27	1	2										
28	11	5										
29	1	2										
30	6	6		2								
31	2											
32	5	1		2								
33		2		1								
34		2										
35	6	9	2		1	1						
36	1	5			1	3						

37 38 39 40 41 42 43 44 45 46 48 50 52 54 55 56 58 60 62 65 70 75 78 79 80 85 88

TABLE 24. Civil and Religious Careers of Household Heads

(Religious)

Age of household head	No office	Nič'nal (1 term)	Nič'nal (2 terms)	Ali?bal, nič'nal	Nič'nal, tatil	Nič'nal, ali?bal, tatil	Nič'nal, ali?bal, tatil (2 terms)	Nič'nal, ali?bal, tatil (2 terms), kobraria	Nič'nal, ali?bal, tatil (2 terms), kobraria (2 terms)	Fiscal	Unknown
19	2										
20	18	5									
21	6										
22	11	1									
23	1	11	1								
24	5	2									
25	11	10									
26	3	3		1							
27	1	2									
28	16	9	1								
29	2	1									
30	2	9	1	1	1						
31	2										
32	2	5		1							
33				1	1						
34		3									
35	3	11	2	1	1	1					
36	1	4		3	1	1					

37 38 39 40 41 42 43 44 45 46 48 50 52 54 55 56 58 60 62 65 70 75 78 79 80 85 88

TABLE 25. Number of Civil and Religious Offices of Household Heads over 50 Years of Age as Related to Wealth

Age of household head	Wealth		No. of civil offices	No. of religious offices
	Land in hectares	Head of cattle		
54	3	4	5	3
55	3	8	2	3
65	3	11	6	2
50	2½	2	4	4
75	2½	4	6	6
55	2	8	2	4
55	2		4	3
60	2	2	2	4
65	2		6	6
75	2	7	4	3
78	2	6	2	1
50	2½	2	3	4
50	1½	2	6	5
55	1½	6	2	6
58	1½		1	2
60	1½		6	6
60	1½	4	4	4
60	1½	8	4	5
80	1½		4	5
88	1½	7	6	6
50	1	10	2	3
50	1	1	3	3
54	1	4	6	6
54	1	4	6	6
55	1	6	2	3
56	1	4	3	3
58	1		5	4
60	1	1	5	6
60	1	2	5	6
60	1	2	4	6
65	1	2	3	
65	1		6	6
65	1		3	3
70	1		1	1
75	1		5	5
79	1		5	5
80	1	2	3	
80	1	22	3	1
85	1	6	6	6

Age of household head	Wealth Land in hectares	Head of cattle	No. of civil offices	No. of religious offices
55	½		2	2
55	½		2	2
55	½	2	2	3
60	½		2	3
60	½		1	3
60	½		4	3
62	½	1	2	3
65	½		2	3
65	½	4	4	6
65	½		6	5
75	½		5	6
87	½		4	4

from six to five. The reason given for this is that there are more people now than formerly.

The second course of civil careers is to serve as síndico and go on to president, bypassing the intermediate and lower posts of the hierarchy and never filling the higher traditional posts. Of seven who have served as president, two served as síndico, two had no previous office, and three had been both policeman and síndico (Table 25). None of the former presidents served in any civil post after being president. Two served as fiscal in their religious careers and had had no other religious service. This is the course pursued by literate men who speak Spanish well. An alternative course is to enter the ejido commission as secretary, treasurer, or president and then serve as síndico, or even directly as president. The president elected in 1964 had served only on the ejido commission. This caused some discontent, but not enough to prevent his election.

The household head enters religious office first as *nič'nal* or junior mayordomo, then serves as *ʔaliʔbal,* or assistant, next as *tatil,* or elder mayordomo of a lesser saint. The fourth position is tatil of San Pedro, after which comes *ḵobraria,* or cofrade, first of San Francisco, then of Santa Lucía or Sacramento. Following his appointment as tatil of San Pedro, the incumbent holds the first gathering of mayordomos in his house. When he completes his term in this office, he may be called upon by neighbors, relatives, and compadres to serve as nakawane in household ceremonials. He may at any time in his career be called upon as alférez. This may occur even before he has served as a junior mayordomo or policeman since the post depends on his own or his father's wealth.

The normal career of an official in the traditional hierarchy involves a balance of civil and religious posts. A man enters these posts according to convenience, not in a rigid alternation between civil and religious wings. The rough balancing of posts can be seen in the careers of men over fifty in Table 25. According to informants, a man should start and end his career in the religious wing. By the age of thirty, forty-three men had filled at least one post in the religious hierarchy, and only twenty-four men had served in the civil hierarchy (Table 24). The religious posts are considered less onerous than the civil posts since the incumbents are in attendance only one day a week instead of every day, and their terms in office last only six months.

Wealth level, except in cases of extreme poverty, does not limit a man's participation in the traditional hierarchy. Of fourteen men over seventy, eight had completed their civil posts and seven their religious posts. Three who had not followed the traditional career lines had served as president. The town is small enough so that career lines have not followed any polarization of the upper levels of the hierarchy as occurs in towns of larger size (Bunzel 1952, Camara 1952, Cancian 1965). Discrimination is based on residence rather than wealth—those Indians who reside in barrios and colonias cannot reach any post higher than that of assistant judge. Wealth level is a factor, however, in the time span of the individual's career, since at some time before becoming second or first regidor he must have filled the expensive post of alférez. Table 25 lists the careers of men fifty years of age and over in order of wealth. It is possible to finish a career in office by the age of fifty, but if a man has less than one hectare of land, it is unlikely that he will finish before he is sixty-five. The Indians of Tzoʔontahal do not however maximize the importance of passing through the hierarchy. It is a duty not a goal, and the reward in prestige is minimal.

The only post in which wealth has been crucial was that of alférez. The incumbent and the household of which he was a member spent 3,000 pesos to carry out the fiestas with which he was charged in his year in office. The president, the four judges, and the four regidores chose the alférez shortly before the fiesta of the saint's day with which he was charged. When the nomination was made, the president sent out the first policeman with the chief policeman to bring the man chosen to the town hall. They expected, and were always confronted with, resistance to the nomination. In order to gain acceptance they got the nominee drunk in a drinking session at the town hall. Liquor was measured out, and all the officials drank only a half cup at each round, but the new alférez was required to drink a full cup. The rounds continued until the new alférez was drunk. If he did not accept at this session, he was put in jail to think it over. Another drinking session took place the following day.

Nomination to the post of alférez was the only situation in which the jail penalty has been brought into effect, since refusal by nominees to other posts simply means that the officials "look for someone else." The reason given for invoking the punishment was "we know he has the wealth and therefore he should serve." Until 1965 the town had always succeeded in recruiting two of the alfereces from Ahk'olnantik and two from Alannantik. Since the upper division of Ahk'olnantik has grown at a more rapid rate than the lower division, candidates were found only in Ahk'olnantik. This unbalancing of the population ratios undermined the institution of alférez, which had always been the most unpopular position. When I returned to the field in 1967, it had been eliminated.

THE FUNCTIONS OF CIVIL OFFICIALS

An analysis of the formally prescribed functions of the civil officials must take into account three sources of data: the functions as prescribed by state legislation, the functions as understood by local officials, and the observed activities of the officials. Table 26 compares the functions of officials as stated in the constitution of the state of Chiapas (Secretaría del Gobierno Departmental de Chiapas, 1828: Decreto 52, Nov. 30, 1825) [3] to statements of informants and to my observations of the carrying out of their official obligations.

3. I have chosen this constitution as the first post-independence statement of the status of local civil administrators.

TABLE 26. The Functions of Civil Officials

Constitution of Chiapas, 1825 *	*Interpretation of functions by villagers*	*Actual functions, as observed*
President: To open and close the sessions at the hour designated in the ruling. To raise the order of the discussion, yielding the floor for or against individuals who solicit it. To designate the affairs which ought to be discussed, giving preference to those of greater importance and interest. To decree to the appropriate commissions the means or projects which are initiated by the members of the corporation or by individuals, in the cases that the law determines. To maintain decorum in the discussions, calling those who disrupt or use harsh expressions in which they lack respect and consideration owed, without loosing the moderate liberty which they ought to have in discussions. To call extraordinary sessions when he judges it convenient or when some circumstances make it necessary. To care for the present ruling; to impose fines of 4 reales up to 2 pesos to those individuals who without permission or motive do not attend sessions or do not arrive at the fixed hour, to those who commit some faults in them, or are remiss or lacking in diligence in fulfilling their obligations. To handle official correspon-	To order the judges. To pass the banners in the town-hall. To go to the house of the alférez to pass the banners.	Sits in on court cases; assigns fines. Orders the police to bring in criminals, assigns tasks for them. Announces government edicts on loudspeaker of cantinas (formerly police played drum and announced these at street corners). In sale of land, goes with síndico and police to plots of land to measure them. Draws up official acts concerning cases of homicide, sale of communal land, etc. Receives government officials. Signs birth and death certificates; consults calendar to name child. Initiates communal projects such as building the kiosk. Signs acts of matrimony and, recently, divorce. Orders police to bring in debtors. Consults with department officials in matters pertaining to community resources such as forest and irrigation canal.

| | *Interpretation of* | |
| *Constitution of Chiapas, 1825* * | *functions by* *villagers* | *Actual functions,* *as observed* |

dence and to sign the commu-
nications that the corporation
makes.

To sign along with other members of the civil officials all the
acts of the sessions that are included in the book.

To read orders of payment
against the funds of the town,
previously agreed upon by the
civil authority in which they
will specify the quantity and the
object of its destination.

To watch that the police assigned to the civil authority care
for the papers of the archive
and keep them in the best order
possible, not allowing omissions
in the correspondence.

To demand fines of those who
break these orders, previously
agreed by the civil authority in
the cases that are necessary, and
to deposit receipts in the trea-
sury of the town.
Síndico:

The síndico will have a voice and vote in the civil authority. His duties are:	To sit at the table. To accompany the president when he calls upon him. To wait until there is a fight to arrange it.	Attends president in all above functions.
To raise his voice in the ses-sions.		Notes contributions made in communal fiestas by each household head.
To ask and promote before the civil authority what is agreeable to the rights of the people.		Helps fiscal and treasur-er count funds collected.
To intervene and censure what-ever touches on the good admin-istration and investment of mu-nicipal funds.		Succeeds president if lat-ter cannot fulfill term of office.
To examine the accounts which the treasurer ought to present an-nually, to the effect that they		

(*cont.*)

Constitution of Chiapas, 1825 *	Interpretation of functions by villagers	Actual functions, as observed

should fulfill all the specifications following the statement of the respective commission.

To promote the prompt dispatch of such duties which affect immediately the interest of the public.

To represent the civil authority in all those judgements which promote the welfare or in which there is some demand.

To watch over all the objects that are under the inspection of the civil authority, denouncing to them the omissions and faults of fulfillment which are noted.

The síndico should be heard in all the serious affairs and when there is a plea for permission to invest municipal funds which is greater than that covered in the plans. In the naming of the commissions he will have the consideration of the síndico, in attention to the importance and extension of the objects which are under his inspection and care.

Alcaldes:
Exercise the office of conciliators.

Handle civil cases which do not exceed 100 pesos, and criminal cases on injuries and light misdeeds which require only slight punishment and verbal judgement.

Bring culprits to justice. Advise judges.

Set fines up to 100 pesos and labor payment up to 15 days in public works.

Greet the principales with the pat?o?tan.

Hear trials.

Initiate proceedings in courtroom, delivers verdict.

Greet the principales with the pat?o?tan during ceremonies.

Sign official documents involving court cases.

Hear court cases.

	Interpretation of functions by villagers	*Actual functions, as observed*
Constitution of Chiapas, 1825 *		

Have the responsibility of publishing the laws and edicts of the government.

Announce to the townspeople the days for electoral meetings.

Regidores: †

	Sit on the benches inside the town hall.	Bring in officials nominated by the civil authority. Greet them in their houses with the pat?o?tan.
	If there is no judge, regidores order police.	Transmit orders of the president to the policemen.
	Arrange dispute cases with the president and judges.	Pour liquor in the town hall for the other civil officials.
		Sit in on court cases.

Police:

Care for the streets, markets, and public plazas, hospitals and other public places.

Inspect the quality of foods of all kinds in the interest of the public and the sellers.

Care for the drainage of swampy places and free standing and unhealthy waters.

Name a permanent commission charged with maintaining the health of the place.

Ensure that the public fountains are well kept up and have abundant water.

Ensure the punctual attendance of the children in school.

See that the equipment distributed by the army is done with equality.

Help the alcaldes tend to the execution of the laws, rulings, and agreements of the civil officials.

	Interpretation	*Actual*
	Sit on the benches, outside the town hall.	Maintain town hall, plaza, road from highway to town. Adorn town hall for fiestas.
	Summon children absent from school.	Cook common meal for civil officials following court cases when fines have been collected.
	Maintain public buildings and streets.	Collect money for fiestas from each household.
	Distribute portions of bull slaughtered for a fiesta to those who have paid 20 pesos.	Buy liquor for use in town hall.
		Round up truant school children.
		Bring in criminals.

(cont.)

Constitution of Chiapas, 1825 *	Interpretation of functions by villagers	Actual functions, as observed
Secretary: In each civil administration they should have a secretary who will earn an annual salary of 144 pesos. To attend the office on non-holidays. To be present all the time that the sessions last. To take notes in order to draw up acts and minutes. To set in a book the acts after approved and signed by all the individuals of the civil administration that are persent at each session. To pass on to the respective commissions the affairs with which the civil authority gives accounts, setting down the understanding in the corresponding book, and taking care to note in the margin when it is undertaken. To give account of all the negotiations that occur in the following order: (1) the acts of the former meeting, (2) the official communications that they receive, (3) the proposals that the members of the civil authority make, (4) the representatives that say the particulars, (5) the dictations of the commission. To sign in union with the president all the official communications, arranging them in order to form them in the points agreed to by the civil authority. To put in the best possible	If there is a major task for the pueblo, the secretary does it. Call the secretary to write the act. Arrange things if there is a homicide. Take a culprit to San Cristóbal if there is no settlement in court.	Writes all official documents. Attends president and síndico in most official trips out of town. Writes official documents such as birth and marriage certificates.

	Interpretation of functions by villagers	*Actual functions, as observed*
Constitution of Chiapas, 1825 *		

arrangement and with an exact inventory all the books, acts, and papers of the archive, not permitting that anyone take them without express permission of the municipality and leaving the corresponding understanding in order to know where it was stopped and to take it up in the appropriate time.

To present each month a list of the affairs that have passed in the commissions, of those that have been dispatched and those that are hanging.

To pass each month to the municipal president a list of the individuals who had failed to meet in the sessions without legitimate cause in order that they can exact the fine corresponding, arranging for that in the acts.

To meet in the extraordinary sessions when called by the president.

When the secretaries fail in some of their obligations, mentioned in the former articles, they can be fined by the civil authority 2 to 10 pesos without prejudice from the remaining punishments to which they make credits.

As to the election and replacement of the secretaries they will be covered in article 162 of the law of the 20th of March, 1837.

* Translation and paraphrasing of Constitution of Chiapas, 1825.
† Not given in this constitution, perhaps because of the ceremonial nature of the post.

The statement of functions of the civil officials as codified in the state constitution contrasts with that of local informants first of all in the brevity of the latter. This indicates the lack of functional specificity in the role as conceived by Indians in contrast to its Spanish-derived model. The latitude of acceptable performance in the role is best indicated by the statements concerning why a man is relieved of office. A man might be dismissed because he "fights a lot," because he "gets drunk and fights," or because he "steals a lot." The qualification "a lot" suggests the difficulty of actually ridding the town of an incumbent who has caused difficulties while in office. There are only two posts in which deposition actually has occurred: those of president and fiscal. Both these posts represent mediating roles between local and national interest groups. The deposition of the president Augustín recounted in Chapter 9 indicates the kind of community action which can be mobilized. Significantly, failure to perform prescribed duties is not mentioned.

Second, it is the presence of the officials, not their specific obligations, which is of significance in the local context. "Sitting" therefore is a central and active duty. Each morning at about seven o'clock the officials gather to sit on the benches on the porch of the town hall. The president and síndico sit inside at the table. They return at six in the evening to sit again. The line-up of the civil authorities at their appointed places each morning and evening is a statement of social control. Their presence gives evidence of an authority ready to act against offenders.

A third feature of contrast is that the local statement of functions includes many of the ceremonial activities of the civil officials. Thus the president has the significant duties of seeing that the banners pass into the town hall at the time of a fiesta, and of going to the house of the alférez when the banners are moved in procession. The holiness of office is associated with the holy symbol of the banners. For the police, collecting the 20-peso portions of meat when a bull is butchered for ceremonial meals is as significant as apprehending criminals.

RITUAL BEHAVIOR

In ritual behavior, the status of officials is projected in role performance. Relative position in each ceremonial setting is an index to rank.

Priorities in service and salutations validate the prestige of the incumbent. Rituals also provide the occasion for noting social change. Divergencies between expected and enacted sequences are a clue to shifts in authority and prestige. Conflict between competing interests often comes to the surface when structural features are made explicit in ritual performances. This is particularly true in these Indian villages where drinking liquor releases inhibitions. The inaugurations of officials in the civil and religious hierarchies are analyzed below to show how they reflect both continuity and change.

Inauguration of civil officials. Legal provision for the installation of the civil officials is minimally stated in the constitution of the state of Chiapas (Secretaría del Gobierno Departamental de Chiapas, 1841:4):

1. The judges and regidores elected will present on the 30th of December their credentials to the Secretary of the civil branch in order that he will put an account of them in a book.
2. Having verified this, he will give an account to them on the following day in the town hall, for which he will name a commission of three people who will identify the people named.
3. On the 1st of January of each year the first judge will meet in the meeting room and present the oath before the civil officials, chaired by the Prefect or Subprefect along with the remaining members of the group, as is stated in article 164 of the law of the 20th of March, 1837. The form of the oath will be the following:

   "I swear to God to preserve and to have others preserve the constitutional laws decreed and sanctioned by the National Congress in the year of 1836". To which the response will be, "Yes, I swear."

   Concluding the oath, they will take their seats. The outgoing officials will cease their functions, and they will be withdrawn from the place of the meetings.

The elaboration of ritual beyond the requirements of the law in household settings as well as in the town hall reveals the significance of ceremonial acts in these small, endogamous communities. The inauguration is a crucial ceremony for the following reasons: (1) Most of the officials are changed simultaneously, so that, since there is neither carryover in a civil service nor tenure officials, the act of transferring authority carries a greater burden in preserving continuity; (2) The official is integrated in a prior set of kinship and other social relations such that he cannot act anonymously in his official capacity as judge or policeman. Thus one of the functions of the inauguration is a disengagement from the preexisting network of obligations and a priority commitment to the obligations of the office (Parsons, 1951:80–84; Gluckman 1962:34; Cancian 1963); (3) The household ceremony preceding the inauguration provides a setting in which the individual who is about to assume the office learns what is expected of him (Fortes 1959:82).

The inauguration is patterned on a series of acts which symbolically communicate to performers and villagers who participate as observers the desired social goals. The settings in which the change of civil officials is carried out are (1) the house of the incoming official, (2) the town hall, (3) the plaza, and (4) the church. In each arena, the validation and support of the new officials is publicly defined before overlapping sets of participants and observers.

The activities of the inauguration observed in 1965 are recorded below:

On New Year's eve, household celebrations are held in the house of each new official. The houses are decorated with pine needles on the floor and juniper boughs on the porch. The visitors arrive about eight in the evening bearing pitch pine and wood to light the house and provide fuel for cooking. The helpers and guests who attend the evening celebration in the house of the president include relatives, compadres, and neighbors who will support him in his term of office. Primary support is given by the official's wife, without whom he would not be serving in the hierarchy. His advisors and councilors in the household are the nakawanehetik, or household officials. These are men who have passed through at least four religious offices and who are somehow related to the new official. A second group of supporters in the household setting are the b'alnialetik, young men who are either brothers, brothers-n-law, sons, compadres, godchildren, or neighbors of the houseowner, and who serve as errand boys and assistants. A third group are the školtawanehetik, *the female helpers, usually wives of the b'alnialetik or widows who are part of the official's or his wife's family. A fourth group are visitors,* yulatak, *who come to congratulate the new official. [The visitors at the house of the first judge are shown in Figure 7.]*

The new official addresses the first nak̯awane with the following speech:

Official: "Holy evening, Mamtat, to your health."
Nak̯awane: "Holy evening, Mamtat, to your health."
Official: "Lord, how are you, Mamtat? You are alive, word of God, this holy evening. There is no illness behind your heart."

Fig. 7. Relatives at House of First Judge on Eve of Inauguration

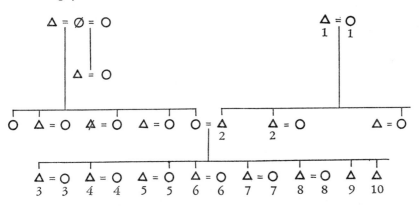

Nak̯awane: "I live. I feel no illness."
Official: "Lord Mamtat, give pardon with God, with the Virgin Mother. Give holy pardon your mothers, your fathers, with God.

"Give pardon, Lord, give pardon. Virgin mother. Here we are gathered before you where we are seated, our soil, our mud.

"How are we going to succeed in what we will have to do in this holy new year for our patron Lord? Here again in the dawning of the holy hour, let us look into our heart, there where we are going to receive the holy oath inside the holy cold house, the cold hall, where we go receive the work and suffering of the holy staff, the holy wand this holy day, this

holy year. And so we shall be able to do what our mothers and what our fathers did here where the holy Father sees us and the holy Mother sees us."

The formal prayer, using elements of all the addresses of pat?o?tan, presages the events which will take place and announces the continuity with the past in following out the work the ancestors have done. The civil authorities, like the religious authorities, assert that they are taking on a holy responsibility. There is, in the words of the pat?o?tan, no distinction between profane and sacred obligations toward the village.

Following the drinking and prayers, liquor is served. Drinking order always follows the elder to younger pattern which, in household settings, is always coincident with prestige ranking. At midnight, coffee, bread, and bean-filled tamales are served.

The second series of household gatherings takes place on the morning of New Year's Day in the houses of the new president, the first judge, and the first policeman. It is the duty of the fourth regidor to assemble the other three regidores, and of the assistant judge to assemble the other judges. The two groups, regidores and judges, meet in the first judge's house and are served coffee and liquor. They then proceed to the house of the president. As the judges and regidores arrive there, the visiting group greets all of the assembled guests at the president's house with a prescribed greeting, the sak'inaltat and the hand-kissing, called ?utzk'aab. The first judge exchanges an extended pat?o?tan with the first nakawane of the president and then liquor is served to all those gathered. The assembled group next stands and "turns toward the rising sun." This is said to be a "defense against the entry of the devil."

While the higher officials meet in the house of the president, the policemen join togther in the houses of the first policeman on each side of the dual division. Just as in the house of the president, the ceremony consists in serving liquor and coffee. They await the sound of the firecrackers set off in the yard of the president's house before setting out for the town hall. With this announcement of the departure, the officials at the president's house and at the two first policemen's houses set out for the town hall.

Gathered in the town hall are the old officials along with the alfereces and the principals. The new officials enter two by two, the president and

*síndico first, followed by the two first judges, the assistant judges of the
barrios, the regidores, the judges of the colonias, the two first police, followed by the rest of the police in pairs. As they enter, they kneel and
make the sign of the cross, or "measure their noses" (sp'is sniʔik), an act
which shows respect to the holy banners that the alfereces have delivered
from the church and laid on the table in the town hall. On this same table
are strewn orange blossoms and leaves of laurel with the newly peeled
canes of the police and the old staffs of office of the higher officials. The
new officials put on their rosaries as they prepare to receive their staffs.*

*The principales, fairly inebriated from drinking all morning as they
awaited the arrival of the new officials, pass out the staffs assisted by the
old president, who helps direct them as they wander in a daze from the
table to the line of waiting officials. The second principal picks the staff
from the table and hands it to the first principal who passes it on to the recipient. The act of passing over the staffs is a significant index to their role
in the hierarchy. They are the only "permanent" officials—permanent so
long as they are in good health and not impoverished. They are the link
between the outgoing and incoming officials.*

*The oath of office was given in Spanish by the Ladino schoolteacher the
year I observed the ceremony. Formerly, this was performed by the Ladino secretary, but a contest of power in the community resulted in this
shift in role performers [Chapter 9]. The inventory of the town's possessions is read by the "old" president[4] and each item is inspected as it is
passed on to the "new" president.*

*After the ceremony in the town hall, all the old officials scatter to their
homes and the new officials, wearing their rosaries, go to the church. The
principales wait in the town hall for their return.*

*The new officials follow the alfereces out of the town hall in a proces-
sion. The four alfereces, holding their banners, line up before the town
hall and dip their banners toward the town hall and then toward the
church. They lead the procession of new officials two times around the
plaza, stopping in front of the church to dip the banners toward it and the
town hall. The order of the procession indicates the rank order of the offi-*

4. The officials who have completed their year in office are referred to as "old," and the
incoming officials are referred to as "new" at this event.

cials, from the last policeman to the first and second judges. The procession makes two turns "to show [the townspeople assembled in the plaza] who the new officials to remain in office are."

Awaiting the arrival of the new officials in the church are all of the mayordomos. Their function is "to watch the officials as they enter to see who they are." The new officials enter two by two and proceed to the altar rail where they "speak to God," asking for health so that they can fulfill their obligation to the town. They kiss each of the saints' pedestals and then leave the "holy mother church" to return to the "holy father cabildo."

The first order of the new president is to ask the fourth regidor to buy two liters of the "gift of the ancestors," contraband liquor. When the liquor arrives, the first judge rises and goes to the principales. Standing before them while they remain seated, he asks permission of God to "receive the gift," or drink the liquor, saying, "Give pardon, Mamal Krinsipal; let a little enter and warm your body."

The policemen, after leaving the church, enter the kitchen shack attached to the town hall. The first new policeman orders the fourth policeman to bring a little trago, and when he returns with the liquor, the first policeman orders one of the policemen of the colonias to measure the drinks. They drink one liter, after which the first policeman of the lower division addresses the first policeman of the upper division in the pat?o-?tan. After the spatbeyo?tan, or formal address, the first policeman wonders "whether they can endure a little more. Can they drink more liquor without getting drunk?" It is his responsibility to receive any orders from the president, and he wonders, "What should happen if we get drunk? We won't know if there is an errand for the mamal judge and we cannot help. Better rest a while, and if there is an errand we can help a little. If there is no errand, let us drink a little more until midday." At twelve noon both groups retire to their homes to rest their hearts.

Inauguration of religious officials. The change of the mayordomos occurs twice annually, once on January 6 and a second time on the Day of San Pedro and San Pablo, June 29. San Pedro is associated with the functions of the caretakers of the church because, one informant said, his image shows him holding the keys to the gates of heaven.

The ritual of the inauguration begins on June 29, a day called Pas Kantelero, *prepare the candle holders. The old mayordomos who have served for the past six months scrape the candle sticks, while two of the group play the drum and blow the flute. Others sweep the church and clean the interior. Then the fiscal and the mayordomos gather outside the church. A table is brought out, and the money that has been collected from each mayordomo by the two cofrades to be used for the purchase of candles is counted. When the money has been counted, two mayordomos ring the bells in the bell tower. Two servings of contraband liquor are passed out, one called "arrival of our food," before the meal, and the other called "wash down the meal," afterwards. Formerly a meal, consisting of a male turkey, or beef soup if the mayordomos could not afford a turkey, with tortillas and chile, was prepared and served in the church yard. This is now eaten in the home of the cofrade because the priest objected to the preliminary drinking session.*

On the second day of the fiesta, called Wišpereš, *the mayordomos "make a fiesta" which consists of beating the drums, playing the flute, and drinking trago. Early in the morning the priest gives a mass for San Pedro and San Pablo attended by the old and new officials and the women.*

A series of house celebrations takes place in the houses of the cofrades. The new mayordomos go first to the house of the cofrade of Santa Lucía. There they are offered the mouthwash, a bowl of cold water with which they rinse their mouths, followed by a round of two drinks each. The Cofrade of Santa Lucía then speaks to the Tatil of San Pedro the Martyr:

Cofrade of Santa Lucía: "Good day, Mamal Tat. Thank you. How do you look, Mamal? Thanks that you are alive, word of God, at daybreak. What will we do? What have we done? We have to speak of what is in our heart, our soil, our mud. So it is as we did in the past. We are all together as are the old officials, where we hear and see with our eyes. Where are we on the very day of his fiesta our saint and our judge San Pedro and

San Pablo? So it is that we are here and that we are united in front of the house. Pardon us, if it is not much, you elders. Where we are gathered together there is nothing flavorful nor is there much. It is only a little to warm your body, the water that washed his body, his hand our old saint San Pedro and San Pablo [reference to liquor]. God thank mother and father, mam kobraria."

As the mayordomos prepare to leave the house, the following exchange takes place:

Tatil of San Pedro the Martyr: "What are we thinking? How shall we rise to enter the house of the Kobraria Sakramentu? Why is it he does not want us to drink too much? It is good, we would not remember. It is enough. If you will remember, you will say little, mayordomos. Are we not ready with our rosaries and with our kerchiefs and our candles? Is there anything you want to say?"

Cofrade of Santa Lucía: "It is good. I am going to ask you all if you are ready with your rosary and with your cloth to take the holy candles."

Mayordomos: "Yes, good, we are ready, thank you."

Cofrade of Santa Lucía: "Only one more thing do I have to say. Do not drink too much trago. I do not want you to walk like a mad man. I do not want anyone to say that the kobraria did not say anything to advise you."

Mayordomos: "Yes, thanks. It is good. Let us go now. Let us raise our mud, our soil [reference to body]."

The group goes on to the house of the Cofrade of Sacramento who is awaiting them with his nakawanehetik, his b'alnialetik, and the female assistants in the house. They enter saying "Good day, Mamal," greeting first the b'alnialetik, then the third nakawane, then the second nakawane, and finally the first nakawane. The Cofrade of Santa Lucía stands before the first nakawane and recites the spatbeyoʔtan. Then he goes on to speak to the meʔil k'op, or woman speaker, who is referred to in this instance as the meʔc'ukušaʔil, "woman who nursed us."

The women of the kobraria's kindred, the sisters and first cousins and wives of his brothers, remain inside the house as the men sit on the benches on the porch. The nakawane orders the b'alnialetik to serve the mouthwash which is followed by coffee and tortillas. After another

*mouthwash, the b'alnialetik lay a cloth on a small table which is put in
the center of the porch, and two liters of trago and a measuring glass are
laid on this. The Cofrade of Santa Lucía rises and asks permission of the
women, the mayordomos, and all the b'alnialetik to drink the liquor, saying: "God, mother who nurses us, give permission to us so that the water
of his body, the water of his hand, the gift will pass in our bodies, that
which is the gift of the meʔtiktatik. God speaks, tat nakawanehetik and
b'alnialetik. Give us permission to hand the gift that will pass in your
body from the meʔtiktatik. God, Jesus, Mary, only one commander God is
three persons. Bless what we eat and what we drink and bless in the name
of God the father. God, take the gift, meʔeštateš."*

*The mayordomos, b'alnialetik, and nakawanehetik then make the sign
of the cross. The Cofrade of the Virgin Santa Lucía blesses the liquor, saying, "In God's name, God the father, name of God, God the son, Holy
Spirit. Yes, I can endure doing what they did, what our mother and what
our father did, with my hand which has sinned and my feet which have
sinned. Yes, we are changing office on this holy day, this holy year the
holy saint, with the holy oath and in the name of God the Father."*

*The mayordomos drink four measures of liquor, then raise the rest of
the drinks to their lips without drinking and take the glass over to one of
the nakawanehetik. In this way they show the restraint to which they
have been urged in the speeches. At eleven o'clock they leave for the
church, putting their red kerchiefs around their necks along with the rosaries. As they set out, the elder nakawane says so the new mayordomos:
"May you all get up and go to the church. May you all enter inside the
church. May you take the oath inside the church before the face of the
fiscal. After you take the oath, make the sign of the cross before the face
of the Tatik Jesus Christ. After you have made the sign of the cross, when
you enter inside the door of the church, the mamal new kobraria will give
the account to the mamal old kobraria."*

*Sitting within the church are the old mayordomos and the fiscal who
have remained there after the mass. They are awaiting the new mayordomos. Two of them play the drum and the flute. The new mayordomos
enter, the elder and junior mayordomo of each saint walking together,
and kneel before the image of Tatik Jesus Christ. The church has been ar-*

ranged with a large table in the center, the candles allotted to each mayor-domo laid out in bundles of nine. On the table is a little cross of the cruci-fied Christ. The priest blesses the new mayordomos and the old mayordo-mos. Then the fiscal gives nine candles wrapped in a napkin to each may-ordomo. The nič'nal, junior mayordomo, of each saint first takes the can-dles allotted to the tatil to the latter's house, and then takes his own to his house. After the oath, the new mayordomos return to the house of the Cofrade of Sacramento where they drink until prayer time in the evening.

On the sk'ak'alel Sk'in, the true day of the fiesta, the new mayordomos go to hear the mass along with women prayer-reciters at seven in the morning. They then go to the house of the Cofrade of Sacramento, leav-ing three junior mayordomos to play the drums and flute at the door of the church. In the house of the cofrade, they count the money of the Vir-gin and of San Pedro the Martyr. This fund of money is passed over from the outgoing officials to the incoming officials along with interest. It is now being loaned out to local entrepreneurs. The Virgin has a fund of 228 pesos, and San Pedro the Martyr has 40 pesos. The fiscal supervises the counting of the money, and records the sum, after which the pat?o?tan is recited and drinks are served.

In the behavioral sequences of the inauguration, several features of the structure and functioning of the hierarchy can be noted. First, one can see in the actions of the officials that the hierarchy of civil officials is not a smooth step ladder but a segmented order. The categories of officials, the alkaletik, rehiroletik, and mayoletik, act in concert, move in unison, and sit in the same area in all the settings. Each of the three categories has its internal hierarchy, ranging from first to fourth (and in the case of the mayoletik, from first to fifth, physically denoted by the order in which they sit and drink. Those who speak the greetings are the men in the first position of each category. They command their group or the group immediately below them. Thus, the judge orders the fourth regidor to get liquor, and the first policeman orders the police from the rural colonia to get liquor. By these behavioral indices one can see the ordering and group-ing by age, skill in praying, and territorial identification within the seg-ments of the civil-religious hierarchy. These principles apply, however, only to ordering between segments; because of the uneven civil careers of the incumbents, a man in the lower ranks within a segment may be older than another in the same rank because he started his career later.

A second significant feature of the inauguration behavior is the sacred quality of the acts, indicated by the words of the patʔoʔtan—"holy office," "holy cold house," "holy staff, holy wand," "holy day and holy hour." The presence of the alfereces, the observation of the new civil officials by the religious officials, the movement from the town hall to the church and back to the town hall are the behavioral links between "our holy mother church and our holy father cabildo."

The behavioral elements in the inauguration of the religious officials parallel those in the inauguration of the civil officials. As in the case of the latter, the ritual takes place in both domestic and public settings—the house of the new officials and the church. In both inaugurations, the same feature of "raising" (rounding up for gatherings) the officials occurs: those of lower rank gather in the houses of successively higher officials, finally entering the house of the highest official. In each setting, the same ritual acts are performed—the formal greeting, the serving of coffee and bread followed by bean tamales, the request for permission to drink, and the serving of the "gift" of liquor. In the household setting for both civil and religious officials the same role performers—nakawanehetik, b'alnialetik and školtawanetik—lend their support.

In the religious hierarchy the symbolic "tools" of office of the mayordomos are candles while those in the civil hierarchy are canes. In the case of the inauguration of the religious officials, the inventory involves counting the money collected for each saint rather than accounting for the possessions owned by the town. An inventory of the saints' clothing is not made as in other towns, possibly because the lay sisters living in the town maintain this stock of equipment.

The formalized speech of the patʔoʔtan is an important social tool in both public and private ceremonials. Characteristic of the speech are the elaboration of simile and metaphor (*meʔbaʔal, wokol:* poverty and trouble in reference to one's house; *lumiltik kač'aletik:* clay and mud in reference to bodies; *snuk shoy:* his joined one, his companion in reference to one's wife; *sapil yok' sapil sk'aab k'a santuetik k'a peroltik:* the washings of the legs and arms of our patron lord, Jesus, in reference to liquor). The prayer-like intonation, together with repeated invocation of the gods, gives a sacred quality to the words.

Liquor, referred to as "the gift of God" or "gift of the ancestors," is of crucial significance in both civil and religious ritual. Receiving an offering of liquor is tantamount to accepting part of the spiritual essence of the donor. Drinking in each of the domains—the house, the town hall, and the church—serves to tie together different sets of participants in the obligation system of service to the community. In Mauss' terms (1954:11) receiving the gift defines "a pattern of spiritual bonds between things which are to some extent parts of persons, and persons and groups, that behave in some measure as if they were things."

In both inaugurations an attempt is made to control the intake of liquor so that the officials can function in the ritual. This is shown in the civil inauguration when the first policeman thinks about whether the police can take another drink and still carry out their duties. It is more explicit in the religious inaugurations when the cofrades warn the mayordomos that they should not drink so much that they "walk like madmen." The mayordomos then pass on the drinks served to them to the nakawanehetik who drink them and fall into a stupor.

In noting the difference between elicited and performed ritual, minimal changes in behavior provided clues to structural change. The change of custom as to where the meal of the mayordomos takes place (it now is given at the house of the cofrade rather than in the courtyard of the church) indicates a significant shift in the relation between the priest and the local religious leadership. The priest has gained control over the church since he has taken up residence in the parish house. The incident in which the confrontation took place is described in Chapter 9. Divergence of the performed from the expected ritual in the inauguration of the civil authority occurred when the schoolteacher delivered the oath instead of the former Ladino secretary. This revealed the schoolteacher's increasing power in his competition with the former cacique.

The rituals of both civil and religious inaugurations reveal the sense of the sacred obligation to the ancestors. Although both the roles and the scheduling of events are derived from outside the culture, the necessity for undertaking the burden of office is still phrased as a means of maintaining the internal system of security. Tying the new official to personal supporters in the household setting is a significant means of integrating the Spanish governmental system with the preexisting authority systems.

The emphasis on continuity is evident in the prescribed pattern of behavior stressing repetition of bodily and verbal performances. Repetition of behavior, the essence of all ritual, provides that fulfillment of expectations which links the present with the past.[5] The nakawanehetik, who are the repositories of knowledge of the customs of the ancestors, are stage directors of acts performed in the house. Behavioral replication is reinforced by verbal references in the pat?o?tan to performing "that which our mothers, that which our fathers did." When any act has lost the wider context of belief in which it must at one time have been embedded, the reason given for the performance is simply "so was the custom of our ancestors." As an example of this, the officials in the president's house on the day of the inauguration stand and bow in the direction of the rising sun. A few informants have heard of the God of the East, Santo Ariyó, the saint in charge of household gods who gave to the people corn, wheat, beans, and cattle, and they say that it is in recognition of him that people turn to the East and bow their heads in all household performances. They further state that in this act they defend the house against the entry of the devil. But the mythological context which might explain the logic of this association is lost. These behavioral sherds, when cut off from the belief system which they dramatized, survive in perpetuating the customs of the ancestors.

The link with the past is also seen in the presence of both new and old officials in the town hall, providing a setting in which the succession of the new officials is acknowledged by the old. The role of the principales is of the greatest importance in establishing continuity, significantly emphasized in the fact that it is they who hand over the symbol of authority, the

5. Bunzel (1952:251) has pointed to this familiarity of ritual sets in a variety of ceremonials as providing ties with the past in the inauguration in Chichicastenango, and Vogt (1966) has shown the significance of replication in the ceremonials of Zinacantan. Another function served by behavorial replication is that which Leach (1967:2) pointed out for verbal replication in myths and prayers: it overcomes the "static" of less significant background interference.

newly cut pine canes of the police and the old carved and painted staffs of the higher officials.

Order and measure, respect and deference are the social effect achieved in the ritual performance of the inaugurations. In the act of drinking, these principles become behaviorally explicit. The drink is carefully measured out and passed to the first principal, who asks permission to drink it of each set of officials in order of their ranked positions in the hierarchy. Each official must receive the drink, whether he is a teetotaler or not. He will then perform the action of drinking, which is sufficient to express his good will as part of the group. The symbolic act of pretending to drink— receiving the "gift" and raising it to one's lips without imbibing—reveals the importance of acts *as such* in social interaction. This is expressed in the Tzeltal loan term *ʔaksion,* from the Spanish *acción,* the pretended act, which demonstrates in this case one's good will in joining in the communal act. We have a tendency in our culture to downgrade the act, stressing motive specific to the immediate goal of the act. If performance is motivated by other goals, we express it in phrases such as "He is only acting," or "It was all a big act." In Tzoʔontahal, the play is the thing, and everything can be justified by reference to traditional expectations.

Before describing some of the organizational changes which are affecting the civil-religious hierarchy, I shall at this point assess its viability on the basis of structural criteria. These criteria include the effectiveness of the system in (1) coordinating roles such that conflict is minimized in carrying out tasks, (2) motivating people to enter into office and fulfill obligations, (3) absorbing changes without structural modification.

The primary devices for coordinating roles in the hierarchy are those of relative age and residence in the dual division. The major challenge to the age-respect pattern has been the introduction of young leadership in the roles of president and síndico. This shock to the system has been somewhat overcome by the retention of the ceremonial primacy of the principales. The president and síndico are considered outside the traditional hierarchy. This conceptual isolation of the roles becomes obvious when one asks informants to list the civil officials, for they never include the president and síndico in the first response. They are mentioned in response to repeated enquiries as to whether there are other officials.

The principle of balancing posts according to residence in the dual division is maintained in the traditional civil posts but fails to be effective again in the case of the president. Increasing population in the upper division meant that the expensive post of alférez had to be filled primarily from the side with the highest population. This unbalancing of the sharing of these burdensome posts eventually led to revolt and the post was abolished. Since it was the key post in learning prayers, its loss may mean the end of the traditional rituals in the home.

The hierarchy fails to provide sufficient prestige or power to motivate people voluntarily to undertake some posts. The most vulnerable post was that of alférez. In fulfilling obligations to the saints, alfereces used to spend over 3,000 pesos, twice the normal income of a man in one year. They were assisted by members of their immediate households either in loans or in the sale of pottery to help pay for the house fiestas. The show of wealth at these fiestas, when up to one hundred guests were fed, excited the envy of neighbors, often among the invited guests. It was felt that this provoked witchcraft, and every former alférez I knew maintained that he suffered some catastrophe following his year in office. In the last few years before its demise in 1966 the post was accepted only under duress, and all those who had been nominated at first chose to go to jail. The reason that it survived as long as it did was the insistence of those officials who served in this post that it was essentail to maintaining good fiestas. The resolution of the contradictions by abolishing the post contrast with that of Zinacantan, where men sought the prestige-conferring posts that involved large expenditures of money as a validation of wealth (Cancian 1965).

Another contradition which minimizes the motivation to undertake the traditional posts is that the highest post in the ladder, that of principal, is one associated with embarrassment and shame rather than prestige. Shorn of his roles in decision-making and in guarding public funds, the principal is reduced to holding the plate in which donations for the major fiestas are placed. The ceremonial role of the principales will probably survive, however, since the old men of the community who have retired from active work in the fields enjoy the drinking sessions in the cabildo sufficiently to compensate for the shame associated with the role.

The internal structural contradictions have to be considered in the context of strong sentiments supporting an independent civil authority. The adaptations which have been made within the existing structure are a tribute to the strength of the sentiments associating survival of tradition with office-holding in the civil-religious hierarchy. Chapter 9 will deal with the capacity of the structure to absorb change.

Chapter 8

Taking Care of the Lord Spirits

Religious behavior is concerned with two major goals: maintaining a given state of prosperity and protecting the community against disaster. In the words of one informant: "All of the goods which we enjoy—the corn, beans, and wheat that we eat, the animals which work for us and give us food—are the gifts of the Lord spirits." The technique for maintaining the flow of goods of the world is the annual cycle of fiestas for the saints. The strategy for protecting the community against disaster is through avoidance of offense and special offerings to the gods identified with pre-hispanic deities and spirits. Responsibility for the ceremonial cycle is assigned to officials who represent the community, but everyone is responsible for the avoidance of disaster, since any transgression of moral behavior by an individual can cause their wrath and bring destruction of crops and animals. The protective rituals involve beliefs continuous from pre-hispanic times; maintenance depends on Catholic saints.

KINDS OF LORD SPIRITS

Religious behavior is based on an understanding of the personality and rank of each deity in a hierarchy of power. The people distinguish two major categories of gods: the lord spirits of the heaven, *č'ultatik ta č'ulčan,* and the lord spirits of the church, *č'ultatik ta č'ulna.* The prefix *č'ul* in all of these terms can be translated as spirit. All growing things—people, plants, and animals—have a spirit. *Tatik* can be translated as our lords, elders, or fathers. The categories of spirits discussed here differ from the č'uleletik (Chapter 1) since these are spirits possessed by the place in which they dwell, as indicated by the possessive form of the noun with the prefix *s.*

The two groups of spirits differ in their traditional characteristics and functions. The spirits of the heaven "look to see where everyone is going," "look and listen to all that people say," "are very alive," and "are of the world." In contrast to them, the spirits of the church "are not alive," "do not speak," "do not do anything," "are only of the pueblo." Thus the spirits of the heaven are universal; those of the church are particular. The saints' images which are kept in the church of the town are not considered to represent the same person as these same images in other towns. This conception of saints as local and distinct personalities is found in other Maya Indian towns and differs from that of orthodox Catholicism.

The lord spirits of the heaven. The spirits of the heaven are God the Father, *Tios Tatil,* God the Son, *Tios Nič'anil,* and the Holy Spirit, *Spiritusantú.* Table 27 indicates the identification made between these major figures and pre-hispanic spiritual entities.

TABLE 27. Pre- and Post-Hispanic Equivalents of the Lord Spirits of the Heavens

Post-Hispanic spirits		*Pre-Hispanic spirits*
Tios Tatil (God the Father)	=	B'alamilal (The World)
		B'ankilal (Elder Brother)
Tios Nič'anil (God the Son, Jesus Christ)	=	Sčeb'al B'ankilal (Second Brother)
Spiritusantú (Holy Spirit)	=	Tatik K'ahk'al (The Lord Sun)
		K'oš (referential, Last Child)
		Šut (vocative, proper name)
		ʔihtz'in (Younger Brother)
Meʔ Santú (Virgin Mary)	=	Meʔtikčič ʔu (Our Grandmother the Moon)

The "mystery" of the Trinity is "explained" in the following story in which pre-hispanic deities are identified with the Christian deities.

Many years ago, the Lord Sun [Tatik K'ak'al] *did not walk as now. He was only hanging in the heavens. Our Grandmother the Moon* [Meʔtik Čič ʔu] *bore three sons named God the Father* [Tios Tatil], *the Elder Brother; God the Son, Second Brother; and a third named K'oš, or Last One. The first brother did not turn out bright nor did the second brother. It was the youngest brother, K'oš, who was the brightest. When the Elder*

Plate I. Head of Palm where the ancestors stand and watch over the town. The cross, standing about twelve feet high and adorned with an arch of pine boughs and flowers, tops a jutting rock about thirty feet high. Behind the rock is the hill with the cave in which the ancestors were reputed to live.

Plate 2. The view the ancestors had of the town from the Head of Palm shows the proximity of the village center to the Pan-American Highway just to the right of center. The church, which can be discerned in the center of the major settlement, is the dividing marker for the dual division. The barrio of Yetawitz is shown just to the left of the major settlement. The barrios of Madronal and La Grandeza are found at the mid-level of the hill in the far left, on the other side of the road which goes to Pinola and "hot country." The Ladino town of Teopisca lies just beyond the hills to the right along the Pan-American Highway. From this site, the ancestors were able to see clearly all of the thoroughfares within the town and guard against the entry of evil.

Plate 3. A father and his two sons, walking in order of age, leave the village to go to their milpa. The father, walking in front, is wearing the old-style costume with a wrapped over-shirt concealing short undertrousers. His sons wear western clothing. All of the men carry net bags on a tumpline, with their backs protected from their burdens by a sheepskin. They all carry machetes, and the boys have rifles.

Plate 4. Farmer showing the arada plow. He is holding the handle, and the shaft, made of a long tree post, is propped on the ground.

Plate 5. Men assisting the women of their household in the firing of canteros, or water jugs. They have just removed the still-smoldering logs which were propped on the outer perimeter of the pyramid of jugs.

Plate 6. Woman scraping a cantero that has been sun-dried in the porch of her home. Behind her is an altar with pictures of the saints. Photograph by Marcey Jacobson.

Plate 7. Types of pottery produced:

a decorated water pitcher

b water storage jar

c bowl

d water-carrying jar

e toy: man astride donkey

f flower holder shaped in form of duck

g candle holder

h vase on an ashtray, pedestal with three frogs

Photographs by Jean Simmons.

Plate 8. Women of a household and their helpers grinding corn and making tortillas with a press in preparation for a house ceremony. They are all dressed in the traditional costume. Most of such food preparation is done inside the house except at the time of large festivals. Photograph by Marcey Jacobson.

Plate 9. Curer sitting next to the center post where he has just arranged the candles and branches of spring bushes in preparation for the house fiesta. The basket contains the protective crosses, bound with palm fronds, which he will nail on the house posts. The basin contains springwater, and the gourd in the foreground contains the powdered medicines which will be added to the water and drunk. Photograph by Marcey Jacobson.

Plate 10. Future members of the household line up with the branches of spring bushes with which the curer will brush them. Photograph by Marcey Jacobson.

Brother was in heaven, there never was night. He never rested from his work.

One day K'oš said to his brother, "Let us go for a walk. We will get honey and eat it. I know where there is a tree." He told his mother to make tortillas to take with them. She made many tortillas for K'oš to eat, and in addition made two small tortillas.

His mother asked K'oš, "Why do you want to go out walking?"

He replied, "I am going to find honey. Wait for me to return."

K'oš and his two older brothers walked until they arrived at the tree with the honey. The Elder Brother said, "I shall climb very high."

K'oš said, "I too will climb."

The Elder Brother said, "Do not climb. Wait and I shall throw the honey down. You cannot climb the tree, Šut" [for this is what they called K'oš].

K'oš just waited for his brother to throw down the honey. K'oš got very angry because the Elder Brother just threw down beeswax.[1] An animal entered the trunk of the tree and started eating the root. The tree shook, frightening the two brothers. They called out, "What are you doing, Šut?"

"Nothing. I am not doing anything. Why don't you give me good honey?"

"Go on and drink it," the older brothers said.

"I don't like it. It isn't any good," replied K'oš.

He did nothing for a while. Then the tree fell. K'oš saw the tree fall. He went and got the two small tortillas his mother had packed in his lunch, and he put one on the Elder Brother's nose. His brother turned into a pig. He tried to put the other tortilla on the Second Brother's nose, but he could not seize him. The Second Brother turned into a wild boar, and fled into the forest. He brought the Elder Brother to his house. When he arrived at his house with his little pig, he said to his mother, "Mother, I have brought a little pig to raise."

"Where did you find it?" his mother asked.

"I just brought it," replied K'oš.

---

1. In recounting this passage, the narrator laughed, and when I asked why, said that the word for beeswax is also the word for excrement. She commented that K'oš was very bright because he would not tolerate this.

"Is there food for it?" asked his mother.

"I am going to plant a milpa to feed the little pig. You stay here and watch the little pig and I will go."

"Yes, I will care for it," said his mother.

K'oš went to plant his milpa. As he was leaving, he said to his mother, "I will return in the afternoon."

His mother said, "I shall await you in the afternoon."

When K'oš returned, his mother asked, "How is your milpa?"

He replied, "It isn't ready. Tomorrow I am going to burn it because it is just a forest."

The next day, K'oš returned to his milpa. Everything he had cut had grown back in his milpa. He asked himself, "How did it spring up? I am going to wait and see who is causing the trouble." He waited and saw a bird entering the milpa. The bird said, "I don't want to have the woods burned!"

K'oš said, "I am going to start the fire."

He started the fire, and then he said, "I am going to where the day meets the heaven." He picked up the fire of his milpa, saying, "My brother does not know how to walk. I am going to walk around and return."

Now the day walks in front and the night walks behind.[2]

The story has an aftermath which describes the continuing relationship between the Lord Sun, K'oš, and his mother, Our Grandmother the Moon.

The Lord Sun sees all of our sins and puts them in a book. If anyone has sexual relations in the milpa, he puts it down. When he sees this, he gets angry because he walks alone. He wants to end the world since he does not endure our sins. But Our Grandmother the Moon does not want

2. There are other versions of this story in neighboring Tzeltal-speaking communities. Castro (1959:24–31) gives an Oxchuk version in which the identification of the three brothers with the Christian Trinity is not made. Šut, the vocative term used in the Tzo?-ontahal version, is given as the name of the youngest brother, who succeeded in giving a new sun to the world. But in outwitting his brothers with the honey, Šut killed them rather than turning them into pigs. A Chol version (Whittaker and Warkentin 1965) is closer to that of Oxchuk.

the sun to kill people. She is afraid that if all the people die, other people will come who have just one hand and one foot. They will not be able to work. Our Grandmother the Moon wants things as they are. So she fights the Sun, and then there is an eclipse. For this reason, people say that she bears our sins.

The tales occasionally try to bring the old gods into focus with the Christian gods and to explain certain cosmological events, for example the eclipse and the movement in the heavens of the sun and the moon. The synthesis is incomplete. First of all, the small part Jesus (Second Brother) plays in the first myth, in which he finally disappears into the forest, shows a failure to fit the three gods into the pre-hispanic format which included only two main characters. Secondly, the myths fail to synthesize the codes of morality stemming from Maya and Christian sources. In Christian mythology, the deities are conceived of as perfect. They are not identified with the sun, but are the power of creation which brought forth the sun and made it move. Destructive forces come from the evil power of the Devil. The deities of the Indians incorporate both good and evil. Cosmological forces are the gods acting directly either to promote or destroy man's work. Even the Grandmother Moon, who shows compassion for her grandchildren, can be piqued into destroying their crops.

In another tale the personification of good and evil in separate characters shows greater influence from Catholicism. Jesus emerges as the hero who, with the collaboration of the Virgin Mary, outwits the Devil.

After Jesus was crucified, the King of the Jews[3] *called upon people to sow a staff to prove who moves the world. Jesus planted the seed, but the Jews did not let them grow. He did it again, and only one leg came out and one hand came out. Therefore the plant did not stand because the "King of Evil" was watching.*

Jesus and his mother had an idea. He spoke to her, saying, "What do you think, Mother?" She replied, "The only thing I can say is, what can we think of?"

The Lord Christ replied, "Our children and offspring [the milpa] do

3. The Devil is alternately called King of the Jews [Statal Jurio], King of Evil [Statal Pukuh], and the Devil in the story.

not stand. Only one stands—he who does not respect us." The Virgin Mother said, "Yes, I saw another one who walks well watching our children." Jesus asked, "Did you get a good look where he walks?" His mother replied, "Yes, indeed, I saw him." Christ asked, "If you know, what are we going to do there where he walks?" "I do not know what we shall do," said his mother.

Then, after a pause, Christ said, "Now I know what we will do! Do you know what hour he passes?" The Virgin answered, "Yes, I do."

"Good. I am going to make a little house and put a Victrola, an accordion, and also a violin in it. I will put a marimba, a guitar, and a harp on each side of the road. And I shall also put trago and beer, everything that is good to drink. When you see him coming, we will begin to play the marimba and guitar and all the music on both sides of the road. When you see the King of Evil, we will begin the dance and drink trago—everything there is—and he will look at what we drink."

The Virgin said, "I will invite him to dance a little." "Yes, you remain here dancing, and I shall go for a moment to see his children [corn plants]. Continue dancing while I go out to look," said Christ. The Virgin answered, "Good. Good."

And so the Devil passed by. When Christ left, the Virgin began to dance with the Devil. They drank more liquor to make him "lose his heart" [get drunk]. The Virgin did not see that the Devil put his tail in half of the bottle. It is because of this that the people say liquor is one-half Devil and one-half God.

Meanwhile, Jesus arrived where the children of the Devil were. He made no more than the sign of the cross, and all the children of the Devil died. It is after the Children of the Devil died that Christ seized control of the world.

And so it is true that we are his children who came out of Jesus Christ.

In this tale, evil is personified in the enemy of the Catholic Church, the King of the Jews who is also the pre-hispanic "King of Evil." The Virgin Mother is concerned with preventing the world from reverting to the situation in which people were born helpless, with just one arm and one leg, as it was when the Devil was in control. To prevent this, when the moon is "sick" or in eclipse, the people must call her back to life. The strategy is to make a great deal of noise by striking hoes, firing rifles, blowing the horns of bulls, and striking gourds. The logic of this behavior can be understood from the following statement of an informant: "The sickness of the moon is a result of the conflict of the sun with the moon. The noise we made frightens the father sun so that he will stop fighting the moon. If he were to win, the people would die, and new people would be born with only one leg and one arm." [4]

We have in this story what appears to be an overlay of post-hispanic mythology, in which the Devil personifies evil forces, superimposed on a prehispanic mythological identification of the powers of both good and evil in single cosmological deities. Whereas in the previous myth it is the Devil, the King of the Jews, who caused all of the children of Jesus to die and to be reborn with only one arm and one leg, in this statement it is the sun who can effect the same reversal of nature. The sun, Tatik K'alik, has the power to cause the milpa to grow, but by staying out too long, it can burn the crop. Similarly lightning, Tatik Čaʔuk, may bring rain, but can destroy the milpa with the winds that precede the rain or kill man and destroy his house. Man is responsible for determining how the force of the gods will be directed.

The guardianship of the sun and the moon over the people of the world serves to control or at least restrain the behavior of people. Since both of them "walk alone," without companionship, they become jealous if they see sexual relations performed by people in the milpa. Since all legal sexual relations are carried out in the relative privacy of the house, it is only those who seek illicit relationships who retreat to the milpa, and so this restraint has a prohibitive effect on unsanctioned sexual behavior. If the moon sees someone in the milpa at night, she refuses to retire and stays out, not letting her son the sun rise. Similarly, when the sun sees someone in the milpa in the daytime, he refuses to retire, burning the milpa with his hot rays.

The lord spirits of the east. There is another category of spirits which is ill defined and not many people know. These are the spirits of

4. The same behavior, that of making noise during an eclipse, is found in the Maya Indian community of Cantel, Guatemala, but there it is interpreted as a means of calling the sick grandmother back to life by showing that her grandchildren care about her.

the east. Each of these is responsible for giving something to men: one gave corn, one wheat, one bulls, one horses, and one pigs. These spirits are recognized in the context of the household only: at the end of each household ceremony, the assembled guests stand and look to the East where the gods reside in a place called Santo Arió, somewhere in Guatemala. Since their gifts to mankind are products which are produced and consumed by the household, and since they are recognized in the context of the house, there is some basis for thinking of them as old household gods. Calnek (1962:61) has pointed out that among the ancient Maya, household gods were part of "a hierarchically ordered series of deities, worship or propitiation of which progressively links him not with other individuals conceived particularistically, but to all larger social units of which he is a member."

The only case I know in which an identification is made between these household gods and the saints concerns Santa Teresa:

Once long ago the owners began to harvest their milpas, and they put the corn in a pile. When the harvest was finished, they began to beat the corn from the cob. When they carried off the corn, some of the seed [sb'ak'] remained.

A man passed by and heard a saint talking. He asked what she said, and she replied, "Nothing. I said that you should tell the Padre to pick me up and put my body (also sb'ak') in a church. I want a church for myself, and I shall wait here until you come to carry me inside the church. I do not want any companion. I don't want you to throw away the corn seeds, nor do I want you to burn the seeds because they are my bones. Make a good fiesta and bring me into the church with firecrackers and with prayers. Raise me high on a pedestal because I do not want to be kissed, I only want my feet to be kissed."

And now there is a church for Santa Teresa standing in a milpa outside of Comitán, in which she lives alone since there is no companion for her.

The lord spirits of the church. Among the sixteen saints of the church, four "big saints"—Sacramento, San Pedro the Martyr, Santa Lucía, and San Francisco—are distinguished from the others. All four are considered by the Indians to be patron saints of the pueblo, although the priest lists only one, San Francisco. Only these top four are hierarchically ordered. The big saints are supposed to be able to make miracles, but there are stories only for San Pedro and Santa Lucía. San Pedro Martyr, *Tatik Martil,* is the only saint possessing a soul. The image of San Pedro shows him with a hatchet in his head, blood dripping over his face. According to legend, San Pedro was the first patron saint of the town. The following story recounts his transformation:

Tatik Martil was of a very foreign kind of heart. He gave permission to the witches to bring sickness. Only those who knew how to make illness spoke with him. They went and asked permission to make the illness continue. People heard he was very evil, and they threw him out of church. They cut off his head, saying, "You only give evil. You do not give any miracles. You have given the old ones permission to give evil."

San Pedro received a new head in Pinola. Now he is good and is of one heart with the Virgin Santa Lucía, with Sacramento, and with San Francisco.

The logic by which San Pedro is cast as leader of the witches is implicit in judgments concerning guilt in cases of homicide. Any man who is killed is referred to as the guilty person, since protecting the village from witchcraft is the main motivation for homicide. When an early priest set up an image of San Pedro in the church, this must have inspired fear and foreboding. He was transmogrified by the people into the leader of the witches, and they burned the church to the ground. (Its foundations are still visible in Alannantik.) Whether the priest at that time (around 1746) convinced the people that, with a new head purchased in Pinola, San Pedro was transformed, or whether the people invented the story, we do not know. Despite his reformation, San Pedro still inspires fear. He is identified with the Lord of Lightning, Tatik Čaʔuk. The following is a typical account of his power:

This power comes from his possession of an animal spirit. Whenever the lightning strikes, people know that some sin has been committed. The old people say that he asked a son-in-law to put down a lightning flash. The son-in-law couldn't do it—I don't know why he couldn't do his work—

and so he returned and the Lord of Lightning gave him another job—that of making lightning flashes.

San Pedro now gives protection to the people from the power he wields. During his fiesta, palm crosses are distributed to everyone who attends mass; if a man walks with a cross tucked in his hat or a woman wears one strung on her neck, he or she will not be struck by lightning. The houses are similarly protected with palm crosses.

Santa Lucía is the only other saint in the local roster who is described as being "very powerful." She is supposed to be able to cure diseases of the eyes. The image of her in the church shows her holding two eyes reflected in a small mirror in the palm of her hand. The story which explains why she holds them was told me with an expression of complete belief, and other informants vouch for its authenticity:

Formerly, Santa Lucía used to "talk with" [a euphemism for "had an affair with"] Santo Tomás of Oxchuk. Santo Tomás loved her because she was pretty. Santa Lucía was so in love with Santo Tomás that she gave him a gift of her eyes. He did not want them—he was frightened by the gift—and he returned them. From then on, she did not speak to him. Now, when a child has sickness of his eyes, his mother buys medicine and takes it to Santa Lucía who gives her blessing, and the child gets well.

They say the lightning struck the church in Oxchuk, and it was the fault of Santa Lucía. But then a few years ago it struck our church. And that was the fault of Santo Tomás. He is very strong.

"I am going to see how she will pay for that!" said Santo Tomás.

And in ten years a storm came and broke the tower of our church. There was a meeting of the principales. They said, "Let's sell the cattle of Santa Lucía so that we can build a new church." The tower was struck another time. All the married men had to contribute forty pesos each. We made it out of metal this time, because Santo Tomás is very strong.

On a conscious level, most people know that the earth is round, and that the sun revolves around it, but the motivating power behind natural phenomena is still conceived in personalized terms. One informant, when asked why the sun rises and sets, ventured cautiously, "I have heard that our Father, the Sun, revolves and that he goes down below the earth. But

I do not know if it is so. I just heard that in a story told." He then referred back to the story of K'oš, the younger brother who took over the task of carrying the sun from his elder brother, to explain how the sun's movement started.

Misfortunes caused by lightning, winds, and drought are explained as failures in social relations among people of the community or between the members of the community and the spirits. Restraint in their own conduct, fulfillment of their ceremonial obligations, and show of respect to the spirits are the only safeguards against such casualties.

CARING FOR THE LORD SPIRITS OF THE CHURCH

The relationships established with the spirits of the church contrast to those with the spirits of the heaven in the following ways: First, the upkeep and maintenance of the spirits of the church is delegated to appointed representatives, the mayordomos, who carry the burden for the community; "all the people of the world," on the other hand, are responsible at all times for avoiding behavior which would incur the wrath of the sun and moon. Second, the obligations to the spirits of the church are standardized, while those to the spirits of heaven are ill-defined and involve avoidance of offense rather than positive expectations. Third, duties toward the church spirits are performed in repetitive events following the calendrical cycle of fiestas, while obligations to the spirits of the heaven are fulfilled sporadically, as during an eclipse of the moon or a drought.

The major strategy in dealing with the spirits of the church is to give them a fiesta. Big fiestas are associated with the big four saints. These fiestas have been the responsibility of the top mayordomos, called kobraria, and until 1966, of the alfereces. Big fiestas also occur on the Day of the Dead, the Day of Santiago, the Day of San Pedro and San Pablo, the Day of the Kings, and during Easter Week. The pattern of fiestas will be described first, followed by a detailed description of the inauguration of the alfereces, witnessed in 1965 before the institution was abolished the following year, and the fiestas of Santiago and Easter Week.

Religious fiestas occur in an annual cycle of ceremonies based on the Catholic calendar. In Tzoʔontahal the Maya calendar no longer exists, even in the twenty-day cycle that constituted a month found in the neigh-

boring towns of Oxchuk, Larraínzar, and Chenalhó. The ceremonial calendar is given in Table 28.

TABLE 28. Ceremonial Calendar

| | Big fiestas | | Small fiestas |
Date	Fiesta	Date	Fiesta
Mar. or		Jan. 20	Tatik San Karalampio
Apr.	Tatik Kušibal	May 6	Tatik San Migel
Apr. 29	Tatik Martil	May 15	Tatik San Isigre
July 25	Tatik Santiagú	May 26	Tatik Spiritu Santú
Aug. 29	Tatik San Pransiskú	June 11	Tatik San Antonió
Nov. 29	Santuʔ	June 29	San Pegro-San Pablú
Dec. 13	Meʔtik Santa Luciá	July 15	Tatik Korasón
		July 20	Tatik San Huan
		Oct. 2	Meʔtik Rosario
		Nov. 12	Meʔtik Guadalupe
		Dec. 12	Tatik Santo Tomás
		Dec. 25	Meʔtik Paskú, Tatik Ninyo

In every fiesta drums and flutes are played, liquor is drunk, candles
burned, and church bells rung. During a big fiesta, which continues for
three days rather than for a single day, these additional activities are
added: contributions of 5 pesos per household are collected, the church is
adorned with flowers and greens, mass is held (this may occur in minor
fiestas as well if the priest happens to be present), a common meal is prepared for the mayordomos, and the people celebrate with firecrackers,
saints' processions, dancing, house fiestas in the homes of the alfereces
when they were still being installed, and a fiesta in the houses of the kobraria with a bull slaughtered for the meal.

During fiestas, time is measured in liters of liquor consumed and in cigarettes. The liquor, or "gift of the gods," is the basic element of all fiestas
and assures the participants that the celebration will be successful. Safeguards were built into the management of the fiesta in the role of *alisiles,*
who used to act as attendants to the alfereces and who watched to see that
the alfereces and the guitarists did not get so drunk that they could not
perform.

The following story about the origin of liquor illustrates its great importance to the fiesta.

Well, hear now how liquor first appeared. They were looking and look-
ing for a bullfighter. But there was none to be found. There was no one
drunk enough to make a fiesta. With no one to make a fiesta, there was
no fiesta. Therefore Santa Lucía and Santiago wanted to make a fiesta.
Santa Lucía said, "There is no one to make a fiesta. I better go take a
bath. When the water comes to wash me, then we can have a fiesta. It is
because now you are very frightened. You cannot mount on horseback.
No one will fight the bull because there is no liquor. You are not prepared
because you have to have a liter of trago."

"Good," said Santiago. After Santa Lucía and Santiago spoke they took
the water from Santa Lucía's bath and took out of it one liter of trago.
They distributed one liter to all and we changed. They built a beautiful
corral and everyone in the town gathered.

Well, when they had arrived, they gave a little liquid in the little cup.
After drinking a little, it gave strength. Well, everyone changed greatly.
Those who drank the trago found strength with each drink. But since
many drank, no one got drunk. They finished one liter and then another,
but no one got drunk. "Better get another," said someone. They got one
more liter, and with this they began the fiesta. One after another mounted
on horseback, and fought the bull. Thus they fought, one horse tied to an-
other. How they fought that fiesta! Thus they went on, getting more and
more drunk, until the women hid it.

It is thus that liquor appeared by the grace of our patron God. It is for
this reason that we say in the pat?o?tan "the washings of his legs and of
his arms our saint and leader Jesus Christ, the great master holy Jesus
Christ, Santiago, Santa Lucía. So we gather at the door, our clay, our
mud." We speak these words because of the liquor, because God gave the
trago only by washing himself, only by his powerful urine. There was no
trago for the old forefathers because the washings were given to their
offspring. So it is that liquor appeared according to this story. Later it was
related in the pat?o?tan. Now it is the custom for everyone.

This story is somewhat confused since it is Santa Lucía who took the
bath and Jesus Christ who is given the credit. Others have told me that
the first liquor appeared when Jesus was taken from the cross and his

body was washed. The confusion may come not from error, but from an identification of the patron saints with Jesus. The importance of the story is that liquor, as the gift of the gods, is the medium for releasing people from their fears.

The small fiestas are the responsibility of only the two mayordomos, the elder and the junior, who are assigned to the saint. They ring the church bells, light the candles, and play the drum and flute until noon. In the large fiestas all the mayordomos are active, as well as the fiscal and the priest, the prayer-reciters, and formerly the alfereces. The entire pueblo participates in the mass given at the large fiestas and assembles to "see the saints" when they emerge in the procession.

The proceedings of the fiesta take place in the church and the church yard, the house of the cofrade of the major saint whose fiesta it is, the plaza, and formerly, the house of the alférez of that saint. In each of these domains different sets of actors are tied together by acts performed in carrying out responsibilities to the saints. The chain of command is established in each setting: in the church the mayordomos are directed by the fiscal; in the household the eldest nakawane orders the b'alnial and receives the visitors with the pat?o?tan. He is the master of ceremonies, as in all household gatherings, and his female counterpart is the woman speaker. She orders the women helpers in the preparation of the food, which is then served by the b'alnialetik. Religious officials hold ceremonies in their houses only after they have served five times in office.

In the household, religious ceremonies replicate civil ceremonies. A mouthwash is served, followed by coffee and bean tamales, another round of mouthwash, an offering of thanks for the liquor by the nakawane, and a serving of liquor. Musical instruments played in the household differ from those of the church yard: a guitar and gourd rattle provide the accompaniment to the drinking episode here. Fiestas held in the household of the alfereces were terminated with a dance.

Choosing and Installing the Alférez

Formerly the alfereces were the chief figures in maintaining the fiesta cycle. During my stay in 1964 and 1965 the officials were experiencing more and more resistance from those named to undertake the post. Finally, in 1966 the officials were able to recruit only from the growing division of Ahk'olnantik. There had always been two representatives from each side in the past, and the role was a symbol of the division and of its unity in ceremonial occasions. I predicted at that time that the institution would not survive because the imbalance in representation destroyed the structural premises of the role. When I returned for a brief visit in 1967 I was told that indeed 1966 was the last year the alfereces were inaugurated and that the institution had died. I would expect this to further weaken the structural opposition of the dual division. This case of structural breakdown is a good example of the behavioral feedback one can analyze with an equilibrium model of change. The following description of the fiesta is based on an inauguration I witnessed in 1965.

Formerly, the role of alférez involved both civil and religious functions. At the time that I observed the institution in action, it provided the ceremonial link between the civil and the religious hierarchies, but the duties of the alfereces were only ceremonial. In the words of one informant, their function was "to put on a good fiesta, to drink, and to dance, and to bear the sacred banners in processions."

The alférez was chosen by the four judges and the four regidores with the help of the president and the síndico. About two months before the installation of a new alférez, which occurred during the fiesta for the one of the four saints with which he was associated, the civil officers sent out the first policeman and the martomorey, or elder policeman, to bring in the appointed alférez. The martomorey greeted the alférez with the pat?o-?tan, and the appointment was made known. The standard response of the chosen alférez was, "I don't want it. I have no money. I cannot bear it [the post]." The martomorey and first policeman said, "Good, we shall return another day." On their return, if the nominee still refused to accept the post, they brought him to the jail, where they left him for two or three days before bringing him before the civil officials. There they "took his heart" to see if he would accept. A fairly standardized conversation ensued:

Nominee: "I do not want it; I cannot bear it."

Judge: "By force you must receive it. You do not have to give as much. You only have to receive the sacred banner."

Nominee: "But if I don't give a fiesta, the pueblo will speak badly of me."

Judge: "It is not important what the pueblo says. Pardon us, let us drink a little trago."

[*All the officers drank, contributing jointly to buy the liquor. Each officer took one sip from the measure, but the nominee drank the entire measure on each round. When he became intoxicated, he yielded to the persuasions of the officials and agreed.*]

Nominee: "Good. I am going to see how it goes."

[*The two regidores carried the new alférez to his house.*]

The activities of the alférez in preparation for the fiesta during which he was installed in his post are summarized below.

Making pottery. *The new alférez prepared for the fiesta by organizing his household to make the pottery that was to be sold to cover the expenses. His brothers and brothers-in-law went on horseback bringing fifteen or twenty loads of clay. The women got the sand, carrying it back with the tumpline. The men went on horseback again to collect the limestone temper, which the women would grind and mix with the clay for cooking pots. The next week, the alférez went with a gift of 2 pesos' worth of bread and one liter of liquor to ask the woman who knew how to make large ollas, pots in which the festal foods are cooked, to help him. The sisters and sisters-in-law of both the alférez and his wife joined together to grind the temper and mix the clay. In addition to the special large pots, the women made bowls, soup plates, and water jugs to sell.*

When the pottery was ready to be fired, the men brought the wood and the women tended to the firing. After the pots were fired, the men sold them in the markets of San Cristóbal or Comitán. They usually made about 26 pesos per dozen, which netted them about 500 pesos.

Learning the patʔoʔtan. *Each evening, an elder of the family of the alférez who knew the patʔoʔtan, or prayer, came to teach him. This*

*might have been his father, an uncle, or a godparent who had already
served as alférez.*

Buying festal foods. *The following items were purchased in the
neighboring Ladino town of Himšol: 120 pesos' worth of bread; one-half
a slaughtered bull for 600 pesos; 6 almudes of beans; 10 kilos of coffee;
and 5 pesos' worth of brown sugar. If the alférez owned a bull, he slaughtered it and sold one half.*

Preparing liquor. *The alférez rented a still and, with the help of
his father and brothers, distilled 7 garafones (126 liters) of liquor, using
brown cane sugar.*

Preparing special clothing. *The following items were purchased
or bought: jacket for 50 pesos; shirt for 55 pesos; hat for 30 pesos; pair of
boots for 32 pesos; red waistband for 16 pesos; and red kerchief for 9
pesos.*
  *The hat was made by a man in the town. When the alférez went to ask
him to do him the favor of making a hat, he brought 1 peso's worth of
bread, 1 liter of trago, and 40 cents' worth of chocolate. The alférez borrowed black leather leggings and a black towel. To each of those who lent
him clothing, he gave 1 liter of trago, 1 peso's worth of bread, and 40
cents' worth of chocolate. When he returned the clothing, he gave the
same gifts.*

The installation of the new alférez. *During the four days of the
fiesta of the saint with which he was charged, the new alférez was initiated into his duties in office. In taking on each of the functions assigned
to him, that "dialectical connection between the actor and his part, the person and his roles or status or office," was effected (Fortes 1959:57).*

The first day (Paswamal). *On the first day of every large fiesta,*
Paswamal *(literally, "to make the boughs or decorations"), the women of
the household and the sisters and sisters-in-law of the new alférez and his
wife gathered in his house to cook the food. The men slaughtered the*

bull, and the women prepared beef stew and made tortillas and coffee. The floor of the house was strewn with pine needles.

At noon, two alfereces led the procession of police, judges, síndico, and principales as they collected money for the fiesta. The alfereces held the banners with an embroidered cloth. The movements of the procession were initiated with church bells ringing and rockets set off by two junior mayordomos as they left the church and as they arrived at and left each of the seven "stands," locations marked by crosses at the intersections of the major streets of the village. When they arrived at each stand, the alfereces stood holding the banners and the other civil and religious officials sat on the side of the road, smoking and drinking. The five police scattered, going to collect 5 pesos from each household. When they returned, the síndico noted the amount received and the principales held the money in a tin tray.

When the group arrived back at the church at two-thirty, the alfereces put the banners in the rear corner of the church. They went to the altar rail, knelt and prayed, crossed themselves and kissed first the image of Santiago, then all the other images. The music of drum and flute was played in the church courtyard, and firecrackers were set off. A table was set up to the right of the door of the church, and there the money was counted. As the officials came out of the church, they made the rounds of the seated officials, greeting them with the pat?o?tan. The officials arranged themselves in the traditional pattern: The fiscal and town treasurer stood at the table counting the money before the assembled officials. The principales and judges, stood immediately before the table watching the fiscal and treasurer; their position indicated their guardian role. Bills of the same denomination were set in piles under stones to prevent their blowing away, and then tied into bundles with palm fronds. When all the money had been counted, the principales put it in a manila folder, and the treasurer wrapped this in a red kerchief. The striking of the church bells announced the end of the counting.

All the relatives—the yermanotak, or "brotherhood" group, including bi-laterally-extended brothers and brothers-in-law and their wives, compa-dres, and neighbors—were invited to partake of the meal in the afternoon at the houses of the alfereces. The nakawanehetik and b'alnialetik, rela-

tives whose positions in this household fiesta are established on the basis of their age and experience in office, took up the established positions for these roles in the house of the new alférez. The first nakawane blessed the liquor; two bottles were measured into shot glasses and served to the guests. After this the meal was served.

The second day (Wišpereš). All the nakawanehetik appointed for the new alférez gathered in his house at nine o'clock in the morning to drink. The first and second nakawanehetik went to the cabildo to ask the judge and president when the new alférez must take out the holy banner. The president replied that it would be in two days. The question was rhetorical: everyone knew that the ceremony of taking out the banners occurred on the fourth day of the fiesta, and the day itself was named Šlok' Krus, taking out of the cross (the banner has a cross adorning the staff). What was being communicated to the civil officials by the question was the recognition of responsibility to the new alférez by the nakawanehetik. In the afternoon of this day, another meal of beef stew and tortillas was served to the same guests assembled on the previous day.

The third day (Sk'ak'halel Sk'in). At cock's crow the parents of the new alférez awakened him. Gathered in the house were the woman speaker, the guitarist, and the nakawanehetik. Under the direction of the woman speaker, the alférez' wife helped him put on his clothing, and the guitarist accompanied this procedure with music. When he was dressed, the new alférez danced a turn before the assembled guests to show his new clothing, and reviewed the patʔoʔtan with the nakawanehetik who had taught him. He then went with his guitarist to raise his companions. First he went to the third alférez and awakened him. He greeted the nakawane of the third alférez with the patʔoʔtan, and was invited to sit down; he was served coffee and bread, followed by a mouthwash. The third alférez dressed, and after the two were served liquor they danced a turn. In this same fashion, the new alférez raised all of his companions. The assembled group went to the cabildo.

The nakawanehetik and the b'alnialetik, after drinking coffee and eating bean tortillas, went to collect the things needed to receive official

guests. *They borrowed benches from neighbors; they cut juniper and pre-*
pared the resting place for the sacred banner; they borrowed seed-gourd
rattles and two tables, and they adorned the house with pine branches and
fruit. In the afternoon, all the relatives, the compadres, and the neighbors
were invited. Two alisiles were appointed (this term is probably a Tzeltal
rendition of alguacil, *in Spanish an office corresponding to high bailiff or*
peace officer). The alisiles were charged with watching to see that neither
the new alférez nor either of his two guitarists got too drunk to carry out
his functions.

The two alisiles called out the women to dance, first asking permission
of the woman speaker. The dance was the most important act in the set of
performances on the third day, which was sometimes referred to as the
"afternoon of the big dance." The dance was a highly charged event be-
cause the women were for the first time cast in a public role. Fear and
shame, the two conditioning mechanisms of socialization in Tzo?ontahal,
had to be overcome when the women became involved in the dance. Spe-
cial precautions were taken: the alisil formally requested the woman
speaker to take the women out:

> *Lord, women who nursed us, give pardon with God, the Virgin*
> *Mother. Give holy pardon mother and father with God and with the*
> *Virgin Mother. We have gathered here, collected together your child,*
> *your offspring, where it is not very pretty, not very flavorful, at the*
> *door of your holy poverty, holy suffering, for the holy office, the holy*
> *prayer. Again our clay, our mud comes to speak here to the mothers*
> *who nursed, who give us fear and embarrassment.*

Then the altereces took off their hats and kerchiefs and brought them to
the women. This act was described by an informant: "The women cover
their heads with the kerchief and put on the hat. The girls want the hand-
kerchief and the hat of their husbands in order not to be ashamed to be
seen by a boy. They want the kerchief to hide their faces. If they do not
want the hat, it is when they are mature women and do not have shame.
The wives of the altereces do not have shame because it is their job." The
use of the kerchief which was draped over their head, partially covering

their eyes, the posture of dance in which they clasped their hands at their stomach-band—all of these manifested the shame that they were overcoming. Whether they really felt the shame or not was irrelevant since they were being judged in terms of their behavior. The wives circled around with a two-step, their eyes downcast and their hands clasped over their stomach-bands, while their husbands stepped up and down in place in a ring around them, shaking the gourd rattle and joking.

When the dancing was terminated, a joking session was initiated by the naḳawane. The signal for this was the lighting of the first round of cigarettes. Smoking, like drinking, was required of everyone and was rarely indulged in privately. The women sometimes put aside the cigarettes, but they had to accept them. At midnight a meal of bean tortillas and coffee was served.

The fourth day (Šlok' Krus). *The four regidores arrived early in the morning to raise the alférez and take him to the cabildo to receive the oath. In this function the regidores were referred to as* personaetik *or "persons." The Spanish term* persona *signifies the exterior appearance by which men of merit were distinguished, and in its Latin derivation* persona *is the mask by which role is indicated. I think it is in the sense of assuming a new identity that the Indians incorporated the term as a reference for specific roles assumed by the regidores at this time. The alcaldes, or judges, were on this day referred to as* koronaetik, *or colonels. This reference term evoked the military ranking system, as did also the term alférez or captain, and established the relative ranking of the two sets of officials in the cabildo on the day of receiving the banners. The alfereces were given titles to indicate the order of their entry into office. The seating order of the four in the cabildo followed the succession pattern, with the first to take office sitting nearest to the door.*

The new alférez, with two of his four escorts on either side, sat on the visitor's bench along with the higher officials, themselves once alfereces. The first regidor, or persona, addressed the first judge with the pat?o?tan. The fourth regidor distributed a liter of trago to the assembled officials, first to the judges, then the president and síndico, the alfereces, the person-

aetik̗, and finally the new alférez. The first judge spoke with each set of officials, saying, "God, we have finished the gift of your ancestors"; and the departing alférez said, "So it is, elders."

The new alférez took his banner from the table and went outside with the four personaetik̗, followed by the other alfereces carrying their banners, and by the president, the síndico, and the k̗oronaetik̗, who carried their staffs of office. They went in a procession to the home of the outgoing alférez; at the fence of his house, they lined up their banners in the stand provided. The wife of the outgoing alférez, with the nak̗awane, brought burning incense from the house and placed it before the banners. The first nak̗awane exchanged the pat?o?tan with the first judge. In a column of paired officials, they approached the house and seated themselves on the porch. The judges went to the first nak̗awane and greeted him with the pat?o?tan; then, standing at the door of the interior of the house, the first judge repeated the greeting with the woman speaker.

The nak̗awane ordered the b'alnialetik̗ to bring the fermented corn gruel. After it was served, the b'alnial put a small table in the middle of the porch, covered it with the embroidered cloth, and set two liters of liquor on it. The nak̗awane rose and gave the pat?o?tan to the first judge. He asked permission of the woman speaker to drink, and when this was granted, the b'alnialetik̗ measured out and served the trago.

After the two bottles of trago had been consumed, the alisil took the wife of the outgoing alférez, and the dance began, following the same pattern described above. The dancing was followed by a procession to the church in which the new alférez carried the banner, thereby asserting his succession to the office. The old alférez remained in his house with his assembled guests.

In the movement of the banners by the alfereces, one could see the symbolic military behavior: the procession to the house was a mock column of march; the military titles of the alfereces and the "colonels" were carried out in vocative and referential titles in the prayers. The handling of the banners was always done with show of sacred respect: cloths were used to handle them, and they were always set carefully in appointed places so the pole never touched the ground; incense was set nearby when they were unattended. In the cermonial movment from the houses of the al-

*fereces to the cabildo, back to the house of the former alférez, and finally
to the church, the old alférez was divested of his post and the new alférez
took it on. The theme of continuity and change were exemplified by the
rotation of this office just as in the case of the other ceremonial offices. The
dialectic of role identification could be seen in the final act of relinquish-
ing the role: the old alférez wept at the altar as he thanked the gods for
permitting him to carry through the task. In serving in this office, it was
said that the alférez "learns some understanding and speaks with understanding." He became eligible to be nakawane in the household celebrations of others; he learned the commitments to office, the fiesta needs in
terms of liquor, wood, and money for food. This office, more than any
other, was a rite de passage for acquiring the skills and becoming eligible
for higher ceremonial office in the household, church, and cabildo settings.
Those who had served in office became aware of its significance, and, despite the resistance and finally outright refusal of young men to accept the
post, they were convinced of its importance in the comunal life.*

*An attenuated version of the post of alférez was retained in the barrio
of Madronal for the fiesta of San Antonio. Those who had passed in the
office in the center referred slightingly to the post in the barrio, pointing
out that the alfereces there did not spend as much money, that their clothing was not as elaborate, their pat?o?tan shorter, and the meal given at
the house less adequate since they did not kill a bull and then did not
have as many nakewanehetik. All these components combined to give the
office the prestige it still possessed in the eyes of the villagers. The value of
the office was clearly measured in the costs involved; the very factor
(money) which made it hard to get recruits gave luster to the post. Scal-
ing down the costs in an attempt to make the post more attractive to those
nominated, would probably have diminished its significance and led to a
quicker demise.*

OTHER FIESTAS

The acts described for the inauguration of the alfereces are carried out
for each of the major fiestas: those in honor of Sacramento, Virgin Lucía,
San Pedro the Martyr, and San Francisco. The only exceptional acts occur

during the fiesta of Santiago and Easter Week. These are described briefly
below.

Fiesta of Santiago. *On the third day of the fiesta the new alférez
went to "raise" his three companions. First he went to the house of the
alférez who had recently served. There he greeted the nakawanehetik
with the pat?o?tan, drank a measure of liquor, and went with the third
alférez to the house of the second alférez. The same greeting was exchanged with the nakawanehetik, and the two drank another measure of
liquor. They went to the house of the first past alférez, and there they exchanged a greeting with the nakawanehetik in which they comment on
the "flowery and flavorful" fiesta for "our old saint and commander, the
great angel man Señor Santiago." From there they mounted their horses
and began the races.*

*Each of the horseback riders was given a quarter-liter of liquor and a
cigarette. Three liters of liquor were distributed at the holy cross (site of a
cross no longer standing). The four alfereces stood at the cross, removed
their hats, which they stacked one on top of the other, and put them
nearby. The four took turns kissing and bowing before the others. They
said, "Holy good afternoon," and gave two holy thanks for the gift (the
liquor), embracing each other. After the four alfereces greeted each other
and the three alisiles, the leader of the races gave the pat?o?tan with the
past alférez:*

> *And good day. What do you see, Mam compadre? You are alive,
> word of God this holy afternoon. You have not heard of any sickness
> behind our heart this holy afternoon, Mam compadre? There is no
> fear, shame, Mam compadre. Give another pardon Lord with Virgin.
> Give me holy pardon, Mam compadre. See us gathered before you
> seated our bodies, our clay, our mud, Mam compadre. What can we
> do, what can we make here where we have arrived again? Speak,
> raise godchild, afternoon of holy fiesta godchild afternoon of holy
> child's fiesta of him our saint, our commander. What can we do,
> what can we make when we have found this holy hour, this holy day
> of our lord Santiago Calixtro, for our patron god? Where now is the
> water of her legs, the water of her hand [liquor], our saint, virgin*

mother? There is nothing but holy suffering, holy penitence here before our sinful clay, our sinful mud. Again we gather here where others have gathered before in the company of our ancestors, the holy alisiles with the liquor bearers. It is your burden the four of you, the holy work, your holy office for his godchildren again give his godchild at the gate of the door of the church our saint, our keeper, the great father Señor Santiago Calixtro for our patron God, again we gather before this doorway our bodies, our clay, our mud with the holy alisil with our costume. Only give a little liquor, the gift of your mothers, your fathers, mam compadre.

The two alfereces of Ahk'olnantik received one liter of liquor, and the same quota was given to the two alfereces of Alannantik. They drank some and poured off most of the measured shots into the bottles carried by the liquor bearers; then they smoked a cigarette. When they finished this, they raised their banners and entered the plaza on horseback. The bell of the church struck as they entered. About four o'clock, two columns of horsemen formed, one behind the two alfereces of Alannantik and one behind the two alfereces of Ahk'olnantik. One year I observed thirty-eight horsemen from Ahk'olnantik and fifteen from Alannantik. The imbalance in representation for the two sides of the dual division grew sharper each year as the population increased in Ahk'olnantik. Before starting the race, the four alfereces crossed themselves, facing first the church, then the cabildo. As the race began, the mayordomos played the drums and flute in the church yard and the nakawanehetik sat in front of the church wall.

When the racers made four passes across the plaza, they came to drink another trago and smoke two cigarettes in front of the church. At the end of the race, they again drank and smoked the same measured quantities as the pat?o?tan was recited by the leader of the races.

On Sk'ak'halel Sk'in, the same procedures occurred as on the previous day. The final act of the fiesta took place when, after the races, the alfereces dismounted and the nakawanehetik went to them and drank one liter of liquor before the leader of the races. The two most recently appointed alfereces entered the cabildo, where the banners were laid out on the table among orange and lemon leaves. The president, síndico, two judges, and the regidores were seated in their customary places; the alfereces sat on the visitors' bench. The two former alfereces went before the two newly appointed alfereces and gave an account of what was going to take place, instructing them on "how they should make a fiesta."

When the two former alfereces entered, they went to the president, saying, "How does the Lord see you alive on this holy afternoon?" They then went to the síndico and the regidores and ended with the judges, exchanging a pat?o?tan.

The alfereces went out, mounted their horses, and were handed the banners by the regidores. The two old alfereces received their banners first. All four made the sign of the cross, first facing the cabildo, then the church, and then rode in procession, preceded by the flutist, two drum players, and a guitarist, and followed by the other horsemen. They stopped before the church, dipping their flags, first toward the church and then the cabildo. The president, síndico, and first judge walked across the plaza to the church as the church bells were rung, and all the musical instruments played—the marimba, bell, drums, and flute. The alfereces dismounted and put their banners in the church.

The final day, called Lahinbahel Sk'in, *was spent sobering up, putting things back in order, and returning borrowed items.*

Although Santiago is not one of the major saints, a major celebration is given in his honor because of the high value placed on horsemanship in this community. Before the construction of the Pan-American Highway in 1953 everyone in town had horses which were used to carry the pottery to market. Riding skills were developed in the free-swinging *macho* (manly) style of northern Mexico's cowboys. Even today when horses are not as economically useful the horse culture has survived. The running of the horses in the fiesta is not competitive. Each rider does his best to tear at high speed across the plaza, but there is no specific goal. Since the drunken riders often fall and are injured, some of the excitement is based on the potential danger.

The behavioral data on which the analysis of rituals depends are included because they provide a basis for comparison with neighboring towns and explain small-scale change over short periods of time. The contextual description of behavioral details may eventually overcome the lack of replicable events available to laboratory science. By specifying all the conditions of the ritual, it is possible to separate the unique from the patterned components. At one level, the analysis consists in indicating the repetitive patterns and the continuity of beliefs which these exemplify. At another level, rituals can be analyzed as psychodramas in which the individual adopts a social role. The dialectical connection between the new official and his role is established in the obligations he carries out.

When people are asked "why" something is done, they continually shift between the social and psychological levels. "We do this because it was the custom of our ancestors," they will frequently say. When pressed further, they reduce their level of response to the individual, saying, "The women don their husband's ceremonial hat because they wish to hide their face because of embarrassment." Both answers are true interpretations, differing only in the level of social complexity at which the enquiry is directed. One can go farther in elaborating the latent significance of the ritual acts. To continue with the same example, the dance drawing the wife into a public performance was performed because, as one informant said, "she too has done work for the fiesta" (she made pottery to raise the money). The dance gains the favor of the saints, as is demonstrated in the Virgin's tactics with the Devil, and in the curing rituals with the spirits of the house and of the springs. Dancing establishes a relationship to the group: the women dancing in the center of the circle formed by their husbands revolving around them are incorporated as an integral part of a sacred social unit.

Rituals provide a key to the psychic dynamics of the group since they deal with these explicitly. The ritual acts are predicated on expected individual responses. For example, since liquor overcomes embarrassment,[5] it

5. Bennett and Zingg (1937) have stated the even more dramatic social significance of liquor among the Tarahumara. Social intercourse in this mountain tribe is impossible without liquor. Conditioned as they are in isolated nuclear family groups to retreat at the sign of an outsider, the Tarahumara need something to relax their embarrassment and fear in large gatherings. Landa (Tozzer 1941) has commented at length on the compulsory drinking at ceremonials of the Yucatecan Maya.

is served when the expectations are that the individual will feel embarrassment. These occasions formerly occurred when the company arrived at the house of the alférez before the dance and when the alfereces mounted their horses. Cigarettes signal relaxation, and when the first round of cigarettes is served in the house setting, the company abandons formal restraints and, led by the chief nakawane, indulges in joking.

Carnival and Easter Week. Carnival has changed over time more than any other religious ceremonial in the town. Until five years ago, a group of masked jokers visited the houses of the captains of the fiestas. They wore Ladino clothing, including vest, pants, and shoes, and they hid their faces behind masks or painted them black. They danced a "Ladino dance" (paired couples), first in the church and then in the houses of the alfereces. While dancing, they made sexual allusions about unmarried women. Their joking emphasized their strangeness to the villagers; for example one of the jokers might say, "You do not know what type of person I am. An airplane made me." They carried small stuffed animals which they made "cry." Pretending they were the husband of a woman, they would go to her and tell her to take care of her "baby." The woman speaker would sometimes respond to their jokes, saying, "Who are you? You are not good looking, you little black boy. You must be from Germany or from the other side of the water. Maybe you are from Patwitz or Yetawitz, and your father is kurik." People say the custom was discontinued because it was too expensive to give liquor to the jokers.

Another carnival custom which has been lost is the "common meal" of squash on the five Fridays of Lent. Formerly the wives of the four kobraria brought squash from hot country, cooked it, and brought two gourds each to the church. The assistant divided it, giving two pieces to each of the mayordomos. This custom was stopped during the typhoid epidemic of 1928 and has never been resumed because, it is said, the people did not want to lose work time. These changes may be a response to the priest's attempts to modify some of the excesses of carnival. Whether or not this is so, the people prefer to attribute change to their own decisions.

The events of Easter Week as recounted by an informant are outlined below.

Monday: Nothing

Tuesday: Nothing

Wednesday: All the mayordomos gather at the church. Some go to carry wood for the cross while others look for flowers to make a "bed" for Jesus, Tatik Eskipulas, *to lay Him on after he has been crucified. The mayordomos arrange the table on which he will lie very beautifully. They tie boughs of evergreen on all four sides. Some of the flowers [a small variety of orchid which was possibly of some importance in pre-Catholic rituals] are very fragrant. When all is arranged well, they take out a box so that Tatik Eskipulas can lie where the flowers and branches are. They put this table at the foot of the cross. After the mayordomos have "planted" the cross, they adorn it with pine boughs. They put flowers on each arm of the holy cross. Then they drape it with the holy cloth* [the purple banner]. *At eleven o'clock some of the mayordomos begin to play the coronet, matraka, flute, and drum. Tatik Eskipulas arrives at the cross with the male and female prayer-maker.*

Thursday: Half of us finish making the cross, and the other half arrange the "prison" inside the church where Tatik Eskipulas will spend the night. After we make the prison, we make the Jew. We look for his pants and shoes, his hat and his tie, his mask, his gourd, his bag, his shirt, his cigarette. After we arrange him, we raise him with a rope in front of the church, and leave him hanging for the pueblo to see who killed Christ. Meanwhile, others put Tatik Eskipulas in prison. When night time arrives, four men with rifles watch Tatik Eskipulas to guard Him as the holy evening passes. The mayordomos gather at the church and play the sad flute and the old coronet. They play the matraka. At midnight they play the drum and coronet.

Friday: Very early in the morning of Friday, the four guards of God are changed as the dawn enters. All day, the guards will watch the Lord. They will see Him rise on the cross and descend from the cross. Then the four go to their house to drink a little liquor. At eleven o'clock in the morning the mayordomos will give a sign on the elder coronet, the elder matrake, and the sad flute and the drum. They will play three times to summon the townspeople instead of sounding the bell. When all the women and men arrive, they hear the prayer announcing that Tatik Eski-

pulas has risen on the cross. After they have seen Him rise, all the pueblo will go out. At two o'clock in the afternoon, they will again play the sad flute, the drum, the coronet, and the matrake. All the pueblo will collect and will make another prayer to see the Tatik Eskipulas lowered from the cross. When He is lowered, they take Him out on a procession with the priest, the prayer-makers, and all the men and women of the pueblo who will hold candles, and the four guards with rifles. The first mayordomo knows how to blow the old coronet, and another mayordomo knows how to blow the sad flute, and anther plays the drum, and another plays the old matraka. After the procession goes in the plaza, it returns to the church and leaves Tatik Eskipulas in the middle of the church. The mayordomos sit outside the church and drink a liter of trago, and then go to their homes.

Saturday of glory: Very early in the morning of Saturday, they give a prayer with the sad flute and drum, with the old trumpet and with the matraka. Three times it is sounded for the pueblo to gather and hear mass. After the mass, the judge goes to speak to the police to look for a horse to mount the Jew. When the horse arrives, they take the figure of the Jew down from the church and tie him on top of the horse. A mayordomo leads him by the bridle, and he goes out in the pueblo with the flute and drum to ask for contributions. Those who know fiesta [the curers] give fifty or twenty cents or if there is nothing, they give an egg. Afterward, they return to the church and the Jew is taken from the horse. The people set fire to his straw body. When they finish burning this, they check to see how much money they collected. All the mayordomos count the money in common. If there are twenty or thirty pesos, the mayordomos make a fiesta with drum and flute.

Sunday of Resurrection: Mayordomos gather and sweep church. After sweeping they play the music to open the mouth of the bell. After the mass, they go drink fermented atol with bean tortilla. They eat a hen or rooster to make a fiesta for our Holy Lord because he is resurrected and because all the town is happy. They give the mayordomos fermented atol to drink. Then they return to the church and take out the lord cross, take out the jail, and the bed where the Father Eskipulas slept.

The informant failed to mention the following actions which I observed:

1. In raising the figure of Christ on the cross, the four regidores, in this context called *apuštol* (probably from apostles), entered the church. Two of them stood at the head of the cross to receive the image raised from below by the other two.

2. The image was always handled with cloths so that no one's hand would be in contact with the surface.

3. The priest, standing behind a cloth screen, guided the figure up on the cross.

4. The priest gave a sermon about the significance of Easter and the life and death of Christ. He spoke of the crime of the Jews in killing Christ.[6]

In comparing the elicited and observed accounts, one can see clearly the censoring of the priest's role in the perception of the people. Even while the ceremony is in process, they ignore his appeals. For example, as the body of Christ was lowered from the cross, the priest exhorted the congregation to cry and give vent freely to their emotions in this most holy moment. There was no response from the audience, even after he waited several moments, pleading with them again not to feel embarrassment at their show of emotion, and becoming visibly annoyed at their impassivity. Finally, a woman dressed in Ladina clothing, rewarded him with the stylized wail of mourning.

Observation of the ceremony reveals evidence of attitude and belief coded in the staging, the costuming, the postures and gestures of respect or derision which cannot be elicited. Each element is an interpretative comment by those who direct and act the play. We are told that the Jew is the anti-Christ, but we learn that he is also a Ladino through his clothing, the cigarette, and the horseback ride. The Indians do not state that they castrate him in hoisting him upon the church, but their comments and ac-

6. Despite the fact that the Vatican had exonerated the Jews of the guilt for the murder of Christ the year before (1965), the priest spoke of the crime of the Jews. This time lag in communicating doctrine to the hinterlands would be an interesting problem to investigate.

tions betray the intent. As he is hauled up by ropes and hung from the bell tower "to show the world that he killed Christ," the mayordomos on the ground who are assisting those up in the bell tower jab him with long poles. In this horseplay they symbolically castrate him: I heard one mayordomo say, *"Me?čunun,"* (transvestite) as one well-directed blow struck Judas. On Saturday, he is let down and given a ride on horseback around town. Formerly riding a horse was the prerogative only of Ladinos in the department of San Cristóbal Las Casas (Colby and Van den Berghe 1961). Placing Judas on a horse possibly has a symbolic value in identifying him as one of the hated dominant group who asserted this privilege. As he rides around town, the mayordomos solicit gifts from the people. Everyone gives fruits except the curers, who donate money. This transaction may indicate an obligation they feel toward Judas as one source of their power over witchcraft-derived illnesses. The money is used to buy liquor, called the "washing of the arms and legs of our Lord Eskipulas." The drinking is mandatory for all the mayordomos who have participated in the hanging of Judas.

The Judas figure, which was the church's symbol of the hated Semite, is made to appear as the enemy of the Indians, the Ladino. He symbolizes the sexual license of Ladinos with Indian women, the oppression of Indians by Ladinos, and the killer of Christ. In retaliation, the Indian symbolically castrate and hang him, and finally burn his body, thus dramatically vanquishing the alien in their midst. So far as I know, the priest is unaware of the identification Indians make between the Jew and the Ladino. He prevented the ride from taking place the year I witnessed the Easter Week ceremonial on grounds that it was a pagan ritual; when he left town on Sunday, the mayordomos took Judas on his customary rounds.

The attitude toward Jesus, as the hero of the morality play, is ambivalent. Martyrdom is not the way to win in Indian society. The feeling is that power goes to the one who makes the sacrifice, and since Jesus was a Ladino sacrifice, they have more power than the Indians. During the Caste War in Chiapas in 1868, the Indians crucified an Indian youth in the hope that they would find a savior as powerful as Jesus. To this day, Indians of To?ontahal seem not to identify Jesus as one of themselves, and they show little personal concern with his fate in the reenactment of the Passion.

The ceremonies by which the Indians care for the spirits are Spanish introductions, but within these forms they have found a means of containing the powers of the spirits and making them work for the benefit of Indians. In the reenactment of the Passion they caricature and symbolically kill their own enemy, the Ladino, without his being aware of it. Through reformulation of introduced ideas and practices, the Indians have preserved a sense of the past in an idiom meaningful to themselves.

Chapter 9

The Competition for Power

Changes in the organization of the civil and religious hierarchies since the constitution of 1927 can be traced in a series of events remembered by members of the community. Their selection of significant events and the interpretation they make of them give the best clues to their response to change. In the remembrance of things past people structure their world and project expectations for the future. Behavior in these events lacks the controls operating in the formal rituals of the officials—age-graded authority, hierarchy, and a code of behavior which conceals the open show of power. The strategies employed in these organizational changes reveal other rules or transformation of the old rules characterizing social interaction.

The structure of roles in the civil and religious hierarchies has remained intact. What has changed are the bases for according prestige and authority and allocating roles. The pivotal positions in which change is occurring are the mediating roles between local and national power structures, specifically those of president and secretary in the civil authority and of fiscal and priest in the religious authority.

The contest for power and "control of the town" has centered in five blocks of competition: (1) the opposition of new young leaders with skills in speaking Spanish, literacy, and knowledge of the idiom of behavior in the national culture to the established succession of an age-dominated authority system; (2) the challenge by the civil authority to the control of the curers who rely on power derived from possession of an animal spirit; (3) the struggle for political power among factions based on new economic enterprises; (4) the contest among local caciques for domination; and (5) the conflict among religious functionaries. The series of events in which these contests have crystallized and brought about a reorganization of political relations is summarized for each of these conflict areas. Most of the events recorded below are transcriptions of informants' statements given in Tzeltal. I have chosen this method to show how the people interpret incidents and how this leads to cognitive restructuring.

THE CONFLICT AMONG CIVIL OFFICIALS

In the period of consolidation since the revolution, the crucial issue in determining the allocation of power among local civil authorities has been that of incorporating men who have special abilities to deal with external authority without upsetting an age-ranked system. Prior to the 1950s these skills were rare—in 1920 only four young men could sign their names and read. The civil careers of two men, Ceferino, a native of the town, and Augustín, a revistido Indian from Huistán, illustrate the different courses taken by this new leadership in the post-revolutionary period of the 1930s. Ceferino was included in the given structure of power while Augustín used his skills in dealing with Ladinos to gain personal power. Ceferino was one of the first four men of the town to learn to read and write. The civil authorities recognized his potential usefulness in the town hall, and succeeded in incorporating him in an honorific but powerless position as scribe. He described his introduction into local government:

After I got out of school, the town saw that I knew how to write. Formerly there was no one who knew how to write. In the town hall the judges and president needed someone to write down the contributions and the payment for the government agents. Therefore, when the civil authority changed in the new year, they talked to my mother. As was the custom then, four regidores came to "raise" me, bringing a bottle of trago as a gift for my mother. She did not drink it alone. Together with the regidores we finished the trago. After finishing the trago, the first regidor began to speak to my mother in the pat?o?tan, saying, "I am going to bring one of your children, one of your offspring to the place where we look and where we see [reference to town hall]. We ask this favor because he knows how to write. Therefore the judges and the president ordered me to come and raise him and take out his soil, his mud, for this duty for this obligation.

We shall go with your child, your offspring to pass the holy day, the holy year. Thank you, thanks to your heart that you permit your child, your offspring to go. Now we go to receive the holy post with all the elders. The spirit of your child, your offspring shall learn."

When the fourth regidor finished the pat?o?tan, my mother spoke: "Thank you, Take care of him. I do not want him to return to me drunk. He hasn't yet learned to drink."

I went out with two of the regidores on my right side and the other two on the left. When we arrived, the first judge spoke to us in the pat?o?tan: "You have brought before us our writer. It is well that you arrived with him. Enter and sit down."

I sat down in the middle of the regidores. When we sat down, the first judge and the president began to speak. All were gathered in the town hall. [Ceferino then listed all the civil officials by name, a feat of memory which I shall not repeat here.]

We sat down and they brought in two liters of trago. They began the pat?o?tan, and after the pat?o?tan the third regidor came to measure the trago. He gave the first measure to the president, the second to the first judge, the third to the second judge, the fourth to me, the writer. And I was not accustomed much to drink liquor. I took the trago and I drank it. It was killing me. It came out my nose. The judges and regidores saw my suffering when it came out my nose. They patted my back, and with some difficulty the trago went down. Thus with suffering and with trouble, I learned to drink trago. But then I got drunk. I felt drunk, and I told the judge and regidores that I was going to die. The first judge ordered the regidor to go with me to my house.

He said, "Go leave him in his house because his mother said that I should return him to his house. See that you hand over her poor son to his mother."

Since I did not have a wife—I was a bachelor—they gave me to my mother. My mother said, "Thank you." They ordered my mother to send me the next day because we had to see how another day passed.

When I left in 1925, I didn't return to the town hall until 1936 when the pueblo asked me to stay as president.

In the strategy of incorporating new leadership, these tactics are employed.

1. The four regidores are assigned the task of bringing the novice scribe to the town authorities. They are the official recruiters for civil and religious office.

2. The request is made to the parent of the appointed scribe in the formal speech of the pat?o?tan. The appeal is cast in terms of the sacred nature of the task with reference to the "holy" nature of the post to be undertaken on this "holy hour, holy day and holy year."

3. The contractual relationship is initiated as always with a drinking session. The scribe is introduced into the drinking order as fourth in rank. The officials show solicitude as he is taught to drink "the gift of the gods and the ancestors." Once the gift of liquor has been accepted, the recipient has no recourse except to fulfill the obligation.

These tactics, used also in other contractual arrangements, were inadequate to the task of inducting foreign Indians living in the township into the traditional hierarchy. In 1929, a Huistecan Indian, Augustín, who had worked as a laborer in a finca within the township, became president. Although he could not read, he was able to speak Spanish fluently. He succeeded in getting the first ejido grant under the land reform act of 1927.

During his term of office, Augustín was accused of abusing his authority on several occasions, as the following account shows:

When I was very young, my father told me about this land case. Augustín was president then. He tried to get land from my uncle's father-in-law, Juan. My uncle, Bartolo, defended his father-in-law's right to the land because he had good friends in Tuxtla. Augustín spoke Spanish very well, but he did not know how to read. Since my uncle knew how to read well, he gained the case. Augustín was angry. He invited all the curers to the town hall and ordered the police to bring in my uncle. My uncle was given something in a cup of liquor, and in three days he died.

Even if this story is untrue, or distorted because of the family relationship of the narrator and the victim, it reveals the sense of being exploited or abused by leaders from outside the community. Stories by other informants indicate that Augustín took advantage of his power as president. He was accused of charging high fines in court and pocketing the money. Finally a case against him was brought to the Ministerio Publico in the departmental capital. The denunciation is recounted by Ceferino, the scribe, who replaced him as president:

The court's decision was that Augustín had to return the three hundred and fifty pesos that he had forced out of Juan in the land case. Augustín claimed that it was difficult for him to pay the fine. He said he would pay it in installments. Juan wanted it right away. After a month, the money still was not handed over. I spoke to the Ministerio Publico who told Augustín to sell his cattle. The pueblo wanted to seize the cattle. Augustín got frightened, and said he would sell his cattle. He sold them. After this he never returned to work in the pueblo.

There were no killings in this affair. Eight days after he gave the money, Augustín came to the town hall with a pistol. I noticed it and said, "Better come in an register this pistol." He ignored this and spoke to the judge for a while.

I told a policeman, "Go get the pistol and register it." The policeman was afraid. I asked him, "Why are you afraid?" He said, "I am afraid." I said, "You have turned into a woman."

The policeman seized Augustín's arms. I went behind and took the pistol out of his hand. Augustín said, "Why are you taking my pistol? I have committed no crime."

I replied, "You came to bother the people here." I took away the pistol.

Augustín also knew how to wear a watch. His son bought it from a thief for one hundred and twenty-five pesos. We also took his watch because it was stolen. I told him, "Go look for work and earn money. The Ministerio Publico has given orders that you cannot continue working here. You cannot rob here any more."

He went away for two months, and then came back to get his things and moved to Teopisca.

Despite this successful denunciation, Augustín's son, Juan, tried to "get control of the town." He and the other Huistecans of the barrio of Yetawitz had formed a small *cacicazgo* (supporters of a cacique) of armed men. Because of their influence with departmental officials since the land grant, they had secured an order to reassign lots in the center, putting one family from Yetawitz in each block. The reaction of the townspeople to this "invasion" of barrio Indians was immediate and conclusive, as Ceferino's account reveals:

The owners of the house lots here objected to having their lots seized. They went to a lawyer in San Cristóbal, and they also had the help of the professor here. He was a good professor. We walked with the professor. The pueblo was united. We did not have fear. We were in accord with the principles. The people from Yetawitz went to another lawyer in San Cristóbal. They got an order that the people of the pueblo would have to admit the people of Yetawitz. We returned to the lawyer. He asked where these people were from. We said they were from Huistán. They were well armed. Because of this, we went to take over their arms.

When we arrived at their house, Juan asked, "What are you here for?"
We answered, "We came to get your rifles."

They refused to give them up, but we seized their property. We tied up the men and carried them up to the pueblo. We dragged them like dogs up to the jail and put them in.

They asked, "Why are you putting us in jail?" and we answered, "Tomorrow we will arrange the case."

Four police stayed there. The next morning I came to see them. They had planned to go to Las Casas, but we ordered the saddles taken off the horses that were in readiness. We tried them, and they no longer bothered the pueblo.

The Huistecan's attempt to seize power reveals several significant factors in the genesis of cummunity political institutions. In the 1930s in Chiapas, the land reform act of 1927 was taking effect. Translation of law into reality in the local community required the drive and leadership of the Indians themselves. Literacy and Spanish-speaking skills were of even greater importance than before. The Indians of the center who had not been forced to work in the fincas and who had sufficient resources to resist contact with the outside economy were not in a position to take a leadership role in the new political setting. As a result, it was the marginal Indians, outsiders who had come as did Augustín to work as *baldios* (laborers) on the finca near the town, that were the drivng force behind the demand for land. This was the basis for the new leadership in the early days of land reform. The ejido program, conceived of by Cárdenas as a basis for political development of the campesinos, (Brandenburg 1964) gave these marginal Indians the opportunity to rise to positions of influence in local government. The reluctance of the townspeople to take action against Augustín derived in part from fear, since he reputedly backed his use of force with witchcraft—the imported kind of witchcraft in which poisons are used instead of spiritual force.

Ceferino, the man who finally deposed Augustín, was a member of the traditional community, but because he had been impoverished by burying four members of his family in the typhoid epidemic of 1928, he had been forced to work in the fincas. There he had learned Spanish and some of the ways of the dominant society. His leadership potential had developed in the role of *caporal,* or gang leader of the pickers in the coffee finca, and he had been a leader in the trek of recruited laborers down to the fincas in Soconusco. Under the old authority structure, in which all officials including the president were recruited through the hierarchy, he would never have reached a prestigious position. But in this crisis, he was the only man willing to confront the incumbent and take over the operation of civil affairs.

Ceferino did not take advantage of the situation to emerge as a cacique himself. As he explained in his narrative, "The pueblo was united. We did not have fear. We were in accord with the principles." The way in which he had been introduced into the cabildo as scribe had successfully neutralized his own ambitions to attain power, if he had any. He accepted the ideal of a united pueblo, recognizing the authority of the principales.

The increasing scope and frequency of relationships between the nation and the locality since the revolution has emphasized the roles of president and síndico at the expense of the authority and control exercised by the principales. The ceremonial significance of the principales in rituals is retained as a symbol of continuity in the change of officials, but their functions have decreased. Their major responsibility is to hold the plate in which the contributions for the fiestas are deposited by the police. Formerly, the fact that the principales also held the money until it was spent lent dignity and prestige to this function. Now that the money is turned over to the treasurer, who also keeps the accounts, passing the plate gives them a sense of shame. When I asked why the principales lost authority, the first response was cast in terms of behavior: my informant, a former president, pointed out that it was because they did not attend the town hall every day. When I asked why they did not appear, the reply was reformulated in functional terms: they did not come because the laws and acts that are raised and interpreted in the town hall are written in Spanish, and the principales could not read or write. As a consequence, the balance of power has shifted to the posts of president and síndico, while the framework in which the officials act has remained.

CHALLENGE BY THE CIVIL OFFICIALS OF THE POWER OF THE CURERS

The autonomy of the highland Indian corporate community has rested on the retention of social control by local leaders. This local leadership, which has survived over four hundred years of domination by Spanish colonial and national rule, is based on power derived from two sources: (1) control over life and death by men who claim to possess an animal spirit and/or (2) ability to devine or predict the future, such as the calendar priests have (Nuñez de la Vega 1702:19).[1] The belief in power derived

---

1. Bishop Nuñez de la Vega repeatedly inveighs against the "maestros Nahualistas." This is summarized in an excerpt, which I have translated, from his book (1702:19):

> Almost two hundred years after the light of evangelism dawned, the Indians in most of the Kingdom of New Spain and Guatemala are found full of their primitive errors, superstitions, and misdeeds such that there is hardly a single pueblo where each year there are not deaths brought about by witches, and houses and families known to have, as an inheritance acquired from father to son, evil powers so abominable that they are viewed with great fear by the rest of the Indians. With only a glance and certain words, with which they invoke the Devil, they can end life or cause their victim to go mad with great pains and stupendous illnesses, and the result is that they inflict their rivals for very slight pretexts. We exile them and other spiritual performers from the church, and when the ministers and judges try to verify what happened to the sick ones, all

from animal spirits was probably influenced by the Toltec belief in nahualism, or transformation of people after death into animals (Calnek 1962:22). The Toltec belief originated in the period of Mexican influence but had many local indigenous manifestations (Foster 1944). The integration of the two systems of power was brought about by calendar priests controlling the distribution of animal spirits (Calnek 1962:19). The degree of retention of calendrical knowledge and of belief in witchcraft gives us one of the best indices of acculturation in the area.[2] In Tzo'ontahal there is no remnant of calendar divination for ceremonial or predictive use. However, witchcraft based on belief in animal spirits continues to be an important factor in the contest for power. The technique of secrecy, of presenting a united front in the face of attempts by the outside Ladinos to tamper with the local social control system, persists to this day in the town.

An endemic problem in communities dominated by belief in witchcraft is control over the evil power of witches. The traditional control system in Tzo'ontahal operated through the guardianship of three sets of power-holders who checked up on each other: the ancestors, the curers, and the judges. The guardianship of the ancestors consisted in preventing any child possessed of a swayohel from the devil from growing up to abuse his power and in keeping any evil spirits from entering the town. The curers,

---

the Indians, whether out of cowardice or deceit, withdraw their accusation or claims, so that it is impossible to convict the evildoers for punishment; and for lack of sufficient proof they cannot be punished, or if there is enough basis to put them in prison, they sometimes disappear and flee to another jurisdiction and hide, denying their place of origin or changing their name.

2. In Oxchuk, calendar experts with the ability to divine the future still set the days for carrying out Catholic fiestas according to the twenty-day Maya ceremonial cycle. Each of the spirits symbolizing the twenty days wielded the power of good or evil. This provided the basis for predicting. When Villa Rojas studied the town in the 1940s, elders of patrilineal lineages controlled the behavior of members by causing sickness brought by their *lab,* or animal spirit (Villa Rojas 1947). In San Pedro Chenalhó, the principales exercise power through their *wayhel,* or animal spirit (Guiteras Holmes 1961). Nahuales of leaders of the patrilineages and principales are feared and respected in Larraínzar, although there is a growing discontent with their oppressive control (Holland 1963). Men believed to have thirteen nahuales figure as guardians and avengers for individuals in Pinola society, although the Indians of this community no longer have a hierarchy of civil offices through which their prestige can be publicly validated (Hermitte 1964).

as the direct agents of the ancestors, guarded the streets of their own side
of the dual division. The judges, with the supervision of the principales,
were responsible for guarding against the abuse of power by the curers or
others possessing a swayohel in their review of witchcraft cases in the
town hall. The three sets of functionaries—ancestors, curers, and judges—
are classified in a lexicon of role function in the stem *me? . . tat . .* ,
common to the terms applied to them, me?tiktatik, me?iltatil, and me?e-
štateš.[3]

The system of control over the use of power has been in a state of
uneasy tension. In a series of incidents recounted below, the growing suspicion that the judges and the principales were not countering the witches
because of their fear of falling victim to them, and that the curers themselves were exercising the witchcraft becomes apparent.

In the following case, the system of checks and balances was upset by
the entry into the presidency in 1940 of Mam Nicolás, the leading curer of
Allannantik. Nicolás combined the skills of operating in the traditional
culture with those of dealing with the Ladino world. Despite the fact that
he was a graduate of the boarding school operating in the town in the
1930s, which had far more extensive effects in acculturation as well as
formal education than any prior school, he practiced curing. The case is
recounted by Ceferino, the scribe:

Formerly the dead president Mam Nicolás left at midday from the
town hall and went to his house where he ate a meal. A neighbor, Fran-
cisco, came to talk to him. They drank a half a liter of trago, and then
began to drink a second and got drunk. They began to say goodbye, and
Francisco left Nicolás' house. When Nicolás saw that Francisco went
out, he grabbed his shotgun. He saw that Francisco was now far away,
and he fired many shots. One got him right in his back. When Francisco
felt it, he shouted. The police heard him and went to get the judges who
came to see also. His [Francisco's] wife came. She raised his head and
cried when she saw he was dead. An elder sister brought a new mat to

3. The suffixes *-eš,* and *-tik* refer to pronominal forms, as in "you judges" and "our
ancestors." *-il* is an article, as in "the curers." In prayer, the ancestors may be addressed in
the second person, or the judges may be referred to with the first-person-plural possessive,
but these forms are rare in those contexts.

carry him. When the new mat arrived, the judge ordered that he be brought to his house. The judges saw that the shot had entered well. They ordered the police to seize Nicolás and put him in prison. They saw that Francisco died.

The night entered, and the judges ordered the police to guard the killer throughout the night. At dawn he remained in prison and stayed there the entire day. On the third day, they "took his heart" [questioned him] to see what his crime was. He said that Francisco had blamed him for giving witchcraft and that it was not his fault, that he was not a witch. He got angry and shot Francisco. The judge heard the case and raised an act. They sent him to San Cristóbal and the síndico, Simón, took over the presidency. He remained in power in the pueblo.

People heard that the new president could not arrange things in the town hall. Illness entered the pueblo. Word was left that Juan, Ebaristo, and Antonio had brought in the illness. All those who "knew how to make fiestas" [reference to curers functioning in curing ritual] gathered together in the town hall. The two leading curers came with a garrafón of liquor. The curers drank until nighttime.

The president remained in prison. When the night had entered well, he slept. And although he had heard many rumors about what was going to happen, he slept well. At dawn, the president was "of one heart" [content]. A policeman arrived and said that Antonio had been brought to jail.

"Why?" asked the president. "For what crime has he been put in prison?"

The policeman said that it was for witchcraft, and that they had gone out to get the other witch Juan, but he had escaped into the Cave of the Star. Although there were fifteen men after him, they couldn't seize him. They had also gone to catch Ebaristo, but he was not in his house, and they did not find him. The crime of the three was that they had brought in the illness.

Meanwhile, everyone was saying that Nicolás was also responsible for letting the illness in the town. People said that he had vowed that if the authorities seized him, he would let in the illness. The townspeople got drunk.

Eight men of Alannantik wanted the interim president, Simón to re-main as president. But the people of Ahk'olnantik did not want him to re-main as president. The townspeople began to talk, saying, "Why should he remain as president since he stole twenty bulls? We don't want him. Let us get another president. We shall walk with Ceferino."

They wanted me for president since I was first regidor. It is for this rea-son that I entered as president, but I didn't think that I would be able to stay on as president. Simón received an order from the [state] government that he should return as president. He came with soldiers, and when they took me out of office, the lieutenant said to Simón, "Now you enter."

And so I gave over the archives and seals and everything in the presi-dency to Simón, and I left the presidency. And the people saw that it was the order of the government, and they did not say anything. The town remained silent.

The incident is given as it was related to me in Tzeltal. I have sorted out the steps in which the conflict developed in order to clarify its mean-ing.

1. The traditional checks and balance system of the civil authority over the curers was initially upset by the entry of a leading curer into the post of president.

2. When he committed a murder while in office, the judges seized control and had him put in prison.

3. His replacement by the síndico who was from the same side of the dual division, aroused the opposition of the people of the opposite side, Ahk'olmantik, who believed that the epidemic, which followed the president's removal from power, was caused by the curers of Alan-nantik under the direction of the president who was in jail.

4. The leaders of the revolt in Ahk'olnantik chose as their replace-ment the first regidor, Ceferino, who was from their side.

5. Leaders from Alannantik rejected this replacement and were able to get official backing from the state government to replace their representative.

The process illustrates the way in which a conflict, precipitated by a clash between civil authorities and the curers, was cast into the idiom of structural opposition between the two sides of the dual division. In this case, resolution came with the intercession of federal troops.

When curing was a controlled profession, with a hierarchy legitimizing entry and exit, the power of the curers was directed toward guarding the village against evil as well as curing. In the 1940s, the loss of one leader by death and the other's jail sentence meant loss of control over entry into the profession. A growing suspicion and discontent with the curers as a group, laying upon them the responsibility of much of the witchcraft, is reflected in the account of another older informant:

Formerly when the curers J. C., A. A., S. K., and J. D. were alive, they walked in common. The people were in accord with the curers because they watched over the peublo. They knew about medicine, and so people of Alannantik went to ask them favors to cure them and also the people of Ahk'olnantik went to ask them favors.

But then, after they died [about 1940], the principales did not dare fight the curers because they had animal spirits, and the principales themselves didn't—they were just honorable people.

The doubt about the civil authority's control over the curers has increased since young leaders have taken the leadership in the town. One informant said, "When there are young people in the cabildo, they can't keep control of the curers, but the old people in the cabildo can." With the relaxation of restrictions on entry into the curing profession, following the loss of leadership and the ranked hierarchy, curers were no longer restrained by professional standards. When drunk, they bragged of their power to do evil as well as to do good. The first killing of a curer accused of being a witch occurred in 1937. He was working in Pinola when he was shot. The dead curer's widow wanted to bring his body back to be buried in the town cemetery, but the request was refused by the judges. This suggests that the town authorities agreed with the accusation, since it is the custom to return the dead to the town for burial. Other assassinations by individuals occurred in 1943 and in 1950. During this period, the civil officials sanctioned the assassinations of persons accused and convicted of witchcraft. When someone wished to kill a man suspected of witchcraft, they would go to the town hall and ask for permission. After a review of the case by the judges and the other civil authorities, the president would have the suspected witch locked up in the local jail and then give the key to his enemy. The following story illustrates this procedure:

When we were still part of the township of Teopisca [sometime before 1931] F. went and asked permission of the authorities to kill his enemy, a curer, whom he thought was bewitching his brother-in-law. The president arrived at the house of the suspected witch with the order to imprison him. He said that they were going to Teopisca to put him in jail. The group of authorities set off with the suspected witch. On the way another group met them and asked them where they were going. The President replied, "To Teopisca." The group which had encountered them asked them if they would like a drink to "heat their body." They gave one cup and then another. They then cut up the suspected witch with a machete and put his body in the cave of me?tiktatik that goes to Chiapa de Corzo. When the widow enquired the next day where her husband was, the president said that the man must have gone to the finca.

After telling this story, my informant concluded, "Therefore, little by little, the pueblo is getting better because we scared the curers with the permission of the president to kill them." He felt that this was the point at which the power of the curers, who were more and more frequently being accused as witches, was broken.

While the usual course of action, once a man was accused of witchcraft, was to kill him so that there would be no danger of revenge, the following case illustrates punishment by beating.

The time was 1935. There was a very bad curer who stole much cattle. One man who heard that he had stolen his cattle wanted to kill him, but the curer met the man and killed him in an old house. The town authorities seized the curer and forced him to pay one thousand pesos for the bull. The principales punished him by tying him to a tree and beating him five or six times. They beat him well for the town. After they beat him they brought him to prison in San Cristóbal and gave him over to the Ministerio Publico to arrange the case. He did not return to the pueblo but went to another place. In five years he returned to his pueblo.

When he arrived here, he did not hear any word that they would kill him. He persisted in his custom of stealing. And the pueblo seized him and put him in prison. The whole town seized him although he had heard no word.

They tied him to a tree and said to him, "You do not have shame. You are a curer, father of the pueblo, [respect term for curer], and yet you behaved badly and truly stole. The town sees you are a bad man, Emilio. They call you their father, but now I am going to tell you that you ought not to be called father. You're a bad one."

He wanted to be called father, but he was only a bad one. He returned again to San Cristóbal because of two crimes. He did not hear the words. He remained in prison, and when he came out someone else came and killed him.

Since 1938, nine of the thirty-seven homicide cases on which I collected data (Table 29) were killings of curers. The increasing frequency of such killings reveals the loss of faith in the guardianship role of the curers, but along with this, retention of belief in their power to work evil.

In the series of successful confrontations, the civil authority has gained strength and overcome some of the fear of the people. In May 1964, during a severe contagion of measles, a rumor started that the disease was being spread because of witchcraft. The president called together the curers. The consensus of this gathering was that a certain curer of Alannantik had buried the "heat" which was causing the deaths in the milpa of his enemy. The people of Alannantik gathered with the curers and the civil officials in the milpa of the "enemy" to dig it out. The curers dug out a charcoal brazier which is the sign of illness and threw it in the Cave of the Star. That evening the suspected witch was killed, presumably by his neighbors.

In the most recent confrontation between the civil authorities and an individual curer, in March 1966, the civil authorities showed a united front in denouncing the use of witchcraft to threaten any official. The entire group of practicing curers from both sides of the dual division were called to witness the denunciation before the assembled civil officials in the town hall. The only one absent was the curer accused of attempting to cut short the life of the president because of envy of his position. The assembled

TABLE 29. Time, Victim, Suspects, Crime, and Outcome in Selected Homicide Cases, 1938-1965

	Victim or other				
	Curer or other	Age	Killer	Suspected crime of victim	Outcome
1938 *	Other	50	Unknown	Witchcraft	No one apprehended
1945	Other	65	Drinking companions	Drunken quarrel	Two companions went to jail
1946	Curer	48	Brothers: 1 elder, 2 younger	Witchcraft	One brother went to jail for five years
1946 *	Other	38	Unknown	Witchcraft	No one complained to authorities
1946	Curer	45	Unknown	Witchcraft	No punishment; no suspect apprehended
1946	Curer	50	Unknown	Witchcraft	Wife of victim complained, but no witness would testify
1958	Curer	27	Father of boy who had died of witchcraft	Witchcraft	Before dying, dead man revealed name of killer. Wife reported it to authorities, but no action taken
1960 *	Other	60	Son-in-law	Witchcraft	Son-in-law fled town
1960	Other	24	Cattle owners' paid killer	Stole cattle	Released killer on bail
1960	Curer	60	Brother-in-law	Witchcraft	No one apprehended
1961	Curer	70	Neighbors	Witchcraft	Neighbors, who felt he was responsible for contagion, were not apprehended
1961 *	Other	30	Wife's brother	Very abusive, fought when drunk	Suspect fled town

(cont.)

| Year | Victim | | Killer | Suspected crime of victim | Outcome |
	Curer or other	Age			
1961 *	Other	45	Neighbors	Witchcraft	No one apprehended
1961 *	Other	37	Unknown	Witchcraft	No one apprehended; wife agreed he was a witch
1962	Other	18	Rival for girl	Fought over girl	No one accused
1962	Other	20	Cattle owners' paid killer	Stole cattle	Went to jail but released on bail
1962	Other	35	Brother-in-law	Revenge for death of brother; political conflict	Killer declared he had killed, paid fine and was released
1962 *	Other	20	Rival for girl	Fought over girl	No one accused
1962 *	Other	50	Leader of cattle association	Stole cattle	Unknown
1963 *	Curer	36	Unknown	Witchcraft	No one apprehended, but victim's brother tried to find killer
1963	Curer	45	Indian of neighboring town whom victim had accused of witchcraft	False accusation	No action taken
1963 *	Other	Unknown	Drinking companions	Barroom brawl	One of assailants went to jail, and other two bailed out
1963	Other	70	Sons of a man whom he was accused of having killed	Witchcraft	No action taken
1964 *	Other	30	Killer paid by victim's brothers	Stole cattle	Brother fled town but jailed when he returned
1964 *	Other	34	Unknown	Witchcraft	No one accused
1964	Other	30	Ladino liquor distiller of another town	Denounced distiller to authorities	No action taken

	Victim Curer or other	Age	Killer	Suspected crime of victim	Outcome
1964	Other	30	Brothers	Witchcraft	One brother fled; other put in jail but he claimed first brother did it
1964	Curer	65	Neighbors	Witchcraft in contagion	No action taken
1964	Other	22	Close friend of victim, hired by cattle owners	Stole cattle	Killer freed on bail
1965	Other	45	Unknown	Witchcraft	No one accused
1965 *	Other	45	Unknown	Witchcraft	No one apprehended
1965	Other	42	Unknown	Unknown	No one accused
1965	Other	27	Brother-in-law	Had relations with 14-year-old sister-in-law	Brother-in-law tried but not sufficient evidence
1965 *	Other	35	Unknown	Stole cattle and corn	No action taken
1965	Other	42	Son by first marriage	Failed to provide dowery; also witchcraft	Widow spread rumors against step-son, but insufficient evidence
1965	Other	20	Rival for brother's girl	Mistaken identity—brother's rival took him for competitor	Unknown

* Occurred during a fiesta.

group walked to the hill where the curer had been reported practicing his
witchcraft. There they collected the evidence: fourteen candles of all colors, crosses of wire placed on a photograph, and a gourd. The curers present lifted the evidence and threw it in the river to get rid of the evil. A
transcription of the proceedings in the town hall is given below:

*President: "We are gathered together here because something which is
not good has happened. See here,* Tatinel *[to the leading curer], we do
not know if it is witchcraft or not."*

*First Curer Feliciano, of Yetawitz: "The old men [elder curers] have
pulsed our children. All the pueblo has helped. We have just brought in
the candles. He is a very bad witch. We walked out there and we found it.
For this we have gathered together, but if there is an owner of the witchcraft, we have not heard."*

*Second Curer Emilio, of Alannantik: "But this owner is not good. Thus
spoke my compadre. This is not good. So my compadre and Mam Pelise
[Feliciano, first curer to speak] have spoken. Whoever did it has not advised us. The ancestors did not want this. Now who wants it? Who
speaks with the holy word? You do not announce whether it is a curer or
whether it is or not. We do not know where it is or what it is that he did.
But when someone does give an illness, it is a good custom to see where
this comes from. This we do not know. It is for this we went to the cave
to know where he found it."*

*President: "Therefore we had to look for it and see who did it;
whether it is someone who knows how to do both witchcraft and curing.
But he will pay here in the presidency for what he did, because we are
going to announce it, we are going to reveal the crime. Now your hearts
are content and truly you cannot do it. Now we know a little, compadre.
Truly we have seen and know where it [the magic] was kept."*

*Feliciano: "Now you speak a little to God who gave his little child.
And what if tomorrow you should come? Now is the time we speak to
God, we speak to the Virgin Mother. Don't kill and don't give suffering.
Better not do anything. Please don't do anything at night; please do noth-
ing as I have told you. Thus your children [the younger curers] have*

heard our hearts. The people will hear that we didn't do anything. The true curers looked. We came to the place and we found it."

The curers left the town hall, one by one, saying the pat^ʔo^ʔtan to the judges as they left. The judges remained.

President: "We have heard clearly what we waited here to hear. They have brought back a little soda."

Judge: "So it is for your work [referring to the soda], what you went to do there [in the hills]."

President: "It is good what you did, but you are afraid because of that."
Judges laugh.

The curers in public performances nominally recognize as leading curers the two major speakers for the group, Feliciano of Yetawitz and Emilio of Alannantik. However, these men are not recognized as true leaders. Feliciano lives in the despised barrio of Yetawitz and is associated with the kuriketik, (the inhabitants of the colonia of San Vicente), while Emilio himself has been accused of witchcraft. But the situation required someone to represent the group from each side, and so there was compliance with this temporary role.

In the public gathering, the curers refrained from accusing anyone, and denied that they had knowledge of the witch. The older curer (not recognized as leader but serving in the place of an elder) warned the group not to kill anyone as a result of the meeting. That evening, the president and his brother announced on the loudspeaker of the cantina that they did know who was trying to murder the president, that it was the curer who was absent, and that he should desist. The curer responded by announcing on another cantina loudspeaker that he was innocent. On the following day, the accused appeared in the town hall with two family-sized bottles of beer. He said that he did not want the president to continue accusing him, since he was not guilty and had truly been sick. (He had consulted the I.N.I. clinic nurse rather than one of his colleagues and had received treatment for a headache. This was commented upon by his opponents, who interpreted it as showing his lack of faith in traditional curing practices.)

The open confrontation by the civil authorities with the suspected witch, in which they warned him to stop before violence resulted, represents a new strategy in the contest between officials and curers. Formerly even when there was strong suspicion against a man, the principales and judges kept quiet. If they acted, it was to kill the suspect without forewarning. The new strategy reveals the position of strength from which they now operate. That the president could joke in the town hall about the fear of the judges in dealing with the accused curer (see his final remark above) is indicative of a changed attitude. Incidents such as that of the curer consulting the clinic nurse instead of his fellow curers, which was noted and commented upon by the brother of the president, may further serve to undermine the townspeople's belief in the power of the curers.

In the weeks following the incident, the president and his brother discussed the incident, pointing out their fearlessness in openly confronting the witch. The curers clearly tried to deny any responsibility as a group with the remark: "Whoever did it did not advise us." They expressed the feeling that it is against professional ethics: "Whoever did it is a very bad witch"; but they refuse to name him or admit knowledge of who did it. "We do not know where it is or what it is that he did." The behavior of the curers in this incident is clearly defensive and stems from their loss of control and initiative.

Political Parties and Factions

In 1950 the first contest for the post of president was started by two brothers who had secured the backing of the Partido Acción Nacional (PAN). Never before had anyone initiated his own candidacy outside the traditional nomination procedure through the old officials in the town hall. The brothers lived in the new barrio of Yut Hok, the ejido land grant of Ahk'olnantik. The candidacy disturbed the customary alternation of posts between Ahk'olnantik and Alannantik. Threatened by the imbalance, the leaders of Alannantik secured the backing of the Partido Revolucionario Institucionalizado (PRI) for their candidate. The PAN candidate won the election. However, he was never able to consolidate political support. At his death, he had no successor, and "the town remained in peace."

In this first political contest, the conflict was interpreted as opposition between the dual divisions. Factional disputes and the sense of political responsibility and control were contained within these parameters, and any conflict was conceived of as a threat to territorial balancing mechanisms.

The new factions that have developed since 1963 are tied to economic rather than territorial competition. In 1960 the first truck-owning cooperative was organized under the leadership of the former Ladino secretary. The twenty shareholders of the town had only a small amount of capital in the truck, and the controlling interest was in the hands of the secretary's wife. The cooperative was merely a device to gain business in carrying pottery and wheat from the town to the market centers. In 1963 a new truck-owning cooperative was organized by local Indians. The two brothers, Santiago and José, secured capital to buy the truck from thirty residents of the town without any assistance from outside. The shareholders of the new cooperative came from both sides of the dual division, and from the outlying barrios.

When the leaders of the new cooperative tried to get permits and certificates to license the car and the operator, they were refused by the town president who was a shareholder of the first cooperative. The Indians then hired a Ladino truck driver from the neighboring town, and the son of one of the shareholders served as assistant. They realized that it was necessary to get control of the local political positions in order to extend their operations. With the help of the schoolteacher, they got eighty-one signatures on the petition for the PRI candidacy of one of the brothers, José, in the presidential nomination of 1964. He was opposed by a ladinoized Indian living in one of the barrios who was backed by the Ladino secretary who was leader of the competing trucking cooperative. The opponent did not have a chance of winning, as the leaders of the new cooperative pointed out, because of two strikes against him: he was not a resident of the center and he had only PAN backing. The Indians are aware that nothing can be gained politically by a PAN-backed president since PRI is now the party in control of regional and national offices.

After José's election, the Indian truck driver was able to get a driving license. With the help of the schoolmaster, the cooperative was able to get permission to extend operations to hot country where the Indians of the town held ejido land. This territory had been controlled by the state-wide trucking sindicate whose monopoly was protected by government permits. On the basis that they were poor, nonprofit-making ejidatarios, the Indians were granted the right to truck corn from the ejido colonies to the highlands. Whenever the cooperative leaders planned to go to the departmental capital to make their appeals, the schoolmaster counseled them to wear their Indian costume—the white shirt and pants with red sash, sandals, and woolen kotonč̆u—in order to play the role of simple campesinos more convincingly. He was aware of the effectiveness of this pose in pro-Indian governmental circles.

The PRI leadership in the department capital is neither aware of nor interested in the local factions which seek their support. Their concern is only that the vote is solidly behind regional and national candidates of the party, and they support the group that can mobilize the largest number of votes. A policy of favoritism toward Indians, based on an ideology of *indigenismo,* pro-Indianism, is coupled with a policy of permitting local autonomy. The national committee's program for promoting literacy has never reached this community nor any that I know of in the area. The party's promotion of Indian welfare consists of supporting demands made by Indian constituents and bringing them to the attention of civil service officials assigned to these functions. Party officials thus act as intermediaries between the voters and the bureaucracy of the government, channeling complaints and demands.

In the development of factions around new economic interests, the Indians have shifted from an ideology in which the dialectic of conflict was cast in traditional dual-division opposition to one in which the conflict is seen as Indian versus Ladino domination of enterprises. Since these interests cut across the territorial divisions, the economic factions have not crystallized along territorial lines. It is this shift in perspective which makes for the "qualitative" change in local political organization.

COMPETITION BETWEEN CACIQUES

There are several dimensions to the role of cacique in Tzoʔontahal. First, it is a role created by outside interests and occupied by someone marginal to the community, either a foreign Indian, as in the case of Augustín, or a Ladino, as in the cases of the secretary and schoolmaster described below. The only indigenous candidate for the role was recently killed. It provokes too much envy for someone socialized in the community; fear of being accused and even killed as a witch or a power-seeker is justified by several such precedents. Those with the skills to become caciques have until recently been effectively incorporated in the existing hierarchy as firmanetik.

Second, the cacique is a gatekeeper, channeling information, goods, and services from the outside to the members of the community. In this capacity, he prefers to pose as a benefactor when he may actually be no more than the distributor of government welfare goods and services.[4]

Third, the role of cacique is one in which the incumbent operates in a local sphere, but depends upon a network of compadrazgo and professional ties outside of the community to assure his position in the community. He must be sufficiently aware of the local idiom in order to avoid making enemies.

Finally, the role is monopolistic. This results in part from the fact that the outside world prefers to deal with a single representative for reasons of expediency. However, new governmental agents are more and more dealing directly with Indians, a factor which has shaken the position of the cacique. The monopolistic quality of the position also stems from the fact that the profit to be gleaned from the community is small. A Ladino from a neighboring town commented that it was worth the time of only one man to exploit an Indian community of the size of Tzoʔontahal. The extractable profit is diminishing as the Indians become more aware of their rights.

The change in character and range of activities of local caciques is illustrated by the recent careers of two residents of Tzoʔontahal. In the 1950s and until 1964, the Ladino secretary, Don Ramon, had filled the role of cacique. He took advantage of this role not only by collecting a salary and a percentage of court fees, but also by earning money for using his influence in Ladino official circles outside the community. He lent money for interest and subsidized some enterprises such as growing cabbages with Indian

---

4. Goldrich (1965) points to this tactic of politicians who distribute government goods as though they were their own gifts.

partners. He sold a few shares of a truck he and his family owned to Indians, but he retained the controlling interest. His wife was reputed to be a witch, and was an active curer, combining old and new treatments of illnesses.

His position was challenged in the 1960s by the Ladino schoolmaster, who had been remarkably unsuccessful from his arrival in 1953 until that time in gaining personal power and influence. His intercession in a local homicide case involving a father's murder of his son outraged the townspeople, some of whom threatened to kill him. His attempts to have water installed aroused the curers against him since they were accustomed to bathing their patients at the source of the spring from which they were debarred when the plumbing was installed. His demands that children within the legal age limit should not only attend school but should be prohibited from marrying until they had completed their schooling caused the anger of parents who wanted to give their daughters in an early and profitable marriage.

Gradually, however, the schoolmaster extended his own base of support. He minimized his attack on local customs, adhering only to those laws affecting the school population, over which he had a great deal of control. Some of his support came from the orthodox Catholic members of the community; he extended his control through compadre relationships with over eighty members of the community. He showed movies which he acquired from the United Nations and other educational film sources and gave away medicines acquired from the health officials in the state capitol who were his friends. From one of these sources of philanthropy he acquired wool shawls which he gave to every woman in the town.

The professor demanded no return from the townspeople other than their respect and admiration; he was a person who enjoyed commanding others and needed an arena in which to project his own personality. In his early years in the town, he had to satisfy this need by capturing stray tourists and plying them with soda pop or coffee. His first opportunity to gain leadership in the local sphere came in 1963, when he supported the new truck-owning cooperative. He used the influence of contacts in the state capital, including compadres, friends, and relatives of his wife's family. He promoted the cooperative's attempt to gain the presidency. One of the first acts of the new officials was to fire the Ladino secretary and install an Indian for the first time. The schoolmaster had won his battle for recognition. In every legal dispute in which the town became involved, the schoolmaster accompanied the town officials as they went to visit departmental and state leaders, acting as their spokesman. He never accepted even expenses for these trips. His satisfaction was in giving advice to the officials on all matters, in being the man whom outsiders consulted before anything could be accomplished, and in finding an audience.

The schoolmaster consolidated his position by drawing together all his supporters in a parent-teachers association, which served as a captive audience for his extended monologues. I was called upon as a witness to the installation of the members, and I took advantage of the occasion to record some of the schoolmaster's rhetoric as he addressed the "parents." In attendance were the president, his brother, four members of their truck-owning cooperative, and about ten other representatives. The teacher told me that they were the best people in town—not one of them had killed anyone! The excerpt below is not complete, but there was sufficient repetition in the schoolmaster's discourse so that nothing is lost.

Schoolmaster: "I don't fight with anyone. We do not come to fight. A schoolmaster is a guide to teach respect. I have thirty-three years teaching in pueblos of campesinos, poor people like you. I am your brother. I am your teacher. The ignorant people do not want to send their children to school. This is a good school, and there are those of you who have succeeded by learning. Ramon Leon was a boarding school student for two years. He and seven others have received scholarships. They accuse me of not working, but they do not know what is happening in the school. Those who know give congratulations to the school. The children of this school won the competition at the conference of teachers. It is neither a poor school with poor students, nor a rich school with rich students, but all are together. They say we do not teach. Compadre" (to president), *"is this so? They say we only dance, but at the conference our students won the prize.*

"This school is yours. It is better organized than any other. The flag which we had we gave to Villa Las Rosas because they are campesinos;

they are my friends. I prefer to send it there than to Teopisca, because they are campesinos.

"*I have proved to you I am a friend of campesinos and of the poor. I don't have to say anything if I see that some are killing, that some are distilling liquor. This is an affair of the civil authorities, not of me. If some come to tell me that so and so has killed someone, I close my ears.*

"*What is more important in life is what is in your head, not your clothing. Do you understand me?*"

All reply, "*Yes, maestro.*"

"*If we are going to win over Teopisca and Villa Las Rosas, our children have to work hard. I had the luck of receiving a medal because I am one of the principal teachers and know the preparation of teachers. The Jefe of Operation put a medal on my breast and gave me an* abrazo. *Here is the picture taken two years ago—Lupe get the rag!*" *Schoolmaster dusts photograph with rag.* "*Here you see me with the medal on my breast.*

"*Who is more important—the one who accuses me and has to put his finger to sign the declaration, or those of you who can write?*

"*Now the schoolmaster does not give permission to let the children stay away from school. We do not have authority to release the children except for illness. Those children who go most often to school are those who get ahead. They speak* idioma [*native language*] *when they play, but when they enter the school they speak* Castellano [*Spanish*].

"*Now you know everything. I am happy with you. If there are some who are not happy that I am here, then I shall go happily. There are schools where schoolmasters hit the children. There is a school where the Indian teacher hit a child three times. This is a crime!*

"*I know where all this talk comes from. Don Ramon* [*Ladino secretary who supported opposing candidate mentioned above*] *has a truck—he and Doña Juana. They buy wheat and corn at half price. If the Indians do not pay off, they get double the return at the next harvest. My compadres have come and told me. Those who are with him are traitors to the pueblo. They are being exploited by him. They have two trucks in Teopisca. They come and ask people to sign a paper supporting their candidate. People sign because they are afraid she* [*Juana*] *will use witchcraft.*"

President: "Ramon left her, but then he went back to her because of witchcraft."

Schoolmaster "This is the group which is against me and is against the pueblo."

Schoolmaster's wife: "You see how happy the pueblo is." She waves her hand to plaza where marimba is playing for the fiesta. *"Everything is well organized. Not as it was formerly when Don Ramon was in town."*

President: "You see how the pueblo is learning. The children are learning to knit. Everyone knits."

Schoolmaster, giving oath of office to parents: "In the name of the Secretary of Public Education, I ask you to serve with faithfulness to the pueblo. The school is the defense of the country. It is preparing you for tomorrow. The society of parents of the school represents you. Your children represent the future of the country in the sign of the three colors, and you have the obligation to defend the country. The country will become great when all the children know how to write. When Mexico has need of its children, the children will be prepared to die for the country. You should see that schools prepare the children. See Mexico is a country united.

"I have been here since 1953. It is not now as it was then. We have water, a highway. You are not in the state you were then.

"Today we see a kiosk." He waves hand to plaza. *"Tomorrow we will have a telephone, telegraph, and a factory. It will be a grand pueblo, a civilized pueblo. There was a schoolmaster here who worked two days a week. I have worked every day since 1953. I secured eight scholarships for the children. If there are some who didn't go, it is because their father does not send them. If there are those who say the school does not function, they are traitors to the pueblo. Honorable Society of Fathers of Families, I am the schoolmaster. I shall explain. Give an applause."* Applause.

The schoolmaster's discourse reveals several aspects of his position in the town. He indicates the lesson he has learned in avoiding interference in the town's social control system ("I don't have to say anything if I see that some are killing, that some are taking out trago. This is an affair of the civil officials, not of me"). He identifies himself with the Indians in the fight against the competitive trucking cooperative ("Those who are with him [Don Ramon] are traitors to the pueblo. They are being exploited by him"). While he does not accuse Ramon's wife directly of witchcraft he implies this in saying that people sign their candidate's nomination petition for president because they are afraid Juana will use witchcraft. This is a characteristic mode of attacking one's enemies in the town. He claims credit for all of the innovations in the town which have won public approval—the highway, the water supply, electricity, and so forth.

The profit motive is inadequate to explain why Ladinos want to play the role of cacique in these corporate Indian communities. One must seek for an explanation instead in the social status they gain. While their jobs are limited and usually frustrating and they can never be completely integrated into the community, political activities offer them a larger arena in which they can derive personal satisfaction. The contrast between the schoolmaster's position in Tzoʔontahal before he became a political leader and his position after finding local supporters illustrates this. In the early days of his residence in town, when he built a chicken coop which extended a few feet beyond the grounds allotted to the schoolhouse, some Indians threatened to kill him. In 1957, I saw him trying to summon a policeman from the town hall, which was adjacent to the schoolhouse, to remove a boulder from the path so that a visiting friend could pass in his automobile. No one heeded his urgent shouts or the whistle he used to call children to school, although they were well aware of what he wanted. But by 1965 there was not a single important transaction which did not require consultation with the schoolteacher. Campesinos from as far as Villa Las Rosas came to request his advice and his help in approaching government agents. In projecting his political role, he gained support for projects which were of interest to him. When he had succeeded in getting the government to install water pipes and electricity, he talked the civil authorities into building a kiosk, or bandstand, in the plaza. This was a fulfillment of his ambition to make the town over in the image of a colonial Spanish pueblo. His final statement in the speech quoted above, "Today we see a kiosk, tomorrow we will have a telephone, telegraph, and a factory!" reveals the symbolic significance it had for him.

Conflict among Religious Functionaries

Conflict in the religious domain stems from the opposition of the traditional religious hierarchy and more recently that of the young leadership in the civil authority to the increasing power of the priest. In this conflict the fiscal is a middleman who often gets knocked by both sides.

The priest. The priest visits thirty other Indian communities of the department of San Cristóbal Las Casas in addition to Tzoʔontahal. In the fifteen years he has been working regularly in this town, he has gained increasing authority over the cofrades. He is assisted by two lay sisters who maintain the church and lead the evening prayers in his absence. He admits that, without them, his own work in the town would be more difficult because of the sexual jealousy of the townsmen. His relationship to the group of about forty *resadoras,* or female prayer-makers, who attend the evening prayers regularly and are the most vocal respondents in the mass, would be suspect without the presence of the lay sisters.

The priest tries to play the role of parish leader as well as spiritual leader. When medicine is available from missionary sources, he gives it to the sick. In his sermons, he advises people to use injections, which he makes available, against contagious diseases. He attempts to counsel the people, advising them not to kill, to steal, or to have illegal sexual affairs. In his role as pastor, the priest is influenced by missionary efforts of American Catholic organizations which have sent supplies to the area.

In recent years, the priest has challenged the authority of the head cofrade in activities occurring within and at the door of the church. The following incident, recounted by the son of the elder cofrade, marked a shift in control in these domains:

In 1961 the elder cofrade of Sacramento was drinking with the other mayordomos at the door of the church. The priest came out and demanded that they stop because this was the house of God. The elder replied that it was the custom of the pueblo, and he and the other men refused to leave. The priest went back into the church and returned with a gun in his hand. The mayordomos seized wood which they had gathered to cook their meal in the yard of the church. They threatened to beat the priest with the wood, and he retreated into the church. He later announced that he would not give mass, or weddings, or baptism. We did not mind that he did not give the mass or would not give weddings, but the people were frightened if he would not give baptism. The mayordomos had a meeting, and they agreed to give up drinking in the church if the priest would continue to give baptism, but they would no longer care for the pigs or bring wood for him without payment. We pay him fifteen pesos for an ordinary mass and forty pesos for a singing mass, so he should pay us for help. The priest was in agreement with the mayordomos.

As a result of this edict, the drinking has stopped and the mayordomos no longer eat the common meal in the church yard. Drinking was an act linked to eating, since the round of liquor served before the meal was "to prepare the stomach," and the drink after the meal was "to wash down the food." The shift to the house of the cofrade was a ready alternative in this community where the household is a recognized ritual domain.

The priest's control over the church has extended to control over the donation boxes and the saints' images. He now receives the money donated to the saints and does not permit a public accounting of the funds. Because of this, the civil officials accuse him of stealing some of the money. A recent incident recounted below by one of the prayer-reciters led to even more severe censure:

The bishop visited our church, and when he looked under the silk robes of the Virgin Santa Lucía he found a wooden dress covered with gold paint. He told the priest to have the cloth dress removed. The people were very upset by this since they are very proud of the dresses bought for the Virgin. One of the prayer-reciters dreamed that the Virgin appeared before her in tears, saying she did not want to appear nude in public. We [the group of prayer-reciters] went to see the bishop to demand that the Virgin should wear her dress in church and that the priest be sent out of the town. The bishop refused. He said the Virgin did not feel cold because she was just a statue. Ha! How could she not feel cold?

The issue of the Virgin's clothing has increased the attacks on the priest. These have been aired in public meetings which take place on Sunday. Opposition to the priest has shifted from the old cofrades to the young leadership of the pueblo, men who wish to extend internal control over the church as well as the town hall. They tried to enlist the fiscal's help in getting rid of the priest, but he refused to cooperate. The president's brother, who serves as town treasurer, recounts the following exchange he had with the priest:

I saw Padre Juan take money from the box when I was mayordomo in the church. All of us mayordomos went to talk with him. I asked him how much money was turned in during the fiesta.

"The madres [lay sisters] know," he said, "I don't."

He called them, and they said, "We haven't counted the money. Come tomorrow."

The priest was very angry that we asked for an account. Pablo [the fiscal] was too afraid to talk with him. When we left the church, I told Pablo, "You are in charge of the church. Why didn't you demand an account of the money in front of the church? We never got an account."

Then we began to fight. Padre Juan doesn't want to leave the town. He has it too good here. He has a good yard with many fruit trees and a nice house. The Ladinos in Teopisca don't let him stay in their convento overnight. They are sharp, those damned Ladinos! We pay the padre thirty pesos every Sunday. Before he lived here, we used to have good music and more firecrackers for fiestas. Now he wants to stop all this. He was the one who ordered that all the money be collected. We wanted to go buy a gross of firecrackers. He said, "Why do you want firecrackers? It is the mass that has value. The saints don't want firecrackers or music."

He is very smart, the padre. He wants to keep the money for himself. Now we just get two firecrackers each morning of the fiesta and two in the evening. In Teopisca, they fire dozens of firecrackers. Here what is left over from the contributions for the fiesta remains in the box, and he takes it.

I went to get new clothing for the saint. In Comitán they wanted two

hundred and fifty pesos for a dress. The padre said I couldn't buy it there.
He told me to send for one in Mexico that cost five hundred and fifty
pesos. He wanted to make the profit.

The fiscal. As an intermediary between the traditional religious
officials and the priest, the fiscal is the target for both sides of the religious
controversy. The priest selects the fiscal, but his retention of the post depends on his being accepted by the mayordomos. The tendency in the past
fifteen years since a regular priest has been assigned to the community is
to choose a man who speaks Spanish and can read and write, but who can
be dominated by the priest. The following statement by a man who served
in this post in 1929 defines the functions of the fiscal as the Indians see
them:

When I served as fiscal, I knew how to sell [*the Indians use the verb* to
sell *in reference to any propaganda—whether commercial, political, or*
religious] *the catechism. After the prayer, I cleaned the patio. I held the*
key to the church. I saw [*in the sense of watch over*] *all the mayordomos.*
I bought the candles and incense for the saints. At midday the mayordo-
mos and I left the church and went home. There was no padre living here
then, and the padre from San Cristóbal came only on the days of San
Francisco, Virgin Santa Lucía, San Pedro the Martyr, and Santiago. Each
Sunday, the ten mayordomos and I entered the church and prayed in the
true language.

Prayers are now given in Spanish by the fiscal and the prayer-reciters
under the guidance of the lay sisters, who remain most of the time in the
convento. The fiscal, as a consequence, is no longer selected on the basis of
his ability to recite the patʔoʔtan. Since one of the main tasks of the fiscal
is to take care of the church, several recent incumbents have been jeered as
being like women, cleaning house and responding to the bidding of the
priests. Some have suggested that one was a homosexual. They blame the
fiscales for letting control over the domain of the church fall into the
hands of the priest.

A man who had filled the post himself, described the careers of several
former fiscales:

In 1912, Bernardo was fiscal. He knew how to pray well. About nine in the morning, the girls [prayer-reciters] gathered in the church and heard prayer in common. Then he borrowed money from the church and did not return it. He left for the finca with his father and three men. His wife went with her children. He fled because he didn't have the money, and he never returned. He sold his house in town to buy food. He died there in the finca. The girls remembered him because he was a friend, and they bought a candle for twenty cents.

Another fiscal, Antonio, began to give prayers to the same girls who accompanied him. He knew how to pray very well, and he prayed each Sunday. Then he died.

Then Carlos passed as fiscal. He knew how to pray from memory. The same girls learned, and all sang the prayer. Then that fiscal sold the table-cloths; he sold the candle holders; he sold everything. Therefore the cofrades did not want him. They said, "Go away because you are not good." God was going to punish him because he sold everything in the church.

In 1929 the pueblo named Ceferino [the informant, who refers to himself in the third person]. He served until he was made president in 1937.

In 1938, Antonio was chosen by the pueblo, but soon they did not want him because he was always ordering the pueblo to do work. He charged a lot for the fiestas, but he did not buy firecrackers or clothing for the saints. In a mass meeting they asked him to leave.

In 1939 Miguel put himself in office. The pueblo did not choose him. He did not know how to pray. He knew a little by memory because he heard what Antonio had said in his prayers, but he did not know the catechism. He didn't want to leave the church, but the pueblo spoke much against him.

The padre was against Miguel because he had begun to take advantage of the trips with the priest to sell the contraband liquor that he distilled. Some maintain that it was during his period as fiscal that the power shifted from the cofrades to the priest. He was accused of stealing the money donated to the saint, a sum of about 300 pesos. Although the money was returned, he is still considered guilty.

Miguel's successor, the present incumbent Pablo, served as president

while he was fiscal. He let control over the key to the church and the donation boxes slip into the hands of the priest. His opponents accused him
of weakness and failure to act in the interest of the town. The careers of
these fiscales illustrate the pitfalls for those filling the post. First, there is
the temptation for personal gain, since the fiscal has access to the money of
the saints: in the past three fiscales have been charged with robbery. Second, there is the problem that the fiscal serves two masters, the priest and
the head cofrade, each of whom has different standards of conduct for the
role: when the selection of the fiscal was in the hands of the cofrades, they
chose a man who knew the pat'o'tan and who was to deal directly with
the curers in rituals at the cave of the ancestors and in the homes of the
cofrades; now he is chosen by the priest who prefers a young, literate man.
If the fiscal follows the commands of the priest, he runs into problems
with the cofrades. This was the difficulty with Antonio, who was put out
of office by the cofrades because he yielded to the priest's demands to improve the convento and the church. As long as the conflict in interests between the priest and the traditional authorities exist, there is no successful
position for the fiscal to take.

Conflict and Social Change

In the contest for leadership which has and is occurring, the following
observations can be made on the basis of the events described.

1. The community has successfully incorporated the young, literate
men into the framework of the traditional hierarchy. This has been
accomplished by expanding the scope of activities of the president and
síndico and by relieving them of serving in the lower posts of the
hierarchy.

2. The ceremonial role of the principales serves as a symbol of
continuity in government both in the tie they have with the past and
in the annual changeover of officials.

3. The threat of foreign Indians in the township misusing their
skills in dealing with the outside world has been overcome by removing
them from office and preventing them from filling high posts.

4. In a series of confrontations, the civil officials have challenged the social control functions of the curers. Witch-killings in which many of the victims have been curers have minimized but not overcome the power of these men.

5. The priest has succeeded in establishing control over the church, but the Indians may yet succeed in deposing him, a plan they were putting into effect when I left town.

The Indians are now aware of their rights to limit—or eliminate if necessary—the self-appointed caciques. The new cacique promotes the community welfare not only in his rhetoric but in the services he performs for the officials. His involvement in political affairs is tolerated, not encouraged, and the officials are ready to turn to alternative sources of aid in their activities.

The involvement of the PRI in local elections has not introduced a new center of power in the political arena. Political factions are based on economic interests contained within the town, and the autonomy of the town has in no way been affected by leadership from party headquarters in the state capitol. The community and the party use each other for their own ends in almost complete ignorance of what is occurring in the domain of the other.

The system of beliefs and understandings has changed along with these organizational changes. The most significant change has been the waning belief in the guardianship of the ancestors. The absence of the curers at the fiesta of the caves means that they no longer have this ritual occasion to validate their claims by communicating with the ancestors. The loss of leadership and of a hierarchy of prestige within the ranks of curers has removed internal controls over the profession and further undermined their position. The diminishing respect with which they are treated in the town hall and the increasing number of murders of curers accused of witchcraft is directly related to the loss of belief in their power as guardians. Since they were not an integral part of the civil-religious hierarchy, as the curers were in Oxchuk (Villa Rojas 1947), this has not upset the hierarchy, but it has changed the balance of power in the wider community.

The diminishing significance of the leadership of the principales is tied to the loss of belief in the curers. The principales were formerly conceived to be overseers of the curers, men who, because of their advanced age, could determine whether the curers were acting in the interest of the town. With the loss of this social control function, along with the loss of other functions such as holding public funds and helping the judges to interpret the law, they have declined to the level of ceremonial figures dissociated from political action.

The forms of political organization remain the same, but there has been a shift in the balance of power from leaders whose authority rested on guardianship linked with the ancestors to leaders who can deal with the external power structure. The emergent forms of political organization can be partially assessed in the meaning participants assign to the events which precipitated this process of change. To paraphrase George Herbert Mead (1938:liii) it is the "organization of perspectives" concerning the past events and the present conditions which will effect the emergent forms. The analytical problem can be phrased with the questions, "In what dialectical terms is the conflict cast?" and "What changes do the members of the community perceive as an outcome of the struggle?" Whereas in the colonial period the conflict between the Indians and their Spanish conquerers was seen as a struggle for control between Catholicism and traditional religion, today the conflict is phrased as one of opposed economic interests. In the civil sphere, factional opponents seek the support of extra-communal power holders to gain their ends. In the religious sphere, the Indians see the conflict as one in which their control over the church and the income derived from it is opposed to the priest's growing influence.

In this reorganization of perspectives, the Indians share some of the goals of the dominant society, but they continue to oppose themselves to the Ladino world. For this reason they are willing to preserve the form of the civil-religious hierarchy as a means of asserting their independence from the dominant society. They see the community not only as a defensive screen against the outside world, but as a springboard for entry into the national economic and political life. They are now consciously taking advantage of pro-Indian sentiment to secure a preferred position in this society. Their awareness of their advantage over the deculturated Indian is made explicit in the contrasts they make between their conditions and those of the migratory mestizo laborers who work in the sawmills and fincas in the area. They comment on the fact that these workers have no political representation and that they and their children are illiterate and do not attend school. The significant factor is that the Indians of the corporate communities not only have advantages over the mestizo worker, but they perceive these advantages and are acting in terms of them. The preservation of community traditions is seen as a means of retaining community-owned assets and of maintaining a sense of self which is threatened or destroyed when the individual Indian enters into the national society.

The rules of strategy for moving in the direction of change are a transformation of the rules of the game that the Indians hve played in the four and a half centuries since the Conquest. The overall strategy is still defensive and aimed at preserving local independence, but their tactics include new skills acquired from Ladinos. In opposing the old power elite of the curing hierarchy, the present leadership uses the same tactics of the witch-hunt that their opponents used in the past to punish deviates, but they are beginning to confront them openly when sorcery is suspected. Leaders of the new cooperatives state that their aim is to increase opportunities for the whole community, not to make individual profit.

Because the conflict has been contained within community boundaries, the statement of goals remains the same. These goals include the retention of control by local leaders over judgment of guilt or innocence, in ceremonial affairs, and by all townspeople over land. This retention of local control is the key feature of a moving equilibrium in a model of change that puts the emphasis on continuous adjustments and adaptations. In the usual models for discussing modernization, the confrontation is conceived as one between the indigenous society and the outsider representing western influence. In Tzoʔontahal, young leaders within the community have confronted old in the stated interest of preserving tradition. Occasionally they may make alliances with the old leaders as in the conflict with the priest.

These "shifts in the focus of political power within a given system" (Leach 1964:9) are the prelude to structural change. Tzoʔontahal as a case example demonstrates the large input of local energies in bringing about change, both the changes that lead to internal restructuring of the distribution of power as well as those necessary in the introduction of new technology and organization of economic activity. It defeats the notion of the non-western segment of the world as a passive recipient of the gifts of the West.

Chapter 10

Roles, Persons, and the Evaluation of Performance

Categories of roles, time, and place structure the expectations of social groups. The following three chapters summarize the preceding data according to these cognitive modes. Role behavior and system, which will be analyzed in the present chapter, provide only a partial explanation of social interaction. It is the "proliferation of behavior beyond roles" (Linn 1967) that is of greater interest for the study of change. Consideration of place and time helps to make role categories explicit and to structure behavior that exceeds role expectations. Changes in the use of space and time can reveal adjustments in role relations before change occurs. Space and time perspectives will therefore be analyzed in the following two chapters.

Cooperation is possible when actors not only take into account the responses of others but also anticipate those responses. Anticipations are based in part upon understanding of conventional roles, but the rights, duties, and obligations invested in roles do not encompass all of the relevant expectations which make coordinated social interaction possible. Individual repetitive behavior in role play gives an image of what kind of person each actor is, and the groups of individuals are further categorized as "kinds of people." As an example of the first kind of classification, we have persons characterized as bright, dull, honest, crafty, etc. The second set of categories puts different personalities in socioeconomic classes such as rich and poor, or in political classes such as radical and conservative. Tzoʔontahal, along with other small societies, emphasizes personality categories since it lacks well-defined socioeconomic or sociopolitical classes.

Social continuity depends upon events which call for the participation of groups defined by roles as well as on socialization processes that under-

269

write beliefs that give coherence to these roles. Whether these events continue to be scheduled, and in the process of being presented "prove" the postulates upon which structural relationships are based, depends upon acceptance of the belief system.

A fundamental understanding governing behavior in Tzoʔontahal is that people ought to do as the ancestors did. Both "knowing" and "remembering" are expressed by the same verb, *ya sna,* while "learning" and "memorizing" are expressed by the verb *ya snop.* The behavioral corollary of this association between knowing and remembering is that one should accept the word of the ancestors as a guide to behavior. The importance of obeying one's elders as the intermediaries in the transfer of ways of behaving from one generation to another is stressed in child training and is restated in the prayers uttered at ritual performances enacting the ways of the ancestors.

In this chapter I shall consider the integration of behavior based on roles, personality, codes of morality and etiquette, and the ideological and behavorial changes which are disturbing this system.

The Role System

Coherence of the role system in Tzoʔontahal depends upon (1) similar premises for role recruitment and continuity in transition from one role to another; (2) alternation in office and linkage of separate domains by special offices; and (3) standardized etiquette of role interaction. Uniform standards of evaluation of performance provide a sanctioning system ensuring social integration.

Recruitment and transition. Relative and chronological age combined with consideration of sex are the fundamental principles for assigning role categories. The age principle categorizes the entire town in role pairs of respect and deference. Sex differentiation is not made in children until after infancy. An infant of either sex is called *ʔunin,* also a term for the new moon, until the age of eight months. The sex of parent rather than that of the child is designated: a woman calls her offspring *ʔalal* whether boy or girl, and a man calls his offspring *niĉʼan.* Sex distinction is made in speaking of toddlers: boys are called *htatil* and girls *ḳantzil*. After five years of age, a boy is referred to as *č'in ḳerem,* "little boy" and a girl as *č'in ʔačiš,* "little girl." The term for younger sibling, *ḳihtz'in,* which is extended to all of the people younger than oneself on one's own side of the dual division, is not sex marked, but the terms for all people older than oneself are. Sexual segregation begins at the age of five in sleeping arrangements as well as in public gatherings, when little boys stand with their fathers. The modifier "č'in" is dropped after the age of nine, and the terms "kerem" and "ačiš" are used until marriage. At the age of fifteen, a girl is referred to as *ʔantz wištal,* "just arriving at womanhood," and when she is married she is classified as an *ʔantz,* or woman. A boy is referred to as a kerem until he is married, when he is called *ač' winik* or "new man." A woman with children is referred to as *meʔeliš,* and is a full-fledged member of her sex, the *meʔil.* A man's reference term does not change with paternity. When a young unmarried man dies, people say with sorrow that it was a pity "he did not try out life," and that "he did not try out a woman."

In her youth a woman's role is tied to the reproductive cycle, but after menopause she is released from the restrictions of childbearing women. She need not appear as modest in public, and can drink and dance at fiestas. A noticeable personality change can be seen as women move out of the chrysalis of their reproductive cycle. Some older women begin to take a keen interest in sex, and widows in particular may have sexual relations with young unmarried men. It is after menopause that a woman takes her first role in ceremonials as a woman speaker.

In the man's life cycle, leadership roles are related to age. Paternal roles are the prototype for both familial and public authority positions. Thus the term for father, *tat* is the stem for the term for leader, *statal.*

In the relationship between the sexes, women are considered to be under the control of a male protector, either their father or husband. However, there is a kind of equality between the sexes which is not found in Ladino society. Usually there is only a small age difference between husband and wife, even in second marriages, and parents resist giving a young unmarried girl to an older previously married man. Mutual respect is stressed in the advice given by elders at marriage. There is no double standard for extramarital sexual relations, although men abuse the prohibition more often than women, judging from court cases. The ability the women has to assert herself rests on her economic contribution in pottery-making and on the fact that female household help is not part of the labor market.

Female sexuality has the connotation of negative power over male sexuality. A woman should not step over a man's feet or his clothing since she could affect his virility. This negative power emanates from the odors of a woman's body, and is captured by anything in contact with it. A woman's skirt cast over the head of a bull can tame him, and the water used by a woman to wash her body, particularly the vagina if she has had children, is drunk to cure snake bites because it is very "cold."

Sexuality is seldom extended beyond persons to material objects. There is some feeling that a man's tools, especially the machete and hoe, are male and that a woman's tools, especially the grinding stone, are female. Corn is a crop of men, while beans are a woman's crop, identified with the Virgin. But I could not get much farther with such distinctions.

The accidents of birth determine the recruitment of successive generations into the family of orientation. There is no outright adoption, but a child may be "lent" to a childless couple, usually by a sibling of one of the spouses, or a grandchild may take up residence in the house of a grandparent when all the children have moved to separate residences. Parents discipline a badly behaved child with the threat, "I am going to sell you to care for someone's house," but I have never known of a case of outright sale of a child.

The selection of a spouse is a decision based on both universalistic as well as particularistic considerations. Both the boy and the girl should be hardworking, sober, and dutiful residents of the same section of the dual division. It is considered to be of greater importance that the boy feel affection toward the girl than vice versa. The "taking of the heart" is a test of the strength and exclusiveness of the boy's interest in his chosen mate, and there is no counterpart for the girl. Although there is no term for romantic love, the closest approximation being "want" or "ask for" a woman, there is an awareness of the importance of a warm, affectionate basis if a marriage relationship is to last "at least until the day after tomorrow." A suitor is accepted if he is known to be a hard worker and if he does not drink or have a record of fighting. Character traits are given more significance than wealth, since the minimal differences which distinguish rich from poor can be lost within a few months if a man drinks heavily or does not work. The close identification among siblings means that in accepting a suit the girl's parents will take into consideration not only the boy's reputation, but those of his brothers. If they are considered to be disobedient, lazy, or frequently drunk, their brother may have difficulty finding a woman.

Positions of ceremonial importance in the household celebrations are filled by any of the elders who have acquired knowledge of the prayers. The nakawanehetik are chosen from among any of the bilaterally-extended relatives, compadres, or padrinos who have served five times in religious office. They are selected not only on the basis of how well they know the prayers, but also on their behavior when required to drink. A man who can hold his liquor and still speak well or who quietly goes to sleep rather than fighting when drunk is preferred. The me?il k'op is selected from among the female complements of these male relatives. She acquires her knowledge of the prayers in familial settings. The b'alnialetik are chosen from the kihtz'inal (younger siblings and cousins), or from among compadres or members of neighboring households. The rank order between the two sets of roles—the nakawanehetik and b'alnialetik—depends on relative age; thus the older nakawanehetik have greater authority.

Familial roles provide both a pattern and a springboard for other roles in the community. The father-son role pair is extended to the relationships between senior and junior officials in both the religious hierarchy and the curing hierarchy. For each saint, the elder mayordomo is called "father" (*Tatil Martoma*), and the younger is called "son" (*Nič'nal Martoma*). A man must fill the junior post at least two times before taking on the senior post. For each side of the dual division, the elder curer (when there was a recognized leader) was called "father" (*Tatil ?u?ul*), and the younger was called "son" (*Nič'nal ?u?ul*) or sometimes "youth" (*Biktal ?u?ul*). The term *me?il* (woman who has borne a child) is used in the reference to ceremonial roles played by women in the household, as in the case of me?il k'op (woman speaker) and me?il č'om (mother of the betrothal).

Familial role requirements must be fulfilled in order for public roles to be undertaken. A man must be married in order to enter into even the lowest posts in the civil and religious hierarchies.

Only in the case of the alfereces has wealth ever been a criterion for recruitment. These four officials had to be able to spend 3,000 pesos during their year in office. The heavy expenditures failed to give prestige to the official, and the display of wealth excited envy rather than respect. The result was that people called upon to accept the post had to be imprisoned before they would accept.

Recruitment to roles in almost all institutional contexts is based on innate qualities; special skills and knowledge are attributes acquired in office or other role positions rather than requirements for undertaking roles. Curers are recruited because they are recognized as having an animal spirit; they learn whatever skills are required after they have been initiated into the profession. The curers' special position in the society rests more on esoteric powers than on esoteric knowledge. Everyone in the community knows the herbs and medicines which are prescribed, and most men can give as comprehensive a taxonomy of illnesses as any practicing curer.

Economic roles, though largely undifferentiated for each sex, are consciously learned and transmitted. Boys accompany their fathers or elder brothers to the field at about the age of eight and continue working with them until they reach independence. Observation of behavior alone would seem to indicate an unconscious absorption of the role of agricultural worker, but informants recount episodes in which training in field work was explicitly transmitted by their fathers or brothers, and formal approval of their ability to do the tasks announced to their mothers. Parents express fear that school attendance not only interferes with working in the milpa, but that it will cause the child to forget what he has learned in the field. Regardless of what other tasks a man performs, he thinks of himself as a farmer.

Becoming a potter requires an even more explicit training procedure. The fine linguistic segmentation of each act and movement in the schedule of pottery-making is a clue to the explicit transmission of tasks by the mother to her daughter. Informants are able to recount the succession of learning of the tasks, the relative difficulty of each task, and the mistakes they made and how their mother corrected them. Being a potter in Tzoʔontahal is as much a part of being a woman as the role of agriculturalist is of being a man.

Special tasks become crystallized as roles only when few people perform them. Jobs such as caponizing, butchering, net and rope weaving, and wood cutting which are done by almost every man do not have role terms. Bonesetting and curing of certain "good" illnesses, such as swelling caused by embarrassment, are semispecialized activities performed by a few women who have "cold" hands. Midwifery is a fully specialized role performed by two women who are referred to as "the grandmothers of the newborn child."

A new occupational role has been created with the purchase of a truck by Indians of the community. There are now two Indian truck drivers. Recruitment of these particular young men was a result of their fathers' importance in the truck-owning cooperatives, and their skill was acquired in apprenticeship with a Ladino truck driver hired when the truck was first in operation. Both of them are acculturated in clothing and speech. Since they have acquired skills in dealing with the Ladino world, they often act as intermediaries for Indians of the town in their negotiations in the market or the courts of the departmental capital.

The continuity in occupational adjustment from early childhood to adulthood contrasts with the discontinuities in assuming roles in the life cycle. Girls are not advised about menstruation until they see the first signs of it; they describe their reaction to it as one of fear and surprise. Often they have been pregnant several months before they are aware of the condition or its cause, and they have no preparation for the experience of childbirth before it is upon them. Boys are not considered men until they are married, but in order to arrive at this status, they must enter into the "fight to get a wife," as the betrothal is often called.

Since recruitment to roles in almost all institutional contexts is based on qualities of the person rather than acquired skills, failure to recognize the prerequisite conditions of age and experience undermines the validity of the status. Community integration is achieved at the expense of limiting the range of roles through restricted recruitment and validating mechanisms.

Alternation and linkage in office-holding. The principle of alternation between civil and religious posts serves to integrate these officers in a single functioning system and prevents the development of segmented groups. The alternation of offices between sides of the dual divisions helps to integrate the village by pairing or alternating them in the same office. Some roles served as links between the institutional domaines. Principales are the primary symbolic leaders of both hierarchies since they are chosen from among men who have completed service in both hierarchies. The alfereces formerly symbolized the unity of the civil and religious branches in the transfer of banners from the cabildo to the church and in other ceremonial duties.

The regidores and judges have remained identified with the civil authority in Tzoʔontahal, although in other towns in the area they have become almost exclusively identified with the religious hierarchy (Cancian 1965). The regidores were formerly involved in religious affairs during the household celebration for the installation of the new alférez. At this time they were called personaetik from the Spanish term persona, or personage.

Events requiring community action reveal some of the links which unite officials who play roles in different institutional settings. On the occasion of an epidemic, curers are called before the civil authority to "give an account" of who is causing the witchcraft. Formerly the curers were linked to the civil hierarchy by a system of social control in which the principales, as elders, reviewed their actions in guarding the safety and health of the community. This system of checks and balance has been broken by the shift in power from the principales to the president.

The nakawanehetik provide the links between the household and the civil and religious hierarchies. They transmit the knowledge of ritual prayer and acts and officiate at the inauguration of officials. They serve as stage directors in maintaining the traditional household rituals and in ensuring continuity in public ceremonials.

Etiquette of role interaction. The complex system of stereotyped behavior contained in codes of etiquette depends upon role relations. The primary rule of etiquette is to greet people appropriately. In street greetings, one demonstrates that one knows how to "take into account," or show respect to, elders and minors. To elders of the first ascending generation or above, one says, "Good morning, father (or mother)." Those of one's own generation are greeted as elder brother or sister, or younger brother or sister, depending on their relative age. If the encounter is with a compadre, the terms kumpare or kumare take precedence over any other relation. A respected curer is addressed as *tatinal.* Officials are greeted by their titles, preceded by *mam* if they are older. Such greetings are restricted to people who live in the same division of the village. When one enters the other division, it is necessary to greet only compadres or relatives who have passed over after marriage. When younger persons approach elders of prestige, they remove their hats and incline their heads to be touched.

Service of food and drink is strictly ordered by age and sex. At mealtime, small children are fed separately, before or after their elders depending on the child's needs. When they reach the age of reason, about twelve, they are expected to await their turn. The father is served first, followed by his sons in order of age. The mother eats later with the girls.

The etiquette of ceremonial behavior is an extension and elaboration of the everyday forms. Service and greetings are made in order of age and rank, a procedure simplified by the fact that seating arrangements are made in the same order. In house ceremonials, the eldest man sits facing inward, to the right of the door. The rest of the company sits in clockwise order from eldest to youngest on benches lining the porch. Within the house, the seating of women by age begins with the eldest woman sitting at the center post and others sitting in clockwise order.

Preferred modes of behavior in all settings for all roles are "slowness and softness, expressed by a single term, *k'unk'untik.* Deference and respect—"hearing and feeling," *š?awai*—should be shown in all encounters, marked by behavior such as downcast eyes, shawl held over the mouth, avoidance of direct eye contact, as well as verbal signs of agreement and support of whatever is said—repeating the final phrase of the person conversing or injecting supportive statements such as "indeed, indeed," or "so it is." In the dance of the alfereces' wives, for example, women were the model of deference, moving in a self-contained pattern before the assembled guests, with slow, tiny steps, eyes downcast, a shawl covering their heads on which they wore their husbands' ceremonial hats.

Through recruitment procedures, alternation and linkage in official roles, and leadership validated by age and service in lower positions—principles applying to role relations in all institutions—Tzoʔontahal has remained an integrated community. There is a high degree of stereotyping in behavior from one institution to another, and norms of behavior are the same for public as for private roles. However, a remarkably high homicide rate and open conflict in all of the institutional settings indicate basic sources of disruption.

Since 1960 the rate of homicide in town has increased from an average of 1 every 2 years to an average of 5 or 6 per year. Table 29 indicates the role relationships of killer to victim in 37 of over 70 homicides occurring between 1937 and 1964. The highest incidence of homicide (7 cases) occurred between brothers and brothers-in-law. Male siblings comprise the closest cooperating group. Brothers work together in the milpa until the father dies or divides his property among his children during his lifetime. Bilateral inheritance with equal division of land and houses among female as well as male offspring means that brothers-in-law are potential competitors for the same limited resources. Friction arising among brothers and brothers-in-law does not come from the principle of equal inheritance, but rather because of the fact of differing responsibilities and expenses within the family. For example, the child who has remained with the parents and thus assumes the burden of care for them in their declining years often feels that he should inherit a greater share. The disputes arise in the decisions concerning how much this disadvantage should be weighted. The suppression of overt competition may in part explain the homicidal acts. Although the tensions in fact stem from suppressed economic competition, they are translated into witchcraft accusations as soon as anyone in the family becomes ill. Violence against a witch is condoned by the community and provides a channel for latent hostility. Once the accusation has been made, there is no recourse but to kill the man since he may retaliate by killing his accuser (this occurred in two of the cases noted in Table 29).

Conflict between generations in the role sets father/son and father/son-in-law stems from delay in carrying out role responsibilities. Fathers are expected to provide the money for the costs of betrothal, and to give their children shares of the patrimony including both land and livestock. The scheduling of when this should occur is often a matter of dispute, resulting in at least two cases of homicide in the period analyzed.

New economic enterprises have exacerbated the tensions rising from envy. Foster (1965) has suggested that envy stems from the notion of the "limited good," requiring the strategy of a "zero sum game" (Bennet 1966). The fact that the new wealth is evidence of new opportunities, not a subtraction from a given resource supply, has not entered the cognitive awareness of the people. The prospering leaders of these enterprises feel themselves to be particularly vulnerable to the envy of others and thus to the charge of witchcraft. There have been several open attacks on new leaders accused as witches; the leader of the truck cooperative, for example, was murdered in 1966. Six men have been killed as cattle thieves in the past ten years.

The economic roles created with the introduction of new enterprises have not been integrated in the traditional pattern of recruitment and control. In the association of cattle breeders, leadership tends to be based on the size of the herd; in the case of the truck cooperative, amount of capital invested and entrepreneurial skills have determined the leadership of the enterprise, while driving skill and ability to get along in the Ladino world has been the basis for choice of drivers. Such achievement principles as the basis for recruitment into these envied positions are not accepted in the same way that age and passage through a hierarchy of posts validated higher positions in the old hierarchies. The conspicuous expenditure of wealth in the more expensive posts in the religious hierarchy has also failed to lessen hostility aroused by the increasing disparity in wealth, and in fact those who have served as alférez have been even more subject to witchcraft aroused by envy.

EVALUATIONS OF BEHAVIOR

The evaluation of individual behavior is related to role categories, but is not circumscribed by them. Some behavior is universally prescribed, and judgments include all categories of people. This is particularly notable in behavior related to the moral code. Etiquette requires an ability to respond appropriately not only to individual "others" in a setting, but to a plurality of "others" categorized in special roles. This ability to respond to others in a setting and to anticipate what their responses will be has been characterized as "complex syntactic behavior" by Hebb and Thompson (1954). Analysis of complex syntactic behavior must go beyond the summation of dyadic interaction within role sets to exploring the shared values and norms on which judgments are made and expectations predicated.

Judgments of behavior are cast in terms of (1) morality, or the acceptance of prescribed behavior, (2) etiquette, or the acceptance of preferred actions, and (3) competence, or the effectiveness of performance. In gossip, in court cases, in allocating roles of responsibility, in judging professional competence, the assessment of a person is made with reference to his action in past incidents. A person is what he does, and the evaluation of a person's repetitive acts (called *yobra* incorporating the Spanish loan word *obra* and the Tzeltal possessive form *y*) encompasses a personal history.

Morality. Judgments concerning the moral value of a person are summarized in terms of states of the heart. A person who behaves well is said to be of "very good heart" in contrast to someone of "another heart." A good man is "one-hearted" if he takes other people into account. The description may be put in the negative, as "one who does not know how to seek disputes." The expression "two-hearted" is comparable to what English speakers mean by "two-faced."

Violations of the moral code are differentiated from violations of the code of convention or etiquette in that the former are said to indicate lack of fear and the latter are said to indicate lack of shame. These two definitions of social transgression point to the major socializing technique of the community: promoting a sense of shame and fear.

The following list of moral transgressions is roughly ordered in terms of the egregiousness of the crime: witchcraft, theft of cattle, theft of corn, "talking with" a woman (this is a euphemism for having an affair), having more than one wife, killing, and disrespect to parents. There is a fair amount of consistency in the rank order given by different informants. Of five people questioned, all ranked witchcraft first, and theft, without qualification as to what was stolen, second. Subjects questioned differentiated the crime of "talking with" a woman according to the status of the woman —it was worse to have relations with a married woman than with an unmarried girl or with a widow. Killing was listed late or not at all by some because it is assumed that the killer has cause unless the contrary is proved. The dead man is referred to as the guilty one. It is considered worse to kill a consanguineous relative than an affinal relative or a nonrelative. One man remarking on an incident in which a person lost his bull said: "It was a punishment of God for killing his father. If it had been his stepfather, it would be different." Wanton killing is said to be absent in the pueblo, and something that the kurik of the colonias do. The three murders in the past ten years resulting from barroom brawls between "friends" have not dispelled this notion.

Disrespect shown to parents is considered a serious violation of morality. A boy who refuses to listen to his father cannot expect to receive the protection and support of his parents, usually offered a child throughout their lifetime, or of the community. If the son abuses his father verbally or physically in public, the father is supported in whatever action he takes. One father, whose son kicked him in one of the local bars, drew applause when he made the sign of the cross in two deep gashes with his machete on his son's forehead. To beat one's father or mother is a great sin, but to beat one's wife is tolerated, particularly if it is done in drunkenness. If a man other than the husband beats a woman for any cause, she may reciprocate by beating him in court "before the eyes of the judges." One woman who was awarded this privilege when her husband's brother beat her said, "If he were my own husband, it would be all right for him to beat me."

The good man is "of one heart" and reveals it by his humility ("very soft heart"). The rules for demonstrating this are given by an old man who is frequently asked to be a nakawane in his section of the dual division: "I pay respect to my elders. I greet my brothers and my children [extension of kinship terms]. To all I give respect. Thus I fare well. I have not been killed, nor have I been sick."

A good man is a generous host, expressed in the phrase, "he gives many tortillas." He serves his community in public office but avoids the appearance of seeking power or self-aggrandizement. When he gives orders, it is in a soft, low tone, supplicating rather than ordering with the phrase, "If you would please lend a hand." He gives thanks readily for any service rendered both to God and to his fellow man. He avoids any show of anger, and is always careful to show consideration of others. Those who are of "another heart" or "two-hearted" are the opposite, seeking disputes, "thinking small," "being miserly," and of a "very black soul."

The heightened awareness of the state of the heart of others comes from the ever-present fear of witchcraft. Since the people feel their survival depends upon perception of evil heart before it strikes, they develop an acute sense of the behavioral clues that indicate its presence.

Conformity and deviance. Conventional or preferred behavior is characterized as "reasonable." The phrase "ʔič' rason," to take reason or understanding, is applied to a child who is expected to have reason at the age of twelve years or so, as well as to the arrival at agreement of competing parties, as in the case of betrothal.

Reasonable behavior is any behavior conforming to socially accepted understandings of what the world is. These include what a person of non-Indian culture might characterize as beliefs based on faith. They "know" that there are hill spirits, wood spirits who cut off people's heads, and men who transform themselves into animals. Occasionally they subject given understandings to empirical tests: one woman tested the belief that a woman could rid the milpa of insect pests only by walking through a planted field wearing a new skirt; she walked through the field wearing a worn skirt and her belief was confirmed when she found that the insect pests were not killed but just fled and returned later. Empiricism is not lacking; the difference between the content of their category of what is rational or reasonable and ours is based on the premises, not the process of reasoning.

People who fail to conform to the customs of the town are said to lack "reason." This category includes those who do not attend to the advice of their elders. People from outside of town who do not behave in conventional patterns are said to be "of another sort."

Institutionalized patterns of behavior differ as to the degree of explicitness of the association between action and reason. Curing practices are most directly attached to an understanding of why they are performed. Ritual practices in the cult of the spirits are tied to a more general explanatory system in which something should be done "because it was the custom of our ancestors."

Competency. Judgments concerning the intelligence of a person and his ability to adjust to his social and physical environment complement the criteria of morality and reasonableness. Alertness, or intelligence is associated with the possession of more than one soul: a person may have from one to a dozen additional souls. Curers and witches, by virtue of their possession of an animal spirit, are by definition very intelligent. Evaluations of alertness are often made in discussing the personalities of others. In the myth concerning the three brothers and the honey (Chapter 8) God, the Elder Brother, was described as "not very bright," Jesus Christ, the Second Brother, as "a little brighter," and the Holy Ghost, the Youngest Brother as "the brightest." Alertness is usually associated with manipulation for one's own advantage, but is not necessarily antithetical to having a good heart. In the myth mentioned above, the youngest brother outwits his two older brothers to his own advantage, and coincidentally that of the world.

The word *b'ol* is used figuratively to express the opposite of alertness, stupidity. Literally it means one who is mute; the connection is significant. A child born mute is said to have had its soul stolen at birth so that he must exist without speech. The power of speech is highly valued and the prestigeful roles are accorded to those who can speak well in both formal and informal exchanges. It is a dangerous skill, since the ability to talk to the gods gives an advantage to the speaker over the general population. The ability to speak to the earth, a talent which people say the ancestors possessed and which curers in the neighboring town of Chamula still claim, has been lost, as has been more recently that of speaking with the ancestors. But the curers can still enter into communication with the spirit world and in this lies their power.

Industry is valued along with competency. A man is described as industrious with the words, "he carries much wood well," and a woman with the words, "she carries much sand well." These expressions are a kind of synechdoche for general industriousness, since the tasks serve as the measure of willingness to perform one's sexually defined roles.

Judgments made in the choice of working "partners" in the exchange labor system are based on competence in working as well as on considerations of kin and compadrazgo relationship. Women make judgments of others' skill in pottery-making on the basis of both the appearance of the pot and its durability proved in use and transportation without breakage to market. Both men and women known to be hard workers are admired and envied. They may consequently become the objects of witchcraft.

Conceptions of personality are one end product of evaluations of performances and condition people's expectations of individuals in their social environment. For the Indians, personality traits tend to imply other traits. In order to derive a sense of these implications for Tzoʔontahal, I drew up a checklist to identify some of these associations. Informants were asked to state whether each of the traits listed on the top line in Table 30 was correlated positively, negatively, or not at all with each of the same traits listed vertically. A plus (+) sign indicates positive correlation, a minus (−) sign indicates negative correlation, and an equal (=) sign indicates that there was no correlation. Thus being bright is positively correlated with being beautiful and negatively correlated with being evil, fearful, lazy, foolish, gullible, braggardly, gossipy, and miserly. There is no connection between being bright and being of good heart, aggressive, or honorable. This suggests that the heart and the mind are independent loci for a set of traits that stem from them. Metaphors such as bitter, acid, and straight, when used to describe personality, are similar in connotation to those used in English. As in English, immediate sensory experiences of taste and vision provide by extension a means of talking about character.

In studying these personality traits, I sensed that "being" was "doing" things in certain repetitive ways. This impression is corroborated by the

TABLE 30. Personality Traits and Their Implications*

	Bright	Beauti-ful	Good heart	Soft heart	Aggres-sive	Evil	Indus-trious	Fearful	Lazy	Foolish	Gullible	Gos-sipy	Mis-erly	Up-right	Brag-gardly
Bright	+	+	=	=	−	−	=	−	−	−	−	=	=	=	−
Beautiful	=	=	=	=	−	−	=	=	−	−	−	−	−	=	−
Good heart	=	+	=	+	−	−	=	=	−	−	−	−	−	+	−
Soft heart	=	=	+	−	−	+	=	=	+	−	−	−	−	+	−
Aggressive	=	=	=	−	−	+	=	−	+	−	−	−	−	+	−
Evil	−	−	−	−	+	=	=	−	+	−	−	=	+	−	=
Industrious	=	=	=	=	=	=	=	=	−	=	=	=	=	=	=
Fearful	−	=	=	=	−	−	=	=	−	=	=	=	=	=	+
Lazy	−	−	−	−	=	=	=	=	=	=	=	−	−	−	+
Foolish	−	−	−	−	=	=	−	=	=	=	=	+	−	−	−
Gullible	−	−	−	−	=	=	−	=	=	−	−	+	+	−	−
Gossipy	−	−	−	−	=	+	−	=	−	=	+	=	+	−	−
Miserly	−	−	−	+	=	+	=	=	−	−	+	+	−	−	=
Upright	=	=	+	+	−	−	=	=	−	−	−	+	−	−	+
Braggardly	=	−	−	−	=	=	−	−	=	=	=	+	+	−	−

* Response of one informant.
  + Positive corelation
  = No corelation
  − Negative corelation

system of giving nicknames, which is based on behavior typical for an individual but considered unusual by the community (Table 31). Many of these names are acquired in drinking sessions, or they may be passed down from father to son. Women of the community do not have nicknames, perhaps because they do not often drink in groups until they are

TABLE 31. Nicknames

Nickname	*Reason given for nickname*
Mono (Monkey)	He acts like a fool.
Nulkačo (Horn of bull)	He once ate the horn of a bull.
Purga (Purgative)	When he was young, he had a great deal of diarrhea. As he grew older, people asked him how he grew and he said, *"pura purga."*
Soltero (Soldier)	He was once in the army.
Obiskú (Bishop)	When he was young, he made a hat which looked like a bishop's.
Chanal (Town of Chanal)	Formerly he had given lodging to Chanaleños who passed through town.
Mam ti?el mut (Man bitten by a chicken)	He had a chicken who bit him.
Mam čok (Beggar)	He was always borrowing things and not returning them.
Hwečol (Meal of sausage)	When he was president, he used to collect fines and ask his companions what they wanted to eat. They always replied "sausage," and so they had many a meal of sausage.
Mam sel pat (Torn shoulder)	He always wore an old, torn kotonču because he was afraid someone would steal it if he wore a new one when he was drunk.
Lo čiol (Tomatoes)	He ate a lot of tomatoes.
Heowa (Jehovah)	When he was drunk, he used to say to his companions, "You do not know of God, but his name is Jehovah."
Yakan tz'i? (Longbone of dog)	He was an orphan, but he grew quickly like a dog.
Tz'a yok (Short-legged)	He was short.
Rečo (Right [side])	When he was drunk he used to say that others didn't know what the revolution was like, but he did because he was in it. He used to shout, *"Flanko, recho"* (to the right flank).

old and do not have as much opportunity to project their personalities in larger than life terms. Ladinas of the neighboring towns are given nicknames: Me? Sobol for example, was named for her habit of saying when she was drunk, "No soy bola" (I am not drunk); Me? Č'ič'el, meaning Mother Blood, was applied to a woman who sold blood of slaughtered animals.

Behavior is not believed to be totally dependent on innate traits, and the Indians emphasize the socialization processes. A badly behaved youth was said in court to "behave as though he did not have a mother," and to lack fear of his parents. The sense of shame and fear begin at home, and the community relies on the family to instill these controlling influences on behavior.

Notions of Justice and Compensation

Notions of immanent justice, whether acquired from the priest or indigenous beliefs, are peripheral to the morality system. Crimes should be paid for not in suffering, guilt, or remorse, but in fines exacted by the communal authority. Every crime has its price, and most people agree that it is good to be able to pay in money and be exonerated. The scale of values assigned in the fines for crimes is some index to the relative weight given them:

Stealing a bull: 500 to 1,200 pesos, depending on value of bull.
Stealing a turkey: 40 to 70 pesos, depending on value of turkey.
Stealing a horse: 300 to 500 pesos, depending on value of horse.

The range of fines for each act of theft indicates that justice is exacted on the basis of market value of the item stolen. The fine for murder is 1,600 to 3,000 pesos or two to eight years in prison when a killer is captured by the federal authorities. Local authorities rarely try to find the killer. In the thirty-seven cases of homicide analyzed in the period from 1938 to 1965 (Table 29) only two resulted in federal action.

People express doubt about the priest's warning that those who do evil will reap the wages of sin in this life or the next regardless of whether they are found guilty. The pragmatic basis for this conclusion is revealed

in the following statement by a man who admitted to me that he had
killed two men:

*The padre said that those who kill will get killed. The one who kills
also receives all the guilt of his victim and will have to pay for it in the
after-world. But my father said that when he was a policeman, there was
a man in Tejonero who killed for nothing when he got drunk. He always
carried a knife and would kill anyone around. However, he lived until he
was very old. Therefore I do not believe the padre.*

Concern about the afterworld does not act as a deterrent to action in this
world.

Most men ignore the priest's attempts to persuade them to go to confes-
sion. Women, especially the prayer-reciters, confess and take communion.
Their confessions, according to the priest, are a recitation of the sins of
their husbands or their neighbors.

Drinking is often given as a defense for failing to meet standards of behavior. While this serves to excuse minor infractions, a man is supposed to
be responsible for his actions even when drunk. When one policeman
started a fight in public, an elder judge commented to my informant:

*Look at that, younger brother! I drink liquor when I am very drunk, but
I do not fight either my elders or minors. When I passed as president formerly, I used to enter the cabildo, and I spoke well to the judges even if I
was drunk. One time I came to your house very drunk and you were half
drunk, but you did not say anything to me, nor did I. You did not fight.
Thus I walk well. I never fight, nor have I gone to prison, and it is because I give respect to my elders and to my juniors.*

Reflecting on this advice, my informant added:

*And so it is with me also. I have drunk a great deal in Ahk'olnantik [the
opposite section from where he lives] both at day and at night. Whoever
speaks to me tells me to go drink with them a little liquor, and sometimes
I give them a drink or I take them where they sell liquor and we drink.
But I never fight, and I am able to drink wherever I like.*

The community has developed techniques for compensating failure to
meet behavioral norms. The most frequently used is an offering of the

"gift of the gods," liquor, to the party whose interests have been slighted. This is done in the case of a suitor who is asking for a woman of the other side of the dual division; he gives the bachelors of that side a gar- rafón of liquor in compensation for the loss of a potential mate. Liquor has become a substitute for the sacrifice of a child by a man being initiated into the curing profession. Informal offerings of liquor may be made be- tween neighbors or relatives who have been fighting with each other. Liq- uor is a kind of universal social solvent in disputes, and figures impor- tantly in court cases which are always terminated in a drinking session.

Another technique is simply a payment in money to compensate for damages. In some homicide cases, the payment of "blood money" has com- pensated the family of the victim to avoid legal action. This is never done, however, if the community agrees that the victim was a witch. Payment of fines in court is another such form of compensation. These payments or offerings minimize the bloodshed or personal involvement in conflictual relations. Payment by the man judged guilty will ensure his reincorpora- tion into his customary place in the community without stigma.

While it is impossible to elicit from informants a theory of roles, it is possible to formulate the principles underlying roles. These are deduced from behavioral observations and from evaluations made of the performances of others. They can be summarized in the following propositions:

1. There is a clear separation between role and role-bearer. This is seen most clearly in the passage through civil and religious offices with a minimum of "halo" effect. It is also found in the situation of house- hold officials whose authority in directing affairs within a household ceases when the ceremony in which they officiate is over. The separation ensures flexibility in a closed social system, enabling people to shift from one role to another. It also permits continuity in a system which re- quires an almost complete turnover of personnel each year.

2. Function performed is separate from role in which it is per- formed. This applies even in those roles which are designated on the basis of the most important function required of the performer, for example woman speaker, liquor measurer, and basket carrier. All of

these role-bearers have other functions to perform, but the term specifies the most significant of these. Other people may unofficially perform these acts but only the officially appointed person has the other prerequisites for and duties of the role.

3. Recruitment into roles depends on age and sex qualifications. Validation of the role emphasizes, in addition to these ascribed characteristics, innate capacity rather than acquired ability. For example, the curers who are respected are assumed to have been born with an animal spirit, while those who are believed to have acquired it are suspected of being witches. Similarly, high civil officials are expected to be innately clever, not just trained for office.

4. Evaluation of performance emphasizes the state of the heart and qualifies judgments of the person according to characteristics of the mind and of the soul. The heart governs emotions such as contentment or inner turmoil and determines the moral relations a person has with others. The mind enables a man to deal effectively in his instrumental activities so that he can speak and work well. Possession of a second soul means that one is clever and capable, but it is the third soul which gives power over the life and death of others. The exchange of evaluations about others is a crucial area of concern in the tense atmosphere dominated by fear of whichcraft. In the belief that their very survival depends upon knowledge of the intent of others before it is expressed in witchcraft, the people constantly consult with relatives, compadres, neighbors, or the curers, in order to anticipate changes in their relations with others.

5. Sanctions against behavior that fails to meet role expectations depend on the seriousness of the crime rather than on the attitude of the criminal. This means that compensation relieves the wrong-doer of any guilt burden. Most compensation, even for homicide, can be translated into cash payment.

6. Ceremonial behavior in everyday interaction as well as in ritual serves to limit the personal involvement in the encounter and to emphasize the role category. This is particularly emphasized in the initial stage of the encounter. Liquor and cigarettes introduce a more informal behavior in which the etiquette of reserve can be relaxed.

Unorthodox behavior after drinking is less subject to censure than that indulged in without this stimulus.

The social changes affecting the community have not changed the categories of roles. What has happened is a shift in the power and authority associated with civil roles: the president's role for example has assumed importance over that of the principales. A full account of the changes in the role system requires a discussion of the settings in which they are enacted, the timing which gives them coherence, and the beliefs which give them meaning. Summary statements on role coordination will be given in the final chapter.

Chapter 11

Ordering Behavior by Places

People act out roles in a space and time matrix that provides the cues for appropriate behavior. Place is a means of patterning three structural dimensions of role: sex, age, and relative prestige. In societies characterized by multiplex relationships, Gluckman (1962:35–36n.) has emphasized the importance of the setting in establishing what role the individual is playing. One's selection of a particular role from the many possible relationships tying people together is supported by observation of official terms of address and reference in these settings. In Tzoʔontahal, the use of place as a designation of role is even more specific since each person occupying a role is given a special place within the setting.

The social domains, or fields of activity where major systems of roles are defined in Tzoʔontahal, include the house, the cabildo, the church, and the school. Segmentary role relations are limited to the clinic, the corn-grinding mill, and the store. The house has retained its importance as a ceremonial locus not only for life crisis rituals but also for initiating new officials into the civil and religious hierarchies. The institutional buildings grouped around the plaza—the church, the cabildo, the schoolhouse, the clinic, the mill, and the cooperative store—are the meeting ground for outside representatives of national or supra-local agents and townspeople. These provide the settings in which behavioral adjustments to internal changes and to external standards can be viewed.

The Concept of Space

Relevant social space is conceived of as a square. The square shape of houses, of the offering hole for the house sacrifice, of the corn field, and of the planting pattern for corn conforms to a notion of the world as a square. Although this conception is contradicted by knowledge learned in school, the two concepts are not brought into direct opposition. The town still defines the outer limit of most meaningful social relations, and most people are not forced by the circumstances of their lives to deal with an understanding of the world as round. It is enough that the four "sides" of their village be protected by crosses at the points of entry. The important orientation points are the east, referred to as the "coming out of the sun," and the west, referred to as "the sleeping place of the sun." North and south are referred to as lowland and highland because of the topography. Compass orientation is important behaviorally only at death. The body of the deceased is laid out in the cemetery with the head to the east. Indians comment that the Ladinos lay the body out with the head to the west, but Indians of other towns, such as Zinacantan, also do so. The cemetery is located on the western side of the town.

The House

The reference to the house in prayer as "the entry to suffering, inside the poverty" suggests the "cult of poverty" which Wolf (1955:459) points out as characteristic of closed corporate Indian communities. Most people conform to a standard house size of five square meters subdivided into an interior sleeping and living area and a porch (Fig. 8). The walls are made of mud strengthened with lime packed in a framework of poles supported on nine main posts. The roofs are pitched with four sheds rising steeply to a truncated ridge. Tiles are used in most new houses to cover the roof, but there are still many thatched palm or wooden shingle roofs. Corn and beans are stored in the rafters under the eaves of the house.

Inside the house, beds line the two side walls. If there is no cooking shack separate from the house, the hearth is placed in the center of the interior room. The grinding stone, raised on three posts, is placed to the left of the center post.

The porch is the area for ceremonial gatherings and for making and storing pottery. A table with the pictures of household saints set against the inside wall, is adorned with flowers and candles. During house fiestas, men sit on the benches lining the four walls of the porch, while the women sit inside in a semicircle. A house without a closed-in porch is referred to as a "cattle house" since it is considered inadequate for entertaining guests at ceremonial affairs. Townspeople prefer to choose as higher officials those who have houses with porches to accommodate visitors.

Fig. 8. Interior of a House

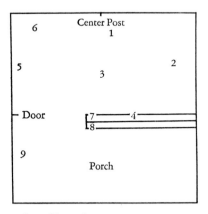

1. Seat of honor for women
2. Bed area for women of house
3. Hearth
4. Bench area for relatives of house
5. Bench area for visiting men
6. Mats or wooden board for visiting women
7. Honor seat for men (when inside house)
8. Honor seat for men outside house
9. Resting areas for male helpers

Each member of the household has his place for sleeping, eating, and sitting. The youngest child sleeps with his parents, and older children sleep with siblings of the same sex or with their grandparents. Newly married couples living with their parents prefer to sleep in the cook shack if there is a separate structure. At mealtime, men and boys sit on small wooden chairs at a miniature table placed against the wall separating the interior from the porch, while women and girls kneel on straw mats near the hearth.

Reference points inside the house (Fig. 8) are the center post where the meal for the house is buried in the inauguration ceremony (Chapter 1) and the door. Left and right are orientation points viewed from inside facing the door. Women of the house sit on mats near the center post. Female visitors occupy the mats to the left of the post and male visitors sit on benches lining the right wall and the interior wall. If it is a large ceremony for the ritual of inauguration or a celebration by the captain of a fiesta, only women enter the house, and the men sit on borrowed benches lining the walls of the porch.

Relative age is indicated by position in the seating arrangement. For women the seat of honor, occupied by the oldest woman present, is at the center post; other women of the household sit on a straw mat or board in order of descending age clockwise around the room. This order is modified by the presence of the grandmother who, if not a woman speaker, retires to the left (facing door from inside) corner. Visiting women sit to the right of the center post with the oldest immediately next to the post and those decreasing in age and stature to her right. For men, the seat on the bench nearest the door to the interior is called the "head of the bench"; this is the seat of the leading nakawane. The rest of the nakawanehetik sit along this bench in order of age. On the bench facing them sits the house owner, with his brothers and other visitors to his right in an age-ranked order. The b'alnialetik sit on the right wall bench.

Since prestigeful roles are usually a concomitant of age, especially in the house ceremonies, there is seldom conflict between age and role status. When conflict does occur, it is only seen at the top level; thus, the grandmother if not active because of age, retires to the corner while the woman speaker, who must order the women in the kitchen and receive visiting dignitaries, takes over this position. I have seen the leader of the č'om take precedence over the leader waiter who was older, because of the important role of the former.

When the family is carrying out a ritual, it is felt that the house should never be left vacant. The role of the "waiters" (maliwanehetik) is specifically that of remaining in the house while others of the celebrants are involved in ritual acts outside of the house. When the members of the betrothal party go to the girl's house, for example, the waiters are left behind; or when the patient leaves with the curer and some of the curing party to go to the spring, at least one relative remains in the house to greet the soul if it should precede the curing party.

Behavior in household rituals is described in Chapters 1, 5, and 8.

THE CABILDO

The cabildo, called by the people of the town the "cold house," [1] was built following the revolution of 1915, when Piñeda's revolutionary soldiers destroyed the original colonial structure. The tiles of the roof were confiscated from a finca which the Indians invaded in 1941 in an unsuccessful attempt to gain additional lands. When they were unable to maintain their hold on the land, they burned the owner's house and took the tiles to the town center where they remain as a symbol of their defiant action. They refer to this event with pride. The cabildo houses the jail, equipped with a barred wooden door, in one of its wings, and the Ejido Commission office in the other.

Within the cabildo, each official has his established place. The cabildo is furnished with a table at which the president and síndico sit on wooden chairs made in the Indian town of Chamula. Four benches lining the walls on either side of the entry provide seating for the civil officials. On the right side (looking out at the plaza) sit the judges in order of rank; the regidores, in similar sequence follow them. The principales, and formerly the alfereces, sit on the left side when they appear for ceremonial occasions. This spatial allocation establishes drinking and greeting order as well. Visitors can go directly from one to another in the formal greeting of a handclasp and murmured "good morning, father," or "good afternoon, father," without violating age-respect patterns.

During court cases, the claimant and his supporters sit on the bench to the left of the door; on other occasions the bench is occupied by visitors or petitioners. The police sit on one of the two benches lining the outside wall, or retire to the kitchen, a wooden slat lean-to on the left wing of the

1. Bunzel (1952) notes that in prayers, the cabildo in Chichicastenango is referred to as "the cold house, the icy house." Although the Quiché term is not given in her manuscript, one can see a similarity in the rhyming couplets and metaphorical allusions in the prayers of the towns.

building. When they leave the cabildo, they take their staffs as a mark of office.

The central room serves as a courthouse, a place for legislating and administering town affairs, for performing marriages, recording births and deaths, and for inaugurating new officials. Everyone who goes to the courthouse has a specific purpose for being there. Regular attendance means that an established seat and place in the order of greeting and drinking is accorded—even to the anthropologist.

Each day the civil officials assemble at the town hall about eight in the morning and take their accustomed places. Sitting is an official act. In listing the duties of the president, for example, "sitting at the table" was given first in order of importance of his functions by two informants, and in the case of the judges, "sitting at the bench" was listed first.

The president opens official mail and dictates responses to the secretary, now an Indian of the village, who pecks out the letters on an ancient portable typewriter. Since typing is a new skill for him, he makes many errors, and his retrials are accepted with patience and sometimes joking by the president and judges. When the president has an order for the police, it is transmitted to the regidor, who in turn passes it on to the police. The police always carry out their orders in pairs. Interruptions occur as petitioners enter. Men come in to announce the birth of a child and receive the name of the saint's day from the president, who consults the calendar; creditors arrive to request that a debtor be jailed for nonpayment of a loan or interest. When official visitors arrive from the I.N.I. or from the Ejido Commission, the president usually rises and stands at attention, agreeing with everything said. If it is an affair of some importance, the discussion may be continued in the schoolhouse, since the teacher has gained political importance in the town. The Indians rarely oppose departmental or federal officials directly; when they are unwilling to comply with an order, they stall for time, figuring that in the long run time is with them.

When the cabildo serves as a courtroom, it provides a setting for airing not only the grievance which precipitated the court action, but also the entire spectrum of personal relations involved. More women than men resort to court, since the drinking customs for men mean that they are more often the violators of norms. Behavior in the courtroom is controlled by a minimum of explicit rules. Very little is ruled out of order, and almost nothing introduced is considered irrelevant. The dialogue is primarily between the judge and claimant and secondarily between judge and defendant. The rural judges join with the regidores, who act as court clerks when a case is heard, in a kind of Greek chorus when consensus is reached regarding statements made by defendant or claimant. The judges indicate clearly their approval or disapproval of the statements being made, and throughout the case, consensual verdicts are made in an apparently spontaneous manner. No one pretends to be impartial. Personal knowledge of the defendant or claimant is introduced into the case.

Courtroom behavior falls into three major acts: (1) the declaration by the claimant, (2) the questioning of the defendant (literally the "taking of the heart"), and (3) the paying of the fine. The judge introduces the first act by asking the claimant to "come and speak" so that they can "listen and hear." This ends formally with the claimant saying, "Good day, Elder Brother." The judge introduces the second act when he turns to the defendant, who stands before the civil officials, and says, "Speak and we shall listen, boy. What goes with you?" The defendant sums up his defense in the questioning period. The president introduces the final act, telling the defendant, "When you give a little fine you will be free."

Both claimant and defendant pay court fees, an acknowledgment of the feeling that both are guilty because they are involved in a dispute. Before the term of the incumbent president began, this was paid in two liters of illegally distilled liquor, a kind of symbolic defiance of federal law. Now, since the president drinks only beer, it is paid in two family-sized bottles of beer. The etiquette of courtroom drinking is prescribed: the bottle, referred to as *smahtan,* or gift, is passed to the judge, who goes to the president and presents it to him with a few words of the pat?o?tan giving thanks for the gift. The fourth regidor then measures out the liquor, giving the first shot to the president, the next to the first judge and so on around the room. If a large fine is paid by the defendant, the president orders the police to buy meat, and a "common meal" is prepared and eaten.

In this society, there are neither veniremen nor specialized advocates. Civil officials other than the first judge act as jurors, announcing their sentiments in unison. The judge, rather than handing down a decision, sums up the consensus of the group. Kinsmen of the claimant and defendant act as lawyers. The defendant is sometimes accompanied by supporters who feel that he has a case. The failure of parents to accompany a defendant, regardless of his age, is attributed to their shame over their child's misbehavior and their own failure to train him properly. The judge does not limit himself to passing judgment but also counsels the defendant as to how he should behave.

The town hall is usually shut and locked at noon unless some business requires more time. In the evening about six, the officials return to take their same posts. They sit with their arms drawn inside their woolen jackets for warmth. After a half an hour they drift home. People rely on the presence of officials rather than particular actions to maintain social control, and it is their appearance at regular hours that assures the villagers that the town is being well run.

Local autonomy depends primarily on retaining social control functions. Civil officials try to settle disputes locally and avoid the entry of Ladino officials from the departmental capital, although the judges and president will threaten the defendant with taking the case to the department if they cannot get compliance. The number of cases referred to the capital has been increasing since 1950 as Table 32 shows. In 1951 the federal government began to fine local officials who failed to report homicide cases and accidental death. The local officials complied, but departmental courts were unable to bring action in over half the cases. No action was taken in 72 cases, or 54 percent, in comparison with 62 cases, or 46 percent, in which action was taken. Domestic cases, except for one of adultery, are adequately handled in local courts and do not appear in the departmental records. The trend shows an increasing number of cases of crimes against persons in comparison to crimes against property, an index to the breakdown in social control processes.

THE CHURCH

The church has been built and on two occasions rebuilt—when the tower was struck by lightning—with funds collected locally from household heads. Damage to the church was attributed to the patron saint of the neighboring town of Oxchuk who, the people say, was fighting with their patroness, Santa Lucía. The townspeople feel that they own the

TABLE 32. Cases Brought to Departmental Court

	Complaint									Action			
	Homicide	Rape	Robbery	Property damage	Assault	Adultery	Liquor distilling	Accident	Misc.	yes	no	unre-solved	Total
1950	2		1							3	1		4
1951	4	1								3	3		6
1952	1	1		1						6	2		8
1953	3		1	1	4	1				6	3	1	10
1954	2		3	1	1		2			8	1	3	12
1955	3		3		2				5	7	1	1	9
1956	3		3	1	2					4	3	3	10
1957	5				3				2	5	4	3	12
1958	4		3		3				2	2	2	4	8
1959	1				4		1	1	1	5	2	3	10
1960	2	2			2		1	2	1	1	1	3	7
1961	4				1			2		5	2	4	8
1962	5				2				1	3	1	2	9
1963	6				3					3	1	5	10
1964	5			1	4					4	2	4	11
1965	9								2	4	2	9	11
TOTAL	56	4	14	5	31	1	4	5	14	62	30	42	134

church, and many resent the intrusion of the priest who resides sometimes two or three days a week in the adjoining rectory. In the past five years, however, the priest has succeeded in asserting more control over the church: he has forbidden drinking in the church or in the courtyard, a prohibition that resulted in an open confrontation with the leading cofrade (Chapter 9); and he now controls the keys to the church and to the money boxes, formerly the responsibility of the fiscal. The two lay sisters who are in residence during the week hold the keys and are in charge of the upkeep of the church.

People always show respect for the church by removing their hats as they pass the entrance, even when they are at a distance. As they enter the church, they always kneel and cross themselves. They may spit on the floor of the church, for this is not a sign of disrespect.

The complementarity of church and cabildo is still formally recognized in ceremonial events: participants bow to the church and then to the cabildo during processions. The transfer of sacred symbols from one locale to the other at the time of the inauguration of civil and religious officials ceremonially signifies the integration of civil and religious authority, despite the growing separation in day-to-day functions in each of the domains.

The church serves as a staging platform for the images and symbolic offerings to them in the annual cycle of ceremonies. During the nine days of ceremony accorded to the major saints, their images are moved to the center of the altar or to the center of the nave. The staging effects are particularly notable during the fiesta of Holy Week, when the reenactment of the crucifixion is performed in the nave. The mayordomos, under the direction of the fiscal and the lay sisters, move the saints about and prepare adornments of flowers and pine needles.

The church is the locus for the weekly mass given by the priest. The men stand on the left side of the church (facing the altar), while the women kneel or sit on the floor to the right. A few benches near the altar are occupied by the Ladinos of the area who attend the mass. The lay sisters indicate to the congregation when they should kneel and rise in response to the cues of the sermon or mass.

In addition to these scheduled events, the church serves as a locus where individuals can visit the saints on their own personal missions. Appendix 3A records the visits of groups and individuals on an ordinary Sunday. Their actions in the church are part of the standardized behavior incumbent upon all those who enter the building.

Communication with the saints is ensured either by touching and kissing their images or, if the images are enclosed in glass cases, by tapping the glass with offerings of money. It is believed that one gains an audience by paying for it. When groups larger than individual clusters of visitors enter the church, sexual segregation is observed (for example, when a male child enters with his mother on the occasion of a mass, he remains with her until more people arrive, then leaves her to stand on the male side of the nave). Ritualized wailing is done by women only. After such a demonstration the women show normal composure, since wailing is a standardized mode of communication, not an outburst of uncontrolled emotion. It is private and concerns the individual wailer and the saint to which she appeals; none of the other visitors in the church indicates any sign of response to these displays. Unless there is a focused activity going on, such as a mass or series of baptisms, each visiting group is an autonomous unit, carrying out its own mission.

People visit the church most commonly in pairs of two. They congregate for mass in a pattern in which women and children enter first, and men, who linger in the plaza until the church is partially filled, enter in clusters and take their places on the male side of the nave. The religious and civil officials enter last, and the mayordomos, whose attendance is one of the obligations of their post, move toward the altar at the front. Men attend church less frequently than do women.

The School

Unlike the church, the school is regarded as an alien structure. Assistance in reconstruction and maintenance is given under pressure rather than voluntarily. Until fairly recently, schoolteachers too remained unintegrated in the community. In the early years of the school's existence, there was a rapid turnover of teachers. The employment of a schoolmaster with a wife and daughters stabilized the position after 1953. The school has become the domain of the schoolmaster, who represents federal influence in the local community. He has rebuilt parts of the structure in the thirteen years he and his family have lived and worked in this building; it was his fortress when the Indians threatened to kill him for building a chicken coop obtruding into the street, and again when he interceded in a case of homicide. He has a small arsenal stored in his bedroom in preparation for any reversal of his position in the community. The school is his platform, the area he controls and from which he shouts to his compadres—the storekeeper, the fiscal, and the president—to come speak with him.

The long building is subdivided into four classrooms and the living quarters of the schoolmaster's family. The classrooms are furnished with crude benches and tables; blackboards and charts of birds, animals, and the alphabet decorate the walls. The back porch, converted to classrooms to accommodate the three hundred and fifty children, overflows with benches. The students' own materials—a notebook, pencil, and erasers— are provided by their parents. When a notebook is filled, the students industriously erase all the marks and reuse the book until it falls apart.

When I was in the village, the schoolmaster often encouraged visitors to share a Coca-Cola with him in his office. Here, surrounded by his books, his collection of artifacts of both genuine and spurious origin, a picture of the district inspector of federal schools pinning a medal on his chest, the flag of the Mexican republic, he could speak freely of the personal attacks and frustrations and of the rare satisfactions he encountered "in bringing civilization to the town." As he began to build up his political power in the community, the president and síndico often consulted with him on town affairs. Agents of the federal or departmental offices who came to town frequently communicated with him directly before going to the ca-bildo. The school became the arena for working out political programs and strategies. The schoolmaster prided himself on being the primary channel of communication between the outside world and the village.

The conflict of interest between the schoolmaster and the parents of the children over attendance in school has been ameliorated in recent years with the acceptance by some of the parents of education as an advantage. In the early years of compulsory education, physical force was used to round up the children. The traumatic experience of his first day in school is recounted by a man now sixty-eight years of age. He was thirteen in 1918, the first year that compulsory education was introduced into the town.

I was in my house when I heard the civil authorities call the children to school. The police came to tell me to go to school. I did not go because my mother wanted me to accompany her on the road to Teopisca. On our way to Teopisca, the inspector saw me and asked me why I didn't go to school. My mother replied, "I am a widow. He came with me because I seek for what we eat. Therefore he must go with me."

The inspector did not hear her words. Since he was mounted on horseback, he said to me as I was walking, "Come here, boy. Don't walk on foot, climb up on the horse." I was embarrassed to climb up on the horse, and I had some fear because I had never ridden on horseback. I began to cry. "Don't cry," he said. "You are only going to school. The schoolmaster will not beat you." It is then that my mother said, "Señor, don't take him. See that there is no one else to accompany me on the road. When I come home, there will be no one to do errands."

But the inspector feared nothing. His heart was hot, hot. A man came by and told the inspector that I did not know how to ride and that I was afraid. The inspector said, "If he doesn't know how to ride, then you take him." But the man replied, "But I don't want to. It is better that I go get wood. You take him by force if you can, Señor. I go before your face" [a way of excusing himself].

I didn't want to go, and I just cried because I didn't want to. The inspector seized me, and put me on horseback. I was afraid to get up, and I cried and cried from fear. He said, "Stop it! Let us go!"

And so he led the horse with me on it. My mother cried when she saw the inspector take me off on horseback. She remained very sad as I left, since she no longer had a companion. I went on to school, and the inspector handed me over to the schoolmaster.

The schoolmaster gave me a paper with my name, which I didn't know. I did not hear what was said in that large school because I did not know Spanish. The schoolteacher asked me, "What are you called, little boy?" I cried a great deal because I felt sad for my mother whom I had left in

Teopisca. The schoolmaster said, "Don't cry, Ceferino. I am not going to
beat you because you will learn to write. It is good to know how to write.
You will speak Spanish because you will hear it, and you will look at the
letters because the letters are the same as they are spoken in Spanish. Sit
down now, and come tomorrow."

Then I told my mother to look for a slate and chalk because every
morning and afternoon I wrote. She was of one heart and did not cry
when she heard how I entered in the school.

For the most part, the teachers rely on authority in their program of instruction rather than encouraging the active involvement of students. In
the early years of the school, there was a rapid turnover of teachers, but
the employment of a schoolmaster with his wife and daughters stabilized
the position after 1953. The children respond with respect and fear to the
schoolmaster, and occasionally with interest and enthusiasm. The following reminiscences by the informant, Ceferino, reflect the fear, tempered by
some pleasure and interest, which he experienced:

The first schoolteacher I had when I entered school was called Chaya.
She taught me to write with chalk on a blackboard. Every time I wrote
badly, she told me to erase the letters and write another. After I finished, I
went to my house at three in the afternoon. The next day I would go back
to school. I would write on the blackboard. Writing was another kind of
thing. The chalk did not stick well on the blackboard. Afterward, we
started to use ink, and I began to learn well. But for a long time, I did not
learn how to read. For one year, I couldn't speak Spanish, but I continued
writing letters. This schoolteacher left and another came, Mista Munda
Gordi. He asked me what my name was, and I told him. He saw that I
didn't write the letters well. He was interested. He told me how to do it.
Then I began to improve, and my name came out well. He said that the
letters were better. He saw that now it was good. "Now you can make
capital letters."

Mista Munda used to beat us if we did not make good letters, but I did
not know how to make capitals. He told me he would beat me, so I began
to do the capitals well. He saw that it was better. When he saw the letters,
he gave me a book. In the first year, I finished the book, and he gave me

another book that added to the letters I knew. He saw that I was doing well. I began to read out loud, and he listened to see if I read well. Then he heard that I did well, and he gave me another letter to learn. Then he gave me another book, to take to my house.

["Was he a good teacher?" I asked.]

He beat us if we didn't do the letters well. He would pull my ear and he scolded very much. I began to make the letters better, and I was writing when the schoolmaster left.

A third schoolmaster came and taught in the pueblo. He was named Carmen Urban. We received him. I learned a little more writing. Now when he asked me a letter, I could reply. He saw that I knew all the letters, and he gave me another notebook. I began to write with a pen. With the pen my writing came out well. He saw that it was good and gave me another book. After I finished all that was in the book, he took another writing book out. He told me that I read all the letters well. He gave me a fourth book and a piece of paper. It was a very fine book! But this schoolmaster stayed only three months. Then he left. I did not continue in school since my mother said I should continue to learn only until I know all the letters.

She said, "You are an orphan since you don't have a father. You eat by my strength only. Now that you know your letters well, I want to see how well you can help me because I alone am buying corn and you are only eating it. Now that you know everything, you don't have to go to school because you must accompany me in looking for corn."

She saw that I was too big to stay in the school. She went to talk with the schoolmaster to tell him that I could not return. She told the schoolmaster, "See before your eyes that Ceferino has no father. It is for this that I want him to accompany me looking for corn." The schoolmaster said that I could not go out because I was now learning well. But my mother began to cry before the eyes of the schoolmaster and the president. He lowered his heart and said, "Well, take him then."

I left then. My mother heard and went happily because her boy had come out. When I came out I said "Thank you" to the schoolmaster. He said, "Now you know and go. Don't forget your letters. Take this book, and go on reading in order not to forget." I began to copy all the letters in the book so that I would learn some.

Despite the beating and the scolding, Ceferino recognized that the schoolteachers cared, and this inspired him to learn. He learned to write without any knowledge of the meaning of the words in his first year of schooling, but this did not discourage him. He was among the first four literate Indians in the community.

The program of education for primary schools today is scheduled by the Secretary of Public Education in Mexico City. The teachers conform to this as best they can in the overcrowded, understaffed conditions. The first-year program, according to the book, includes, in addition to reading and math, health studies—basic knowledge of nutrition, social and personal hygiene, the study of the healthful environment, the prevention of diseases and accidents, and first aid. The second-year course includes the study of nature—the sky, earth, seasons, the various changes in the moon, and conservation of natural resources. In the third year of their training the children learn about social life—the child in the home, school, community, and nation. The fourth year includes creative activities—games and artistic expression through learning to play musical instruments and the formation of orchestras, for example. The fifth year teaches practical activities—the construction of toys, work in gardens and other agricultural projects, and the economics of the home; and the program during the sixth year stresses the study of the national language, arithmetic, and geometry. Each of these six sections has a list of the knowledge, habits, abilities, and attitudes the teacher should have formed in the children by the time they have finished the year. The lists become more detailed with each passing year. The amount of material the teacher is expected to cover is impressive.

Mary Marshall's observation of classroom behavior (Appendix 3B) suggests some of the complexities of communicating this standard program in a class of first-year pupils. Inside the schoolroom almost all behavior is initiated and controlled by the teacher. All communication within the school is in Spanish—the teacher ignores responses other than those in Spanish—although most of the children understand no Spanish when they enter school. The regular pattern of question and response is sometimes broken up by demonstration of objects. The children's response is greater when the teacher reverses the pupil-schoolteacher role and lets them ask the questions she tells them. The scarcity of materials imposes a greater burden on the teacher already laboring with the barrier in communication. Despite these difficulties, the children manage to learn the basics of reading, writing, arithmetic, and Spanish in four years of schooling. The teachers are devoted and spend at least seven hours in the classroom each day.

During the recess period the children play individual competitive games except when organized games are introduced by one of the teachers. There is a tendency toward ganging up on weaker individuals in fights, that occur, but I have never seen signs of marked brutality. Since the Ladino children are a small minority in the school (there are no more than a half a dozen among the three hundred and twenty-four students) the Indian children do not face the discrimination found in schools with a greater proportion of Ladinos (cf. Romney and Romney 1966).

Discipline is no longer as strict as it was in the early years of public education. The teacher allows someone who has been hit to hit the aggressor but does not herself intercede. Threat of punishment may be made by the teacher, but I have never seen it carried out, and it is never suggested as a solution to failure to learn.

In comparing the domestic, civil, and religious domains of activities, the following features emerge:

1. In each domain, a hierarchy of power is present. In the house, males take precedence over females, and older members over younger. In the cabildo, the power hierarchy takes the form of a rank order coordinate with age in most of the offices, while in the schoolhouse, power is polarized with all authority vested in the schoolteacher. In the church, the conflict between the priest and the cofrades (Chapter 9) has not been resolved. Within the ranks of the mayordomos, relationships between the elder and junior mayordomo establish a graded ranking system (Chapter 8).

2. Behavior in each domain is standardized. Relative rank is reflected in seating order, greeting order, and drinking order. Autonomous behavior is most marked in the domain of the church. Focused interaction is predominant in the school, where order and control are based on absorbing the attention of the child in a learning task.

3. Categories of role-bearers sit and act together in all the domains. In the home the meʔeletik, the nakawanehetik, and the b'alnialetik have established seats and act in concert. Similarly in the cabildo, four ranks of officials, the principales, judges, regidores, and police, move and act together. In the church, elder and younger mayordomos move in pairs of two.

4. Sexual segregation is present in the home, the church, and the cabildo, but is lacking in the school. This rejection of the community standard for a group situation was the basis for some parents holding their children out of school until coerced by the federal authorities backed by the local officials.

5. Attendance in all domains involves coercion as well as voluntary action. Coercion is most marked in the school, but resistance by the parents to forced attendance and mixing of the sexes is fast wearing down in this domain. In the cabildo, the defendant is required to attend the court hearing and may even be jailed if he does not pay the fines charged against him. Coercion is covert in the home; the lack of alternative housing arrangements makes residence in the household of orientation or of procreation mandatory.

6. Sacred symbols are present in all the domains. The symbols of the cabildo and of the school relate the community to the nation with the national flags and the portraits of the president. The canes of office which are assumed as each official acquires office are symbols of local authority. The universalistic symbols of the church—the saints images, portraits, and banners—are acquired from Catholic orthodoxy, but have been encapsulated with local sentiments and beliefs. Sacred symbols are treated with respect and avoidance, both in the church and the home. The "holy cross" or banners are touched only with sacred embroidered cloths binding the hands of those who carry them. Saints' images are kissed, but as a mark of respect, not intimacy. The Mexican flag, with which less awe is associated, is saluted.

Each of the domains provides a setting for the recognition and validation of authority figures in the community. Values which are communally shared or imposed from outside are formally instilled in these settings. Extra-institutional supports are still lacking for the school, which is not yet fully incorporated into the community framework.

Replication of behavior in all of the institutional domains except the school provides a measure of social integration in the community. Patterned behavior, such as the set speeches of the patʔoʔtan, the formalized drinking procedure including the blessing of the drink and the serving of it in accordance with age and authority ranking of the participants, the etiquette of greeting and leave-taking, the embrace signifying ritual guardianship, occurs in the home, the town hall, and the church. These sets of stereotyped behavior, specified according to roles, simplify the movement from one institutional setting to another and contribute to continuity in role performance by the individual. The new patterns of behavior introduced in the school—desegregation of the sexes, competition in performance, grading of achievement—are not modes of behavior which have spread. However, as the skills acquired in school assume greater importance in the community, it is likely that the socializing procedures with which they were transmitted may spread to the home.

Chapter 12

Ordering Behavior by Time

The structuring of social acts depends upon shared understandings about how others use time as well as space. Scheduling of activities in the daily and annual cycles minimizes decision-making by individuals and provides a set of expectations that facilitates cooperation.

The Sense of Time

The abstract noun for time, *ḱalal,* is derived from the word for day, *ḱal.* Time began when k'oš, the youngest son of Our Grandmother the Moon, took the sun from his elder brother and carried it around the world so that there was a succession of day and night (Chapter 8). Time past, (*name?iš*), is a general state of being in which the ancestors lived. The future is at best a recapitulation of the past.

People judge time by the position of the sun during the day, and by that of the moon or the stars at night. In winter, the appearance of the group of stars called "the sandal" and in summer of the "seven stars" indicates two o'clock in the morning. The appearance of Venus, called "the big star," announces the arrival of dawn.

In addition to these natural indicators, there are three timepieces in the town—in the school, the parish house, and the store. In the morning the policemen check the time with the lay sisters or the schoolmaster before mounting the tower of the church to strike the bell at eight o'clock, the time for rounding up the schoolchildren, at noon, the time for closing the town hall and the church, and at five in the afternoon, the time for evening prayers.

Despite bells and nature, however, people are not very accurate in calculating the time of day; when I questioned them as to the hour, they were often as much as an hour off, usually behind.

Most activities are ordered with reference to the Gregorian calendar, but the twenty-day Maya calendrical month, defined as "twenty days or a month" is used in much the same way that we use "a fortnight." The Indians consider the moon to be an uncertain indicator of time, since "she does not walk well." But the moon is important in the culture: people note its different phases and are especially aware of the phase under which a child is born—an important sign for the newborn's future. If a baby is born at the full moon, he is expected to mature more readily. The full moon also signifies a propitious time for undertaking certain activities, such as cutting wood for the main posts of a house and cutting palm for the roof.

The Daily Schedule

Daily activities are organized by traditional economic pursuits. The woman is the first one to rise in the morning. She gets up at dawn, lights the fire, and sets a jar of water to boil for coffee. She grinds the nixtamal cooked the night before on the stone grinding board, or takes it to the mill in the center. She then makes tortillas either by hand or with a press; a recent innovation made of two hinged pieces of wood in which the ball of dough is set between pieces of plastic paper.

The men of the household are served first, followed by the boys; the women and girls eat last. As soon as they have eaten, the men and boys who have finished the required three years of schooling go out to the fields to work. They walk single file even in the streets of the town, the father preceding his sons. Each carries a machete, net bag, tumpline, and sheepskin back-protector if he plans to carry any loads. Many bring shotguns as well in order to hunt for field rats, raccoon, or the burrowing animals they find in the fields.

After the men leave, the women go to the porch and "seize their work." The children go to school, which begins at eight-thirty in the morning and continues until five o'clock in the evening. They return home for lunch, a meal of tortillas, coffee, and sometimes beans or chayote when it is in season.

Women work steadily at making pottery. Older girls help with household tasks from the time they are six in order to permit their mothers to make pottery. They bring the water from the faucets installed at every other corner of the streets in the center, degrain corn, and when they are about ten years of age assist in grinding corn or bring the cooked corn to the mill. In three-generation families, the older woman tends to the tasks of preparing the meals while the younger women make pottery.

The men work uninterruptedly at agricultural tasks, taking only a noon break to eat a lunch of tortillas, coffee, and sometimes beans. During periods of intensive activity, women or children bring a hot lunch to the fields. At about three-thirty they return home, sometimes stopping to collect firewood along the way. When they arrive home, there are no greetings. They deposit their loads of harvested crops, firewood, or *zacate* (leaves and grasses to pack pottery). The children pick these up and bring them into the kitchen with no words spoken. The men sit on the bench of the porch, sometimes assisting their wives with degraining, and "rest their heart" until supper is served about six o'clock. The final task of the day is cooking the nixtamal for the following day's meals. The family retires about eight o'clock.

The weekly scheduling of household celebrations indicates the thorough absorption of the Catholic calendar into the social schedules of the town. The choice of Saturday and Sunday for most household celebrations is geared to a week in which Sunday is a day of rest.

Other significant days of the week are Thursday and Friday. Thursday is thought to be the day when "the earth is open." House curing fiestas are scheduled on this day since the earth of the house floor can receive its gift of liquor. This is also the appropriate day to visit the caves to ask for crops and cattle, or to make payment with candles. Friday has a sacred quality because of the crucifixion, but except during Holy Week and Lent the townspeople ignore any proscription on eating meat.

THE ANNUAL CYCLE

The annual ceremonial cycle of religious rituals and life crisis events establish the pattern by which the people schedule their economic activities. Since the township gained dependence in 1931, there is no forced labor on communal projects for the neighboring town as there had been formerly. The peasant is master of his own time.

Tables 33 and 34 summarize the number of days and percentage of time accorded to various activities for men of two households. The first family consists of a man forty-three years of age and his wife. All of their own children died in infancy, and an adopted daughter recently left home to live with her husband and child in a new ejido plot. The second family consists of a man, his wife, two adult sons, and an unmarried daughter. In this family, the father of sixty-five is retired and his two sons perform all of the agricultural work. Table 34 includes only the activities of the sons. The two schedules provide some contrasts:

1. The forty-three-year-old man has many more ceremonial obligations than the youths. This is a factor related to the life cycle in which men over thirty-five years of age are involved in more familial and community celebrations. During the year this schedule was taken, the man was serving as a mayordomo.

2. The older man has fewer productively employed days than the youths (only 54 percent of his time is spent in productive activities) in contrast to 76 percent and 79 percent for the youths). The difference is accounted for by wage employment the youths have undertaken. In order to pay for the cost of betrothal, the elder son worked 56 days (37 percent of the time accounted for) in a neighboring sawmill.

3. The youths were not involved in any exchange labor arrangements; until they become independent heads of households working their own fields, the men do not contract reciprocal exchanges.

The fact that men spend only 54 to 79 percent of their time (using these tables to provide minimal and maximal limits) on productive activities means that there is a great deal of flexibility in the use of time for ceremonial responsibilities. Everyone takes an average of twenty days off for celebrating fiestas in addition to fifty-two Sundays.

The high proportion of time spent in family or communal ceremonials suggests the high value placed on them. The preference for leisure to pursue these activities is proved in cases such as that in which the additional profit in cultivating cabbages was not sufficient to motivate one agricultur-

TABLE 33. Activity Schedule for September 1 to June 29 of Man Owning
1 Hectare of Land and 2 Ejido Plots of ½ Hectare Each

Activity	Days spent	Percent of total time
Agriculture		46
Preparing land		
Clearing irrigation ditches	12	
Repairing and mending fences	11½	
Clearing land by cutting and burning brush	11	
Irrigating land	8	
Plowing	11	
Planting	6	
Cultivating crops	21	
Guarding crops against animals and birds	3	
Harvesting	34	
Milling sugarcane	8	
Exchange labor	13	
Walking to hot country	4	
Hunting for and tending animals	25½	9
Collecting firewood	13	5
Religious activities		23
Performing duties as mayordomo	26	
Attending Sunday mass and cleaning church	24	
Fiestas, attending mass, participating in playing drum, flute, etc.	21	
Kinship and social obligations		6
Attending funerals	7	
Attending curing ceremonials	3	
Attending betrothal ceremonials	5	
Helping in house-building	1	
Marketing		3
Buying	9	
Selling	1	
Communal labor		2
Cleaning irrigation ditches	1	
Repairing threshing shelter	4	
Business affairs of cooperative	4	1
Assisting town officials	4	1
Outside work	12	4
TOTAL	303	100

ist to continue growing this labor-intensive crop (Chapter 2). The low propensity to consume, maintained by community-shared standards which inhibit the display of wealth, further reduces the incentives to expand production (Schultz 1964:27). The major reward for hard work is land which, in his middle years, the agriculturalist can turn over to be worked by his sons, thus relieving him of daily toil.

TABLE 34. Activity Schedule for September 1 to February 28
for Two Unmarried Youths

| | Younger brother | | Elder brother | |
	Days spent	Percent of total time	Days spent	Percent of total time
Activity				
Agriculture		41		25
Preparing land				
Clearing land by cutting and burning brush	26		6	
Irrigating land	3		3	
Plowing land	1		1	
Planting	1		1	
Harvesting crop	11		7	
Doubling over stalks	4		4	
Working in hot country	16		16	
Collecting firewood	6	4	2	1
House maintenance		12		6
Plastering house walls	13		6	
Bringing lumber	2		2	
Making pigpen	3		2	
Pottery		1		1
Bringing clay	2		2	
Agricultural work for others		8		8
Harvesting and carrying corn	3		3	
Plowing	2		2	
Planting	6		7	
Nonagricultural work in sawmill	16	11	56	37
Religious activities		18		21
Attending fiestas	3		3	
Attending mass and relaxing on Sundays	25		28	
Sickness	8	5		
TOTAL	151	100	151	100

The assumption that leisure is a concept unique to highly civilized societies is denied by peasant behavior in this community and many others like
it in which the members are masters of the greater part of their time.
What differentiates their scheduling of leisure-time activities from that of
most western societies is that theirs is based on community decisions
rather than individual predilections and that it is set in the frame of sacred
rather than secular performances. Community standards are most notable
in the way people dress for fiestas: women wear their newest embroidered
blouses; their hair is neatly braided with ribbons. Men wear a kotončŭ
with their cleanest shirt and pants. The children, except for the youngest,
wear clothes like the adults'. Villagers "care for" the celebration by sitting
on their porches, greeting neighbors, smoking and talking. When a public
performance is held in the church or plaza, they participate as observers.
Arduous work of any kind is proscribed. Special foods are prepared and
served at regular mealtimes. A special mark of all days of fiesta is the serving of fermented corn beverage. Meat or chicken is more likely to be
served on Sundays and holidays than on other days.

TIMING AS A STRATEGY IN INTERPERSONAL RELATIONS

The preferred mode of action is "slow and soft." This applies to motion,
especially in rituals, as well as to the scheduling of actions in a series of negotiations. The people are sensitive to the use of time in bargaining as an
index to the relative resources of the negotiators. Withholding power in
the market gives a marked price advantage in the sale of crops. Sale in advance of harvest means a loss of one-quarter to one-half of the price which
could be gained if the crop was sold after it was cut, and corn sometimes
doubles in value if withheld for six months or more. Interest as a time
payment for the use of money is accepted on the basis that the borrower
could put it to work. There is no feeling against the evil of usury, although the rates are relatively high in town—five percent per month.

This understanding of time as an indicator of relative strength extends
to social functions. Time serves as an interval to build confidence on the
part of both parties entering into contractual arrangement. In the betrothal, both parties are prepared for a long series of visits before the suit

is accepted. Precipitous action on either side reveals a weakness of which the other party might take advantage, or which might even stop procedures.

Timing of activities is so specific that it can be read as an equation of social relations: People who come to the house after nightfall are either intimate members of the family, or are members of the circle of me?tiktatik invited for a special household celebration—night is the time when spirits wander, not a time for casual visiting. Arrival of the betrothal party at the house of the girl's parents after ten o'clock in the morning indicates that the suit has been accepted.

Sequential timing expresses relative prestige and a sense of priority. In "raising" the officials for the official ceremonies, the lowest ranks of officials rise first to go to the house and awaken each of their companions in order of rank. The sequence in serving order has already been discussed with respect to rank and prestige. Another principle of sequence operates at a more subtle level: women go before men when there is expectation of a fight since their presence evokes less hostility. This is evident in the betrothal: the me? č'om precedes the mam c'om in the initial proceedings when strong resistance and hostility is anticipated. When drunken fights start during house ceremonies, women intercede with calming effect.

Time always is on the side of the Indians when they wish to resist national orders. Verbal agreements to pay fines imposed or to assist federal agents in the capture of criminals are frequently followed by deliberate negligence in carrying out the orders. Usually the order is forgotten or interest wanes at a higher level. Government agencies such as the INI learned to bide their time much as the Indians did. Expecting opposition to any proposed change, they waited for the initial reaction to die down, and then proceeded as support from those who benefited overcame internal resistence.

When called upon to perform jobs that require regular appointments, the Indians respond easily to the daily scheduling. Resistance comes against scheduled requirements that involve long spans of time and interfere with communal and familial ceremonies. Work away from home is undertaken only on the premise that it will be of limited duration. This control over their own time is a value which Indians will not easily yield.

These time and space patterns provide the individual with a cognitive structure which enables him to function appropriately in a given setting and to plan his future actions. Having one piece of information, people can derive the other understandings necessary to adjust their own behavior to the expectations of others.

Time as a measure of value has been affected by changes occurring in the past two decades. Men are less willing to expend time in ceremonial activities than formerly. The first ceremony given up was Carnival, which has not been celebrated for over a decade. Most recently, young men have refused to become alfereces, and their resistance on the basis of loss of time and money was formally recognized in 1966 when the institution was abolished. The resistance parents used to show to their children spending, or wasting their time in school has given way as some of the more modernized parents have seen the advantages of education.

The tempo of life has accelerated with the increasing importance of bus and truck transportation to market. Women's time has always figured as importantly as that of the men because of their pottery production, and they have quickly accepted time-saving innovations such as the tortilla press and the corn-grinding mill. They have not shown any inclination to adopt time-saving technology, such as the potter's wheel, in pottery-making since they have no knowledge of it, and using it would require re-learning basic tasks.

The ceremonial cycle still provides the major consideration in programming other activities in the community. The Indian as an agriculturalist remains master of his own time, and he plans his work so that he can fulfill his ceremonial obligations.

Chapter 13

Belief and Behavior in a Changing Society

Continuity is the theme stressed in the rules of the game that apply to living in the square world of the community. The framework of continuity is the landscape itself with the ancestral hills and devils' caves reminding people of the moral order of the past. Repetitive behavior in rituals symbolically projects the past into the future, and behavioral schema in pottery and agricultural production reinforce the belief that all remains the same. The conditions making for change stem from the very attempts to preserve the existing equilibrium. A rising population on a limited land base using colonial techniques of cultivation is bringing about an increasing reliance on outside markets for the sale of labor and the purchase of goods. The ejido program which has perpetuated the system of subsistence cultivation has at the same time increased the dependency on external political influence and undermined dependency on parents. Some of the rules of strategy that have developed in response to changes coming from outside the community can no longer be justified by the beliefs that govern behavior within its boundaries. The community is now in crisis: people are losing faith in the old beliefs and have not yet developed a meaningful ideology for new strategies.

The crisis does not affect all institutions equally. It is absent in the traditional economic activities of milpa cultivation and pottery production. It is incipient in the households, especially where there are wage-workers in nonagricultural jobs. It is more apparent in the civil than in the religious sphere, and it is most manifest in the new economic activities. The school, as an externally imposed institution, generates awareness of the conflict between old beliefs and the ideology of nationalism, but until recently receptivity to these ideas has been limited. The behavior described for each institution in earlier chapters will be summarized as a mode of adjustment or adaptation in relation to the beliefs that give it meaning and purpose.

ECONOMIC ACTIVITIES

Learning agricultural tasks and pottery-making in the household is part of adjusting to membership in the community. Parents are responsible for teaching the value of industriousness and are held accountable throughout the life of the child. Agricultural tasks are scheduled in a yearly cycle that provides sufficient flexibility for a man to carry out community and familial ceremonial responsibilities. In milpa agriculture, there is no specialization of tasks. Small-plot agricultural production with a simple technology has been reinforced by the land reform program. Since the lands incorporated under the Ejido Commission in the 1930s were attached to the community, agriculturalists were not forced to adjust to new ecological conditions. Politicalization was minimal since the local commission operated within the old civil hierarchy. In the recent expansion of ejido colonies in hot country, Indians from the community have developed alliances with non-Indians in asserting claims to the land. Without any preexisting civil hierarchy, these ejidatarios have not had to adjust their activities to a given structure of authority, but have developed independent political organizations as an adaptation to their new environment.

Women's work in pottery is less subject to changes in techniques and organization than is men's. The schema of production in simple tasks in a fixed sequence makes it easier to teach girls each process and reinforces a given pottery tradition. My guess would be that if wheel production were introduced, it would liberate the creativity of each potter by freeing her of established routines.

Pottery production is not surrounded, as is agricultural production, by ceremonials. There is no god to whom one lights candles or gives offerings to ensure success, although there are hazards in production, particularly at the time of firing. Agricultural productivity, on the other hand, is thought to depend on the proper relation between the spirits of the heaven and of the church with the spirits of crops.

In the new economic activities, the Indians have shown both adjustive and adaptive responses. With the expansion of cattle raising, Indians have organized associations adjusted to the traditional dual division. The association for each side of the dual division mobilizes labor for maintaining the watering holes. The failure to organize communal corrals means that inefficient herding techniques, damage to the milpa, and frequent loss or theft of cattle persist. The association reacts to the last problem by hiring killers to get rid of those suspected of theft, but this adaptive response is limited to dealing with particular incidents and has not solved the problem.

The manufacturers of contraband liquor have succeeded in organizing a syndicate strong enough to maintain a monopoly price for both the internal and external markets and to provide security for themselves against federal agents. The syndicate mobilizes for specific actions, such as raising the bail bond for imprisoned members or punishing informers. As a community-wide organization ignoring the dual division and age-ranked seniority, it represents an adaptation in response to extra-community pressures.

The cooperatives that have been organized to manage the local store and the trucks provide permanent managerial operations that are an adaptition to growing interaction in extra-community economic activities. Cooperative owners are able to raise the capital to maintain and expand these operations. It is within these structures that entrepreneurial skills are being developed. The organizers gain the advantage not only of socializing the risk of loss but also of making a profit in a community where belief in witchcraft, fostered by envy, is rampant.

Activities in the new economic enterprises are not supported by any supernatural belief. In order to gain acceptance for the new enterprises, the entrepreneur Santos, who had organized the trucking cooperative, recognized the need for an ideology. His rhetoric drew upon the sense of deprivation Indians feel in their relations with Ladinos. He justified his own ends as an attempt to gain for all the community the profits that only Ladinos had been able to gain through trucking and crops resales in the regional markets. The ideology he had begun to formulate stressed economic and political independence from both the Ladino entrepreneurs of neighboring towns and government agents who tried to promote welfare programs in the interest of "civilizing" the Indians. This formulation involved a basic contradiction between the goal of moving into regional and national networks and that of keeping the old autonomy and independence of the corporate community. He never had to face that contradiction. Unable to gain adherents other than the small group of profit-sharers in the cooperative he organized, he was killed by opponents within the community.

THE FAMILY AND HOUSEHOLD

The core of the traditional culture lay in the local power hierarchies patterned on the familial model of age-ordered paternal authority institutionalized in the me?iltatil. The me?iltatil of the household have provided a flexible institution for adjusting conflict within the kin group. Their role in directing ritual performances preserves a sense of continuity in life cycle changes.

The institutionalized authority of the elders has not been upset by the trend toward residence based on nuclear families, which is an adjustment to the pressure of limited space in the town center. Kinship ties are continually reinforced by rituals that draw together the me?iltalil as sponsors of ceremonies marking baptism, marriage, and death. This group of sponsoring relatives has absorbed the institution of compadrazgo, adding compadres to the network of affinally-and bilaterally-related kin. The procedures for adjusting conflict among members of the household and extended family networks reinforce the authority of the elders. When adjustive processes in the house and court "arrangements" and in curing ceremonies fail, the only recourse is for one of the disputants to leave the community or commit homicide.

Ceremonies within the household provide a model for the rules of the game that apply to adjustive behavior in the community. The household officials introduce new officials into their role, teaching them the prayers and directing the proceedings. Their authority depends upon age and prestige acquired in office. The me?iltatil, as the elders of the family, are the direct link with the ancestors. They and the nakawane provide the strongest force for preserving the ways of the ancestors.

Religious Behavior

Socialization of the child includes teaching him how to adjust to spirits of the house and of the surrounding hills and springs as well as to people in his social environment. He learns the obligations he owes to these spirits in the rituals of house inauguration and curing. Place spirits are given an ethnic identity. The ancestor figures who live in the cave are Indians from whom all the people originate. The Ladino spirits residing in the houses and springs are a mythological projection of a conquered people who have learned to coexist with their conquerors by paying tribute of candles, food, liquor, and entertainment. If the spirits are not won over, they will admit the evil spirits who bring sickness and death. Their presence is known only by the trouble they permit rather than by good occurences; the miracles they perform are an undoing of the harm they have permitted.

The belief in the potentially dangerous nature of these spirits when their envy or appetite is aroused is linked to an understanding that men and gods alike are jealous and vindictive. It generates behavior that is in conformity with that of the ancestors. A sense of security is reinforced by the protective symbols of incense, the cross of palm hung on the entrance posts of the yard and house, candles which "blind the eye of the devil," and garlic mixed with hot herbs which exude an odor that evil spirits dislike. When the uneasy contract between spiritual and human coresidents is upset, a curing ritual is performed to make everyone "of one heart." Behavior with respect to both spirits and people stems from a policy of appeasement through entertainment and liquor provided in household ceremonials.

Behavior differs in regard to the category of saints called "spirits in the heaven" and those called "spirits in the church." Spirits of the heavens have incorporated pre-Conquest deities with those introduced by the missions. They are a more powerful force influencing human moral behavior. Illicit sexual relations carried out in the milpa by day are believed to arouse the envy of "Our Father the Sun" who will cause the milpa to burn by refusing to give way to rain. Similarly "Our Grandmother the

Moon" will not give way to the sun if her envy is aroused by seeing such things. These spirits of the heavens have greater control over natural forces than the spirits of the church, or saints. The saints have only limited influence over the souls of particular crops and chickens; people say "they are just of the pueblo."

The distinction between the "big saints of the church" and the lesser saints is recognized in the rituals accorded each group. Four of the saints are given big fiestas which are longer, require more expenditures, and involve more people than the fiestas for the lesser saints. Few distinctions are made between the personalities of the big saints and those of the lesser saints. They are big because their fiestas are big. The fact that the townspeople have selected four from the rostrum of saints given them suggests a link with the four guardian gods of the pre-Conquest pantheon, but except for San Pedro the Martyr's identification with Chac, or Chaʔuk in Tzeltal, I could not make any other associations.

To say that there is a system of beliefs does not rule out inconsistencies. Some contradictions can coexist without giving rise to tension. Awareness of incongruence either between beliefs, or between beliefs and behavior associated with them, arises in specific events in which the conflict becomes apparent—that is, when the participants must make choices between alternatives that affect their interests.

The people do not recognize any division between pre- and post-Conquest spiritual entities. Sometimes two personalities from Catholic sources may be equated with one of pre-Conquest origin in order to fit a story format, as in the case of Jesus Christ and the Holy Ghost, with K'oš (Chapter 8). The priests, who had a special dispensation to make whatever cultural translations were necessary in teaching the doctrines of the church (Doctrina Cristiana Lima 1584 III, 3, Recopilación de Leyes, Ley 22 lib. cited in Lamb 1956:531), are responsible for some of the reworking of the two traditions. But local elaborations reveal indigenous cognitive patterning.

Contradictions in myths concerning the origin of crops show some gaps in the union of pre-and post-Conquest legends. The gift of corn is attributed in one myth to the patroness, Santa Lucía, who received it from the patron saint of the neighboring town of Oxchuk. Another myth gives

credit to insects who carried it from the hills. Still another myth synthe-
sizes both pre-Conquest and Catholic agents: San Antonio, seeing an insect bearing a kernel of corn, persuaded a woodpecker to break open the
rock which blocked the entrance to the hill where the corn was stored and
then organized the insects to bring forth the corn. The contradictions in
these myths do not motivate the people to bring the several versions into
line with one another because the rituals associated with beliefs concerning
crops provide an overall insurance rather than a specific contract. The Indians do not trust their security to any one saint or even group of deities.
The two candles lit in the milpa following the harvest are an offering to
the "owner of the earth"; along with this, offerings of corncobs are made
to the saints in the church and to the house saint. Even the birds are left
an offering of corn kernels in the fields after the harvest so that they will
not be jealous of the farmer.

These myths fail to provide specific charters for action. What they do
provide is a set of dispositions to behave in certain ways. The underlying
disposition is that of self-imposed guilt and recrimination. The ancestors
left their cave because the people failed to give them a fiesta; the spirit of
money left the town because the religious officials in the past failed to
adorn the church and improvidently strewed the floor with green peso
notes in place of pine needles. Sickness and poverty are attributed to their
own failures.

Another disposition is that of appeasement through ceremonial entertainment. This is carried out in the fiestas for the spirits of the church and
the spirits of the heaven just as for the spirits of the house, caves, springs,
and hills surrounding the town. Community-wide disaster is interpreted
as a direct result of failure to perform rituals establishing reciprocity
with the spirits. When individuals face crop loss, they review their own
ritual obligations to see what went wrong. The curing ceremony is another effort to appease the devil whom the witch has persuaded to give
illness to his victim.

A third such disposition is to project human conflict into the supernatural sphere. The conflict between Santa Lucía and the patron saint of Oxchuk, Santo Tomás was taken to be the reason for the church tower being

struck by lightning on two occasions. The solution was to rebuild the tower of metal so that Santo Tomás could not demolish it if he struck again, a defensive reaction which is typical of the Indians in their extra-community relations. When an eclipse of "Our Grandmother the Moon" occurred during my stay in town, everyone went to her assistance, banging metal tools and pots, in what was believed to be a fight with the sun.

The emphasis on self-recrimination and guilt in explaining failure minimizes the build-up of protest. Economic hardship attributed to a man's own improvidence in relation to his fellow man and God are accepted as his lot in life. The drama of the curing ritual projects the Indians' sense of their own guilt for the suffering and poverty they endure.

POLITICAL BEHAVIOR

The structure of the civil hierarchy has been maintained but organizational changes have occurred which have weakened the basis for it. The alternation of offices between church and civil positions survives in the lower levels, but the new leaders in civil affairs now begin in the Ejido Commission, and few of those who pass as president take on posts in the religious hierarchy. The appearance of continuity has been maintained in communal rituals in which the principales provide the link with the past and the alfereces, until 1966, were the link between civil and religious wings; but in the day-to-day running of the town, the officials do not act on these premises. The balance between officials from each side of the dual division has been upset by the population increase on one side. The abolition of the institution of alfereces gives public recognition to the growing awareness of imbalance. Moreover, the factions based on the new trucking cooperatives that cut across the dual division reduce the effectiveness of the dual division in channeling conflict.

Behavioral deviation from the norms is present in all societies and is not in itself an index to structural change. This comes about when new interpretations are given to events that undermine confidence in existing institutions and leaders. Political conflicts in the past were interpreted as a contest between members of the sides of the dual division and hostility was channeled along existing lines of competition. During my stay in the community from 1964 to 1966, most conflicts were attributed to economic competition between the two trucking cooperatives. Along with this, the waning of the position of the principales has undermined the confidence of the people in the system of checks and balances in which the principales watched over the judges, the judges watched over the curers, the curers watched over the people to see that no one brought in evil, and the ancestors watched over everyone. Curers are more and more often accused of witchcraft and are frequent victims of homicide. The sense that they are the guardians of the pueblo and the agents of the ancestors is nearly dead. They are consulted only because the people feel that, because of the evil in them, they can fight the evil caused by others.

The shift in power from the old leaders to the new has not been accompanied by a shift in ideological allegiance. The new leaders cannot offer the security the people felt when they were living in the eyes of the ancestors. The curers remain as a powerful group because of their claims of being able to fight evil, but there is no longer a legitimate authority controlling their use of destructive forces.

A system of authority based on rule by elders is a structural correlative of a behavior pattern in which people act out the ways of the ancestors. This applies to the schematized behavior contained in rituals and in traditional productive activities. The ideology of a seniority-based prestige system persists at the explicit level at the same time that behavioral changes in contradiction to this are occurring.

Social control in a system of behavior based on what was done in the past depends upon the belief that people are carrying out their lives "in the eyes of the ancestors." Ritual behavior in Tzoʔontahal seems to confirm this, but in view of the waning belief in the presence of the ancestors and the loss of confidence in their agents, the curers, this behavior is a kind of social lie designed to perpetuate the old code of morality. In their everyday behavior, people no longer act on the same premises. The social lie is perpetuated because the people who enjoyed power in the old social system—the curers and the elders—do not wish to relinquish it. It will last only so long as they can find successors, and with the abolition of the recruitment through alfereces, this should not be for long.

Summary and Conclusions

The preceding generalizations anticipate conclusions that will be stated in terms of the hypotheses raised in the Preface.

1. *The stability of the society varies directly with the efficiency of its procedures for adjusting conflict.* The rising homicide rate is a behavioral index to the breakdown in procedures for adjusting conflict. The elders and cures still officiate in rituals to settle conflict, but their judgments are no longer as effective in overcoming fear and suspicion. The principle of age-based authority on which their authority rests has been undermined by ejido lands giving married sons earlier independence from their fathers and by young leaders assuming positions of power in the civil authority. More dispute cases have been referred to the departmental courts in the 60s than in the 50s.

2. *The stability of the society varies directly with the ability to validate behavioral innovations in terms of existing values.* Leaders in the new economic enterprises and the political factions based on them have tried to justify their efforts by stressing the goal of increasing their independence from the Ladinos. Their attempt to develop an ideology emphasizing the need for cooperation to overcome the dominance of the Ladinos is handicapped by the rampant suspicions about other members of the community and pessimism about the chances of the cooperative to succeed in the wider world. The conflict in the individual between desire for improvement of his welfare and fear of exciting envy is exacerbated by each innovation that raises the level of living. The leader who was most explicit in formulating an ideology for adapting to the new, the entrepreneur Santos, was a victim of the conflict he tried to interpret. There is no expression of pan-Indianism that could support the goal of cultural separatism of Indians from Ladinos. Indigenismo is the ideology of national leaders who have left behind the cultural heritage they extol. The Indians of Tzoʔontahal are as suspicious of neighboring Indians as they are of Ladinos. The retreat into separate communities which has ensured their survival in the four and a half centuries of colonial rule and independence makes it difficult to mobilize

support for cultural independence as economic interdependence grows.

3. *The stability of the society varies directly with the effectiveness of its procedures for transforming old power positions into ceremonial posts.* The community demonstrated the effectiveness of its technique of cooling off old power-holders as new leader usurped the authority of the principales. The struggle going on between the curers and the new civil leadership had not been resolved in ceremonial absorption of the curers' power when I left the community. The community was ridding itself of these fear-provoking agents of the supernatural by resorting to homicide. The loss of the institution of the alférez marked the waning of these old techniques of ceremonially incorporating leadership into a traditional hierarchy and linking civil office with religious obligations.

4. *The lability of the society varies directly with the gap between expectations and experience.* The Indians condition themselves to expect the worst and so are not disappointed by it. They pray only that they may maintain a given level of suffering and poverty. They are not caught up in that revolution of rising expectations that makes for discontent when experience does not match them. The Indians know they are better off than they were, and they contrast their present prosperity with the famine of 1915 when revolution and banditry depleted their crops and cattle, and with the typhoid epidemic of 1928 when hundreds died and the rest did not have the money to bury them properly. An attitude of pessimism about the future limits the problem of adjusting to it or of making adaptations to improve it. One could predict neither revolution nor moral collapse.

5. *The lability of the society varies directly with the degree of dissonance between traditional and contemporary interpretations of events.* The old explanations are still applied to current events. Disaster is blamed on individual or communal failure to carry out ceremonials. Sickness and death are attributed to witchcraft motivated by envy or malice. The paranoic theories of human nature are confirmed by every illness or death that occurs. Even the gods are characterized as envious and vindictive. Containment of blame for misfortune within the community minimizes the political involvement of Indians in the wider society and limits the changes that might affect them.

The material conditions making for equilibrium are breaking down within the community, but the failure for protest to develop means that old beliefs are not challenged by new ideologies. Adaptations and adjustments made in response to changes are still forced into this framework of understandings and expectations. But without any stated changes in belief, Indians are themselves transforming the internal structure of the society by undermining the old gerontocracy and shifting the locus of power to the innovating young men. A binary model of change that poses a transformation from traditional to modern might ignore these internal changes that maintain a given equilibrium intact but that provide a reordering of power making possible a successful adaptation to larger social orders. Tzoʔontahal is a case in point proving that the external conditions are not sufficient to explain fundamental restructuring of the society. People continue to act out a faith in the ways of the ancestors at the same time that adjustments and adaptations are made in response to increasing interdependence in regional and national institutions. The same framework of government is retained as shifts of power give scope to a new kind of leadership. Continuity in forms has the positive effect of preserving a sense of security. The social costs are a slowing down of adaptive responses and a high investment in the "ceremonial fund" (Wolf 1966). The benefits can only be measured by comparison with cultures that have lost these controls.

The universal problem which this community is in the process of working out has been stated by G. H. Mead (1938:22): "How is a society to find a method for changing its own institutions and still preserve the security of those institutions?" The present phrasing of the problem in the community is: "How can we preserve the solutions of the past and apply them to the present?" So long as the problem is phrased in this way, the solution is to exile or kill the deviants or innovators who attempt fundamental change. The threat of witchcraft continues to maintain conformity, and fear subverts the search for an ideology to phrase behavioral adjustments and adaptations in such a way that they will be congruent with future goals. Such an ideology cannot be imposed. Only the people themselves can work out the ways in which meaning and understanding are given to technological and social change.

Appendix 1

Settlement of Domestic Cases

A. House Arrangement of Separation

The following transcription of a tape recording concerns the house arrangement of a domestic dispute involving Alberta, the niece and adopted daughter of Mariano. She left her husband and returned to Mariano's home with her one-year-old child because of her husband's abusive treatment. Mariano invited all of the members of the betrothal party, as well as the maliwanehetik who had assisted in the marriage negotiations and Victorio, Alberta's husband. The leader of the betrothal negotiations was unable to attend because he had been drinking all day at another betrothal party. The arrangement proceeded with the padrino of the wedding, Pablo, and Alvino, Victorio's uncle and another elder in the betrothal negotiations, leading the discussion. I asked Mariano to tape the session so that my presence would not be an interference. In the joking session, the tape recorder became a target for the men's humor when, trying to replay it, they found that one section had not recorded clearly.

Pablo opened the discussion by asking the errant husband's elder representative, Feliciano, if the family wanted to take the girl back. Feliciano agreed that that was their purpose in coming, and that they must hear what happened to cause the dispute between the couple. Maria, the foster mother of Alberta, summarized their complaints against Victorio and his family.

Maria: *It is almost as though the child [Alberta's year-old daughter] has no father. We have been feeding her because we have had to support both of them. When the child became sick with diarrhea the father did nothing to help.*
Pablo: *Yes, we have to think of that. The child was frightened by her father and became ill.*
Maria: *When he came to our house, he fought Alberta, and the child was ill. Alberta went to the courthouse to complain about his behavior.*
Pablo: *It couldn't be arranged in the courthouse. It is better to settle the dispute here in the house.*

Maria: *Whenever he came to see her, he was drunk and came in fighting.*

Victorio: *It is a lie. I came, but I was not only fighting. I wasn't always very drunk. I came there sober to speak to you. I asked about how my wife was. Then I went to see my uncle in Grandeza. He told me that if he couldn't order her to come, then I better come here to hear what is said. When I went there, I was sober. I brought two bottles of beer. He said, "Ah, it is you," when I arrived at his house. "Come in and sit down." I sat down. I took off the cap of the beer and measured it out. "What have you come to say?" he asked me. "I am unhappy, father," I said. "What has happened to you?" he said. "I went to see Alberta," I said. He asked me if I had beaten her, and I said, "No, we only spoke a few words."*

Santia: *But if you hadn't hit her, why would she have come back to her father's house?"*

Victorio: *I only wanted to come to an understanding with her.*

Alvino: *So it is, you came to speak to me.*

Victorio: *It was in order to arrive at an understanding as you had told me. But I didn't succeed then.*

Alvino: *You didn't succeed in what you wanted?*

Victorio: *No, nothing.*

Alvino: *Well, when nothing happened, you could have gone later to ask with good words.*

Victorio: *I returned late in the afternoon. I had been drinking a little beer, and I was a little drunk. My father-in-law came with me. He had a fourth of liquor inside his shirt. We arrived at prayertime. My father-in-law was in the church since he was mayordomo at the time. We came in good faith to hear what was wrong.*

Mariano: *But then he came another time. I had gone to hot country to work. He came to the house and wanted to break it. He pulled out two of the tiles in the gate and entered. That was his crime.*

Victorio's father: *That wasn't good. You shouldn't go drunk when you can't understand anything.*

Maria: *We are not at fault. We spoke to him with good words. We told him he could take his wife.*

Elder woman of Victorio's family: *We told him he ought not to come when he was drunk.*

Pablo: *But now he wants to change for the better. You ought not to drink. It is better to eat meat and vegetables, and find corn and beans for your wife and child. Now we have arranged it, and you can take your wife and child to your house.*

Mariano took out cigarettes, and the group relaxed as all lit up the cigarettes and smoked. They discussed my tape recorder as they listened to the tape replayed. When they came to the section that did not record well, they decided that they should take it out and urinate on it. One man suggested that they should put it in prison, and another said that they should shoot it. This provoked general laughter. They went on to discuss the smoking habits of Ladinos. Pablo remarked that Ladino lawyers do nothing but sit in their offices and talk and smoke. Mariano and Victorio's father joked a great deal, the latter maintaining that Pablo had threatened to castrate him. This was picked up by Pablo who said that then Mariano would be a madrina to his godmother, Martina (the woman speaker in the betrothal negotiations). This provoked a great deal of laughter among the women. They then joked with Mariano about Pablo's other madrina, a Ladina from the neighboring town who sells the blood of slaughtered bulls. They refer to her as *me? Skitaoo*, the fat one. Mariano remarked to the women that Victorio's father must be a witch, and someone would try to kill him on the road. The conversation turned from the danger of going alone in the woods to a discussion of hunting. Feliciano bragged that he had an excellent hunting dog which he bought from a Ladino and which he referred to as "the Ladino dog." Mariano asked what Ladino they bought it from, but Feliciano denied knowledge of who the man was. They suggested it was nothing but a Huistecan Indian who changed his clothing. The joking and drinking continued until midnight, when the assembled company finally broke up. The next day Alberta went to live with her husband in the new house he had built.

B. Court Arrangement of Separation

Persons present:
  Judge
  Father of Plaintiff
  Mother of Plaintiff
  Plaintiff
  Husband of Plaintiff
  Regidor
  President

This case concerns a husband who had been separated from his wife and wished a settlement so that she would return to him. The man had been married before, and he occasionally returned to his first wife. When he got drunk, he announced on the loudspeaker of the cantina that he was a poor man who had to maintain two wives. This caused embarrassment to his second wife, who asked for the hearing in order to separate from him. He was working in the sawmill and had not provided for her support. The text is a translation of the transcription of a tape recording in Tzeltal.

Judge [to father of Plaintiff]: *Come, Mam compadre, and give evidence of what has happened.*
Father: *This isn't the first time he has left his wife. It would be different, Mam compadre, if he had only left her once, but he has left her several times.*
Judge: *Why do you keep on leaving her and coming back? It would be better to get her out of your system once and for all.*
Mother: *He goes to his mother's house but then comes back just to fight.*
Judge: *You ought to stop your fighting when you go to your wife.*
Father: *So it is, Mam judge. If it had just been a few words or one visit, but he is always coming here to fight. Even if you drink, you should speak well when you come to our house.*
Plaintiff: *He said he had nothing to eat but dry tortillas. I said to him, 'Go heat your tortillas. You're going to have to live like a woman if you get rid of your wife. Who is going to watch for you at the gate since I no longer intend to? There is nothing to eat in the house because there isn't any money.'*
Judge: *She says this because she is angry.*
Mother: *She speaks because she isn't a fool. He can't answer that.*
Judge: *They are still young, but they will learn. Also, he ought not to continue drinking.*
Mother: *He doesn't obey me. Eight days later, and he repeats the same abuse.*
Judge [to husband]: *Why do you want to do this?*
Husband: *I want a woman who takes good care of me.*
Father: *Does his wife have a lover, that she leaves the house uncared for?*
Husband: *We're fighting because she is always going off to my mother-in-law's house.*
Plaintiff: *Every time he gets drunk, he comes shouting. Why shouldn't I leave so that the child doesn't see us fighting?*
Husband: *I get drunk because of the fighting. If there wasn't any fighting I would just want a soda.*
Plaintiff: *Who wants that? There wouldn't be any fighting if you didn't come.*
Mother: *God can say that we don't want the embarrassment. I said, "Stop fighting. It isn't good. She doesn't give you tortillas or atole because you are always*

fighting. You ought to speak in sobriety. Why do you always want to fight and argue?"

Plaintiff: *At first it was the fault of a little board. For the crime of giving my mother a little piece of wood I had to come here the first time* [*refers to dispute arising over some wood which plaintiff had lent or given to her mother, and for which Husband wanted money*].

Mother: *I am supporting the children he comes and "asks for"* [*refers to the fact that husband impregnates wife, and then does not support the family*]. *The child cried a great deal when we were inside the cabildo. It was I who had to feed him. Why would I want this, my compadre judges? A husband who leaves you . . .*

Father: *How is the child going to grow up? And he keeps asking for another one.*

Mother: *You treat your wife like a mule, like a horse when you go to work. When I asked him to get some wood, he said, "Have I turned into your husband? Don't tell me what to do."*

Plaintiff: *If he gave something it would be good, but he never has supported me or even pays anything when he comes here.*

Mother: *He is never coming back to our house. We have spoken to the Ladino* [*Ramon, the former secretary who wrote out the marriage act*]. *We went to San Cristóbal to see what they would say.* [*Speaking to huband*] *But you don't listen to what he told you. You don't pay any attention because you are a devil. What good is it for us to go up to San Cristóbal?*

Father: *You should go, but you go on fighting as you started.*

Judge: [*to husband*]: *You should stay sober.*

Mother: *If he came to me sober, I would give him atole or sodas, Mam compadre. I returned the little board he had lent me, but he broke it.*

Plaintiff: *I gave him money for some soap, but he never gave account of that.*

Judge: *Now are you going to go with him?*

Plaintiff: *I am never going to go with him, elder brother. Even if he says he wants to take me back to his house, because I am not in his heart.*

Judge: *Ah, no. Let us explain.*

Mother: *Do you want to hear worse? No one is going to stay just to cook tortillas.*

Father: *It would be good, compadre, if she split with him.*

Judge: *They cannot split up because they are married.*

Father: *Well, compadre, if they* [*husband's family*] *take her back, then I am not going to return here. I am going to have to go to San Cristóbal.*

Regidor: *What has been arranged isn't good. There are small children, and he cannot support them.*

Judge: *But what else can they do, compadre? Better go to the man's house and make a fire there [a metaphorical allusion to acting as a wife in keeping the home fires burning].*

Plaintiff: *Although you speak to him, he doesn't listen. He never listened to his father.*

Husband: *What do you want to bring up my dead father for? He never ordered me, nor has any other person.*

Plaintiff: *I am not a fool. You gave me a wound, you broke my tooth. We want to stop all this and finish with the trouble you cause.*

Mother: *Let's come to some understanding. If it is only the trouble with the board, then I will give him the money and see if it is what he says.*

Judge: *This is not good, my compadre. It isn't going to content your heart.*

Mother: *I want to return and take out the marriage paper. It was Don Ramon who married them.*

Judge: *It isn't good for you to go do that. We are trying to arrange things here. The president has charge of the archives.*

Plaintiff: *He told me he was angry. I said, "Why do you want to sell the boards?" [This refers to the wood she had lent her mother.] He said, "I am going to bring more." I asked him again why he wanted to sell the boards. He said he had received money for them. He asked me where the boards were, and I said I had lent them to my mother. "Go get them if you want them," I said. He never gave me back the payment for the soap that I gave him. He spent it for liquor. I said to him, "Where is the soap?" and he said, "I spent it on liquor." When he gets drunk, he begins to fight me. He doesn't want me to talk back, but what does he expect? He said he was going to get another wife, that I was very lazy and very slack. I told him, "Why don't you go out and cut some wood?" He said, "Where do you think I am going to get some wood?" I was ashamed to go before my brother-in-law with my child and ask him. He never wanted to cut wood or ocote.*

Judge: *It is not good what he did. He should do what is necessary in the house.*

Plaintiff: *It is for this reason that I don't want to go with him, Mam Judge. He is always saying that his first wife was a very good worker. If I didn't have a husband or if there were no children, I would bring the wood, but I am not going to do it while he is around.*

Judge: *What would you say if he brought you back to his house?*

Plaintiff: *But I don't want it. What does he want me for? You heard him say I am a whore. He said I was a bitch. He said, "You are an old shit!" I don't want to have anything to do with him. What does he want me for if I am an old whore as he says? He said she [first wife] was a better woman than I.*

Father: *The judge told him before, "Go give your wife some support." We had three settlements before this. Mam Ramon said he was sick of seeing the woman in court so often.*

Judge: *First we will try to settle things here, and if he doesn't go in accord with custom, then you can go up to San Cristóbal.*

Father: *Here me, Mam judges, everyone fights occasionally, maybe makes two or three trips to court. But every time he gets drunk, he looks for a fight. I told him to stop fighting, but he doesn't listen. If I let my daughter go with him, he just takes her and produces more children. I have always had to support her then. He doesn't come around either drunk or sober. If he had come and told me what her fault was, then it would be good. When I had asked him what sins she had committed, he didn't say anything.*

Husband: *She just told me, "Leave me here and you go with your mother. I shall go back to my house."*

Plaintiff: *I left word with him that I was finished because of all the fighting. I don't want to go with a drunkard. [To husband] Even if you drink, you shouldn't beat me.*

Judge: *If you want a woman, you ought to support her. You shouldn't fight.*

Husband: *She told me, "You aren't the only man in the world. There are plenty of men who would want me."*

Plaintiff: *I never said that! You're looking for a fight!*

Husband: *What do you mean you didn't say that? My mother heard it.*

Plaintiff: *Go bring your mother. She didn't want to come because she is ashamed. It isn't the first time we are settling things in court.*

Judge: *You ought to go with him this time, but if it happens again, we will split you up. What else can we do if you don't obey our advice?*

Father: *When he goes to work, Mam compadre, he ought to look and see how much pay he is getting and how it will stretch to support his wife. Then she will make his tortillas for him contentedly, and there won't be any fighting.*

Judge: *We say that when he comes home from work he should ask his wife what she wants to spend for coffee or salt and all the things she will have to buy.*

Plaintiff: *He doesn't give any account of his little pay.*

Husband: *I don't want to say how much there is because there are still debts from when I was asking for her [refers to betrothal expenses]. When the debt is paid off, then I can.*

Judge [to wife]: *You heard that he will have to pay off the debt. Now go with your husband in one heart. [To husband] Go with your wife. If you have enough money, ask your wife if she needs some coffee or if she needs salt and wants the payment of it. You have to give some money in order to live contentedly.*

Father: *So it is, Mam compadre. It is good to be content and see the fire in the hearth. One time he came to my house and I said, "Come in. Let's take a look at what money you have earned." I told him to go save his money, give it to his wife to keep it for him. That is what I said to him.*

Regidor: *And it wasn't to deceive him. It would be good if he would believe [obey] this advice. They have been paying him double because he is a labor agent.*

Judge [to father]: *So it is, Mam compadre. Let it rest there.*

Regidor [to husband]: *The day after tomorrow, don't come back here with a couple more children and say you don't want her. Go back to your mother's house. You are lucky to have a wife. If you don't have a wife, you go get drunk every day. But with a wife life is good. She will give you coffee and corn to eat. Don't go on fighting when drunk or sober. Both my compadres have advised you [refers to judges].*

Mother: *So it is, Mam compadre. I am going now, Mam compadre. [Rises and leaves].*

Judge: *Go then, my compadre.*

The father and the husband give money for the fourth regidor to buy beer, and the group of men sit and drink the two family-size bottles which are purchased.

Appendix 2

Bloodletting in a Witchcraft Case

The following conversation is from a transcription of a tape recorded in Tzeltal at the home of the curer during a curing ceremony for a man whose illness was diagnosed as caused by witchcraft. The patient arrived at eight-thirty in the morning. Present are the patient, his wife, the curer, his two sons, their wives, his wife's father, and the interviewer who helped me collect the data. The curer's family helped in the bloodletting because his hands shook so badly with palsy that he could not control them.

Curer's Wife: *How did it begin, compadre?*

Patient: *It began in the month of April when I brought my horse to the threshing mill at six o'clock in the morning. As the other horses entered, one pushed his hoof into my stomach. My body was frightened, and I could not bear the pain.*

Patient's Wife: *He couldn't do anything but cry when he came out.*

Interviewer: *Where did the pain begin?*

Patient: *It began in my leg. My whole body and my leg ached a great deal. It was so numb I couldn't feel anything. My child stayed in the threshing shelter three days. A little later I went to hot country and stayed there. My son asked if I was going down to hot country, and I said, "Yes. I am going to look at my horse. I will return soon." I was of one heart until yesterday, and then I lost my heart. A man told me that he wanted another horse. It was Emilio Čilol who told me, "Boy, I want another horse." "It is good. I will get it," I said. "Yes, I will get it." I went to get it yesterday with another horse. I caught him and handed him over along with his companion. Then the pain began. I felt I couldn't bear it. It is for this reason that I came to you.*

Patient's Wife: *Take the gift, father. [Hands liquor to curer.] It is for this that I came. His illness is much stronger today.*

Patient: *Truly I could not endure it when I arrived home yesterday. I felt I should come to the elder to be cured and hear what he says. It is for this that I came asking for a favor.*

Patient's Wife: *There he was lying down for the day.*

Patient: *It is the first day I have stepped foot on soil.*

Patient's Wife: *It is today.*

Patient: *I have endured it for days. So I wanted to go get help from your work. He [Emilio] told me, "Go get the horse to work in the wheat." "Good, I am going to get it. Afterward I am going to leave him in the threshing shelter." When I returned in the afternoon, I could not bear walking.*

Patient's Wife: *I told him, "Better not go yet to caponize your horse."*

Patient: *We had another little horse we were thinking of caponizing this year. But now I couldn't think of it. You have heard how it is with me. Let us see what God says.*

Curer's Wife: *Yes, give another [speaking to liquor pourer who was passing out liquor] to the women.*

[*All the company were given drinks. Drinking order was: father of curer's wife, curer, his two sons, wife of curer, interviewer, patient, his wife, wife of curer's two sons.*]

Curer: *Do you want a little more?*

Patient: *No, it is good.*

Curer's Father-in-law: *With your permission.* [*Drinks his liquor.*]

Curer [to Father-in-law]: *Enter!* [*Meaning, "Drink the liquor."*]

[*The curer began to bleed the patient. He had eight gourds which he applied three times. He took the basin into which he poured the blood out to the yard and buried it, saying, "We cannot burn it inside because it was witchcraft."*]

Curer [to patient]: *Can you endure it again?*

Patient: *I can endure it.*

Patient's Wife: *Please, father.*

Curer: *It is good. You don't have to endure it again.*

[*Drinking continues.*]

Curer's Father-in-law [*pouring blood into a saucer*]: *Look, it is black.*

Curer's Younger Son [to elder brother]: *It is not good, elder brother.* [*He had noted that the last gourd did not have much blood.*]

Curer's Father-in-law [to interviewer]: *Ah, God, it is not now as it was before. There is much witchcraft.*

Patient's Wife: *Let us see what came out.*

Curer's Father-in-law: *It is black because the witchcraft is well lodged in his body.*

[*Curer points to his son where to make another scratch.*]

Curer's Elder Son: *Where truly?*

Curer: *There truly.*

Curer's Elder Son: *It is the same [meaning, the gourds are yielding the same kind of blood]. Please, Čiko, help a little.*

Curer's Younger Son: *Yes, I will help a little.*

Patient's Father-in-law: *Is there a little water? [He wanted to know if there was a little more water to dip his flower, the* čiliwet, *to sprinkle water on the patient.]*

Patient: *It pains a lot, man!*

Curer's Younger Son: *Yes, it does.*

Curer's Father-in-law: *It is coming out very well with this larger gourd.*

Patient: *I can stand it.*

Curer's Wife: *Whoever comes, he [her husband] can bleed.*

Curer's Father-in-law: *The women are tired now.*

Patient: *Because they are beginning to feel drunk.*

Women: *No, we only smelled the cup! [Laughter; drinking continues.]*

Patient: *Oh, I am tired.*

Women: *It [the bleeding gourd] is very big.*

Curer's Father-in-law: *Do you have another gourd? There is one over there.*

Curer's Wife: *Where? Me? Angela lost it.*

Curer's Father-in-law: *Did you find it?*

Curer's Wife: *No, it stayed there. Look, look well. I will put it here. My sister wanted a bloodletting, and she did not endure it. She got drunk.*

Curer's Father-in-law: *He endured well.*

Curer's Wife: *Why didn't you bring back a little liquor? You are deceiving us.*

Liquor Pourer: *No, because you did not drink it. I am going to bring another.*

Patient [to Curer's Wife]: *Did you drink liquor at the other bloodletting?*

Curer's Wife: *No. We only ate what they gave us.*

Curer: *I don't drink. I used to drink when I was well. When I bled Manuel, I did not get drunk for that.*

Curer's Wife: *When the curer went to see Manuel, one of his arms did not work.*

Curer: *That man endured curing very well. We have to endure. What can you do?*

Patient: *Yes, it is the same sickness he had. There is much air in your hand. It [gourd] is not sucking any more.*

Patient's Wife: *Your blood is afraid. So it is.*

Curer's Father-in-law: *When there is much air in the hand of the curer, you have to take wax and glass.*

[*Curer's Wife passes cloth to wipe blood.*]

Curer: *Another pull.*

Patient: *Please, favor of God!*

Curer: *Formerly I did everything. I pricked the skin, I put on the gourd. I did everything when I was well. Now I cannot do it. My illness has lasted a long time.*

Curer's Wife: *He cannot even get up well. He doesn't eat. When he takes coffee in his hand, he cannot drink well.*

Curer: *I cannot eat beans or beef.*

Curer's Wife: *He can only drink coffee.*

[*The curing is over. The patient and his wife leave shortly.*]

Appendix 3

Observation of Behavior in Public Places

A. Observation in Church

Sunday morning, August 1

5:40 The mayordomos are sitting on stone benches in front of the church. They are quiet.

6:10 Two men go up and ring the bells.

6:23 A man kneels in front of the altar and prays.

6:35 Two men come down from the bell tower. The mayordomos have now moved to the opposite side in the front of the church and are standing around talking.

6:45 Two men go up to the bell tower, ring the bells for three minutes, then repeatedly with no intervals.

7:05 Two women and a boy in Ladino dress kneel in front of Santa Lucía.

7:15 Two women and two girls (five and seven years of age perhaps) kneel in front of Santa Lucía. One of the women has two candles; she lights one. The other women with fresh flowers places them in front of Santiago, touches her candle to him, and then places it in one of the glasses on the altar that is near his statue.

7:23 Two women and a little boy carrying two candles come in and kneel in front of Santa Lucía. A boy of about twelve or thirteen who came in with the first two women had been sitting in front of Santa Lucía but now that quite a few women are here, he has moved over to the men's side.

7:30 One man comes down from the bell tower. All mayordomos come in and light the candles in front of their saints, then leave church.

7:35 Two men genuflect in front of the baptistry (facing baptistry), make the sign of the cross, and then kneel facing the main altar. (Genuflection is a sign of adoration officially and is only supposed to be done facing the Blessed Sacrament.)

7:45 Miguel, the former fiscal, enters, goes to the left side of the altar, prays a few minutes, goes to a stool in front, and sits there. (He is the only Indian who uses stool to kneel on.) A man with a little girl goes to Santiago, kisses his statue, then kneels and prays in front of him.

7:50 One remaining mayordomo (the rest went home) enters and speaks to the women. Some are leaving now. They kiss altars on the way out, sometimes making the sign of the cross before they kiss the altar. Two women come to me to tell me, "There is no mass."

8:00 Two of the women take out the old flowers in the vases and add the new ones.

8:10 Another woman tells me, "There is no mass." All the women except one have left. The two who fixed the flowers are carrying the old flowers out with them. The woman who stayed is praying out loud now in front of Santa Lucía.

8:20 Two men enter, face the door, make the sign of the cross, and then go up to the front of the church, kneeling now and praying out loud. A man, barefoot, in Ladino dress and carrying a bulging leather bag, enters and kneels in front of the main altar to pray.

8:40 One woman is still wailing (about one-half hour now). A man enters, kneels for one minute in front of the side altar facing the main altar. He goes to Santa Lucía, kisses the altar, goes to all the other altars except one in the front left, and then leaves. The woman stops wailing. She picks three daisies from the vase, touches them four times to the glass front of Santa Lucía's case, kisses them, and leaves them lying on the altar. She kisses each statue on the way out except the statue to the left front.

8:45 Of the mayordomos who are now coming back, five enter the church. One takes Santiago and puts him in the baptistry, then leaves. Two more make the rounds of the statues, pausing a moment in front of each one, then kissing it and moving on. One of them puts money in the coffin-case slot for offerings. They all leave within five minutes. One of the men takes two of the drums with him.

9:15 Men are talking and laughing outside. Once in a while it is quiet. Some begin to play the drum and flute. This lasts for three minutes.

9:20 Another piece is begun, lasting four minutes. One man comes in, kneels facing the front side altar, and after two minutes leaves.

9:45 Two mayordomos begin to play music but don't continue.

10:45 The mayordomos are drinking the liquor left from Santiago's fiesta.

11:00 Some mayordomos are playing the drum and flute.

11:30 The mayordomos ring the bells again. A man says it is twelve o'clock.

12:00 They go home, leaving the door open and the church empty.

B. Observation in the School

Morning

The schoolrooms are exceedingly crowded with three hundred and fifty children in four rooms and an open porch. The babble of the children's voices reciting their lessons drowns out the voice of the teacher, who has to shout to draw their attention to a new lesson.

All the teaching is done in Spanish. On one occasion, when no one in the class understood what was said, the teacher asked a little boy to translate for her. When she talks, usually about only half or three-quarters of the class pays attention. When the children are singing, all but two or three students participate.

In taking roll, the teacher calls the boys' names first. This order is reversed when the children leave the classroom, with the girls going first. Seating order on the long benches set before tables is not segregated by sex, although there is some clustering.

In teaching the children to read, the teacher writes the vowels on the blackboard in alphabetical order. The children are asked to repeat them after her. She does this seven or eight times. She has a number of the children come up and use the pointer to indicate certain vowels while the rest of the children repeat their names. She leads them in singing the song she has taught them before about the vowels. She mixes up the order of the vowels, pointing to them and asking the children to name them. She asks how many there are and writes a number under each vowel. She drills the class in the names of the vowels and the corresponding numbers for about five minutes more. Using sticks (the majority of the children have five sticks which they carry in their bags, and those who don't use their fingers) she leads them in practicing their numbers up to ten. She asks for volunteers to count from one to ten. When a child falters, she repeats the numbers with him.

The teacher uses a doll to teach the children parts of the body, giving the name in Spanish first, and afterward asking, "What do you call this?" She takes the doll to small groups of children sitting at their desks and lets them handle it. They show much interest, crowding around the doll. She then shows

them a mirror, tells them what it is called, and lets the children look at themselves in it. About one-fourth of the class responds. She pastes a picture on the
blackboard of a man carrying a valise accompanied by a dog and a boy. She
asks what each object is called in Spanish and practices the name of the object
with the whole class. Visual aids are pictures cut from coloring books or maga-
zines, things she draws on the board, as well as articles from a box stored in
her desk including a comb, mirror, glass, flag, color wheel, cut-outs of a boy,
girl, chair, table, bear, soldier, flower, and leaf. After practicing the names of
each, she stands in the back of the room and tells different children to bring
the various objects to her. After drawing two ducks on the board and getting
no reaction from the children when she asks them the name, she tells them
and then leads them in practicing it.

She asks them the name of the town, of the school director, of the school,
and when they fail to respond, she tells them and has them repeat the words
over and over.

She leads the class in about five different songs she has taught them. The
number of children who know the songs varies from one-fourth to three-
fourths, with about one-fifth never singing. Some attempt a word every once in
a while. She sings the elephant song, which most of them know and which uti-
lizes their knowledge of numbers from one to five. Twice, when a few children begin to sing on their own initiative, she tells them to be quiet. She asks
them, "Do you like to sing?" and all respond, "Yes, teacher."

The teacher seldom smiles at the children. As they leave the room in single
file, she rebukes any who attempt to run out or pair with another.

Recess. Two boys are fighting and three others join with one of them.
The one who has been ganged up on finally gets away, and they do not chase
him. Boys around ten years old play keep-away with a ball on their own initiative. There isn't much teamwork. Often one boy will get the ball and run with
it, the other boys after him. Finally he will throw it to someone or someone
will take it away from him. The girls sit in groups, sometimes embroidering or
knitting. Some boys just stand by watching those who are playing.

In the classroom after recess. The teacher shows the color wheel and
asks the names of the colors to which she points. A couple of girls put their
hands in their ears while the class is reciting. When the teacher asks for a vol-
unteer to hold the color wheel in the demonstration, approximately twenty out
of the fifty-four children raise their hands. One little boy in the back pays

no attention; he was one who had sat by himself on the bandstand at recess.

They practice counting from one to five. The teacher then writes the numbers on the blackboard with A E I O U written above them. They practice these for about five minutes. She says them first; they repeat. She then picks a child to point to them, and the class repeats after the child. More children pay attention when the child is directing the class. She has ten volunteers for this job. They use sticks when counting to ten, passing them from one hand to the other. A few are doing it right. Although some count correctly, they do not have the right number of sticks correlated with the number spoken. They proceed to copy pictures the teacher has drawn on the board. The teacher asks one girl why she isn't drawing. The girl says she has no pencil. The teacher says nothing and goes on down the aisle.

The children are dismissed from class and line up, each grade together, in front of the school; the teacher tells them to be sure to come that afternoon or she will punish them tomorrow.

Afternoon

The teacher comes in to say a few words to the children (for my benefit, I suppose). She calls up one little girl and reprimands her in front of the group for coming to school with her hair uncombed and with dirty clothes. The child is frightened and hesitant about coming forward, and the teacher shows more impatience. The child's head is cast down all the time her teacher speaks to her.

Vowel practice is resumed. The children are told to erase the vowels they have written in their books and write them over. The teacher has each of the aisles recite the vowels in turn. She asks which of the aisles is best. There is no response from the children; she never says which is best.

Two little boys are writing numbers in their books while some of the others are reciting. The teacher takes the pencils out of their hands and puts them on the table. They pick them up when she is no longer looking and continue writing. A little girl begins to cry. She says, when the teacher asks why she is crying, that the boy in front of her hit her. The teacher tells her to hit him back, which she proceeds to do. The boy shows no reaction at all.

They drill about twenty minutes. A few leaders answer while the rest chime in. "Take out pencil and notebook," the teacher orders. About two-thirds respond. She asks them what things there are in the plaza. One little boys replies, "Č'ulna" (Tzetal for church). She ignores him and names in Spanish the buildings in the plaza. She then draws two men and three pieces of fruit. She stands and watches as the children draw the figures in their notebooks. Many of them show each other what they have drawn. One little boy draws a bus, with seats inside and people sitting in them.

She shows them a cut-out of a chair. The first time she asks them what it is, a few answer "bear," a word they had been practicing before. She asks one child who responds correctly. They practice the word "chair." They practice the difference between *niño* and *niña* (boy and girl). She uses cut-outs of a boy and girl in western dress. Two make mistakes when she asks them to state which is niña and which niño; four get it correctly after they have practiced. She shows a picture of a boy with a train. "What is he doing?" she asks. *"Juganding"* (playing) replies one. The teacher teaches them *"está jugando."*

Some are writing, some looking out the door; others talk in small groups. The majority are watching the teacher as she talks and demonstrates different objects and says their names. They know door and window when she points to these and asks them to name them. She now puts all the visual-aid objects on the table and tells various individuals to bring them to her when she asks for a specific object. "Chair, niño, niña," "Bear," "Soldier," "What thing is lacking yet?" The children answer, "A table." The teacher sends a child to get it. They seem to like this game. There are volunteers to go and get things. They know the objects and so are sure they can bring the correct ones.

The children tend to kneel on the benches, which are high for the smaller ones. The teacher is continually telling them to sit down. A couple of little girls begin to sing. She reproves them and when they continue, she says to them, "Do you remember the animals?" "Yes, teacher," they chorus. "What animal would you like me to draw on the board?" Finally, one boy says, "Chicken." After she has drawn the chicken, the students copy it. She goes around the class and puts a line through the drawing if she approves of it. She finds all of them satisfactory.

The teacher next shows the students a flag, which they are to draw in their notebooks. A bigger girl helps a small boy. The Teacher then asks who knows the recitation about the flag. Three students raise their hands, and sing a song about the flag. Three girls in the back are still drawing in their notebooks. They spend a lot of time erasing so they can use their notebooks over again.

One little girl helps a little boy who has no pencil draw his picture. Another little boy does not draw for the same reason, but when he tells the teacher his problem she does not respond.

She draws pictures around vowels and doesn't explain them to the children, simply telling them to copy the drawings in their notebooks. Their drawings seem to show that they have not seen the connection with the vowels.

She then sings a song that has accompanying gestures (points to stars, hands covering face, hands under head as when sleeping, and so on). A few students seem to know when to do what and understand the words; most of the others copy them.

At four-thirty the classroom teacher tells the children to line up in single file, girls first. She shouts, "No!" as some attempt to run out together. As they line up, each grade together in front of the school, the schoolteacher tells them to be sure to come the next day or she will punish them.

Glossary

ʔahc'al mud; body (in religious metaphorical usage)

alférez captain of religious fiesta, pl. *alfereces; ʔlperés, ʔalperesetik* (Sp.)

ʔaliʔb'al assistant to religious official

ʔalisil attendant to alférez

ʔalkal judge, pl. *ʔalkaletik; alcade* (Sp.)

ʔapuštol apostles

b'alnial male in-laws; applied to assistants in household ceremonies

b'atz'il genuine; *b'atz'il k'op* genuine language (i.e. Tzeltal); *b'atz'il winik* genuine man (i.e. member of the community)

bersinatak neighbors

cabildo town hall

cacique local leader; *cacicazgo* supporter of a cacique

č'om betrothal

compadre co-parent in godparenthood relationship

firmanetik signers; literate men who sign documents in the town hall

fiscal assistant to the priest

h-meʔtikčič'u Our Grandmother the Moon

huʔel official, pl. *huʔeletik*

ʔič' haʔ baptism

ʔič' rason taking of understanding

ʔič' yoʔtan taking of heart

kašlan person of European culture; non-Indian male; *castellano* (Sp.)

kobraria brotherhood; head of brotherhood in religious hierarchy; *cofradía* (Sp.)

koronaetik judges during the installing of the alférez

k'oš the last one; youngest child

kotončuh jacket or tunic of indigenous man's costume

krinsipal elder leader who has served in office, pl. *krinsipaletik; principal* (Sp.)

ƙumare co-mother in godparenthood relationship; *comadre* (Sp.)

ƙumpare co-father in godparenthood relationship; *compadre* (Sp.)

ƙuriƙ country hick, pl. *ƙuriƙetiƙ* Indians not of the center

Ladino male non-Indian

Lahinbahel sƙ'in last day of a fiesta

la ventosa cupping

lum soil; *hlumiltiƙ* our flesh

maliwanehetiƙ people who "sit and wait" in household ceremonies

martomaetiƙ caretakers of the saints; *mayordomos* (Sp.)

mayoletiƙ policemen; *mayores* (Sp.)

meʔč'om mother of the betrothal

meʔeletiƙ women prayer-reciters

meʔeštateš ancestors, when applied to judges

meʔiltatil ancestors, when applied to curers as guardians and guardians in household ceremonies

meʔtiƙtatiƙ ancestors

naƙawane household officials, pl. *naƙawanehetiƙ*

nič'an child, what a man calls his offspring

nič'nal lowest post in the religious hierarchy

nič'nal martoma junior mayordomo

padrino godparent

pasaró man who has served in office, pl. *pasaroetiƙ; pasado* (Sp.)

Paswamal Decoration Day; first day of all big fiestas

patʔoʔtan prayer form

personaetiƙ persons; used in reference to regidores during the installing of the alférez

puƙuh evil, devil

síndico assistant to president

smeʔispetb'aƙ ceremonial embrace

spatbeyoʔtan prayer form of speech

Spiritunsantú Holy Spirit

statal ʔuʔul leader curer

tamohel soul calling

ta sit meʔtiƙ tatiƙ in the eyes/presence of the ancestors

tat father; elder

Tatiƙ K'aƙ'al Lord Sun

Tatiƙ Martil St. Peter the Martyr

Tatil Martoma Lord Mayordomo

Tios Nič'anil   Jesus
Tios Tatil   God the Father
ʔuʔuletik   curers
wayohel   animal spirit; *swayohel*   his animal spirit
Wišpereš   Vespers; eve of a fiesta
yermanotak   his siblings
yol balamilal   center of the world; navel

Bibliography of Works Cited

Adams, Richard N. ed. 1957. *Political Changes in Guatemalan Indian Communities*. Tulane University, Middle American Research Institute Publication 24. New Orleans: Tulane Press.

——. 1964. Rural Labor. In *Continuity and Change in Latin America,* ed. John Johnson, pp. 49–78. Stanford: Stanford University Press.

Adams, Robert M. 1961. Changing Patterns of Territorial Organization in the Central Highlands of Chiapas, Mexico. *American Antiquities* 26:341–60.

Arensberg, Conrad M. and Solon T. Kimball. 1965. *Culture and Community*. New York: Harcourt, Brace and World.

Bennett, John W. 1966. Further Remarks on Foster's "Image of the Limited Good." *American Anthropologist* 68:206–09.

Bennett, Wendell C. and Robert M. Zingg. 1937. *The Tarahumara, An Indian Tribe of Northern Mexico*. Chicago: University of Chicago Press.

Berlin, Brent. 1967. Categories of Eating in Tzeltal and Navaho. *International Journal of American Linguistics* 33:1–6.

Blom, Franz and Oliver La Farge. 1927. *Tribes and Temples: A Record of the Expedition to Middle America*. Tulane University, Middle American Research Institute Publication 1. New Orleans: Tulane Press.

Brandenburg, Frank R. 1964. *The Making of Modern Mexico*. New Jersey: Prentice-Hall.

Bunzel, Ruth. 1952. *Chichicastenango*. Publications of the American Ethnological Society 22. New York: J. J. Augustin.

Calnek, Edward E. 1962. Highland Chiapas before the Spanish Conquest. unpublished Ph.D. dissertation. University of Chicago, Department of Anthropology.

——. n.d. Los Pueblos Indígenas en Los Altos en Chiapas. unpublished manuscript.

Camara Barbachano, Francisco. 1952. Religious and Political Organization. In *Heritage of Conquest,* ed. Sol Tax, pp. 142–73. Glencoe, Ill.: The Free Press.

Cancian, Frank. 1963. Some Aspects of the Social and Religious Organization of a Maya Society. *Actas y Memorias 35eme Congreso Internacional de Americanistas.* Mexico, pp. 335–43.

———. 1965. *Economics and Prestige in a Maya Community. The Religious Cargo System in Zinacantan.* Stanford: Stanford University Press.

Carrasco, Pedro. 1961. The Civil-Religious Hierarchy in Mesoamerican Communities: Spanish Background and Colonial Development: *American Anthropologist* 63 (3):483–97.

———. n.d. Sobre La Introducción De Apellidos Castellanos Entre Los Mayas Alteños. unpublished ms.

Castro, Carlo Antonio. 1959. *Los Hombres Verdaderos.* Jalapa, Mexico: Universidad Veracruzana.

———. 1965. *Narraciones Tzeltales de Chiapas.* Cuadernos de la Facultad de Filosofía, Letras y Ciencias, 27. Jalapa, Mexico: Universidad Veracruzana.

Chayanov, A. V. 1966. *The Theory of the Peasant Economy.* Homewood, Ill.: Richard D. Irwin.

Chevalier, Francois. 1967. Ejido y Estabilidad en México. *América Indígena* 27 (2):163–98.

Colby, Benjamin N. and Pierre Van den Berghe. 1961. Ethnic Relations in Southeastern Mexico. *American Anthropologist* 63 (4):772–92.

Conference Board Economic Almanac, The, 1967–1968. *Business Fact Book.* New York: Collier-Macmillan International.

Day, Christopher. n.d. Report on San Bartolomé, unpublished manuscripts of *Man in Nature Project,* National Science Foundation. University of Chicago, Department of Anthropology.

de la Fuente, Julio. 1964. *Educación, Antropología y Desarrollo de la Comunidad.* México: Instituto Nacional Indigenísta.

de la Peña, Moises T. 1951. *Chiapas Economico.* vol. 1. Tuxtla Guitierrez, Chiapas: Departamento de Prensa y Turismo Sección Autografico.

Edel, Matthew D. n.d. Zinacantan's Ejido: The Effects of Mexican Land Reform on an Indian Community. unpublished report on the Columbia, Cornell, Harvard, Illinois Summer Field Studies Program 1962.

Faron, L. C. 1964. *Hawks of the Sun; Mapuche Morality and Its Ritual Attributes*. Pittsburgh: University of Pittsburgh Press.

Flavell, John H. 1963. *The Developmental Psychology of Jean Piaget*. New Jersey: D. Van Nostrand.

Fortes, Myer. 1959. Ritual and Office in Tribal Society. In *Essays on the Ritual of Social Relations*, ed. M. Gluckman, pp. 53–88. Manchester, England: Manchester University Press.

Foster, George M. 1944. Nagualism in Mexico and Guatemala. *Acta Americana* 2:85–103.

———. 1949. Sierra Popoluca Kinship Terminology and its Wider Relationship. *Southwestern Journal of Anthropology* 5 (4):330–44.

———. 1951. Report on an Ethnological Reconnaissance of Spain. *American Anthropologist* 53 (3):311–25.

———. 1961. *Culture and Conquest: America's Spanish Heritage*. Wenner-Gren Foundation for Anthropological Research, Viking Fund Publications in Anthropology 27. New York.

———. 1963. The Dyadic Contract: A Model for the Social Structure of a Mexican Indian Community. *American Anthropologist* 65 (1):1173–92.

———. 1965. Peasant Society and the Notion of the Limited Good. *American Anthropologist* 67 (2):293–315.

Frake, Charles C. 1963. The Diagnosis of Disease among the Subanum. *American Anthropologist* 65 (1):113–32.

Friedrich, Paul. 1962. A Mexican Cacicazgo. *Ethnology* 4 (2):190–210.

———. 1965. Assumptions Underlying Tarascan Political Homicide. *Psychiatry* 25 (4):315–27.

Geertz, Clifford, 1966. Religion as a Cultural System. In *Anthropological Approaches to the Study of Religion*, ed. Michael Banton, pp. 1–46. Association for Social Anthropology 3. New York: Frederick A. Praeger.

Gluckman, Max. 1962. Les Rites de Passage. In *Essays on the Ritual of Social Relations*, ed. M. Gluckman. pp. 1–52. Manchester, England: Manchester University Press.

Goldrich, Daniel. 1965. Toward the Comparative Study of Politicalization in Latin America. In *Contemporary Cultures and Societies of Latin America*, eds. D. B. Heath and R. N. Adams, pp. 361–78. New York: Random House.

Goodenough, Ward H. 1965. Rethinking 'Status' and 'Role': Toward a General Model of the Cultural Organization of Social Relationships. In *The*

Relevance of Models for Social Anthropology, ed. Michael Banton, pp. 1–22. Association for Social Anthropology 1. New York: Frederick A. Praeger.

————. 1966. *Cooperation in Change.* New York: John Wiley and Sons.

Guessous, Mohammed. 1967. A General Critique of Equilibrium Theory. In *Readings on Social Change,* ed. W. Moore and R. Cook, pp. 23–35. New

————. 1947. Clanes y Systemas de Parentesco de Cancuc. *Acta Americana* 5:1–17.

Jersey: Prentice-Hall.

Guiteras Holmes, Calixta. 1961. *Perils of the Soul: The World View of a Tzotzil Indian.* Glencoe, Ill.: The Free Press.

Hebb, D. O. and W. R. Thompson. 1954. The Social Significance of Animal Studies. In *Handbook of Social Psychology* vol. 1, ed. G. Lindzey, pp. 532–61. Cambridge, Mass.: Addison Wesley.

Hermitte, Esther M. 1964. Supernatural Power and Social Control in a Modern Maya Village. unpublished Ph.D. dissertation. University of Chicago, Department of Anthropology.

Holland, William R. 1963. *Medicina Maya en los Altos de Chiapas: Un Estudio del Cambio Sociocultural.* Mexico: Instituto Nacional Indigenísta.

Hoogshagen, Searle S. and William R. Merrifield. 1961. Coatlan Mixe Kinship. Southwestern Journal of Anthropology 17 (3):219–25.

Hunt, Eva, n.d. Report on Chanal. unpublished manuscripts of *Man in Nature Project,* National Science Foundation, University of Chicago, Department of Anthropology.

Kluckhohn, Clyde, 1962. *Navaho Witchcraft.* Boston: Beacon Press.

———— and Henry A. Murray, eds. 1953. *Personality in Nature, Culture and Society.* New York: Alfred A. Knopf.

La Farge, Oliver. 1947. *Santa Eulalia; The Religion of Cuchumatán Indian Town.* Chicago: University of Chicago Press.

———— and Douglas Byers. 1931. *The Year-Bearer's People.* Tulane University Middle American Research Series 3. New Orleans: Tulane Press.

Lamb, Ursula. 1956. Religious Conflicts in the Conquest of Mexico. *Journal of the History of Ideas* 17 (4):526–39.

Laughlin, Robert M. 1962. El Símbolo de la Flor en la Religión de Zinacantan. *Estudios de Cultura Maya* 2:123–40.

Leach, Edmund. 1964. *Political Systems of Highland Burma.* Boston: Beacon Press.

———. 1967. Genesis as Myth. In *Myth and Cosmos,* ed. J. Middleton, pp. 1–14. New York: The Natural History Press.

Leeds, Anthony F. C. 1964. Brazilian Careers and Social Structures: A Case History and Model. *American Anthropologist* 66 (6):121–47.

Lévi-Strauss, Claude. 1966. *The Savage Mind.* Chicago: University of Chicago Press.

Lewin, Kurt. 1951. *Field Theory in Social Science.* New York: Harper Torchbooks.

Lewis, Oscar. 1963. *Life in a Mexican Village: Tepoztlán Restudied.* Urbana, Ill.: University of Illinois Press.

Linn, Erwin L. 1967. Role Behavior in Two Dental Clinics: A Trial of Nadel's Criteria. *Human Organization* 26 (3):141–48.

Lombardo Otero, Rosa María. 1944. *La Mujer Tzeltal.* Mexico.

MacArthur, H. S. 1961. La Estructura Politico-Religiosa de Aguacatán. *Guatemala Indígena* 1 (2):41–56.

Mauss, Marcel. 1954. *The Gift.* trans. Ian Cunnison. New York: W. W. Norton.

Mead, George Herbert. 1938. *The Philosophy of the Act.* Chicago: University of Chicago Press.

Merrifield, W. R. 1959. Chinantec Kinship in Palantla, Oaxaca, Mexico. *American Anthropologist* 61:875–81.

Merrifield, W. R. and Searle S. Hoogshagen. 1961. Coatlán Mixe Kinship. *Southwestern Journal of Anthropology* 17 (3):219–25.

Mintz, Sidney W. and Eric R. Wolf. 1950. An Analysis of Ritual Co-Parenthood (Compadrazgo). *Southwestern Journal of Anthropology* 6 (1):341–69.

Moore, Wilbert. 1963. *Social Change.* New Jersey: Prentice-Hall.

Mowrer, O. H. and Clyde Kluckhohn. 1944. Dynamic Theory of Personality. In *Personality and the Behavior Disorders,* vol. 1, ed. J. McV. Hunt. pp. 69–138. New York: The Ronald Press.

Murdock, George P. 1965. *Social Structure.* New York: The Free Press.

Nader, Laura. 1964. *Talea and Juquila: A Comparison of Zapotec Social Organization.* Berkeley and Los Angeles: University of California Press.

Nash, June. 1960. Social Relations in Amatenango del Valle: An Activity

Analysis. unpublished Ph.D. dissertation. University of Chicago, Department of Anthropology.

———. 1964. The Structuring of Social Relations in Amatenango. *Estudios de Cultura Maya* 4:335–59.

———. 1966. Social Resources of a Latin-American Peasantry. *Social and Economic Studies* 15 (4):353–67.

———. 1967. Death as a Way of Life: The Increasing Resort to Homicide in a Mexican Indian Town. *American Anthropologist* 69 (5):455–70.

———. Rhetoric of a Maya Indian Court. In press, *Estudios de Cultura Maya*.

Nash, Manning. 1955. *Machine Age Maya: The Industrialization of a Guatemalan Community*. Memoir of the American Anthropological Association 87. Menasha, Wisc.: Geo. Banta.

———. 1960. Witchcraft as a Social Process in a Tzeltal Community. *America Indígena* 20 (2):121–26.

———. 1961. The Social Context of Economic Choice in a Small Society. *Man* 219:186–91.

Nuñez de la Vega, Francisco. 1702. *Constitucionas Diocesanas del Obispado de Chiapas*. Rome: Imprenta de Caretano.

Parsons, Talcott. 1951. *The Social System*. Glencoe, Ill.: The Free Press.

Piaget, Jean. 1952. *The Origins of Intelligence in Children*. New York: International Universities Press.

Pitt-Rivers, Julian. 1966. Honour and Social Status. In J. G. Peristiany, *Honour and Shame*. pp. 19–78. Chicago: University of Chicago Press.

Reina, Ruben E. 1962–63. The Potter and the Farmer: The Fate of Two Innovators in a Maya Village. *Expedition* 5 (4):18–31.

Romney, Kimball and Romaine. 1966. *The Mixtecans of Juxtlahuaca, Mexico*. New York: John Wiley and Sons.

Sartre, Jean-Paul. 1963. *Search for a Method*. New York: Alfred A. Knopf.

Schultz, Theodore. 1964. *Transforming Traditional Agriculture*. New Haven, Conn. Yale University Press.

Secretaría de Gobierno Constitucional, 1893. Roll 78, *Microfilm Series of Chiapas*. México, D.F.: Museo de Antropología.

Secretaría del Gobierno Departmental de Chiapas. 1828; 1841. *Colección de Decretos del Congreso Constituyente de las Chiapas,* vol. 1.

Siverts, Hennig. 1960. Political Organization in a Tzeltal Community in

Chiapas, Mexico. In *The Social Anthropology of Middle America,* ed. C. M. Leslie. special edition, *Alpha Kappa Delta* 30 (1):14–28.

———. 1964. On Politics and Leadership in Highland Chiapas. In *Desarrollo Cultural de Los Mayas,* ed. E. Z. Vogt and A. Ruz L., pp. 363–84. México: Universidad Nacional Autonoma de México.

———. 1965. The "Cacique" of K'ankujk'. *Estudios de Cultura Maya* 5:339–60.

Tax, Sol. 1937. The Municípios of the Midwestern Highlands of Guatemala. *American Anthropologist* 39:423–44.

———. 1941. World View and Social Relations in Guatemala. *American Anthropologist* 43:27–43.

———. 1950. *Field Notes, Panajachel* Microfilm Collection of Manuscripts on Middle American Cultural Anthropology 29. Chicago: University of Chicago Library.

———. 1957. The Indians in the Economy of Guatemala. *Social and Economic Studies* 6 (3):413–24.

———. 1964. Cultural Differences in the Maya Area: a 20th Century Perspective. In *Desarrolla Cultural de los Maya,* ed. E. Z. Vogt and A. Ruz L., pp. 279–328. Mexico: Universidad Nacional Autonoma de Mexico.

Thompson, J. Eric S. 1964. *The Rise and Fall of Maya Civilization.* Norman, Okla.: University of Oklahoma Press.

Tolman, Edward Chase. 1961. *Behavior and Psychological Man; Essays in Motivation and Learning.* Berkeley and Los Angeles: University of California Press.

Tozzer, Alfred M. 1941. *Landa's Relación de las Cosas de Yucatán.* Papers of the Peabody Museum of American Archaeology and Ethnology, Harvard University, 18. Cambridge, Mass.: Peabody Museum.

Trens, Manuel B. 1957. *Bosquejos Historicos de San Cristóbal, Chiapas.* México.

Valladares, L. A. 1957. *El Hombre y el Maiz: Etnográfia e Etnopsicología de Colotenango, Guatemala.*

Villa Rojas, Alfonso. 1947. Kinship and Nagualism in a Tzeltal Community. *American Anthropologist* 49:578–87.

———. 1946. *Field Notes, Oxchuk.* Microfilm Collection of Manuscripts on Middle American Cultural Anthropology. Chicago: University of Chicago Library.

Vogt, Evon Z. 1964. Cosmología Maya Antigua y Tzotzil Contemporanea, Comentario Sobre Algunos Problemas Metodologicos. *América Indígena* 24 (3):211–20.

———. 1965. Ceremonial Organization in Zinacantan, *Ethnology* 4:39–53.

———. 1966. Replica Estructural y Replica Conceptual en la Cultura Zinacanteca. In *Los Zinacantecos,* ed. E. Z. Vogt, pp. 129–44. Mexico: Instituto Nacional Indigenísta.

Wagley, Charles. 1941. *Economics of a Guatemalan Village.* Memoir of the American Anthropological Association 58. Menasha, Wisc.: Geo. Banta.

———. 1949. *The Social and Religious Life of a Guatemalan Village.* Memoir of the American Anthropological Association 71. Menasha, Wisc.: Geo. Banta.

Wallace, Anthony F. C. 1962. Culture and Cognition. *Science* 135:351–57.

Whittaker. Arabello and Viola Warkentin. 1965. Chol Texts on the Supernatural. *Publications in Linguistics and Related Fields of the Summer Institute of Linguistics* 13. Norman Oklahoma: University of Oklahoma Press.

Wisdom, Charles. 1940. *The Chorti Indians of Guatemala.* Chicago: University of Chicago Press.

Wolf, Eric. 1955. Types of Latin American Peasantry. *American Anthropologist* 57 (3):452–70.

———. 1957a. The Mexican Bajío in the 18th Century: An Analysis of Cultural Integration. Tulane University Middle American Research Institute 17 (3). New Orleans: Tulane Press.

———. 1957b. Closed Corporate Peasant Communities in Mesoamerica and Central Java. *Southwestern Journal of Anthropology* 13 (1):1–15.

———. 1964. *Anthropology.* New Jersey: Prentice-Hall.

———. 1966. *Peasants.* New Jersey: Prentice-Hall.

Zabala, Manuel. 1961. Instituciones Políticas y Religiosas de Zinacantan. *Estudios de Cultura Maya* 1:147–59.

Index

Acculturation, 7, 8, 239
Adams, R. M., 2, 159
Adams, R. N., 79, 160
Adultery, 281
Affinals, 99–100
Age-grading, 97, 98 n., 161, 194, 270, 271;
 behavior in reference to, 277–78, 290;
 position in house, 295; in town hall, 323;
 authority of, 328–29
Agricultural production, 27–43, 112, 321
ʔahau, 138
Alférez: alfereces, xvii, 7, 23, 195, 207,
 210; role of, 163–64, 165, 172–73, 185,
 195, 210–22, 274; installation in post,
 212–24, 276, 278
Alisiles, 208, 216, 221
All Souls' Day, 135–36
Amawitz, 5
Ancestors, 5, 22, 23 n., 25, 45, 142, 238–
 39; as guardians, 276, 323, 326
Anderson, 36 n.
Animal spirits, 19, 205, 237, 238. *See also*
 Swayohel
Annual cycle, 313–37
Authority groups, 101–02; household spon-
 sors, 101–02; civil officials, 102; curers,
 102

Baldios, 236
Baptism, 116–18, 260
Barrios, 10, 162, 163, 164, 165, 219
Beans, 29, 31, 33, 34, 35, 36, 39–41, 42
Behavior, xxiv; structuring, xxv–xxvi; molar,
 xxvii n.; evaluation, xxviii, 80, 287;

schema, 49–50, 52, 96, 147; defined in
 family, 109; ritual, 116, 123, 181–96;
 patterning, 126; of curers, 43; defined in
 civil-religious hierarchy, 161–96; repeti-
 tion, 193, 310, 320; religious, 197–229;
 to be avoided, 207; moral, 280; con-
 formity, 282; deviance, 282, 327; as a
 product of socialization, 287; in court,
 297–99; observation in school, 307; stan-
 dardization in places, 309; in relation to
 saints, 324; validation of, 329; in public
 places, 345–51
Bennett, N., 223 n.
Berlin, B., xxvii
Betrothal, 124–30, 279, 295
Blom, F., 55
Bohwaletik, 25
Boundaries, xxi
Bribery, 77
Brindis, 61, 79
Broker, 89
Bullfight, 144
Bunzel, R., 166, 296
Burial, 113, 131–36
Butcher, 85

Cabbage, 35
Cabildo, 296–99. *See also* town hall
Cacicazgo, 235
Cacique, 236; role of, 252–58, 265
Calendar priests, 237, 238 n. 2
Calnek, E., 2, 159, 204, 238
Calpul, 6, 7 n.
Camara B., F., 160

363